# HUBRIS AND THE MYTH OF SISYPHUS

Michael A. Matrozos

# HUBRIS AND THE MYTH OF SISYPHUS

Copyright 2024 by Michael A. Matrozos

matrozosmichael24@aol.com

Queen Creek Publishing Company (QCPC)

WRITERS GUILD OF AMERICA: 2140310

# DEDICATION

This book is dedicated to my wife Christina. My best friend. My rock. My Clementine. Who loves, understands and tolerates me, with all my idiosyncrasies.

CHE FECE...IL GRAN RIFIUTO

For some people there's a day when they have to come out with the great Yes or the great No.  It's clear at once who has the Yes ready in him; and is saying it.

He goes on to find honor, strong in his conviction. He who refuses, never repents.  Asked again, he'd still say "No".  Yet that No - the right answer defeats him the whole of his life.

C. P. CAVAFY

# TABLE OF CONTENTS

# ACKNOWLEDGMENTS

I would like to thank Terry Snow, my fraternity brother, without whom this book HUBRIS AND THE MYTH OF SISYPHUS would never have even begun. Let me explain. I am a Chemical Engineer by education and experience. I have worked for over 50 years in the Energy field building Power Plants, Refineries, Industrial and Department of Defense Projects throughout the United States. I was to retire at the end of 2020 and fell into a deep depression, because I did not know what to do with my time. My wife and I were invited to lunch at the home of Terry and his wife Coleen Snow sometime between Christmas and New Year's 2020. After lunch I had a heart to heart discussion with Terry over the cause of my depression. He asked me what I wanted to do when I was a child. I told him that I always wanted to be a writer. What's stopping you now to realize your dream? He asked me what was on my mind and I started giving him a synopsis of all the books that had accumulated in my head through my experiences over the years. When I reached the plot of HUBRIS AND THE MYTH OF SISYPHUS he told me: "This will be your break out OPUS. It is an iconoclastic book. It will hit the country and the Justice System like an earthquake and a Tsunami, at the same time." He announced.

We continued our discussion, which overall took 4 hours, so we ended up staying for dinner, also. We left their house and I felt energized. I started writing an outline immediately and on January 6, 2021 I started writing my first book: POSTCARDS FROM LETHE. I completed the first draft in three months and have not stopped writing since. Writing became an addiction. I finished my second book: The SARGO INCIDENT and as soon it was published, I moved to my third book: WAITING FOR THE BARBARIANS, the Honolulu Quartet, Books 1, 2,

3, and 4. Then, with three books under my belt, I started my fourth book, the novel  HUBRIS AND THE MYTH OF SISYPHUS which you are holding in your hands.  Terry Snow read the first draft of this book and meticulously fact checked it and provided me with valuable comments and suggestions.  He believes it will be a Best Seller.

I would like to thank my granddaughter Dimitra Milan a world renown artist extraordinaire, for her original paintings, which became my book jacket front and back.  Her website is www.dimitramilanart.com

Finally, I would like to thank my wife Christina whose unwavering love and encouragement kept me writing.

# FORWARD

Sisyphus, the son of Aeolus, the God of the winds, and father of Odysseus, the hero of Homeric times, emerged as the cunning king of Corinth and the esteemed founder of the Isthmian Games—a precursor to the Olympic Games.

Legend holds that when Death came to claim him, Sisyphus ingeniously chained up Death, halting all departures to the afterlife. Ares, the God of war, eventually intervened, aiding Death, and Sisyphus had no choice but to relent.

During this time, Sisyphus instructed his wife, Merope, to forego the customary sacrifices and leave his body unburied. Consequently, upon reaching the underworld, he earned the right to return home, tasked with punishing his wife for neglecting the proper funeral rites.

Instead of immediately returning to Hades, Sisyphus lived to a ripe old age before experiencing a second death. His display of extreme conceit, a manifestation of Hubris in the eyes of the Gods, demanded fitting retribution.

For his defiance, he endured eternal punishment in Hades. His penance involved ceaselessly rolling a colossal stone up a hill, only to witness it relentlessly descend as soon as it reached the summit.

# INTRODUCTION

Hubris in Ancient Greek tragedy simply meant the revealing tale of how a great man's fortunes shifted from initial prosperity to final wretchedness. The hero, once overambitious, self-confident, insolent, and magnificent, faces a tragic fall.

Hubris, also known as 'amartia' is the tragic flaw; the inherent defect or shortcoming in the hero who, in all other aspects, is favored by fortune.

Tragedy unfolds as a conflict between the protagonist and a superior force, leading to a sorrowful or disastrous conclusion that evokes pity and terror.

The hero confronts a series of disastrous events, grappling with life under the shadow of disaster. Overcoming adversity, he becomes unduly confident, arrogant, and presumptuous, entangled in an intolerable yet inescapable situation, guided by will or circumstances, fatal ignorance, or binding obligation. Ultimately, he faces the workings of an inexorable fate, ensuring an unhappy outcome. The ordeal, however, may reveal dimensions of human grandeur and dignity in extreme circumstances.

The tragic hero, a man of noble rank and nature, faces misfortune not due to villainy but some 'error in judgment.' The hero's suffering, disproportionate to its flaw, involves a cosmic collusion among the hero's flaw, chance, necessity, and external forces, bringing about the tragic catastrophe.

The hero's flaw is elusive; often, tragic deeds are committed unwittingly. If knowingly committed, they are not by choice. An apparent weakness is sometimes an excess of virtue, like extreme probity or zeal for perfection.

Since the hero is never passive, struggling to resolve his tragic difficulty with obsessive dedication, he is guilty of Hubris; an assumption of godlike qualities and an attempt to overstep human limitations.

The hero's Hubris is subtle, sometimes wholly blameless, yet his unbroken spirit under the tragic ordeal suggests an overconfidence the Gods find offensive.

Tragedy delves into the role of man in the universe, questioning his actions.

Why must he suffer?

Why is man torn between irreconcilables like good and evil, freedom and necessity, truth and deceit?

Are the causes of suffering external; in blind chance, the evil designs of others, or the malice of God?

Are its causes within, brought upon himself through arrogance, infatuation, or the tendency to overreach?

Why is Justice so elusive?

# CHAPTER 1

## To Conquer The World

It was a few minutes before ten o'clock in the morning—the official Court-ordered surrender time. The dilemma lingered: trust the government employee who verbally extended the surrender time to just before noon or adhere strictly to the ten o'clock AM written Court Order? Either way, a potential pitfall awaited. Arrive before ten o'clock, and accusations of mistrusting the verbal extension might ensue. Arrive after ten o'clock, close to noon, and risk arrest for defying a Court Order. "What do I do, honey?" he asked his wife, who was driving the rental car.

"I don't know. Typical government. They can play it any way they want and get you if that's their game," she answered without taking her eyes off the road.

The asphalt shimmered in the heat, the temperature already pushing one hundred degrees Fahrenheit at the start of September. They had left the Las Vegas strip a couple of miles back, heading North, and the desert was taking over any signs of development. The mountains were outlined clearly in a cloudless sky, with occasional twisters raising clouds of dust in the foothills. Nellis Air Force Base stood visible a few hundred feet to the right in the middle of the desert—no fences, no barriers, just the desert leading nowhere.

Michael adjusted the air conditioner, and as the cool air enveloped them, he couldn't help but notice his wife's reactions. A subtle change in her physique, a reaction to the temperature shift. He followed the swell of her breast, settling his gaze on her right knee. A nerve flexed her thigh muscle, her right foot easing on the gas as they approached Nellis Air Force Base Area II. He was always keen on concentrating his desire and pinpointing it like a cinematographer. Truly erotic movies could focus the audience's eye, isolating the object of desire and relaying the feeling to that one person in the audience. In the movie "The Lover," as his hand approaches her trembling fingers in the back seat of the Rolls Royce. "Claire's Knee," in the movie by the same name, as she is sitting on the beach.

"Did you see this?" he suddenly snapped out of his stupor.

"See what?" his wife replied.

"The sign at the entrance. Larger than life. Under 'Nellis AFB,' their motto: 'TO CONQUER THE WORLD.' Talk about a capitalistic mission statement. No bones about it."

"I didn't see it. But it wouldn't surprise me."

"We are almost here, and it is exactly ten o'clock," Michael said. "I showed them that I believed and followed the verbal instruction by coming after the official court surrender time but not late enough to cause hassles if they renege on the verbal instructions."

The guard at the gate, a nineteen-year-old Airman with an M-16 on his back, wearing an Air Force uniform two sizes too big, leaned on the driver's side, exposing a red cheek of peach fuzz.

"May I help you folks? It seems like you lost your way. This is the entrance to the Nellis Federal Prison Camp."

"I think we are at the right place. I am supposed to self-surrender. Where do I go?" Michael asked from the passenger seat.

"Madam, just park the vehicle at the designated visitor parking stall outside the gate to the right, and I will call security. They will come down and pick you up,

sir."

"I hope I don't start crying when they take you away. God, I wish I stay strong. I don't want to give the bastards the satisfaction," Christina whispered.

"I wouldn't worry about it, sweetheart. You are a tough cookie. You have not been tested yet, but I know you will pull through."

"Oh, honey, I hope so. I don't know; sometimes these sentences are tougher for the families on the outside. You will be cared for, with a roof over your head, three meals a day; probably eating better than at home."

"Christina, don't get started. I don't want to spend the last few minutes before a thirty-three-month separation arguing. Don't blame the wind. Adjust the sails."

"I know, but it is such a waste of time and talent. The punishment does not fit the crime. I bet the prison is full of decent people that were inadvertently caught in government-fabricated cases of 'Intent' and 'Conspiracy.' They are being forced to serve time away from their loved ones, costing the taxpayers money and hurting the economy in the process."

"You are probably right. But I cannot go through this gate hating the Bureau of Prisons. They are neither the ones who indicted me nor tried and sentenced me. They are just the warehousemen who will keep me and return me in the same condition I was when I self-reported. I will try to leave all my bitterness behind as I go through this gate. I will try to do the best I can to get along with the authorities and the prisoners alike. I see this as a new experience and an opportunity to test my survival instincts."

"You are probably right. You may come out of this ordeal a better person. Who knows, maybe looking back, we might think that this was worth it. It sure as heck makes me feel miserable though at this minute and fills me with hate for our government for putting you here. Totally unnecessary. You didn't do anything criminal. How dare they accuse you of something you did not do?"

"You are right, honey, but look at it this way. I have not been a nice person to the government for over twenty years now. I was arrogant, made them look bad on purpose; I basically spiked the ball after I scored. The government is not smart, but they are tenacious and they've got staying power. I have to show equal perseverance and tenacity in the face of adversity. Call it a test of wills. The Vietcong ethic. Will not succumb no matter what."

"Well, I think life is too short to spend it in a confrontational mode. It does no good for the family. Think of Todd, your son, and your daughter Elli, the little 'begeler'; her daddy in prison..."

"Well, you know Todd graduated from Boston University two years ago. He would still be living in the nest, hesitating to try his wings. Now he can go out and earn his own keep. We've done everything that was expected and more. Don't worry about Elli. She is a survivor. She will be a senior this year at the University of Georgia, and thank God we have prepaid her tuition, room, and board for the rest of the year until she graduates. Don't worry about the kids. They have no student loans to worry about. We have paid for everything. In some ways, what is happening to me may be a blessing in disguise to teach them to start paddling their own canoe."

"Sweetheart, you know it's been over half an hour already. Did the guard call? Shouldn't you check or something?"

"Gee, I don't know. I was on time. It's up to them to transport me from the gate to the facility. Look, I see a bus coming down the hill."

"No, that's not it. It turned towards the Base. It looked like it was full of people in khaki uniforms."

Michael opened the car door from the passenger's side of the car. The dry heat struck him across the face, searing his lungs. Oh boy, thirty-three months of this dry heat. Not a cloud in the sky. My skin will flake and fall off after being nurtured for eleven years in the Hawaiian humidity, he is thinking. The guard remained inside the air-conditioned shack as he approached.

"Excuse me, but it's been over half an hour since I reported. Do you know what's the hang-up? Did they tell you what time they will be coming down to pick me up?"

"I called them as soon as you showed up. They do not have a vehicle to send down. They told me that one will be coming shortly before noon."

Michael walked back to the car, leaving footprints on the melting asphalt. Sand, scrawny cacti, and dwarf chola dominated the terrain. He opened the passenger door and embraced the welcome relief of the air-conditioned car interior.

"The government is experiencing technical difficulties," he told his wife. "It is a safe bet that we will remain together for the next hour, at least."

"See, I told you. We should have come here just before noon, like they told me when I called."

"Right! If we've done that, I would now be on escape status. Just the excuse the government wants, seeking to make it harder on me."

"Well, I hope the car does not boil over. I don't know about these Detroit sardine cans of late. I am amazed that the car engine temperature gauge is saying normal, on idle for forty-five minutes with the air conditioner at full blast."

"Honey, you worry too much. Slow down. Where are you going to go? Give me your hand. Moments like these I realize how much I love you and how unbearably I will be missing you."

"I know. Me too. But I plan to visit you at least one weekend every month. I will try to buy a coupon book special Honolulu - Las Vegas. As a matter of fact, this coming weekend, I plan to stay over and visit you Friday evening, Saturday, and Sunday all day. The problem may be that they require a ten to thirty-day waiting period to put me on the visitors' list. See what you can do to speed up the process. We got three days till Friday. I am not hopeful, but I will stay in Las Vegas over the weekend just in case."

"What are you going to do all alone, in town, all this time?"

"I will not be alone. Nancy is flying over from Phoenix today and will drive with me back to Phoenix. As a matter of fact, her plane is landing at 11:58 AM today. Don't worry, though. I told her to wait for me outside tJust at that moment, a white Ford Bronco with military police insignia and blue flashing lights was slowly making its way down the hill from the Camp towards the gate.

"I think that's it, honey. Remember, don't start crying. I will start crying too, and then the bastards will have their victory. Don't give them the satisfaction."

With that, he kissed his wife tenderly and opened the door. He picked up the two grey garbage bags with his meager belongings inside, allowed by the camp authorities, and started walking slowly towards the white Bronco, not looking back. His eyes were cloudy, with the forming tears. He swallowed hard, bit his lower lip, and got control of his emotions. The desert heat and dryness took care of the moist eyes, so that by the time he reached the Bronco, they were bone dry. He went to the driver's side of the vehicle and handed the driver his papers.he arrivals, and I will be picking her up as soon as you are settled. She knows, and she understands. Good old Nancy. You know, in times like these, you realize who your real friends are. Yes, and Harlow is sending his love also. Here is their phone number. Now I want you to call me at this number collect every night starting today and let me know how you are doing, what you need, and whether you had any success in getting me into the approved visitors' list."

Just at that moment, a white Ford Bronco with military police insignia and blue flashing lights was slowly making its way down the hill from the Camp towards the gate.

"I think that's it, honey. Remember, don't start crying. I will start crying too, and then the bastards will have their victory. Don't give them the satisfaction."

With that, he kissed his wife tenderly and opened the door. He picked up the two grey garbage bags with his meager belongings inside, allowed by the Camp authorities, and started walking slowly towards the white Bronco, not looking back. His eyes were cloudy, with the forming tears. He swallowed hard, bit his lower lip, and got control of his emotions. The desert heat and dryness took care of the moist eyes, so that by the time he reached the Bronco, they were bone dry. He went to the driver's side of the vehicle and handed the driver his papers.

# CHAPTER 2

## Processing

The federal guard at the wheel of the white Ford Bronco appeared to be in his late forties, with a receding hairline and the beginning of a paunch hanging over his belt, giving him the air of a man who had spent too much time in a secretary's seat. He donned black cowboy boots, grey pants, and a white shirt adorned with the Federal Bureau of Prisons (BOP) insignia – a bald eagle caught in mid-flight, clutching bolts of lightning and an olive branch. The prisoner couldn't help but wonder which of these symbols held his fate.

Requesting the prisoner's ID without a word, the guard flicked a switch, lowering the back passenger window. He instructed the prisoner to stow his belongings, contained in two trash bags, in the back seat. Opening the passenger door from the inside, he gestured for the prisoner to enter.

"How long you staying with us?" the guard inquired.

"Thirty-three months."

"What brings you here?"

"Mail-Fraud."

"Just Mail-Fraud?"

"That's all."

"That can't be. It's always Mail-Fraud and something else."

"In my case, it's just 'Mail-Fraud.'"

"Never heard of that. Sounds like you ticked off someone up there. What'd you do? How many counts?"

"Davis-Bacon Act violations; eight counts."

"Too technical for me. You a CEO or something?"

"Yes."

"Figured as much. We get them here all the time."

As they crested the rise after the gate, the camp sprawled into view – five hundred yards wide by a thousand yards long, a grassy parkland punctuated by

sparse trees. Half a dozen flat-top, two-story buildings with a fifties aesthetic composed the Camp compound."

The Bronco came to a halt in front of the second building. The security officer swung open the passenger door, commanding the prisoner to step out onto the unforgiving sidewalk. With a casual toss, he flung the two trash bags at the prisoner's feet.

"Wait here. Don't move. Someone will fetch you for processing."

"How long?" the prisoner pressed, glancing at the unyielding sun. "I reported at ten, as the court papers said. Miss Diane insisted I be processed by noon."

"Jack, you are BOP's concern now. Quit the griping. You're on my time. Just stand there and wait like I said."

The Bronco roared away, leaving behind a faint scent of burnt rubber. High noon. The building's windows reflected the desert sun, mirroring the isolation of the parking lot with its aging vehicles.

The cinder track, the chain-link fence, and the expanse of desert created a desolate landscape. High temperatures radiated from the gravel, leaving no respite. The prisoner, exposed under the unrelenting sun, began calculating his chances of dehydration.

Silence dominated. Waiting became a struggle against the relentless heat. There was no place to sit or lean, no grass—only gravel that radiated heat like a furnace. The minutes crawled in five-minute intervals, marked by the prisoner's Cartier watch, each moment stretching toward an uncertain future.

The sun was directly overhead, casting hardly any shadow. The building windows were dark, reflecting the light like mirrors. The parking lot in front of the building had a couple of dozen cars, the four door Detroit gas guzzler variety, of indeterminate age, dusty, with the windows half way down. Past the parking lot, a twenty foot wide cinder track, standard issue, six foot high chain link fence with a warning sign concerning government property and trespassing, and then the desert rolling for miles as far as the eye could see, up into the mountains that seemed to form a ring around Las Vegas.

High noon. Not a cloud in the sky. Silence. Waiting. No place to sit down. No place to lean against. Not a blade of grass outside the building. Just decomposed granite type gravel that radiated heat which must have been well over a hundred degrees Fahrenheit. Dry heat though that evaporates the sweat before it stains the clothing. The prisoner starts calculating the body area exposed to the sun. Estimating the evaporation rate per square inch. Someone better show up pretty soon or he will expire from dehydration. The minutes drag in five minute intervals that are the only subdivisions in his fancy wafer thin Cartier watch.

"How are you doing? Did you bring your whole household?" A pleasant young female voice rang behind him, which woke him from his stupor.

He turned in anticipation, the video image did not match the audio. A fat, dumpy, bleach blond in her mid forties was waddling towards him from the building side door, on waitress type black rubber bottom shoes. She wore a Bureau of Prisons uniform, but they must have custom tailored it around that body. She came closer and he noticed her gut was protruding further than her tits, which kind of hung over and rested on top of her gut as they were getting squeezed by a size too small bra. The whole effect was that of a hammock swinging side to side as she walked. The face though had traces of being pretty at one time, long ago. Her mouth was small with very succulent pouty lips, until she smiled and exposed uneven rows of teeth that would have made an orthodontist smile with glee at the prospect of having a go at that tiger shark mouth.

"Hi, my name is Miss Bailey. You must be Mr....I cannot pronounce your name, although God I practiced. So I will call you Michael. You may call me Diane. Why don't you grab these bags and follow me. We are going up the stairs to the second floor."

She opened the door for him and he followed her inside the glass glad building assaulted by the coolness of the air conditioned environment that seemed like entering a refrigerated box car after the brightness and heat of the outdoors.

He followed the fat ass up the stairs, at eye level, along a narrow corridor that ended up in front of a door at the end of the hall marked "PROCESSING". On the left, the corridor was lined with office doors with signs on them, like "CONTRACTING", "PROCUREMENT", "SAFETY", "NOTARY". The doors were open and the offices were occupied by young, pretty government secretaries. To the right of the corridor there was a long single window, wire mesh reinforced that looked into a single windowless room with two benches running along the room length by the wall, each side a mirror image of each other.

The prisoner followed Miss Diane to the last room on the left, and was told to leave the two trash bags with his belongings there. He was then asked to empty his pockets and put all jewelry he was wearing on the counter. He was fingerprinted and his picture taken. Diane handed him a clipboard and pen and told him to go to the room across the hall and wait. If the temperature in the building was that of a refrigerator, the temperature in that room with the twin benches was the freezer.

Diane came in a few minutes later bringing two thick folders. One marked "INTELLIGENCE TEST" and the other "PSYCHOLOGICAL TEST".

"You are allowed half an hour for each. So sit on the bench and get started. I will come back in half an hour to check on you and then will give you another half hour to finish. Start with the Psychological Test first."

With that, she left the room and locked the door behind her.

"Were you upset at the outcome of your trial?" Was the first question of the Psychological Test.

"No. I was delighted." He thought. "I got the opportunity to come to Camp Nellis." What kind of a question is that? Of course I was upset at the outcome of the trial. No sane person wouldn't be.

Anyway 'yes'. Next question.

"Were you upset to the point that you wanted to do harm to a government employee?"

"Oh! Now. What do they mean by that? Harm to a degree of Oklahoma City pyrotechnics? Or limit it to the courtroom?" Anyhow this is a trick question. 'No.'

"Have you had thoughts of disabling a Bureau of Prisons employee?"

"Do they mean partial or complete disability?" I better answer this one 'No' also.

And so on and so forth, fifty or so questions to test whether to keep you here or send you to an FCI and throw away the key because you are a menace to the government. Bitter and vindictive.

The answers he provided were those of a bitter man, thoughtful and contrived; ready to put all behind him and have a 'good time' at Camp. The test took all of ten minutes to complete, because the government provided all the 'yes' or 'no' answers and all he had to do was check the box.

The intelligence test was next with some math and language problems that any GED candidate should have no problem completing correctly. It then moved on more complex areas of free association and visualization such as the folding paper tests and other Mickey mouse type exercises. He had it all done in fifteen minutes, since the government again was providing four or five answers with each question and all the prisoner had to do was check the appropriate box.

He set down the clipboard with the paperwork and stretched out on the bench.

"Are you not feeling well?" The sexy voice of Miss Diane rang out from the door that apparently could be opened noiselessly.

"No, Diane; I feel fine. It's just that I am...finished."

"Finished! What do you mean finished? You were here less than half hour. This is not a joke. You are required to take these tests to the best of your ability and if you refuse to do so, you will be placed on lock-up. Is this what you want?"

"Miss Bailey, maybe you did not hear me the first time. I have taken and completed the tests to the best of my ability."

"We will see about that." She said in a huff grabbing the clipboard with the paperwork and disappearing with it, locking the door behind her.

Through the window that was running the length of the room, he saw her making her way down the corridor and opening a closet type door with her key. Then she unstapled the pages and started feeding them into an electronic reader. Five minutes later she made her way from the hall closet, back to the room all smiles.

"I must apologize, sir. We just don't get your caliber here very often. Smart, polite, cute too." She said with a mischievous smile.

Oh, God the prisoner thought. I hope I don't see the day that Miss Bailey starts looking good to me.

"I have never seen with my very own eyes an intelligence test completed within the half hour allotted. You did exactly that and you aced it to boot. No one ever finished the test without a single mistake. I remember one came close but he made a mistake. The BOP intelligence test is designed to measure a maximum of 160 I.Q. Yours is off our charts."

"I am not surprised. The Army in 1970 during the Selective Service process asked me to take the Officers' I.Q. test. I finished an hour ahead of the deadline and it was flawless. The I.Q. test finished within the allotted time was rated for 170 I.Q. However, having finished an hour early my I.Q. was off their charts also. This was one of the reasons I avoided being drafted and sent to Viet Nam."

"You sound like a fascinating person Mike, and I would love to talk to you some more, but time in Processing is of the essence, so, if you could follow me, we have to go back to the room with your belongings and go through them together."

She opened the door for him, blocking the opening so he had to brush against her breasts to get past her, feeling her vibrations of desire. She ushered him back to the original windowless office, closed the door and locked it with a key that was attached to her belt by a half inch thick chain, three feet long.

He felt like the little fly caught in the spider's web as she looked at him like a tasty morsel.

"Oh, before we get started, I need you to sign these forms." She said coyly as she handed him two pre-typed government forms with a space at the bottom for  his signature. Her index finger nail scratched playfully the inside of his wrist. He asked permission to get his reading glasses from the trash bags and scanned the typed text.

"I am sorry Miss Bailey, but I cannot sign these forms."

"What do you mean?  Why?"

"Well, it says here that by signing, I acknowledge receipt of a Bureau of Prisons credit card, I have also received two sets of clothing for which I am responsible, and so on; do I need to go on?  None of these things happened."

At that Miss Bailey became another person.

"You fucking bastards.  You come in here questioning our integrity.  You think the government is out to screw you.  Look here mister, you either sign this or you are out of here to a Maximum Security Facility.  There you will know once and for all who is Boss."

"Miss Bailey, with all due respect, what you are asking me to do, under duress, is to sign false statements.  You of all people should know this.  If these proceeding are being videotaped, the government would have the basis to indict you on Conspiracy at the very least."

This had an immediate calming effect on Miss Bailey and she turned the whole matter into a joke.

"Well, you smarty pants, I will give you all the stuff that it says there you are entitled to.  Then you can sign the forms.  I never met a man who can get me so worked up over nothing.  I am going to be keeping an eye on you."

With that she unlocked the door and placed a call from the telephone on her desk.  A few minutes later a black guard opened the door. Six foot five, at least, two hundred fifty pounds with a shaved head.  He had defensive end written all over him.

"Duane, why don't you take Mr. Michael and give him his clothes." Miss Bailey cooed sweetly.

Duane took the prisoner to the room with the two benches.

"Are you self surrender, man?"

"Yes."

"You just came in?"

"Yes."

"What are you, some kind of CEO?"

"Yes."

"Your first time in?"

"Yes."

"That's what I thought. It's written all over you, man! Wait for me here. What size are you? I make you extra large top, large bottom; close?

"Yes."

"Well, it makes no difference, any who. Them are temporary duds. Wait here, I will be back."

With that he left the room and came back in a flash carrying two huge net bags. He tossed them like feather pillows at the feet of the prisoner. Michael raised his head questioningly towards the black giant.

"The one on your right is your bedding, the one on your left is your temps."

The prisoner noticed the long window behind the guard was no longer empty looking into the blanc wall across the hall. It was filled with the giggling faces of the government secretaries with Miss Bailey as their ring leader. He leaned down to pick-up his bags.

"Hey, man. What's you doing? You got to get undressed." The black guard's voice stopped him as he got ahold the lightest of the two bags. He looked up, beat red from embarrassment.

"Here? Now?" He was able to whisper.

"Yea man!  I got to check you out.  You know, take your clothes off.  I mean everything."

The black guard followed his prisoner's gaze directed behind him and saw Diane and her cohorts staring inside the room from outside the window.

"Oh, man! That's what's bugging you? Don't mean nothing man.  You in Jail now.  See them bitches.  Don't mean nothing.  That fat cow, Diane; only chance she got to see dick, other than them stroke magazines she's reading."

The prisoner went through the whole humiliating process of the strip search with the all female audience.  The black guard was kind and considerate under the circumstances.  At the end he told the prisoner that if he wanted something brought in from the outside, to see him.

"Everything is available for a price." He added.

The prisoner was given a new set of underwear and a khaki doctor's operating room type uniform, elastic waist pants and pull over 'V' neck top, white shocks and white tennis shoes.  His clothes were taken and dumped with his other belongings to be gone over by Diane.

Once a woman sees a man naked, the relationship somehow changes. The prisoner sensed that, once he was locked up in the room with the female guard once again.  The Mike and Diane came out a lot easier, like two lovers who are familiar with each other and that familiarity settled into a comfortable relationship.   His belongings were inspected perfunctorily and Diane went through the excess clothing, tennis racket and boxes of cigars without confiscating them or acknowledging their existence.

At the end she said to the prisoner that she hoped they stayed friends and she would like to see him again any time he had a problem.  With that she gave him back his trash bags  and told him to go to Building 203, which was the one next to the Administration Building where he was being processed.  His room was on the first floor; the second door on his right as he came inside Building 203 from the side door.

"The building side door is the first door you would encounter coming out of the Administration Building.  After you put your stuff in your room, come back for the rest of it.  Make that quick because I want to leave and go home." Dianne added.

The prisoner took his sun glasses out of his pocket, hefted the bags and opened the door marked exit from Building 203 Processing Center.

# CHAPTER 3

## The Roommates

The prisoner moved like a sleepwalker towards the door marked exit. He hit the panic hardware opening both leaves to the exit door at once. The three o'clock sun hit him in the face, temporarily blinding him. What happened in Processing was like an out of body experience. The bright outdoors light shining through the open doorway only reinforced that feeling. The question was whether crossing the threshold, was he entering Heaven or Hell? He put on his sun glasses, hefted the two net and trash bags with his belongings and crossed the threshold in search of Building 203.

The backdoor to the Administration Building, which was the exit door he came out of, had a six foot by six foot landing with four steps leading to the main camp courtyard of approximately ten acres laid out end to end, interrupted every acre or so by a crosswalk that cut across the yard and joined the main sidewalk that circled the entire courtyard like a jogging path.

Scrawny trees and cacti spouted in the middle of the courtyard. A building with a sign 'RED HORSE' and another building named 'RED HORSE MESS HALL', marked the two ends of the compound. Two dormitory buildings named 'Navajo' and 'Sierra' together with the Administration Building on one side and the Library, Education Building and Shops on the other side completed the immediate perimeter. The courtyard was full of inmates dressed in khaki's, milling around or heading towards mail call at locations, he found out shortly afterwards, designated in accordance with the last name initial letter. The temperature was in the high nineties as the prisoner made his way slowly towards Building 203 which he guessed must be the next building to his left.

Everybody stopped what they were doing and looked at the new face in the yard.  The prisoner kept his head high, looking straight ahead through people, without concentrating on any one in particular while keeping his peripheral vision angle on alert and roving.  He noticed the biker looking group staring at him, flexing their muscles and showing off their tattoos; the groups of blacks hanging around, leaning against the court yard wall in groups of fives and sixes, shadow dancing and harmonizing their moves to inaudible music through their walkman head sets, by bopping each other at prearranged intervals; latin groups sporting  common tattoos 'La Onda', paid particular attention to the prisoner, dark haired and tanned from living in the Hawaiian Islands for the past eleven years, greeting him with a couple of 'Hola's'.

The prisoner took all that in, without response, and turned left at the last gate where a young Mexican looking female guard appeared to be waiting for him.

"Come with me sir." She said opening the building door and holding it open for the prisoner to come through.  She had sweat stained underarms and twin sweat bands underneath her breasts; the sweat punctuating the dark areoles showing through her white shirt uniform. The prisoner got a faint whiff of b.o. mixed with perfume, musk and sweat, not an unpleasant smell; something you'd smell in the tropical jungle after a rainfall.  He stopped and took at her small frame, balanced on top of high heeled black cowboy boots, light grey wool pants and white shirt.  Jet black hair, olive skin complexion, fleshy lips and enormous brown eyes.  They entered a narrow hallway that fed into a large room whose walls were lined with beds, mattresses, metal lockers and metal folding chairs.

"This is where you come and get what you need as soon as I show you to your room.  Lucky for you, your room is on the first floor so you don't have to carry a long ways."

He followed her through another metal door at the other end of the room and was staring down the length of a four foot wide corridor extending as long as the eye could see, lined with metal doors on each side.

"You are the second door to the right.  Go on in, set your stuff and go to the Administration Building for two other bags with the rest of your bedding and Camp issue clothing.  Hurry, because the Administration Building closes at 3:30 PM."

The next time he turned his head, she was no longer standing next to him.  He was alone in this corridor to find his room.  What number did she say?  She did not.  She said second door to the right.  How many people are there already?  Is there a bed inside or does he have to get one from the ward room?

He made his way towards the second door to the right and stopped. Room 121.  Is this the right room?  He had no alternative but to take the word of the pretty guard.  He knocked on the door.  No answer.  He knocked again louder.  No response.  What do I do now?  He thought.  Go in?  Stay out here and wait?  How long?  Should I leave my stuff out here in the hallway?  What if they get stollen?   He tried the door knob.  It was unlocked.  He pushed the door slowly and peered inside.  Three bunk beds and six lockers at the foot of each bed were the only furnishings discernible though the diminished light filtering through the blind slats.

The room was ten feet by twelve feet.  All the beds were neatly made except for the top bunk to the right which was down to bed springs.

"What can I do you for?" A raspy voice echoed in the hallway with the door wide open.  A middle aged man with a tennis racket in a case slung over his back, carrying two sleeves of tennis balls, a gallon water cooler jug and a towel, made his way into the room, limping slightly. Both his legs were heavily bandaged with Ace support tape. The right one in particular was growing out of his shorts at a very unnatural angle. The product of a serious accident. His face was puffy from exertion and past drinking binges. His hair was light brown, short on top and on the sides, with a flowing mane behind. He took one look at the bags at the feet of the prisoner and said.

"You must be the trash man or our new homie. From the look on your face, I bet the latter. You must be self report also, because the meat wagon comes early in the morning. There is only one bunk left, so guess which one is yours. Throw your stuff on top and go get the other bags with your bedding and issue clothes. By the way my name is Randy."

"Michael." The prisoner replied with caution.

"You can trust me bud. I am your homie. I will go in the meantime and see if I can rustle you a mattress and a couple of lockers."

The prisoner swung the bags on top of the upper right hand bunk and retraced his steps to the Administration Building. He noticed that no one turned his direction anymore. He was no longer new meat. He felt relieved. He stayed clear of the inmates walking from the opposite direction on the path, playfully pushing and shoving each other and acting boisterously. Instinctively, he sought the security and protection of the guards. There was none in sight. He adopted the thousand yard stare and started walking with measured paces towards the middle building, his heart racing and his stomach fluttering.

Halfway between the two buildings, in no man's land, he had the uncontrollable urge to take a shit. Could he hold it until he made it back to the dormitory? Should he risk the Administration Building? He quickened his pace while tightening his sphincter muscles. That's all he needed. Five minutes in the yard and he shit his pants. That will impress the inmate population. Administration Building here I come. Oh! Oh! Change of plan. The metal side door was closed. Probably locked. Two duffel bags made out of netting material were leaning against it.  He raced towards them.  Picked them up.  Tried the door which was predictably locked and started back towards the dormitory, some three hundred yards away, at a brisk pace.

"Don't sweat it man." A smiling black face startled him to his right. "You will make the count."

What was this negro talking about?  Thank God the foot traffic had thinned out so he was making good time back.

He used the same side entrance.  Raced across the ward room.  Found the corridor and Room 121. Opened the door. Slung the two duffel bags inside and raced down the corridor in search of a bathroom as a blue light started flashing overhead.

What the hell?  Is this the K-Mart?  He smiled amused.  The door to the right opened up ahead and saw an inmate coming out adjusting the seat of his trousers.  Bingo.  Two seconds later he was siting on the throne. Deliverance.  Oh!  The joy of taking a shit in a deserted bathroom after several days of constipation because of the uncertainty of the future. Flush your troubles away my boy, he thought. Ouch!  What the hell was that?  His asshole revolted at the touch of the prison toilet paper.  Man, is this paper for wiping or sanding down?  He made a second pass with another wad pre crumbled to soften it up. No good.

The asshole reacted and sent a warning signal to the brain. 'Hey, who is the Boss around here?  If I am treated that way; it's going to be a blue moon, next time I come to bat.'

The prisoner opened the stall door.  Looked cautiously left and right. Gathered his dignity as best he could and made his way crablike to the row of sinks across the way.  There he wetted two wads of toilet paper. He added soap to one of them and retreated to the privacy of the stall to try again.  A little better.  At least he will avoid the skid marks in his underpants.

Feeling better, he made his way out of the bathroom as the blue light was now flashing in the corridor and someone was yelling.

"Recount! Recount!"

He found Room 121 and entered without knocking. He looked quickly at the five frightened faces counterclockwise. One looking like a mad scientist, a hick who looked like he just returned from milking the cows, a tall black man mechanically stroking his mustache, Randy who he had met earlier, and a wild eyed looking fellow with multiple fascial twitches and uncontrollable body spasms. Randy broke the silence.

"Come in man. Where you've been? You almost fucked us over. I hope no one saw you, because the whole building will be late for chow."

"What are you talking about?" The prisoner asked starry eyed.

"The count man." The black fellow replied. "You fucked the four o' clock count. Now the hacks are thinking someone escaped and got the place on alert."

"I hope dip shit for your own good no one saw you." The twitcher said. "Even if they did; keep your mouth shut and play dumb."

At that moment the room door sprang open and the Mexican guard, that had greeted him to the building earlier, came in followed by a black female guard of Amazonian proportions.

The inmates sprang to their feet. The guards stopped briefly, counted heads and left the room as abruptly as they had come in.

"What was that all about?" The prisoner asked shyly.

Instead of an answer, Randy brought his index finger to his lips making the sign of silence.

A few minutes later, a female voice reverberated along the corridor.

"Clear! Clear!"

All at once the five inmates in the room assumed life, talking all at once; their words drowned amongst the din and rumble coming from the adjacent rooms all along the corridor.

"Double 'D' is blaming Big Stupid right now for the double count."  The mad scientist was saying.

"You are one lucky motherfucker."  The black man added in concert.

"Hey, guys simmer down."  Randy was trying to be heard over the noise.  "I want you to meet our new homie.  Michael is it or Mike?  Which way you want to be called?"

"Either way is fine with me."  The prisoner said with a wide grin on his face.

"Well, this is Bushy - the mad scientist, Ed - the hick, Lew - the black man, Eric - the wild twitcher, and myself Randy, we are your new homies."

# CHAPTER 4

## The Blue Light

The prisoner started unpacking his belongings, which was tantamount to dumping each bag on top of the bunk, which had a mattress now, and sorting out his meager possessions in accordance to their function.

Back to the cot and the cardboard box epoch; he smiled wryly. Ab Ovo,(a literary term of starting a story in the middle and coming full circle to the same point in the narrative) when his business was run solely by him from the guest room of his first home in Hawaii Kai. His life was taking a turn towards childhood returning to the roots of his youth.

It is a story that he liked to repeat to his children when they were leaving their rooms a mess or were disgruntled because they only had two of everything.

"When I was a little boy, I had no room of my own. I had an army cot, bedding and a cardboard box; all of which had to fit inside a broom closet in the kitchen. At night I would unfold and make my bed in the kitchen, sleep there, and in the morning put everything back in the closet before people got up in the morning. The cardboard box contained two changes of clothes, my books and all my toys. Whatever did not fit inside the cardboard box, it was thrown or given away by my parents. Needless to say the cardboard box was always filled to capacity. Every Christmas, birthday, name day and major holiday, I would get presents. The joy of receiving something new, was always hampered by the realization that there was no room in my cardboard box or if there was room for the new acquisition, I had to get rid of something else that was dear to me.  I had the habit of wearing several layers of clothes, because I had no room in the cardboard box to store them."

To date, when his wife was giving him a present, like a shirt for no special occasion other than being on sale and she could not pass up a good deal, he cringed from his childhood memory that he would have to throw away something, probably a garment that took as much or more space in his cardboard box.  His wife who knew the story was stroking his face lovingly.

"Honey, it's OK.  You have a large closet.  You have plenty of room for another shirt.  You don't have to throw away another piece of clothing if you don't want to."

A loud banging noise coming from the room down and across the hall brought him back to his new reality.  The bang was followed by crashing noises, stomping and screams for help.

The six homies looked at each other and Eric placed a metal chair across the room's metal door under the door knob.

The noise spilled out in the hallway.  Bodies crushed against the outside of the metal door, followed by thuds as if a head was being bashed against the outside of their door.  Grunts, cusses, angry exchanges, unintelligible for the most part, were heard through the masonry walls.

The prisoner stood mesmerized listening in silence, the muffled words asking for help from the victims outside the door, while his roommates were going on about their daily routine of reading skin magazines and eating junk food they had bought and brought in from the vending machines.

"What's all that about?"  Asked Michael to everyone and no one in particular.

"Why don't you go out and find out." Answered Ed indifferently not looking up from the centerfold.

"Yeah!" Cut in Lew. "But you cannot go in there and simply ask. You got to step up my man, kick their fucking door in and speak with authority. Motherfuckers, if you don't keep it quiet or take it outside, I am going to kick some ass around here. There, you say that and they will take notice. There is a new man in town."

"Don't listen to them Mike," Randy chimed in, "they are only trying to get you in trouble."

"That's right," Eric said, "it's not our problem. Don't butt in uninvited and bring the trouble to our room, because then we will have to rescue you and this will lead to hostilities with steel pipes and baseball bats and before it's all over we will all get transferred to a maximum security facility, after we get a few days in the North  Las Vegas County Jail so the bad boys there can keep in shape with new punch and kicking bags."

"See!" Lew was able to say before he pulled out his front teeth that were being held together with a plate attached to his other teeth.  "This is curtesy of the bad boys.  There were two motherfuckers with clubs and brass knuckles.  But one mother fucker lost a ball in the fracas.  I wished the fuck I started earlier before they had a chance to get me some good ones.  The son of a bitch would be singing soprano right now."

"Where are the guards?" Michael exclaimed. "They were here a minute ago."

"Oh, yeah! The guards. Double 'D' and stupid." Chimed in Bushy. "They are long gone my friend after the body count.  They will come around after chow, when everything is back to normal, to take down the damage and room number.

They are not interested to break up any fights or care what happens to you. They collect their roll of quarters before they put out."

"I am sorry." Said Michael. "I am new around here and I don't understand. For that matter, I've never been in prison before, detained in any way or gotten even a speeding ticket for that fact. So I don't understand what you fellows are talking about."

"The screws, man, the hacks. He is talking about them bitches, and all the other bitches around here." Lew added.

"Let me explain it to you." Eric finally spoke leaning forward and lowering his voice. "The Camp guards are primarily all female. It's the way for the BOP to maintain the required diversity percentage mandated by the Federal Government. The female hacks around here give head. You know what that is? Blow jobs."

Michael nodded his eyes opening in surprise.

"Double 'D' you know, the white broad with the big knockers. No good man." Eric continued. "Very mechanical, little action, no suction. She and her dyke friend Alphonse, you will see them around holding hands and all, are bubble gummers. They chew, but don't swallow. Big stupid on the other hand. The tall black chick, man she gets those thick lips around your joint and she will suck you   dry till the cows come home. I know she is not much to look at, but in the dark they are all the same."

The commotion in the hallway had stopped by now. Eric pulled the metal folding chair that was jammed against the doorknob.

"Hold it! Hold it!" Screamed Lew. "Drop a towel first in front. I don't want to see blood getting tracked inside. If I see blood on my new Air Jordan's, there is gonna be blood in this fucking room also."

"Mike, you are new here." Bushy added. "It's your fucking job to clean the blood from our door and walls. Don't worry about the floor. The orderly will take care of that."

"Yeah man! Move fast." Eric said. "The screws already know the fight ended and they are on their way to investigate. We don't want no traces of blood in our neighborhood and if they ask you, you saw nothing, you heard, nothing. Capish?"

Five towels were thrown simultaneously at the prisoner from his homies, like snow balls turning into parachutes in mid flight. He opened the door slowly and cautiously. He looked each way. The orderly was two doors down bearing down with his floor cleaning machine like a lawn mower. The prisoner stared at the pool of blood in front of his feet which had started congealing and drying out at the shallow ends.

"Stay the fuck inside!" The orderly yelled. "Wait until I give the OK to come out. And put a towel on the inside, at the bottom of the door."

The prisoner did as he was told. He heard a faint "Clear" at the other side of the door and picked the towel he had set at the bottom of the door. It was pink for the most part. Shit! He thought. I bet they will make me wash it now.

"Don't worry." Randy said reading his thoughts. "Use this towel first to clean the door and walls outside. Use as many towels as you need. Then go upstairs on the second floor and throw all of them in one of their hallway trash cans. The most important thing is to confuse the hacks, so they don't pinpoint where the fight took place. As for new towels, don't sweat it. We got a locker full."

He handed Michael a spray bottle of Windex and hopped on top of the upper bunk by the far wall. The prisoner opened the door. The floor was freshly washed, disinfected and even waxed. Low men on the totem pole crews were busy washing neighborhood walls and doors. The Mexican kid from the room on his left had cleaned the entire wall between the rooms and both doors.

"Hey, thanks amigo." The prisoner whispered.

"Gimme the towels." The Mexican whispered back. "I will get rid of them with mine. Go to the bathroom and wash your hands with soap three times. Three times is good. No trace."

The prisoner nodded that he understood.

"What you in for man?" The Mexican asked smiling widely.

"Oh! It's a long story. How about you?"

"Drugs man! My name is Jesus. What's yours?"

"Michael."

"Miguel my man, you be a Big Man on the outside. Jesus knows. Right?"

The prisoner moved his head in the affirmative, sadly.

"Hey! Don't worry man. You be Big Man on the inside, also. It shows. Jesus Knows!"

The prisoner made his way towards the bathroom which was presently occupied by the combatants, all of them black, in their early twenties, being ministered by a rotund white man in his fifties, with curly white hair, jowls, triple chins and hands that looked like they belonged to a pastry chef. The impromptu doctor looked up from sewing a cut lip and asked in a feminine voice.

"Are you hurt?" He answered his own question. "You don't look hurt. Use the bathroom across the hall. We'll be busy here for a while."

The prisoner made his way across the hall. Washed, scrubbed his hands three times like he was told and dried. Back in the room he asked.

"Hey, I just met the strangest looking creature in the bathroom. He was sewing up the combatants. I don't know if he looked stranger or talked stranger."

"Oh! He must be talking about Dr. Come, we call the 'Sperminator.'" Piped in Eric.

"Who is Dr. Come?" Asked Michael with evident curiosity.

"The 'Asshole of the Month', according to the Penthouse Magazine, this month's edition." Ed joined in.

"You must have heard about him Mike." Randy said trying to keep down the laughter. "He made national news. Where the fuck you coming from, anyway?" "Hawaii."

"Hawaii, eh!" Continued Randy. "Even so I am sure you guys have radios and TV out there. He is the doctor who was getting the women pregnant by slipping them his own sperm without telling them. Can you imagine bringing kids in the world looking like him?"

"Well, this is a Civil matter." Michael said. "If the women felt they did not get what they had paid for, they could bring a Civil suit against the Doctor and his Insurance. How did the Federal Government get involved?"

"You are getting too technical for me, bud." Randy said tossing towards Michael the latest issue of Penthouse Magazine opened at the article featuring the sperm doctor as 'The Asshole of the Month'.

"Go ask him yourself. If I know the government, they probably got him on a Mail Fraud charge, since the broads mailed him a check for servicing them. By the way, what are you in for?"

The prisoner blinked his eyes, swallowed hard and said in a barely audible voice.

"Mail Fraud."

The room erupted in laughter.

"But not for what you are thinking." Michael added belatedly.

"Mickey my man," Bust out Lew, "I had you wrong man, I apologize. I took you for a businessman type, you know CEO, that kind of shit. Only to find out that you been slipping them babes in Hawaii the business. You all right!"

"No! No! You got it all wrong." Michael stammered all red in the face, close to tears. "This is a different type of Mail Fraud. In my case it stems from the interpretation of the Davis-Bacon Act."

"Say what?" Lew cut in. "Dave and Bacon Acts; shit, this sound kinky to me boys."

"Davis-Bacon Act is a labor law," Michel continued above the din and laughter, "pertaining to wage rates on federal and/or federally funded projects. The law simply states that the workers that work on site, must be paid the prevailing wage listed, assigned to the particular Contract for the type of work they were performing on an hourly basis. Reports are being sent to the Government on a weekly basis corresponding to the hourly rates paid based on the interpretation of that law."

"What happened? You failed to file the reports?" Lew asked.

"No. The Reports were sent to the Government and were identical to the actual wages paid. The government indicted me on the basis of my interpretation of the law which differed from theirs as presented during my trial. I interpreted the Davis-Bacon Act to apply only on the hours spent working on the actual job site. The Government expanded the term job site to mean everywhere as long as it was remotely associated with the project."

"So, you cheated your workers." Lew insisted.

"The government is the only one cheating its workers. They don't want competition." Randy added.

"If I had paid my workers on the basis consistent with the government interpretation of the law, I would have made more money, because the majority of our work was Change Orders performed on a Force Account Basis. This was the reason the Government was videotaping all our projects, to indict me and the company for overcharging the government on Change Orders. When this attempt failed, they switched tactics and claimed that I underpaid the employees. The thou sands of hours of video tapes comprising a whole library that would have proven my position and innocence, of course got misplaced or lost during my trial."

"What did the judge have to say about that?" Randy asked.

"The judge ignored the lost tapes and decided that the Government's interpretation of the law was correct and mine was not. Accordingly, he gave the jury instructions in accordance with the government's interpretation of the expanded job site. The Supreme Court a few months after my trial, on another case involving the interpretation of the Davis-Bacon Act concerning the concept of job site, decided that it meant the actual physical site upon which the work was performed. Accordingly, the judge's instructions to the jury in my case were erroneous because my interpretation of the labor law was correct and the Government's was wrong. I am Appealing to the Supreme Court with a 'Writ of Certiorari' on this matter and the constitutional issue of the Judge taking the Government's interpretation of the law as fact and ignoring mine; i.e. of the individual citizen. Instead of presenting them both to the jury to decide."

"Hot damn! Another Mail Fraud dude bites the dust." Bushy the mad scientist exclaimed. "You know what they say in prison? Mail Fraud is a unique law applicable to the United States only for bullshit offenses, fabricated by the Government because they want you and they cannot figure any other way to get you. You've been rolled up buddy."

"What are you in for?" Michael asked him in turn.

"Telemarketing. Man I was the 'Bandit of the Airwaves' as Ted Copple called me during NightLine on television."

"What exactly did you do wrong?"

"I was making people feel good man. I was running an ad during the late-late show on TV for people to write to me and get bumper stickers and other beads and trinkets with slogans, like 'Say No to Drugs'. People were sending money also at the rate of $40,000 per day; or we would contact them after they wrote to us and explain our program and their tax deductible contribution would be appreciated. I told the federal agents when they arrested me in New Orleans coming out of a leased

Lear Jet that I intended to fight the drugs, but had not gotten around to it, yet."

"Yeah!" Jumped in Lew. "Like I told the DEA agents, when they arrested me, that I intended to build a hospital with the drug proceeds in the Bahamas for mother Teresa."

"What was the deal with Ted Copple?" Michael intervened, not letting the subject get away from Bushman.

"I was running a commercial, you see, and I was using part of Nancy Reagan's speech in the beginning. You know the 'Say No to Drugs' speech. Ted Copple was doing a piece on telemarketing which was still in the embryonic stages at the time. So Ted was using our scheme as an example of skirting the existing laws, taking peoples money and getting away with it. So he had one of his henchmen trying to get a line on me. ABC invited me to appear on the show, but I didn't bother to answer their invitation. He tracked me down in New York. His sidekick ambushed me as I was getting out of a New York night club at 2:00 in the morning, with a buzz and a babe on my arm. The bastard followed me down the sidewalk shoving a microphone in my face. I told him to fuck off and got in my red Ferrari Testarossa with my date as soon as the valet brought it up front. His cameraman filmed the whole thing, including me pealing out from the curb. The camera got a close up of my license plate which was custom and said 'BANDIT'. So, Ted Copple named me 'the Bandit of the Airwaves' and gave me Robin Hood type qualities which translated to the feds as 'Robbing Hoodlum'. The night the show aired, I became a target. A couple of months later all good things came to an end and I've been in custody under lock and key ever since, because I represented an extreme flight risk. I got 77 months for it and they confiscated everything I owned under the Forfeiture Statues. And I mean everything. Except what I was wearing at the time of my arrest. My gold Rolex and about a hundred thousand dollars in jewelry which I will try to collect as soon as I am out of here."

"What about you Lew?  What is this about drugs and mother Teresa?" Michael asked.

"Yeah!  Lew, tell us how you got taken, you dumb fuck by a DEA hooker." Eric jumped in.

"At least I did not blow up my sorry ass, you motherfucker." Lew answered playacting indignation.

"You two would have made a great team." Randy added.  "Maybe you should team up when you get out of here."

"I wouldn't talk if I were you flour man." Eric cuts in.

"Thank goodness I am just a burglar." Ed chimed in.

"So," Michael said.  "Eric you are in for explosives?"

"No!  For stupidity." Randy said.  "The dumb fuck sat on the detonator and blew himself up."

"Not exactly." Corrected Eric. "I sat on the remote by accident and woke up in the hospital looking like the fucking mummy, chained to my bed. They charged me for using an unauthorized explosive devise and threw in fire arm violations because they knew I was a gun dealer.  They cooked up some paper discrepancies which they claimed, they've pieced together on site." "Why are they calling you the flour man, Randy?" Michael asked.

"Yeah!  Tell him Randy." The homies said in chorus.

"You dip shit," Lew added,  "you would have been better off with a 'key' of the real thing."

"Well," said Randy, "I was a high class dealer.  You know I supplied blow to the rich and famous.  They rolled me up on a small quantity possession and I did some time.  My rep grew as a stand up guy because I did not rat on my supplier or the users, which were all heavy hitters, and the feds wanted that list of 'Who's Who' so they could see who they wanted to roll and who to put the arm to.  Any who, I wouldn't play so I did  a year.  In the joint, I read about these two guys that got off because they carried baby powder.  So I thought.  Why risk a second conviction.  Maybe, if I get caught out I ought to push some flour, the marks would not know the difference particularly if they were donating it to a party mix.  I got out, went to Safeway, got a five pound sack of flour and hit the ski resorts.  Aspen, Vale, Lake Tahoe.  I was doing great.  So great in fact that I bought a Porsche to get around in style.  My parole officer spotted me in that.  He figured the dude must be dealing again to be able to afford this set of wheels.  They bust in my apartment and they find all the flour.  I figured, all right, they cannot bust me, they can't do shit to me.  Wrong.  They got me on 'Intent' and 'Conspiracy' to   sell and a lot of gobble - goop.  Bottom line, I am doing a dime, that's ten years, and I got a transfer here on the downside of my dime from the FCI."

"See, you dumb fuck, what did I tell you!  With a key of blow, you would only be doing a nickel."  Lew added.

"Hey, guys, the chow line is forming."  Ed said after lifting the blind slats and peering towards the Mess Hall.

With that, the homies made it out the door with Mickey, the new prisoner, in their midst.

# CHAPTER 5

## The Mess Hall

Outside the Mess Hall the line was snaking along the entire length of one dormitory, halfway down the Administration Building back entrance, by the time the six homies joined the quay.

They were still arguing about whose turn it was to check the blue light; its extinction signaling the OK to be outside the building and the start of the dinner line.  By now the inmates had exchanged the khaki's, which were the mandatory uniform of the day until two o' clock in the afternoon, for their civilian clothes which comprised primarily of athletic type clothing.

The waiting prisoners looked like students of an inner-city type Community College campus sponsored by the United Negro Fund. There was much jostling and roughhousing in the line requiring guards to walk up and down, staring at the rowdier of the groups.

Michael's homies were still engaged in animated conversation about the events of the day.  Lew had the floor because he was working as an orderly at the VA Hospital, just across from Nellis Air Force Base, and he always came back with titillating stories about a tit that slipped outside the hospital gown or hospital attire bunched up under the covers giving a fine view of snatch as they were moving a patient.  The stories seemed repetitive, after all how many tits, pussy and ass combinations exist, but the inmates listened each time anew, possessed with almost religious fervor as they vicariously transported themselves to the foot of the bed, silent witnesses to voyeurism at its most desperate.

Michael was wondering how much the tales grew in the mind of Lew between the hospital grounds to give birth to those extraordinary tales of lust and patient exhibitionism by the time the hospital van reached the Camp at the end of the working day, bringing back the inmate orderlies, janitors and grounds keepers.

"Does everyone work in this camp?" Michael asked his homies.

"You better believe it buddy." Randy volunteered. "You either work or you get transferred to a Higher Security Institution."

"Where do you work Randy?" Michael asked.

"I work in construction as a carpenter here at the Camp, but most of the people work on Base. The BOP will fill all the Base requests for labor first and what's left stays here working Custody in the Camp. The BOP gets paid eight dollars per hour minimum for inmates that are doing janitorial services on Base and the prisoner gets twelve cents an hour. The rest is kept by UNI-COR."

Michael moved his head up and down thinking out loud.

"Let's see. There are five hundred inmates at eight bucks an hour that's four thousand dollars an hour times eight hour days, that's thirty two thousand dollars per day income to this UNI-COR outfit, whoever they are, out of this Camp."

"That's for the minimum wagers." Randy interrupted. "A lot of others get higher because the BOP/UNI-COR collects higher. There are four wage classifications. Twelve cents minimum, unless you are left over in the Camp in Custody which pays ten cents an hour, to forty cents the maximum."

"Where do you work, Eric?" Michael asked.

"At the Base Golf Course. I cut the grass and drive the water truck in the afternoon. I get grade two pay at seventeen cents an hour. The Base pays the BOP/ UNI-COR twelve dollars per hour for each hour I work at the Golf Course. I heard that the BOP/UNI-COR on the average makes out over twenty thousand dollars out of each inmate. The inmate sells out his ass and UNI-COR is paying him a subsistence type wage."

"Well," Michael said, "there are approximately two thousand working hours per year so on the average the BOP/UNI-COR must collect a little over ten bucks per hour for each prisoner."

"Yes, very possible, the numbers work out at that rate." Eric confirmed.

"What kind of work were you doing on the outside?" Asked Bushy with open admiration. "You are like a God damn calculator."

"I was, I still am, a Chemical Engineer." Michael replied.

"Oh! Oh! You heard that Lew," Ed chimed in, "the man can mix chemicals and come up with any kind of drug you can think of."

"No!" Michael spoke vehemently. "A Chemical Engineer builds plants, factories, you know, power plants, refineries and the like. He is involved with infrastructure work and processes in the field more, than laboratory work."

"My ex wife was an engineer." Randy added.

"Oh, yeah?" Michael replied. "What kind?"

"A railroad engineer." Randy said deadpan. "You know, she liked to pull trains."

The rest of the homies broke in boisterous laughter. It took Michael a split second later to realize the underlying joke and involuntarily turned red. The laughter attracted the guard they called Petunia and she ambled over to where they were standing. Seeing Michael red in the face and the others laughing, she asked him whether he was all right.

Michael looked at her five foot height, two hundred fifty pound frame and replied that he was all right.

"She was involved in an incident last night." Eric brought up as soon as the guard moved out of hearing distance. "Did you hear about it?"

"I heard something about it." Lew added. "Was it related to the brothers last night?"

"I knew it!" Bushy chimed. "Someone was missing last night. That was the reason for the three counts at ten o'clock."

"What happened?" Michael asked in earnest.

"Four beep boppers, sorry about this Lew, I mean four blacks in their early twenties left Camp after the four o'clock count and went to town for some pussy. The assholes didn't even try to change out of their khaki's. Force of habit." Randy added. "I understand that they been doing this three times a week for months now. You can't argue with success. Why change now?"

"That's good and dandy." said Eric, "But yesterday a North Las Vegas cop spotted them coming out of a whorehouse. The guy was one of the 'nasty boys' so he could not get identified. For you Michael that you are gonna ask anyway, the 'nasty boys' is a North Las Vegas elite undercover police force that when they do a bust, they sport face masks, hoods and other paraphernalia, so even their own don't know their faces. Anyway, one of them dudes spotted the brothers four coming out of the Crazy Horse saloon and getting in the white Cadillac Eldorado. He radioed the North Las Vegas Police Desk with the particulars and they in turn notified the federal Camp. The hacks were all set to catch the joy riders, so they put a couple of them in cars on the road, one on a building roof and Petunia in the Mess Hall kitchen parking lot. The brothers blew in through the gate, without lights and were gone; past the dudes on the road before they could shake the dew out of their lily. The hack on top of the roof checked out the commotion and alerted Petunia in the parking lot. Before the crane could make it in the parking lot to lift Petunia off her fat ass, that Caddy braked, four shadows jumped out hightailing it back to the dormitory, low to the ground and both the car and the dudes were long gone before the dust settled. Petunia claims that they bumped her and spun her around, so she was unable to identify the perps. All I know is that they are wanted for attempt to escape, escape, resisting arrest and assault. The Lieutenant on duty wanted to have a cock sniffing contest for traces of cunt juice but her request was turned down by the Warden, afraid of ensuing Civil Rights violation suits and the results would be inconclusive any who, with some dudes claiming that they were tearing a solitary piece of ass with the hired help. Without DNA testing, which is very expensive, there is no way of pin pointing where the dude took his pleasure. So they rolled a few known black loudmouths and troublemakers to the North Las Vegas County Jail and are trying to beat a confession out of them. They should be back by tonight."

The line moved forward by the equivalent of twenty five or so prisoners.

"Why are the inmates being processed through the Mess Hall entrance in batch type fashion?" Michael asked his homies addressing no one in particular.

"So they can stager the line and give the people that got their food ten minutes or so to eat." Bushy answered. "You will see if you linger on your food too long, a guard will come along and tell you that you had enough, leave your tray and get out. Simple mathematics my boy, you are an engineer. You should know. The dinning room has capacity of 150 people. the Camp has 500 inmates. That means that each seat must be occupied 3 to 4 times during a forty five minute period, which represents the overall duration of the allotted meal time."

"Same reason you got six people to a ten by twelve foot room, when it was originally designed for two." Ed jumped in. "It is called overcrowding, so the Warden can retire with the title of Warden instead of Administrator. The overcrowding gets worse as you go up the ladder in security requirements."

"Take a look at the guards." Added Lew. "Would you hire them if they came to you for a job? They are welfare material. The government however, hires them. All they need is a high school diploma or a GED. Most of them get their GED after they get hired. Most of them don't know how to read and write. None of them can count over one hundred. Haven't you noticed why it takes them three times to count the prisoners? See Slim over there." He said pointing at a tall young black guard. "I know he has to take his shoes off to count higher than ten."

Before the general laughter in the line could subside, Lew did it again.

"See that other motherfucker, we all call Mark Furman. The one with the Aryan supremacy haircut and tattoos?" He said pointing to a young blond guard reminiscent of German stormtrooper in dress and mannerism, as he was harassing a group of young black inmates. "Now I sure know this motherfucker couldn't count his balls and get the same number twice."

"Lew. Lew. Lew." Eric hummed in. "Why do you get so worked up. I thought you didn't give a shit. Never did. Never will."

"I know. We all get institutionalized and accept these mothers...like sunshine," mumbled Lew, "but then somebody fresh comes along, like Mike here and starts asking questions; and then you get to answer them, but before you answer them, he got you thinking, something you forgot you used to do and you realize they've changed you and you get mad. Does this make sense to you?"

"The son of a bitch really knows his shit." Eric piped in ironically.

"At this point, his first day at Camp, he knows just enough to be dangerous." Ed added.

"It beats being fucking brain damaged like you two." Lew retorted.

"My coffee cup has a higher I.Q." Randy said.

"They measured my I.Q. at processing." Michael said. "Their test could only measure up to 160."

"I stand corrected." Randy said in apologetic tone. "Now, I know this homie is real dangerous."

The camaraderie and insult exchange was broken by the guard standing at the Mess Hall entrance signaling the six homies permission to enter the premises. Michael got in only to find out that he was at the tail end of another line along one side of the dinning room slowly making its way towards a cafeteria style food display. A Philippine girl of indeterminate age, with straight back raven hair, in a freshly starched red uniform, was handing out trays and utensils as the line was approaching her.

"Hey Mike, would you do her?" Bushy elbowed him mischievously pointing towards the young Philippine girl a few inmates ahead. "I heard she is really good."

"What do you know Bushman." Eric said. "On one hand I can say from first hand experience that she is nothing special. Just a dependable little cocksucker. Extremely neat. Even combs her pubic hair. On the other hand, stay away from big stupid over by the salad bowl. She is a dirty, filthy, smelly bitch. Flies will leave dog shit to follow her."

"Don't you believe this motherfucker." Randy said after the laughter subsided, pointing towards Eric.

"What do you mean cocksucker?" Eric replied taking a face off position with Randy butting chests. "You got a complaint about my work?"

"No you do excellent work." Randy shot back. "If not preoccupied with pussy."

Michael took at a glance two guards streaking down the line towards the two would be combatants, clubs at the ready. He moved forward increasing the gap with his homies. Oh shit! He thought . Here it goes.

Transfer to an FCI.  He turned and looked back towards his homies expecting the worse.

"What are you doing getting mixed up with these low lives?"  He heard a voice in front of him, that was actually two inmates ahead.  He was startled and turned acutely, almost elbowing the inmate ahead of him.  He made hastily apologies temporarily forgetting the impending disaster for his two homies. The voice that startled him, not so much for what it said, but the language it used.  The unknown inmate up ahead, spoke to him in Greek.

"What's the idea here?"  The Mexican looking hack who arrived on the scene first said in a tone of voice indicating that he had a chip on his shoulder and was baiting either one of the two inmates to knock it off.

"Nothing, sir."  Eric said all smiles.  "Just horsing around.  No damage done."

"Is everything alright?"  The second guard asked in earnest itching for an excuse to knock a few heads.

"Peachy."  The first guard volunteered.  "If I hear from you again while you are in here," he said turning back to the two inmates, "I will personally roll you in the North Las Vegas County Jail for a few days for disturbing the peace.  My own peace.  Am I making myself clear, dickheads?"

Without waiting for an answer, he turned around and followed the other guard towards the entrance of the Mess Hall that was under siege, as a wave of inmates seeing the unguarded doors, made a charge to sneak in and beat the down time, waiting in line.

"Close one."  Randy exhaled.  "Not even a shot."

"What's a shot?"  Michael asked rejoining his comrades.

"A shot is a written reprimand that entails assignment of extra duties during the free period, like picking discarded cigarette butts from the ground." Said Lew in a jailhouse lawyer tone of voice.

Michael was mindful not to lose sight of the inmate who spoke to him in Greek as the homies moved up towards the beverage counter. Water, milk, chocolate milk, two kinds of fresh squeezed juices, coffee, tea, and six flavors of soda comprised the beverage section in the dinning room. Decisions. Decisions. This beats the refrigerator back home, thought Michael. So far so good.

The salad bar consisted of a trough of chopped lettuce, tomatoes, cucumbers, onions, peppers and the standard variety of ranch, thousand island, bleu cheese, Italian and French dressings in separate packets resting over crushed ice. The desert was different types of cakes cut in three by three inch squares. The main course was a choice of quarter section of oven roasted chicken or liver and onions or sautéed mahi-mahi with capers. Mash potatoes or rice. Corn on the cob or beans or peas completed the main selections as you worked towards the bread and rolls table. All in all, not a bad meal considering it was served in prison. Very reminiscent of dormitory or fraternity house food in College back in the sixties, Michael thought.

The six homies made their way through the cashiers together, giving them their inmate numbers in lieu of payment. There were other civilians, evidently working on the Base, that had to shell out cash. No bill was however, larger than a couple of dollars. "Oh, the advantages of eating at taxpayers expense," thought Michael as he followed Lew who was making his way towards the smaller of the two dinning rooms with food laden tray in hand. He made two steps past the cashiers and was getting ready to take a third, when he noticed that the entire dinning room was looking at him.

"Mickey!" He heard a sharp voice to his left that he recognized as Eric's. "Come here man, what the fuck you are lost or something? New guy."

He said as a way of apology to the entire room. "Come here dumb shit and follow me." He whispered menacingly under his breath.

Michael turned 180 degrees and joined Eric who was sitting himself in a five chair table. The others had already sat down and were silently staring at their food. Michael set his tray on the table, took measure of his homies and said in a soft voice.

"What about Lew?"

"Sit down," Randy hissed, "before you make a scene. You almost stepped on this one bud. You owe Eric for saving your ass."

"What did I do?" Michael asked looking up from his food perplexed.

"You just about traveled in the black hole, buddy." Ed said with a smile. "Where no white man has ever been seen or heard from again. Come on Mickey, you can't be so dumb. Didn't you see all them eyeballs staring at you in there? That dinning room is for the niggers man."

"Don't listen to him Mike." Eric said embarrassed. "He is a fucking redneck from Spokane. I don't like it either. But you are in prison. You don't have a choice.

You got to eat with your own kind."

"What about Lew?" Michael said. "Our roommate. How does he feel about it?"

"Lew is cool." Eric replied. "He knows we don't mean anything by it. He has accepted it."

Michael took the room in, trying to spot the inmate who spoke to him in line. There were two possibilities and they were both siting together in a two man table. He was staring at them trying to make up his mind. They both looked Greek, involved in an animated conversation using a lot of hand gestures and body language that's a dead giveaway for Southern Europeans. They were too far away however, to catch even the minutest snippet of their conversation that would have confirmed the fact that they were indeed Greek.  The one facing him, looked up from his plate and winked at him in recognition.  Michael raised his left arm and waved at him.  The man acknowledged the greeting and returned to his food.

"What are you doing, waving at him like that?"  Asked Randy across the table.

"You want us to get killed right in the Mess Hall?"  Piped in Bushman.

"What did I do wrong?"  Asked Michael with a pained expression on his face.

"Do you know that fellow?"  Asked Eric staring Michael intensely.

"No.  I've never met him in my life.  I thought the guy waved at me and I waved back.  That's all.  What's the crime in this?"

"Ignore him man."  Said Ed with passion.  "The man is a 'Rat'."

"A 'Rat'?  What kind of 'Rat'?  How do you know it?"  Michael came back with a barrage of questions.

"Everybody knows that Nick is a 'Rat', a cop, how do you say it, he tells on people."  Eric answered vehemently.

"I've heard that for the first time," said Michael, "and I can summate the meaning of 'Rat' in the prison glossary.  However, you have not answered my question; how do you, meaning Eric, know that Nick is a 'Rat'?"

"Everyone knows man, nicotine Nick is a cop; he is one of them."  Answered Eric with disdain.

"The fact that something is common knowledge does not detract from the fact that it must be proven with first hand evidence."  Replied Michael.

"Oh now!  What the fuck are you talking about?"  Eric turned around dropping his fork on his tray.

"What I mean," Michael said unperturbed, "is that you cannot assassinate the character of the individual on rumor and innuendo, without first hand knowledge.  If you do, you are no better than the people who put you in here."

"Well, I got the proof." Ed said quietly.

"We are all ears." Michael said challenging.

"Nicotine Nick teaches a pre-release course over at education.  It is actually a little more than that, since it is mandatory for all inmates to take, particularly the ones getting ready to go on fur-lows,  halfway houses, home confinement, supervised release and so on.  You get the idea. Well your buddy Nick, Michael, turned in inmates that did not take the course.  So a friend of mine was denied his fur-low.  He had nine years to see his wife, man. He was ready to kill nicotine Nick. And I think he would have done it if he didn't talk so much about it before hand. Next thing you know, he was shipped to an FCI.  Is this proof enough for you Mike?"

"I do not know yet.  Let's analyze what you've said so far and it is my understanding that you have first hand knowledge.  I am assuming that the institution selected Nick to teach this course.  The course consisted of the does and don'ts associated with release and other privileges that could be bestowed on the inmate.  Am I right so far?"

"Yes, that's pretty much how it is done." Replied Ed.

"The institution would not turn loose an inmate, I don't care how much trusted the fellow is.  They will still maintain checks and balances. Under this assumption the BOP must have something of a sign up sheet for the inmates to sign, and the instructor to countersign acknowledging the fact that so and so was there this and that day. They need this document themselves to limit their liability.  The  Willie Horton incident has intensified a few of these 'check and balance' measures, I am sure.  I bet the BOP representative in charge of the

Education program must make occasional appearances, I don't care how much he wants to goof off. Am I going in the right direction so far Ed?"

'Yes." Ed said. "Keep going."

"Now that we've set the parameters of the 'did', let's examine how the 'did' was done. This goes to the teeth of the motive behind Nick's action which colors his behavior as that of a 'Rat' or self preservation or under the guise of something that is unavoidable, triggered by the inmate's action. Were you in class yourself Ed at all times when this incident took place?"

"Yes."

"Tell us what did Nick say when he stepped into the class. I am talking now first day, first class. A group of inmates come in. They sit down. Tabula rasa, which means blank paper in Latin. You don't know what's all about, what to expect. Nick comes in. Go ahead Ed, what happens next?"

"Hmm...He said who he was and what the class was all about. No!...Before that, after he introduced himself, he passed an attendance sheet and asked for everyone to sign and write their inmate number."

"Now, we are getting somewhere." Michael interrupted. "Did he explain why you were doing that?"

"Yes. He said that he was required to turn in the attendance sheets to his boss, a Mr. Lee, together with the other one." "Which other one?" Michael asked.

"The one at the end of the class."

"Let me see if I got everything straight so far." Said Michael with a sheepish smile on his face. "Nick was required by the prison administration to turn in at the end of each session, two documents. One memorializing the people that came to class and the other, the people who stayed till the end of the session. Is this right Ed?"

"Yes."

"Did Mr. Lee or whatever his name is, his Boss, an employee of BOP; did he come in ever during class or before the class started or immediately afterwards to check on things?" Michael asked in earnest.

"Yeah,  A couple of times the first week.  I think even once he took roll call in the middle of the session from the attendance sheet."

"I see." Said Michael.  "Now tell us what happened with that particular inmate that caused you to brand Nick as a 'Rat'."

"This guy, you know, was in for many years.  He came down from maximum security facilities all the way down to Camp level.  You know, tough guy. I think he was a biker. Drugs and fire arm wrap. Tattoos. The whole works.  This guy comes in and signs the attendance sheet and then he leaves the class. Who knows probably to keep drinking with his biker buddies that were huddling outside the class door, waiting for him to come out.  Next day he asked Nick for the second time sheet to sign. Nick told him that he turned it in to Mr. Lee at the end of the class that same day as it was required.  Man, I never seen a man get mad that fast. If people had not grabbed him, right there and then he would have beat Nick's head in.  He was making such a commotion, calling Nick a 'Rat' and all and how he would beat his head in while he was asleep with a piece of pipe that the guards came and rolled him away.  He was transferred that same night  out, together with his biker buddies and Nick was spared."

"See, I told you so." Eric jumped in. "He is a 'Rat'. You got your proof, Michael.  There, your buddy Nick is a 'Rat'.  One of these days he will wake up with a screwdriver through his ear.  Or at night walking through a dark alley, Play ball; with Nick's head boys. I hope you don't get caught at the time near him."

"As I said, I don't know the guy..." Michael said.

"A 'Rat' is a 'Rat' period." Randy interrupted. "There are no exceptions. It's us against them. We got to stick together."

"I am new here." Michael said after he got his composure. "All I am trying to do is understand where you fellows are coming from. However, every issue has several sides to it and closing your eyes or refusing to address them is a disservice."

"What are you talking about?" Bushy said while trying to cut into his liver dinner.

"If someone sees something and volunteers to go to the authorities to report it for personal gain, I have no qualms about labeling this individual a 'Rat'. Now here is where things get a little grey. An individual becomes part of a scene of an incident that violates the BOP regulations. His sole involvement being that he is physically present on the scene. In this instance I believe the participants show disrespect for the individual's privacy and their actions incite his inactive involvement. This unwitting participant becomes involved by his mere presence. If he keeps quiet, he is part of the conspiracy by quiet acquiescence. If he volunteers to report to the authorities, he is no longer a criminal, but his action will be viewed by the inmates as that of an informant. This becomes a tough call. The individual did nothing wrong. However, he will be punished regardless of his subsequent actions. How would you guys respond to this? Remember, based on your answer I reserve the right to pronounce the sentence. Meaning, if you keep quiet, I will extend your sentence by ten years. If you tell, I will do to you bodily harm of varying degree to make it suitably impossible for you to ever inform again."

Above the dinning hall din, you could hear a pin drop at the table of the five homies. The silence was deafening.

"Did you all understand the premise?" Michael insisted. "I am listening. What is the verdict? What would you do and why?"

No one answered, instead they kept their hands busy by moving their food around the plate and looking at each other.

"You see. There are no fast answers." Michael added. "Now let's take the present situation at hand. Nick warns the inmates that the class is mandatory. He goes further to explain the system of checks and balances. That is the reporting of attendance prior and at the conclusion of the session. Nick is forced by the regulations imposed on him by the system to turn in the attendance sheets by the end of the class session. I am sorry guys but I don't see that Nick did anything to deserve labeling him as a 'Rat'. In this case the individual is not only trapped in the breaking of the rules by his mere presence on the scene. He is asked by the perpetrators to become an active participant with total disregard to his rights and wishes as an individual human being. No, gentlemen, you are wrong. I would not label Nick a 'Rat' based on the 'proof' presented."

"I wish, the fuck, you were representing me in Court." Randy broke in. "Instead of that 'Public Pretender' the court appointed; I would not be here now."

"Yeah man! Me too." Joined Ed.

"This guy is dangerous." Said Eric laughing, "Did you see how the fucker set us up? He suckered us in. Seduced us to his way of thinking and reeled us in when we were good and hooked."

"Here! Here!" Sounded Bushy knocking with his utensils. "I want Mike on my side in any Board of Inquiry I find myself into."

"Then, if all of you are in agreement." Michael said. "I don't want to hear any more jailhouse rumor about Nick, because someone hearing it with a room temperature I.Q. may decide to act on it. And you my friends have become accessories after the fact. I for one intend to meet this nicotine Nick and I am sure that you all will make every effort to to dispel these 'Rat' rumors and nonsense."

"I am curious man." Eric said. "For someone as smart as you, how did you end up here?"

"Hubris!" Michael replied laconically.

"Who? What?" Randy asked. "Speak English bud."

"I am. Hubris is in the dictionary. It means extreme arrogance and tempting the divine wrath. It is the common malady of all the heroes in the Greek tragedy. Arrogance that brings divine retribution. Only when the hero has suffered sufficiently to find redemption, the gods take pity on him and restore him. A changed man, in circumstances other than those that got him in trouble to begin with. Even in situations that it was, in many cases, humanly impossible to unravel the plot and reestablish normalcy, the ancient Greek writer invented the 'Deus ex Machina", which means in exact translation the Mechanical God. This was accomplished by introducing one of the Gods, Athena for example, on stage coming down from heaven to take set things right and take care of events and circumstances. The mechanism of bringing the God into the set was pretty much similar to our construction cranes. These were lowering the God onto the stage via the machine, 'Deus ex Machina'. Nowadays the saying is used metaphorically to mean an event so extraordinary in nature and circumstances that this alone can alter events."

"Fascinating." Bushy said. "However, for us mere mortals why don't you just tell us in plain English, what the fuck did you do to end up in this joint."

"I was the President and CEO of an Engineering and Construction Corporation." Michael started with a pained expression on his face. "The firm was specialized in defense and industrial type projects for the federal Department of Defense, Army, Navy, Air Force, Marines and infrastructure projects for the State of Hawaii and the City and County of Honolulu. There are several rules, regulations and guidelines that someone is required to interpret and follow when engaged in that type of work.  The regulation that the government has accused me of violating is the Davis-Bacon Act which deals with wage guidelines.  The law states that the employees engaged in federal and/or federally funded projects, are required to be paid in accordance with the prevailing wage for laborers and mechanics work performed on site.  A law, by the way that I have discovered today, the BOP/UNICOR is violating with impunity.

"The law was established sometime in the late thirties and over the years gave rise to controversial issues.

"The first is the prevailing wage rate.  The government maintains that the prevailing wage is the hourly labor rate paid by the respective unions. This definition on the face of it leads to inequity, because for the same type of work someone may be subjected to different hourly rates, depending under which union's jurisdiction the job description falls under.  Let me give you an example.  Say someone is digging a hole using a small backhoe.  If the hole is to burry a sprinkler or a water irrigation line, he gets paid seven dollars an hour.  If the hole is for landscaping purposes, to plant a tree or a bush, he gets paid eight dollars an hour.  If the hole is for a fence post, he is getting paid at a rate of six dollars per hour.  If the hole is for a pipeline, he gets paid twenty five dollars per hour under the plumbers and pipe fitters union wage rate guidelines.  If the hole could be conceivably tied in to carpentry work, say concrete formwork, shoring and the like, he gets paid thirty dollars per hour in accordance with the carpenter's union.  If you leave the work description blank, then the work is claimed by the operating engineers union and the employee gets paid equipment operator wages at thirty five dollars per hour.  So as you can see, for the same type of work, digging a hole on the ground, someone can get paid anywhere from six dollars per hour to thirty five dollars per hour depending how strong the union he belongs to is.  The government's definition of prevailing wage rate was challenged in several states and has been redefined to constitute the average of the union wage rate and the non union rate paid to employees for the same type of work by Merit Shop contractors. In Hawaii no one has challenged the prevailing wage rate figures, so the government adopted whatever the local unions were paying.

"Another issue that was challenged over the years was what constituted laborers and mechanics work. The government adopted a list of job descriptions that determined and clarified this issue. This list of job descriptions and their wage rates are given to every prospective bidder for a project with the bid documents that latter are made part of the Contract to the successful bidder.

"The third issue that spurred a controversy is the definition of the project site. This last issue takes on particular importance as it constitutes the apple, so to speak, of my Eris with the government. For the past twenty years doing business with the government, I interpreted the words 'project site' to mean exactly what was shown on the Drawings Plot Plan called out under the shaded area 'Project Site' denoting the physical and geographic location of the work site in relationship to the surrounding area and other structures. I communicated this interpretation of the project work site to the government and administered the government contracts in accordance with that definition.

"I really had no choice in that regard. The majority of our work was based on Change Orders or what is called Contract Work on a Cost Plus basis. This means that you added up the incurred costs, applied your mark-up, consisting of overhead and profit and the government paid you based on that invoiced amount. The overhead was established by audit. The Defense Contract Audit Agency (DCAA) conducted the audit based on the Corporation audited Financial Statement at the end of each fiscal year. The profit margin was set by the government at six percent, so the only variable was the incurred cost.

"Applying my definition of the Davis-Bacon Act the government was paying my employees at the prevailing labor rate only for the actual work performed on site. The hours spent off site or between job sites or idle hours on site waiting for government instructions were paid at a lesser rate of ten dollars an hour which in my opinion represented the market value of the individual not performing actual work.  Say, if I had placed an ad for pick-up and delivery at ten dollars an hour, I would have generated demand for the job.  Then that was the market value or the prevailing rate for that type of work.

"By applying my definition of the Davis-Bacon Act, the government saved money on their projects.  Otherwise they were threatening they would indict me for overcharging.  They were taking videos and assembling government inspectors  Reports on a daily basis to document the actual working hours spent on site to insure that they were not being overcharged.

"As soon as the Contracts were completed and final payment was made by the government, they closed the Contracts.  Two years later, the government came up with a novel interpretation of the job site, meaning everywhere hours were spent on and off site as long as as the hours were associated or related to the Contract.  That meant that the hours subject to the Davis-Bacon wage rates applied and encompassed the entire work day schedule regardless of where the employee was at the time.

"Based on this theory, the government indicted the Company and myself personally for Davis-Bacon Act violations.  This in itself was not a criminal offense, but the government made it into one by incorporating the theory of Mail Fraud.  The judge decided that since my interpretation differed from the one recently assumed by the government, me and the company were wrong and the government was right.  Then since we mailed our interpretation and the government used the mail to pay us, it became Mail Fraud.

"We filed a civil suit against the government with the Armed Services Board of Contract Appeals (ASBCA) to recover the money lost to the company on Change Orders applying the same interpretation to the

Davis-Bacon Act as that of the government, in the amount in excess of seven million dollars. The government responded stating that the Contracts were closed and could not be reopened. We responded that the government reopened the Contracts to be used as a basis to seek an indictment. The government responded that the Company and myself were trying to profit from our crime. The ASBCA without reading and/or studying the case, sided with the government and informed me that it was against the law to profit from a crime.

"So, the indictment was issued for defrauding the government. When it was shown during the trial that the government was not defrauded; as a matter of fact it saved money, the prosecution with the judge's blessing verbally changed the indictment to read that the government was not defrauded, but it lost its prerogative to dictate where and how its money was to be spent.

"Now the government never had that prerogative to begin with. They contracted with our company to spend 'X' amount of dollars for 'Y' product. Whom we hired and for what subcontract amount was never within the government's jurisdiction. "Accordingly, based on faulty interpretation of the Davis-Bacon Act and erroneous instructions to the jury, the company and myself found ourselves convicted.

"Several months after the conviction on another case in a different Court of Appeals, the government lost in their interpretation of job site to mean everywhere. The Court of Appeals defined the work site to mean the actual physical site, we maintained all along. The government evidently had several cases going all over the country on the same issue involving different companies and individuals and filed with the Supreme Court. The Supreme Court almost a year later came down with a ruling upholding the Appeals Court decision and further reinforcing the lower Appeals Court decision on the issue of the job site definition.

"I filed an Appeal with the 9th Circuit Court of Appeals but we could not file directly with the Appeals Court. A new law passed attached to the

Antiterrorist Act, requiring the Appeal to be filed first with the original sentencing judge for his approval before it could be filed with the Appeals Court for the jurisdiction.  It would take a very enlightened judge to admit wrong doing.  Unfortunately, our judge was not and denied our right for Appeal to the 9th Circuit Court of Appeals. This left me with no other alternative but to file a 'Habeas Corpus' for a 'Writ of Certiorari' with the U. S. Supreme Court.  The only way the Supreme Court will consider looking into a case filed by the individual, it must have a Constitutional interpretation question.  My question on this is: "The law is the law, subject to interpretation.  Why was the federal government's interpretation considered valid over the individual citizen's; particularly when the government's interpretation of the law proved faulty by the U.S. Supreme Court?" The Supreme Court assigned a docket number, 7011, to my 'Writ of Certiorari', which means they are interested in the issues I raised and shortlisted my case."

The homies were listening quietly all that time to Michael's narrative without moving a muscle or making any kind of noise to interrupt his train of thought.

"So, what it boils down is you got screwed by the government." Ed said. "Welcome to the club.  Half the people here are innocent of what they are accused of and the other half got punishment that did not fit the crime."

"Man, it would take a Revolution to set the record straight." Eric added seething.

"Oh!  Oh!  The mad bomber strikes again." Piped Randy in a mocking tone of voice.

"I don't know, but the system's got to start working at some level." Michael said in a low voice.  "I believe in the system.  It is currently testing the individual.  The individual in turn must demonstrate perseverance and tenacity to facilitate and hope to change the system."

"He may not be entirely wrong." Said Bushy addressing the table in general. "Look at my case. Appeal after Appeal and I won something, finally. Next week I am going in for re-sentencing."

"Hey, man! That's great." Randy exploded slapping Bushy on the back, maybe harder than needed.

"Are they cutting you loose?"

"Shit no! I wish. They let me out of this gate unescorted, Man, I am long gone. No. The turds are going to transport me in shackles and irons from here to LA and the judge will reduce my sentence from seventy seven months to forty four. That's all. But it is something."

On this oxymoron, which was the high note of the dinner table, the homies got up as one man and made their way outside the Mess Hall and the fading sun light.

"What took you?" They were startled by a familiar voice, at the foot of the steps from a figure sitting by the shrubberies half covered by the foliage and lengthening shadows. "The food was not that great."

"You, black motherfucker, you." Randy responded after he almost tripped down the steps. "You keep your eyes closed and your mouth shut and you become the invisible man."

"No really. What took you guys so long?" Lew insisted.

"Well." Ed said. "We got listening to professor Mike here explaining to us the ins and outs of business and high finance and the time got away from us."

"Gee! Look what you did to us, Mike." Eric added in a high voice. "We are going to be late for our Board of Directors meeting."

"You keep fucking around like that and you will end up with the widow and her five orphans tonight." Lew said cryptically.

"That's right." Ed and Bushy said simultaneously. "We almost forgot. We are on for tonight."

"Yeah man! You got to hit them showers before everyone lines up, so you can beat the count tonight." Lew continued. "Petunia won't touch day old meat." "What's happening?" Michael asked. "What are you guys talking about?"

"Oh! You are new here my boy." Ed said, putting an arm on Michael's shoulders and leading him away. "You just come off the street. Wait a few weeks. When the time is right, we'll tell you. Hey Randy, are you coming, we can squeeze a game of tennis before count."

"No bud, I got an early call out tomorrow. I got to hit the rack."

"Where do you work?" Michael asked.

"I work for UNI-COR at their construction division."

"What exactly do you do?"

"I am a journeyman carpenter bud. I've been in construction all my life. Here I am a working foreman. I run a crew of six men. You see this building here? This will be the new Movie Theater. I've been working on this project for over two years."

"You must be getting paid good money then. Since the Movie Theater is on government property, the wage rate is subject to the Davis-Bacon Act which is around thirty bucks an hour."

"I wish; but I do all right. Not like most of the guys here making twelve cents an hour. I make grade two wages at seventeen cents an hour."

With that, the homies split into groups. Michael and Ed sticking together on their way back to the dorm. At the gazebo, outside the building, Ed flipped open his pack of cigarettes and lit up.

"You want one?" Ed offered, as they sat down in one of the picnic tables.

"Thanks." Michael replied. "I don't smoke cigarettes. I smoke cigars or a pipe." He said as he took his Peterson Millennium pipe out of his pocket and started filling and packing his pipe. He tested the draw and lit it. He blew a couple of puffs in the air filling the gazebo area with the aroma of his pipe tobacco.

"Man, that smells good." Ed broke the silence. "What kind of pipe tobacco are you smoking?"

"Erinmore flake." Michael replied. "I will be sad when I run out, though. I bet they don't sell this brand here."

"Don't make me laugh." Said Ed. "If they have pipe tobacco here at the exchange, it would be the grocery store variety. I know their cigars are White Owl, Prince Albert and Roi-Tan. Shit fucking nigger cigars. I bet you smoke something real fine."

"Well." Michael said slightly embarrassed. "The cigars you mentioned are machine made, short filler, mostly non tobacco ingredients and the actual tobacco is inferior. They fall apart on you before you smoke them. I prefer long filler, pure tobacco, hand made cigars, using Maduro or English Market Selection outer leaf wrapper. But if you want to appreciate a smoke, you got to go to custom made cigars using Cuban tobacco, hand rolled on the thighs of olive skinned maidens."

"Man, you really know how to get a fellow excited about something. Do you have such cigars with you? I would give anything to smoke a cigar like that once in my lifetime."

"Say no more." Michael said. "You wished and you shall have. Follow me."

With that Ed flicked his half smoked cigarette in the ashtray. Michael put his pipe back in his pocket and headed back to their room. Inside his locker, he reached for an unmarked wooden box. Broke the seal and opened the cedar lined humidor inhaling deeply the aroma. Inside individually packaged were laying fifty hand rolled cigars, six inch long by sixty ringlements in diameter custom made Cuban beauties. Michael extracted two, offering one to Ed who received it like he was receiving communion in a liturgy. He closed the box lid carefully, so it remained sealed, put it back in his locker and he spined the combination lock. "You must excuse my primitive cigar cutter." He said to Ed, brandishing a pair of round tip seizors. "They confiscated my cigar cutter at Processing. I think mainly because they did not know what it was."

He made a small incision at the head of his cigar and tested the draw by rotating the cigar in his mouth. Ed took the pair of seizors and imitated Michael's procedure and mannerisms. They went outside the building to the gazebo and lit their cigars by using wooden matches and rotating the cigar on the tip of the flame for an even burn. A plume of blue smoke rose majestically in the fall evening, hitting the roof of the gazebo, bouncing back and slowly diffusing into the night.

"Man, this is living! Thank you Mike for the taste of the good life, even in this shit hole of a place."

"Ed, my man. Every place is what you make it to be. Don't get caught in their game. Establish your own program and game plan and go for it. As I always say; don't sweat the petty stuff, pet the sweaty stuff."

After the laughter subsided, Michael continued.

"And while we are on the subject, what was the story with our homies? They were behaving back there like they were going out on a date."

"Let me tell you something about this place." Ed said taking a deep draw from his cigar. "I know you were self report and came here straight from the outside so you got no frame of reference. Now, myself, I've done hard time as we say in the business. I made my way from maximum security facilities to the Camp system. Believe me you don't want to go that route. This place here is the nicest, as places such as this go, in the country. Its security is non existent. You can simply just walk out of here. It is near a major metropolitan area, Las Vegas. You can get anything you want, as long as you are willing to pay for it, and I mean everything. You see that parking lot in front of each dormitory? Did you notice that it is not lit? There is a reason for it. After the ten o'clock count all the action begins. You can have anything sent to you. The hacks are the purchasing agents, for a fee of course. You can have a show girl brought in a van with a waterbed, if you can afford it. For most of us though, this kind of lifestyle is out of our league. That's where the female guards come in. For a roll of quarters, they will do you. All you have to do is take a shower, put a check mark by your name outside your door and leave a roll of quarters on top of your locker. Others prefer to go outside the camp, all the way to the City. This can also be arranged for a price. For some people, life in the Camp is preferable from that of the outside. I know a lot of homeless old people that went to the Post Office and on broad daylight ripped the stamp purchase coin box right out of the wall. They were arrested on the spot and given a year and a day sentence. They are here now and are happy campers. They think this place beats any nursing home or their own home for that matter. They got friends their own age to talk to. Activities to keep their mind active and their body physically occupied and no old ball and chain nagging at them to do this or fix that. They feel they've got it made."

The sprinklers came on to water the grass in the center field and inside the courtyard all around the gazebo saturating the hot evening air. Michael stretched back in his bench seat, threw back his head, closed his eyes and breathed lungfuls of the humid air. He dreamed being back in Hawaii, sitting in his favorite chair on the lanai, breathing in the trade winds while dew from the golf course sprinklers caressing his face and evaporating in the evening breeze before it had time to settle and feel wet. Somehow it was not the same here. Close, but not the same. The air smelled different and he could not hear the crashing of waves on Sandy Beach across the fairway.

He woke up from his daydream. The back walls of the dormitory, with row after row of darkened windows assailed his eyes. He settled on the deteriorating siding and something out there triggered his professional memory. He looked around and slowly made his way towards the corners of the building. There, the siding was broken and hanging by a thread. The byproduct of a collision with a ladder or some sort of garden tool. He tore the loose chip, looked at it closely and closing his fist tightly crumbled it into tiny fiber flakes that fell swirling to the ground like fresh fallen snow. "Like I thought." He mumbled to himself. He returned to his seat under the gazebo brushing his hand on his trouser leg and threw his cigar in the nearby ashtray.

"What was that all about?" Asked Ed with interest.

Michael looked at him for a few minutes silently, gauging his response. Should I tell him? Is he trustworthy? What would be his reaction? He looked at Ed's biceps. He obviously worked with weights. Was he a health nut? Suddenly he changed his mind and turned away. He looked at the Mess Hall siding, the other buildings in the distance, same type of siding. He turned back facing Ed and told him in a low voice.

"The siding in all the buildings in the Camp is made out of Asbestos. Built probably sometime in the early fifties. It is deteriorating and flacking off, filling the air we breath with Asbestos fibers."

"So? What that got to do with the price of cotton?" Asked Ed, not comprehending the significance of the revelation.

"It has been determined by the EPA, the government agency in charge of pollution, that Asbestos fibers are the cause of lung cancer and emphysema, in the mid seventies. There's been a massive effort to remove or contain Asbestos in the buildings. Here we are, twenty years later and the government is doing nothing about it at our Camp. Harming the health of the inmates who are forced to live in these buildings and breath this polluted air."

"Holy shit!" Ed whistled softly. "No wonder you were hesitant to tell me. Shit! All along we thought it was fun to have pretend snow fights, throwing the stuff at each other."

"The symptoms and effect of exposure to Asbestos doesn't manifest itself immediately, but several years down the road.  I bet the government is going to be hit with a Class Action Lawsuit by dying inmates."

"And I bet as usual the government will try to deny it and cover it up." Ed added solemnly.

Michael got up from the bench and started slowly towards the dorm main entrance followed closely by Ed.

"I am going to turn in early." Michael said to no one in particular. "I had a long day and tomorrow I got a visitor; my wife will be visiting me all weekend long."

"Hey man! That's great." Ed said slapping him on the back. "I will be at the Visitors' Center also getting toys and stuff for the children of the visitors. I will be on duty all weekend. I'd love to meet your wife and talk to her. I hope you introduce me."

Ed opened the main door and held it open for Michael to enter and the two homies were swallowed by the long corridor with doors on each side.

# CHAPTER 6

## Visiting Weekend

Beep...Beep...Beep...

Michael wakes up with a start and turns to the right to pat his wife's rump like he's done countless times in the past, affectionately and reassuring that his anchor was there, where he set it last night.

This time though he cracks his head on the metal locker which brings him instantly to a fully awake state. The pain has the mitigating factor that if not for the locker, he would have crashed head first from the top bunk to the concrete floor.

Beep...Beep...Beep...

"Shut the fuck up!" Shouts Eric from across the room and goes back to snoring.

Michael quickly presses the off button that lights the display face. It's 6:35 AM on a beautiful Saturday morning. All the homies are fast asleep. His bunky is making chomping sounds. All that pussy eating talk last night. He hops from the bed and silently slips out the door heading for the bathroom. After he gets the three S's out of the way, shit, shower and save, he throws some clothes on and heads to the Mess Hall for breakfast.

The sprinklers have come on and are forming rainbows in the early morning light. He feels homesick for Hawaii and remembers the countless rainbows he's seen from his villa on top of the Maunalani Heights. He sighs. Another lifetime, or so it seems. The good life of ten years was just a blink of the eye.  Look on the bright side he realizes. Visiting day today.  Wife, conversation and exquisite cigars.  A taste from the past.

Like an automaton, he grabs a tray and pushes it along the rail, silently, letting the Mexican maids take over and fill it up with food stuff.  The place is deserted this time of the morning on a weekend and the few that are eating breakfast that early are chatty, like they are glad to see him; only he knows that he is nothing more than the pebble that broke the surface of their pond of monotony.

The guards must have it worse than the prisoners he thinks.  Very little money.

Resentful for guarding those who had a taste of the good life.  Lack of education.  Most of them don't know how to read.  Their writing resembles that of a first grader.

Boredom sets in as result of repetitive activity, the weather and the overall schedule.  Each day they are required to do the same things they did yesterday, which they are destined to repeat tomorrow. Groundhogs Day all over again, as the tittle and the subject of a popular movie staring Bill Murray demonstrated.  A lot of riots got started for lack of something better to do and inmates dying from boredom.

Talk about math.  If it is past their fingers, it does not compute.  They got their GED through the BOP diploma mill after they signed up.  That's why the daily counts take an hour and a half to compete.  Something that should only take a few minutes.

He picks at his breakfast.  His stomach is in a knot from anticipation.  A few minutes later he gets up and leaves the dinning room.  Outside a few stragglers make their way out of the dormitories, slowly towards the Mess Hall.

Back in the room, he puts his khakis on and tennis shoes and by the light of his reading lamp he brushes his hair one more time.  Too bad his clothes are off the rack.  His custom made khakis are being tailor made out of Egyptian cotton and would be ready next weekend.  Too bad his wife has to see him in his baggy pants and rough shirt.  He strokes his cigar humidor inside the locker as he closes and locks it.  Custom made Cuban cigars are not allowed.  He was allowed to keep them curtesy through Diane in Processing.  Now that he got them, they are better than money.  His two custom made uniforms had cost him two cigars to the BOP warehouse manager and his undying gratitude for anything in the future for 'Mickey the Greek'.

"I mean anything Mickey."  Were his parting words.  "Including all the pussy you want.  You got your pick of my wetbacks working in back sewing uniforms in the sweat shop."

He made his way to the 'bubble' at Building 201 where the inmates who expected a visitor today were already gathering.  The 'bubble' is the Control Room where all the guards were dispatched from and stayed in constant communication with the Lieutenant on duty.  Today he saw the man in charge was the one they called   the Tex-Mex stud.  He got his nickname because of the way he strutted around and the car he was driving.  A shinny three year old Camaro with a set of stuffed dice hanging from the rear view mirror.  He was also frequently been seen in the company of little Mexican girls working as waitresses in the Mess Hall or in the uniform shop at the warehouse; giving them a ride home and bragging the next day to the inmates how tight they were on his detour behind some dune in the desert.

"Hey, listen up.  Which one of you is 84119-022?  Step forward." The Lieutenant shouted over the inmate din and noise.

No one did.

"OK, motherfuckers.  I am going to say one more time.  Who is number 84119-022? Michael...something; I can't pronounce his last name."

Michael got out his I. D. card out of his pocket and verified that indeed he was the owner of the number and took a step forward.

"Come with me." The Lieutenant simply said and led him to a room adjacent to the bubble.

"Don't worry, man, come inside . I want to have a word with you, away from these 'Rats'. You don't want to know what they've done to get to this place." The prisoner stood quietly close to the door studying the Lieutenant.

"Relax, man. You are new around here. I haven't seen your face before; and I remember when I see a face. When did you get in?"

"Tuesday, sir." Michael replied as humbly as he could master.

"Don't sir me." I told you to relax, man. "Were you self report?"

"Yes."

"I thought so. You know you got a visitor in the approved list already and we don't have you in the computer yet that you are with us. My boys around here are pretty nervous this morning. They think you are a 'Plant'."

He stopped and eyed the prisoner to gauge the reaction he got from his revelation.

"I don't think so, sir." The prisoner answered evenly. "You can check the probation report, my PSI. I am sure a copy was sent to your office even before I arrived."

"I will do that first thing Monday, don't worry about it. But I thought we might get acquainted in the meanwhile. See how you are getting settled. Get to know you. You know, meet this dude who got the muscle to get a visitor on the list in one day, when it takes the others ten to thirty days. Don't sweat it, man. You want a soda or something?"

"No sir. I am not thirsty. I just finished breakfast."

"OK. Go on now. Join the rest and enjoy your visit. If something is bothering you, you know where to find me."

Michael found the rest of the inmates in a semi circle with its center, the closed door he came out of. They were all staring at him inquiringly and when he took a step forward they parted a path wide enough to go through, eying him with suspicion. Great he thought. I am starting off famously. The guards think I am a 'Plant'. The inmates think I am a 'Rat'. The atmosphere was weighty. He made his way alone towards the double door facing the Visitor Center and waited silently for his number to be called to leave for the visitor's inmate processing center and relieve the pressure in the waiting room.

When his number was called, he followed the other inmates single file to the small single story stucco building with the six foot concrete block wall fenced back yard across the parking lot. A guard asked for his I. D. card, but did not search him like the others.

"Your visitor is waiting for you in booth number eight, sir. You are free to go anywhere within the compound as designated. Have a nice visit, sir."

He eye searched the room peripherally. He spotted his wife sitting on a chair in front of a coffee table, before he noted that the booth had a number eight that somehow had slipped on its side, designating the sign for infinity.

He never had a chance to look at his wife unobtrusively before, one among the several others waiting for their loved ones to make it through the door. She was a slender woman, who aged gracefully, with drawn features from worry and anticipation. She was scratching and picking at the palms of her hands. A nervous habit she had acquired recently. He was overcome by a warm feeling of love like he never experienced before in his life. Yes, his anchor was there for support, no matter what. Confidently he straddled the doorway leading to the guest waiting area and lost himself in the embrace of his sweetheart.

"Oh, honey. I am so glad to see you." He barely was able to say, before the words chocked him as a lump in his throat and he felt his vision clouding over.

He put his arm around his wife and led her to the courtyard outside in an effort to gather back his composure hoping that the desert heat would dry his eyes before the tell tale signs make their way down his cheeks.

"Let me look at you." His wife said. "You don't look bad at all. Khakis always looked good on you."

"Well, this is a uniform from the rack. Wait until I get the set of clothes that actually fit me. Made with a lot better material. They cost me two bloody cigars. But as monkey suits go, at least they will look like they were sawn for this monkey."

"Speaking about cigars. I brought you some. The guards did not stop me, so I guessed they were allowed."

"Yeah. As long as I smoke them in here. You can take them back. But not me. They will search me when the visit is over. I am not allowed anything back. Including money."

They settled at a table underneath an umbrella and held hands like on a first date. For the first time in their life, they were faced with an awkward silence. Shyness? Embarrassment? Who is going to say something first? The silence was eating into the visiting time, but the communication was present in the eyes, the gentle touches, the awkward smiles, the stroking of the knee.

"We don't want to get a PDA now." She broke the silence reminiscing their college dating times when couples would get a little too amorous or at least amorous past the threshold of the girls' house mother, Miss Merrill, and receive a Public Display of Affection violation, PDA, with its repercussions on future dating. "I don't know. I am new at this." He said looking around and noticing a young couple who were laying on the grass and the guy got ahold of bare tit and was attempting a paps smear test.  Over by the sandbox against the fence, another couple was at it, full court press.  His wife looked at him trying to hide an impish smile that he adored on her.

"It's embarrassing, eh." He said in a soft voice, apologizing for the place.

"It's all right. These poor young kids. Forced to be away from each other. They can't help it."

"Well, they are getting nowhere groping each other, other than frustrating themselves.  The guards will get here pretty soon and will put a stop to it one way or another.  At least that's what the visitor instructions say."

"Let's change the subject, sweetheart."  She said.  "How are your roommates? Did you meet any of the other prisoners? Tell me some of their stories."

Michael took the wrapper of an Arturo Fuente Hemingway series cigar his wife brought him. He used the cigar clipper she had brought and put the flame on it.

"I don't know if they tell me the whole story yet, being new around here and all, but from what they tell me it seems that the government is out of control.  Forget the old saying about the punishment doesn't fit the crime.  I am talking here about clear out and out unbelievable accusations."

"Like what?  Tell me, tell me."  She chatted excitedly like a little kid on Christmas Eve.

"There is a fellow in the next room who is in for eighteen months.  His tale of woes is tracking Peter."

Peter and Pam Gillingham were good friends from Hawaii who owned a thousand acre ranch South of San Diego right on the Mexican border by

Tecate, the Mexican town which manufactures beer by the same name as the town.

"Anyway, this fellow has a good size ranch in Montana, thousands of acres. An area of his property, say quarter of an acre, formed a natural drainage spot so he ended up with a little pond on his property. A Canadian goose spotted the pond   and landed on it. A neighbor of his who was not getting along with him, notified the EPA. Under a bizarre interpretation of the 1972 Clean Water Act, known as the 'glancing geese' test, The EPA can assert jurisdiction over any land with a wet area that might conceivably be used by passing migratory birds. So the federal agents visited him, after taking a picture of the pond with the sole Canadian goose on it, they posted a notice on his door prohibiting him from using his land. The fellow, after the agents left his property, tore off the notice. Grabbed his shot gun and shot the goose. The government gave him a year and a half and confiscated his house and property. Doesn't Peter have a pond on his property with visiting ducks? Tell him what the EPA can do if they find out.

"There is a Mailman, I went through the original orientation with. He was a Mailman in the Phoenix Post Office minding his own business and staying out of trouble. He is black and the Post Office manager is a white woman. She gave him all the South Phoenix routes because they were predominantly black and dangerous. Our mailman filed an internal complaint for discrimination. The Postal Inspection Services last year enacted an internal informant type program called 'Dollars for Collars'. Under this program, informants for the Postal Inspection Service infiltrated the Post Office out of which he was working. The first target was the Mailman, because he had filed a discrimination suit. They accused him of stealing mail. They got an indictment against him for stealing mail. They offered him a small fine, if he admitted guilt on one count, no jail time provided he dropped his lawsuit for discrimination. Sounds familiar? He refused. During the trial, the government had a hard time coming up with the alleged mail he stole, although they put on the stand several witnesses who testified whatever the government told them to say.  They could not come up with the same story: 'which piece of mail the poor bastard stole'.   The government, mid trial switched tactic with the federal judge's blessing they verbally changed the indictment from theft, to Conspiracy to Commit Theft. They started putting witnesses that were testifying that our Mailman 'Confided' to them that he 'Intended' to steal a piece of mail and 'Conspired' to do so. They paraded two dozen witnesses from his and other Post Offices with the same story.  The judge stopped them putting any more and ruled that 'Intent' and 'Conspiracy' although hearsay, if collaborated by two or more independent witnesses is no longer hearsay but the same as committing the crime and gave him a two year sentence and a fine much larger than the one originally offered as a settlement by the Postal Service.  I am really concerned and worried about the mental and emotional state of this individual. You should hear him talk about what he will do to the Post Office he worked out of, the Postal Service and the government when he gets out.   We may have the makings of still another disgruntled employee going 'postal'.

"There is a Navajo Indian that does the landscaping in the Camp. Nicest old fellow you will ever meet.  He is from Harlow and Nancy's neck of the woods, Phoenix, Arizona. He was on social security hanging around downtown Phoenix, in front of the Federal Building in a state of inebriation.  Not mind you drunk so that he can get arrested, but in high spirits with a little 'wind talking' thrown in.  The biggies in the Federal Building did not want him hanging around the front door. I mean he was considered an eye sore plus he was giving the impression to the passerby, holding a couple of unlit cigars on hand, that the Federal Building in Phoenix had a cigar store.  Many went inside the building looking for the cigar store. I understand he looked at some secretaries in a way that gave them the creeps and told on him to their bosses. Bottom line, the Indian was 'persona non grata' for the position of doorman of the Phoenix Federal Building.  The feds sent some FBI types to talk to him to change his spot, to no avail.  They arrested him; but the

ACLU got behind him and the judge told the feds to leave him alone. So, if piss and vinegar failed, what's left? You guess it. A harmless looking dork befriended the Indian and even joined him with a can of beer in a brown paper bag after hours for a little heart to heart. The federal nerd, after a few days of 'Dutch Uncle' talk, told the Navajo that he was new in Phoenix. He spent all his money buying a new house and now he got no money for landscaping. Could the Indian help him out? The Indian was game to help his new friend so the federal creep dropped the idea that one of the cactuses who had several branches and 'volunteer' cactus in front of the Federal Building might look nice in his front yard. The feds wouldn't even notice a 'volunteer' missing. The 'volunteer' cactus was not part of the original landscape. The federal creep would back up his pick up after hours and all he needed was for someone with cactus experience to put it at the bed of the truck. He would even pay a little. The Indian of course volunteered to help a friend out and he did not want money. What are friends for. The fed insisted, because the guys who wired him kept insisting on exchange of money for the deed. So the Indian accepted five bucks and as soon as he placed the cactus 'volunteer' safely on the bed of the pic-up truck, the federal troops rushed him from the nearby bushes where they were hiding. They arrested him, charged him with theft of government property, indicted him, tried him and convicted him. They were asking for the moon during sentencing, but a kind hearted judge gave him six months in prison Camp and a fifty dollar fine.

"Look at me again. I monopolize the conversation. Talk to me. What have you been doing?"

"My time seems boring by comparison. What can I say. I picked Nancy up at the airport. We drove down to Phoenix. I spent a couple of days with Nancy and Harlow, which by the way are sending you their love, and I drove up to Las Vegas yesterday to see you. By the way, what are all these females in uniform?"

"Oh! The 'swallows'? They are guards."

"What do you mean guards?  They got female guards in a men's prison?  And what is this 'swallows' reference?  Does it mean what I imagine it means?"

"In an effort for the BOP to achieve the federal mandatory employment standards, they employee 90% female guards for their Camps to offset the male employee numbers for the higher security institutions.  They make bed checks on us at 10:00 PM, midnight, 2:00 AM and 4:00 AM.  They fly into our rooms like swallows."

"Uh, ha.  What else?  Tell!"

"Well, for a roll of quarters, ten dollars, they will do you as you lay in bed.  So 'swallows' has a double meaning."

"Honey, don't you succumb to temptation and lower yourself to that.  I will be disappointed in you if you weaken."

"Darling, right now I can say for sure No!  I would not stoop to that.  But I don't honestly know how I would feel a year from now?  I think the government is brutal in isolating inmates and not allowing conjugal visits and then putting female guards, laundry girls, waitresses, seamstresses and all sorts of female support personnel which know the inmates needs and come to work in a Camp facility solely to make money on the side.  Did you see the parking lot in front of the dormitories as you came in?  After the ten o'clock count, it becomes lovers lane.  A lot of the women from Las Vegas come and offer sexual favors in the back seat of their cars for a price.  What can you say?  It is the way of life here.  The authorities turn a blind eye because they make money themselves, plus they keep the prison morale under control."

"Oh, my.  The stories that I will have to tell Nancy and Pam.  Sodom and Gomorra right here, encouraged by our government.  Come on let's not dwell on this.  Let's  change the subject.  Check out the 'creamer' to the right, behind you.  She is not wearing underwear.  Look at this place, half the women are scantily  dressed.  They would not walk down the street dressed like that, or maybe they would, but would be propositioned."

"Honey, you cannot judge these people here by your dress code. Something that may be hideous to you, it's cool for them. Think of the taste of Peggy Bundy in Married with Children. The majority of the inmates here are hard core criminals that made it down to the Camp system because they are getting towards the end of their sentence and the system is using the Camps as a pre-halfway house. Others are 'Rats' and informers that have ratted on fellow inmates in medium and maximum security facilities and are here for protection; or they testified, informed and acted as government witnesses in trials and plea bargained easier time for themselves. Excluding the telemarketers who comprise one third of the Camp population, the white collar criminals such as lawyers, CEO's et al, for whom the camp system was set up to begin with, they number less than two dozen. Another big block of inmate population is made of high school dropouts who got caught selling drugs. The Camp facilitates this last group with opportunities to get their GED and get vocational training so they can get a job when they are released. That's the area I hope I can be of help, teaching."

"You were a wonderful teacher in Hawaii. I don't see why not here?"

"If I can teach. Win my Appeal to the Supreme Court. Write one or two books. I would then consider my time here, well spent. Here I go again running my mouth off and not letting you put in a word wise."

"Don't worry about that. I told you before, it is fascinating listening to you."

"You know, if it interests you, it might interest several other people to know what goes on behind these Country Club type Federal Prison Camps."

"I am sure it would."

"Hmm! You are giving me some ideas and I plan to do something about it as soon as I get back to my room."

"Speaking of your room, how are your roommates?"

"They are the hard type cases, originally in maximum security prisons and progressively made their way to the Camp system.  Accordingly, they got that institutional mentality, 'us against them'.  One of them is over there, Ed, he is in for five years.  He was originally in the State Penitentiary for burglary.  He robbed houses.  You would want to hear his hard luck story from himself.  Poor bastard, he gets no visitors and when he heard you were visiting, he begged me to introduce you to him."

"He looks like a farm hand."

"Well, that was what he was.  A ranch hand."  Michael waved his hand towards a slouching khaki clad inmate who was in charge of the sandbox for the kids of the visiting families and was babysitting them together with three other inmates.  He made his way awkwardly to the couple sitting at the table under the umbrella.

"Honey, I want to introduce you to Ed, one of my cellmates.  Ed, this is my wife Christina."

"Pleased to meet you ma'm."  Ed said while extending his hand.  Christina, shook his hand briefly and said.

"I hear you are from Spokane.  This is our old stomping grounds, when we were both at Washington State University.  We used to go skiing on Mount Spokane."

"Please don't remind me of that."  Michael exclaimed.  "Ed, she was skiing.  I was tumbling down the mountain.  I belonged in the black and blue league."

"Well, Ed, how did you end up here?"  Christina asked with focused interest.

"I got out of the military and worked for a while in the mills.  I saved some and put it towards a house.  Time was passing me by, so I decided to do some traveling and rented my house to someone who was supposed to be paying the rent to the bank towards my mortgage payments and I left to see Colorado, Utah and some of the country I've only heard of or read about in books.  I was making ends meet by taking jobs, in construction. Six months later, I returned to Spokane, only to find that I lost everything.  My renter was not making the payments, so the bank foreclosed on my house.  He sold my furniture and he was long gone.  I could not get my old job back at the mill, so in essence I ended up homeless.

"That's when I started drinking and doing some drugs.  I got thoroughly screwed and bitter towards mankind and the system.  So, I started thinking, why them, having all the pretty houses, shinny cars and all that money, and not me?  From that, it was a short jump to breaking into someone's house, when they were not in, and stealing to support myself and my newly acquired habits.  I was living in Spokane at the time, so I was picking targets like remote, rich looking, isolated farm houses.  In one of them, as I was getting into my car to leave with a pillow case  of valuables, the farmer was pulling in his driveway.  He knew immediately what was happening, so he tried to ram my car and hit me head on.  Well, I got away with my damaged car and all, but he got my car license number.  The cops traced it to me.  It was not hard to identify my car because of the damage.  So, I got two years in the State Penitentiary out of which I did fourteen months.  I was not bitter.  I had it coming and was relieved in a way because I got straightened out.

"The day I was getting out, I was served with a federal indictment, arrested and marched right on to a federal maximum security prison waiting trial.  I was charged with  interstate transportation of stolen firearms and violent endangerment.  It seems the farmhouse was in Idaho and among the stollen goods was the farmer's gun, which I transported back home to Spokane, Washington. So the feds got me for five years.  Now I was pissed.  This was uncalled for, because I felt that I had already served my time for what I had done."

"So, Ed, you feel that the punishment did not fit the crime."

"Exactly, Mike.  You took the words right out of my mouth."

"How do you feel now?" Michael's wife asked.

"Well, Christina, let's put it this way. If I get the chance, I will get even, and I intend to get even…" Ed mumbled some unintelligible stuff as he made his way back to the sand box.

"Honey, I think the man is one sick puppy."

"I know. A time bomb. Ready to go off at any moment. I am kind of glad he is being transferred next Tuesday to a Camp in Spokane. I think he said he would join some kind of white supremacy group out there in Washington and Northern Idaho. The government provides psychological counseling everywhere else except to their federal prisons. So the people coming out, if they were remotely disturbed going in, they come out verifiable 'psychos'. The good thing is that they are mad at the government and their revenge will be focused towards that end. But you see what happened in Oklahoma City. Innocent people got caught in the crossfire."

"What about your other roommates? What did they do wrong?"

"Eric, the bomber was experimenting with a demolition device that was not in the government list of approved detonators. He accidentally sat on the remote and blew himself up. He woke up in the hospital looking like a mummy, handcuffed on the bed rail. His wife left him and the government put him away for three years at an FCI, because they could not put him away for more, since he had a license to do demolitions. He is another sick puppy as you called Ed. All he can talk about is about detonation devices, effective killing zone, types of CEMTEX. You see I am getting an education in prison already. He wants to steal my Braun alarm clock because it is the 'terrorists' choice as a triggering devise. He claims it is very accurate and very reliable. He is another one who made it to the Camps because he has only six months to go.

"Bushy, 'the Airways Bandit' as Ted Copple named him on his show NightLine, is a telemarketer. He claims, he was the first one to get convicted. The government made an example out of him by giving him seventy seven months. He used in his TV commercial the Nancy Reagan video and slogan 'say no to drugs' from her speech and was collecting money to fight drugs by giving away bumper stickers and other promotional paraphernalia and soliciting donations, which were pouring in at the rate of $40,000.00 per day. Ted Copple on the air did a live segment in which Bushy's entrepreneurial spirit was featured. He ambushed Bushy getting out of a fashionable New York night club, a call girl in his arm, heading for his red Ferrari Testarossa that was valet parked up front. The license plate on the Ferrari was 'BANDIT' which Ted's crew filmed close up and Ted made a big deal in his commentary. Bushy was portrayed as a modern day 'Robing Hood', who was literally thumbing his nose at the government. From that day on Bushy became a 'target'. No one thumbs his nose at the government. The government started a secret manhunt which ended in a televised arrest of Bushy at the New Orleans airport as he was stepping out of the Lear Jet he was leasing. The rest is history. Except an Appeals judge with a sense of humor is resentencing him next week; so instead of 77 months, he will do 44.

"Lew is a black drug dealer turned jailhouse lawyer. He got caught because of people 'Ratting' on him up the chain of command in his organization until they got to him. He claims he stood tough and silent, so the feds gave him eight years. He has made the rounds of most of the high and medium security prisons in the West when he finally got transferred to Nellis Camp last month. He still got a couple of years to go on his sentence. He is a smart, repeat drug offender and has gotten very savvy about how the system works. He plans to use his knowledge when he gets out to screw the system. I don't know how successful he will be though, because the government is staying one step ahead of the schemes with their new word association game called 'Intent' and 'Conspiracy'.

"This brings us to my final roommate, Randy the baker. He is called that, because he was caught selling flour at cocaine prices. You see Randy was a renowned drug dealer.  Well known in all the jet set playgrounds He saw all his competition being cut down left and right, so, he saw the writing on the wall that his turn was not in the too distant future to take a fall.  So, relying upon his reputation for supplying prime blow, he set camp at Vail during ski season.  He went to the grocery store and bought a five pound bag of flour.  He packaged a kilo of it for show and the rest in consumer size envelopes.  He was doing fine, as his players were taking the stuff at parties and adding it to the communal bowl.  So he was actually helping the government by cutting down the grade of the party mix.  Well, the government broke into his home with a search warrant, uninvited while rounding up the usual suspects.  Randy thought that he was in the clear, because his substance collected from the raid tested negative and he as much as told the DEA fellows that they could take his stuff to their wives and they could bake a loaf of bread, literally.  This did not sit well with the Department of Justice and were concerned that it could establish a precedent and a dangerous one at that.  Because now housewives and grandmas could get into the act and knock down the market value of the product that the government so painstakingly brought in to maintain the high prices.  The Law of Diminishing Returns.  Less guns for friendlies to overthrow unfriendly governments.  Where do they stop?  So the bald legal eagles came up with a sophism. The perpetrator intended all along to sell drugs.  He had a Motive.  He just lacked the funds to finance his evil empire.  Hence Guilty.  Double Guilty in fact because he used his brain towards his evil deed.  Hence 'Conspiracy'.  Double whammy.  Double sentence.  The poor bastard would have been better off selling the real thing.

"So, Christina my love, I live in villa Sierra outside Las Vegas as a guest of our government with my five homies, in a room twelve feet by ten feet.  These people may sound adorable to you, different, victims of government abuse of power and so on.  Don't you believe it.  However, there is a handful of truly innocent inmates of the crime they are accused of.  There is a larger number of people caught in the technicalities of the law and have received punishment that does not fit the crime. I mean you kill some one and you go in prison for three years. There are couple of kids from Guam who killed a turtle to make soup. They got five years  each. Is the endangered species turtle's life worth more than that of a human being?  The government seems to think so.

"My cell mates are uneducated hard core type criminals who were after the quick buck.  Almost ten years later they are still uneducated, hard core criminals that have become well connected, via the federal prison system, and are ready to go out and repeat what got them in, in the first place.  Only this time they think they will pay off cops, prosecutors, judges and other authorities, so they may proceed with impunity.

"I see you are raising your eyebrows. I was shocked myself the first time. I met another Greek who is serving a ten year sentence for drugs.  The government could not estimate the quantity involved other than it was a lot.  The guy was living in Beverly Hills, Los Angeles, drove a Ferrari, I mean he was living the good life. His organization was made exclusively of Greeks.  A stunning looking  DEA agent became the girlfriend of one of his Lieutenant's.  She literally fucked her way into his organization. She testified for the government.  She portrayed him as the Greek mafioso who was bringing all these drugs into the country from Europe. Wrong.  The fellow was not importing.  As a matter of fact he was exporting to Europe.  Where do you think he was getting the drugs? From the U. S. Attorney in Los Angeles. Right out of the evidence room. The U. S. Attorney for Los Angeles disappeared the day Sergio was arrested.  He went to Brazil which has no extradition treaty with the United States. The federal Judge in Hawaii who sentenced him was one of his customers. Do you know who he was? The Honorable judge Fong of Honolulu.  Do you remember he died recently of a heart attack right in his chambers.  Well, he used to do a couple of lines after lunch, according to Sergio, so that he could stay awake for the afternoon sessions.  Coke gets your heart rate up and being overweight and all, something had to give.  Sergio kept his end of the bargain.  Omertà, silence; that was the deal.  You can have all you want, but if you get caught we don't know you and you don't know us. Otherwise you will commit suicide in your prison cell.

"My homies are always breaking the regulations. That's their way of revolting against the system. If they get caught, their punishment will be to be moved to an FCI in shackles. So what? That's where they came from to begin with. They consider the time spent at Camp as vacation time. In a few months, they will con their way back to this or another Camp. However, for me transfer to a higher security facility is unthinkable. CEO types do not survive there. So, I have to find a way out of my existing situation. For the time being I am riding the fence. But this is not acceptable in the eyes of both the government and my homies. They believe that you are either with us or against us. There is no middle ground. Like in our business, you are either the shark or shark bait. I would like to organize a room of intellectuals and CEO's and live in an insulated environment.

"Hey look at that couple laying on the grass. I feel bad that you have to see this kind of behavior. Anyway I am about done with my cigar. We can go inside, which is air conditioned."

They got up, arm in arm and made their way passed the Mexican couple with the girl sitting on the lap of the boy, his hands roaming all over her body. As on signal, the guards moved in and started separating the couples in various stages of foreplay.

"You know," Christina said, "the problem lies with these women. Look how they come dressed. Are they going to a party or to a prison visit? Look at all the mini mini's, halter tops without top support underneath. These dresses are appropriate for beach wear with a bathing suit underneath. Their men are locked in here and they cannot do anything about it. All this kissing and fondling is an exercise in futility."

"Why don't you write a letter to the Warden then and suggest the appropriate dress code. Maybe all the women should come in dressed as muslim fundamentalists.   Dressed with these black shapeless dresses, covered head to toe in a way that disguises the female form."

Christina started laughing at this, which was contagious and both of them started laughing, for the first time since the start of the visit. They made their way inside the Visitors Center.  They found a quiet corner, because the couples were now drifting outdoors in the picnic area and the visiting friends were long gone.

"Are you thirsty?"  He asked his wife.

"I thought you'd never ask.  What do they charge here for soda?"

"Fifty cents."

"Well, this is one item that the government is not trying to overcharge."

He went to the soda machine and punched a Coke for his wife and a Dr. Pepper for him.  He returned to their booth and opened her Coke.

"Just like at the CUB, the Student Union Center at WSU.  Remember our first date?"  He reminisced.

"I remember, but it was not at the CUB.  It was at the Rat House, which they tore down and build the Bookie afterwards."

"You are right.  The first time I tasted pizza.  I remember we were there with another couple.  Billy from your dorm and I forget the fellow's name.  It feels like it was yesterday."

"I don't know where the last twenty years have gone.  They went in a blink of the eye."  Christina commented.

"I know.  Particularly the past ten years in Hawaii.  You remember when I was telling you that I live in a dream?  I was working, but had such a good time at work.  It was like playing a game with the money there to keep score.  I was telling you then, that I wished someone would slap me and wake me up."

"I remember.  Someone, the government, sure hit you over the head with a two by four and rudely awakened you."

"The maddening part is that I did not do anything wrong. Let me correct that.  I did not do what they are accusing me of.  I did plenty wrong for which I am punished in a karmic fashion.  I remember during my fortieth birthday you asked me, when I blew the candles of my cake, what my wish was. I told you I wished for nothing to change. That is committing Hubris to the extreme.  Admitting to God that your cup has runneth over.  You have reached the state of Gaudeamus Igitur.  The Greek tragedies are full of heroes who committed similar sins.  Only God achieves fulfillment.  Admitting to being content is the same as acquiring God like qualities. God will strike the Hero down with a bolt of lightning.  The only hope in the Greek tragedy is for the Hero to achieve redemption through humility. Only then will he be saved by the Deus ex Machina.  That's what I need now.  A Mechanical God to be lowered on stage by a crane and set things right again.  And for the experience, the hero to become a better person.  If I achieve this, I am ready to cry out Gaudeamus Igitur.  Which by just thinking it out loud prevents me from achieving redemption through humility.  Circles within circles, within circles spiraling to chimera."

"Let's change the subject.  Did you find out what type of work you would be doing?"

"I had a few feelers out and so far I have been told they are thinking putting me in some sort of teaching program.  Either teaching students who are studying for their GED or teaching Construction Management to prisoners or a course out on the Base for Contracting Officers, called Changes in Construction Contracts.  They have sent out flyers to Bases all over the country and the World and are waiting for responses to assess the course feasibility.  They will be charging each student $2,500.00 for a two week course.  In the meantime, they have me working on Base, a different job and location each day to punish me.  There is this resentment of government employees in the Bureau of

Prisons towards educated and successful people on the outside, who have become their wards. Themselves, they have a high school education, barely, and are paid twenty thousand dollars a year. So, you see, they are really trying to teach us humility. But then, they realize our skills, and with the construction program going on here at the Camp and on Base, they are bound to use me constructively. Actually, they might get a kick out of pretending to pay me as high as first grade at forty cents per hour for work that I used to be paid over one hundred dollars per hour."

"What construction program are you talking about. Don't they put Contracts out to bid and hire outside contractors?"

"The BOP, through a mysterious organization called UNI-COR, utilizes the inmates by hiring their services to the Base for which they receive remuneration of eight dollars for every hour spent on Base and turn around and pay the inmates twelve cents an hour, pocketing the difference. The majority of the work however, is in construction on projects here at the Camp and on Base. The government goes out and gets bids. They use those bids to get appropriations from the General Accounting Office. The bids they got from outside contractors and became the basis for the amount of the appropriation are based on Davis-Bacon prevailing hourly wages. Instead they use prison labor at twelve cents an hour and pocket the difference. For projects on Base the profit is split fifty - fifty between the BOP and the Air Force. All these transactions are being made through UNI-COR which is a mysterious company owned by numerous trusts within trusts. Bottom line, I was told that the real owners are a number of federal judges, senators and congressmen. The proceeds are used to enrich their retirement fund. I was told that this Camp had a request for a Professional Engineer to the Department of Justice for two years now. They think the sentencing judge finally fulfilled their request by sending me and have written a 'Thank you' letter to the sentencing judge. So you see, the government corruption first hand.  They are perpetrating the crime they accused me of, only on a larger scale."

What a racket." Christina whispered.  "I wonder if people realize this. The government is running a very clever PR program under the heading 'get tough on crime'.  The federal government has become so large and powerful , it poses an immediate threat to the rights and freedom of ordinary citizens.  As an extra bonus in recent decades, millions of Americans have lost the right to control their property, to modify their homes, to own a weapon for self defense, to raise their children as they see best, to learn about new medical treatments and to live without interference from undercover government agents looking to create a case for a manufactured crime."

"Honey, you've changed.  You used to be the most pro government person I've ever met.  Even during the turbulent sixties in college.  You were the preppy All American 'see what you can do for your country' type I've ever dated in school."

"Yeah!  Kennedy opened the sixties with a bang, but his brother closed them with a whimper.  Do you know what he told his secretary when she told him she was pregnant? We will get to it when we cross that bridge."

The visiting room had thinned out of visitors and prisoners alike.  Only the diehards remained wanting to capture and commit to memory every last precious moment.

"I don't want to be the last person to be processed." Michael whispered trying to hide his embarrassment.  "I heard all sorts of stories of strip searches..."

"I would not have believed it, if I had not seen it with my own eyes. Female guards, guarding, strip searching and 'accommodating' male prisoners..."

"What do you expect?  They make twenty thousand dollars a year to start with only a high school diploma or a GED.  Lieutenant's make twenty four thousand dollars.  Look at them.  Would you hire them? Would you look at them twice outside the prison?  You wake up next to one of them is enough to set you screaming with freight or turn you into a stone like Medusa."

They made their way to the visitor and inmate processing corridor. Surprisingly, the guard handed the prisoner his I. D. card and told him he was free to return to his unit, while he waved the prisoner's wife to go through the visitor's exit in the opposite direction.  At the last moment, they both turned and simultaneously waved good by.

# CHAPTER 7

## The Chemistry Class

"Five parts ephedrine, one and a half part red phosphorus and two and a half parts hydrochloric acid." The voice was discernible through the half open door in the second floor of the education building, with professorial undertones.

Michael stopped dead in his tracks. The door opening was facing away from the lecture in progress. Impossible to tell who was in the room, without sticking your head inside. It sounded like a chemistry class.

"You slowly heat the solution and maintain one hundred and fifty degrees while you prepare an ice bath and connect the condenser to to the Elmeneyer flask outlet." The professorial voice continued.

Definitely a chemistry class, Michael thought. He should know. He was after all a Chemical Engineer. The problem was that there were no morning classes, he was told by the administration; only evening. On top of that, it was seven o'clock in the morning. He had been told that the staff did not arrive until eight o'clock. The class sounded like it was in full session for some time now. He had an eight o'clock appointment with Mr. Lee, the head of the Department of Education about a possible job to teach math for the prison GED program. He had not been in the education building before and hated to confront the unknown cold. He did not know what Mr. Lee looked like, only that he would be in his office on the second floor at eight o'clock in the morning. There were entirely too many unknowns in the equation. He decided to cut down the number by conducting a reconnaissance of the terrain before anyone else showed up.

There was a steel door at the end of the dark corridor and a second open door a few feet ahead. Light was coming out of the open door frame. It appeared that it was the second door of the classroom he had been listening.

He retraced his steps down to the first floor. The corridor was deserted. He walked rapidly the length of it glancing inside the dark classrooms and made his way to the opposite end. The back door was locked. He started climbing the steps from the opposite side of the building, slowly, testing each step of the aging staircase before putting his full weight on it. He was glad he wore tennis shoes  this morning rather than the clumsy steel toe work boots. Less noise and a quicker getaway, he thought. He made it to the top of the stairs and opened the steel door. He found himself inside the prison chapel and stopped for a minute to gather his bearings and cautiously made his way towards the far end of the room where he was guessing the second floor corridor was starting. He was right. He closed the door noiselessly and started down the corridor hugging the wall across from the lit, half open door. The voice was a lot clearer now. Deep, authoritative, heavily accented.

"...you now have the first stage of crystal methamphetamine, commonly called ice." The professor's back came into view as he was addressing a class of inmates. The professor was dressed in khaki's, an inmate himself. In his fifties, slight built, slouching posture, animated speech, using a lot of hand gestures.

"The product is ready, but not for street use." He continued. "It contains impurities that give it a yellowish-brown tint. You try selling it and no one will buy it. It could be lethal." Michael was listening with rapt attention, hidden in the shadows of the far hallway wall. Unwittingly, he had walked into an illegal session of how to manufacture drugs.

His legs were getting cramped. He could not move forward nor retreat. The movement would reveal his position. He had heard stories about how inmates dealt with witnesses of such gatherings. He measured the distance to the door he originally came in. If he was still in college form, he would have tried a sprint for it. A forty yard sprint, no problem for a left wing in College level varsity soccer. But for an old man, with twenty five years of living the good life, it might as well been a mile. The back door was out of the question. He heard the click as it locked on his way in. He was trapped and the class was getting ready to get out.

"Who can tell me how to get the yellowish tint out?" Asked the jailhouse professor the class, looking at their faces from one side of the room to the other. As he turned toward the hallway, Michael was able to see his profile.

He looked familiar. Where did he see him before? Think! Think damn it! He scanned his brain memory bank to place the face among the five hundred or so inmates. He saw him before somewhere, and recently at that. The class of the eight Mexican looking inmates were sending puzzled looks at each other trying to come up with the answer. That's him. It came to Michael in a start. The fellow the other day in the Mess Hall. The one siting and having dinner with nicotine Nick. Everything clicked into place. The accent, the mannerisms, everything; the professor was Greek. Taking heart in that he moved out of the shadows of the hallway towards the open door and stopped at that point framed by the light.

The Mexican inmates froze in their seats, their eyes looking frightened passed the professor and boring into Michael. The look they gave Michael changed from freight, to hate, to blank. Hands moved down to their books and flicked open, razors. The professor turned slowly, measured Michael up and down, smiled and asked in a soft almost gentle voice.

"Well, what is the answer?"

Michael felt his throat drying up as he answered in a voice mirror image to the professor's.

"You wash it with acetone."

"Well! Well! Pendejos," he said addressing the class, "you are looking here at the product of higher education in this country of ours. A real Chemist. Class dismissed."

As the young Mexicans were making their way slowly towards the far exit of the classroom, the professor turned his full attention towards Michael.

"You have 'thrasos patriotaki'. I like that in a man. For you ignorant wetbacks," he addressed the retreating class, "it means he got steel cohones." The Mexicans nodded and a few even smiled shyly towards Michael.

"Let me introduce myself. Stellios Panayotopoulos, commonly known as Sergio." The professor extended his hand which Michael gripped a little too sternly. "Michael…"

"I know all about you." Sergio interrupted. "Your fame has preceded you. Mr. Chemical Engineer. Registered P. E. I. Q. off the charts. CEO for a Department of Defense Engineering and Construction Corporation. Fucked over by the government. Does that about cover it?"

"Who are you?" Michael asked a little shocked by Sergio's knowledge.

"All in good time my friend. In the meantime, let's get out of this institution of learning for the lower classes before we get questioned by a wandering guard in search of a quiet place to take a nap or worse yet by the prying eyes of a 'snitch'."

"I got to be back at eight o'clock. I have an appointment with a Mr. Lee for a teaching position. What do you do?"

"As little as possible. I wouldn't lift a finger to work, help or promote the cause of these Barbarians."

"Where are you from?"

"All over. I was born in Volos, Greece; but I lived on the island of Skiathos early on, because my parents moved there to open a confectionary.

Then, I lived in Los Angeles, Hawaii, Switzerland and Italy until they caught me."

"What are you in for?"

"Drugs. What else."

"Where were you arrested?"

"Honolulu. Didn't you see it on television or read it in the papers? It was all over for weeks. The government caught all fifteen of us. Fong, the Hawaii Federal Judge on the case, gave us collectively two hundred years. Can you believe that, two hundred years for drugs that the government was selling us, by a judge who was one of my best customers."

"How did they catch you then, if as you claim the government sold you the drugs to begin with?"

"Ah! Maki, Maki...you are so naive. There are governments within governments. All kinds of agencies that are competing with each other and tripping all over each other for a larger share of the money. This whole thing here, this prison, all federal prisons are nothing more than part of the money game."

"Hold on a second Sergio, you are going a little too fast. Who in the government was selling you the drugs?"

"The Los Angeles U. S. Attorney right out of the evidence room. He told me that he would sell me all the drugs I wanted. But if I got caught, I was on my own. He never met me. He did not know me. He did not want to know me. The Federal judges in LA and San Francisco were in on it too. All the way up to the 9th Circuit Court of Appeals. They were all getting their cut. When I expanded my business in Hawaii, the Federal Judges in Honolulu wanted their cut too. What could I do?

The U. S. Attorney in LA told me I had to pay, in order to do business there. What can I tell you Maki, dirtier government than the one in the

United States I have not encountered anywhere in the world, and I have traveled in a lot of countries and have done business with them.  So, I know."

"Sergio, this is so fantastic; it's unbelievable.  It is testing the outer bounds of logic and credibility."

"Why would I lie to you?  I've got nothing to gain or loose.  I tell you the truth as a fellow Greek, because I've been in prison five years already and I need to talk to someone.  I couldn't say anything when I was arrested, because then my life was not worth anything."

"Why didn't the government kill you anyway?"

"People know.  The people and the government know that I kept my mouth shut.

Killing me now is bad for business.  No one will do business with the government.  Or if they did, they would double cross them.  It's complicated. And at the same time it's simple. There is nothing personal here. It's just business."

"You mean to tell me that that the U. S. Government is selling drugs to someone else; right this minute."

"I am sure of it.  Only some of the players have changed.  The U. S. Attorney is not the same.  The one I was dealing with collected his marbles and disappeared.  He didn't lift his little finger to help me.  The Honolulu federal judge Fong, God to torture his soul, gave me and my boys the maximum under the guidelines, regardless if he was one of my best customers.  You know that one was using, I mean personally.  The others, they wanted the powder because it attracted the young stuff like bees to honey. Dirty old men.  Couldn't get young pussy unless they flashed cocaina first. The money aside. See the money was entitlement. Cocaina was extra.  It was not part of the deal. So I remember they were begging me for it. 'Sergio please bring us some next time you come in'.

And me like a 'malakas', I come to Honolulu loaded with packets like Santa Claus."

"You mean, you came to Honolulu with cocaine packages and no one arrested you?"

"Well, I was good. I had a Greek passport. I was visiting friends and I was bringing each a box of 'kourabiedes', you know Russian tea cakes or Mexican wedding cookies, as they are called coated with powder sugar. Between the first and the second layer, was cocaina. Nobody bothered me. The Honolulu federal judges were happy. I was happy. The Los Angeles U. S. Attorney was happy. The California federal judges were happy. I was living in Geneva at the time. A beautiful house on the lake. I had a sixteen year old wife to look at and say she belonged in a museum. A body that would put Aphrodite to shame. An orphan really, who loved me like a father and husband. I was truly happy and felt blessed."

"What happened to change all that?"

"Who knows really how it all started unraveling. I was outside the country most of the time in Italy taking care of the money trail that was ending in Switzerland. I had fourteen boys in my gang, all Greek, to take care of the product distribution. I new their families in Greece and trusted them. I was expanding so fast though, I was forced to hire some Italians that came recommended from trusted sources. One of them is here at Nellis Camp with us. I will introduce you to him. Marcello from Brindisi. I don't know, they were making money you know, Lieutenant level, between two to three million a year and the others on a sliding scale, but no one was making less than five hundred thousand dollars a year.

"You know looking back, I got suspicious first time I laid eyes on Laura. She was with Dimitri, one of my Lieutenants when he came to pick me up at the LAX.

Beautiful girl. Good natured, shy, innocent looking, virginal. Too good to be true. Now Dimitri had a temper. He could be a prick. He introduced her as his fiancé. Lucky Dimitri I thought at the time, but the girl was making me uneasy. She was a virgin looking and a whore at the same time. I was going to check her out but she set up a party that same evening. Maki you should have been there. A party to end all parties, at the Bel-Air Hotel. She invited half a dozen of her girlfriends who looked like college girls out of the magazine centerfold. Well I lost it. Drugs, sex, food, drink, an orgy of the senses. I decided that Laura was OK.

"Two years, the whore. Two whole years she was fucking him and sucking him dry with clothes, jewelry, cars and an expense account. It turned out she was a DEA agent as were the girl friends she was supplying to our parties. The DEA were fucking piping-Toms filming us for two years. You know what the pricks did, they showed my wife the pictures of me fucking other women; after they had me convicted and all. My wife divorced me and wants nothing to do with me. What snake of a mother, Maki, born such vindictive men? Why did they have to break up my family like that? When I found out what they did, I tried to kill myself. I was in Halawa maximum security in Hawaii at the time.

"That fucking judge, that pig, looking at me like Jaba the Hut. That chink who was begging me last week to bring him cocaina. Now was sentencing me to ten years, like he never saw me before in his life. The Marshal standing next to me was wearing my gold Rolex like nobody's business. I told him that this was my watch and I accused him of stealing it. I made a stink in open court. The judge asked to see it. I told him to see at my initials carved at the back. The Marshal said that he bought it from a fellow with that same initials and the judge gave him back my watch. I cursed the judge in open court and asked God to punish him. The judge gives me fourteen days in the hole for the theatrics. The Marshall drags me in my chains like an animal wearing my gold watch. I scream at the judge that God will strike him dead before I come out of the hole.  The judge died of a heart attack three days later due to excessive cocaine consumption.  Let the pig rot in hell."

Tears were streaming from the eyes of Sergio as he recounted his story. Michael touched his shoulder in sympathy and squeezed affectionately. They sat in silence, Michael for the first time in his life experiencing first hand someone else's pain and anguish.

"How do you feel about your case Maki?" Sergio asked suddenly. "Don't you choke up sometime about the injustice? Don't you want to to get up and scream at them for what they've done to you and what they are still doing?"

"I used to feel that way Sergio. I am past it now. I've stopped dwelling in the past, except when I am working on my Appeal and I have to re-read the transcripts.  You know what bothers me looking back?  Not the fact that I was railroaded or the fact that the government lied and suppressed evidence proving me innocent.  No!  Nothing really that hinges on guilt or innocence from the legal standpoint.  The only thing that bothers me is the character of the accused.  I know the government exaggerated to win over the jury, but still a lot of the things   they said about me were true.  I was not a nice person.  I was vain, arrogant and inconsiderate of other people and of what they thought and felt.  I was taking pleasure out of making the government, my customer, looking like an idiot and was steamrolling peoples feelings and careers  to show them up and hit them where it hurts.  In their pocketbook.  I am reaping now what I have sown for twenty years.  This place is ideal for teaching someone humility without putting the organism in extreme danger and struggle for survival."

"You can say that again, Maki, you are lucky to have ended up in this place.

Here is a college town.  You should see some of the places I've been, the FCI's.  Seven knifings a day.  Twenty two to a cell instead of six. No beds. A plastic sheet to serve as mattress, a pillow and a blanket.  No lockers, closets or chairs in the room. Sleeping each night having a death grip on your possessions, with one eye open and the razor blade at the ready, because in the morning your stuff may be gone and yourself would not wake up to find that out."

"Come on." Michael said. "Quit exaggerating. Razor blades? How can you have razor blades in jail? How could you pass it through?"

"You laugh, eh! I have one even here. I cut a place in my bible spine. I trust no one. I sleep holding my bible in one hand at all times. I trust you, so I tell you. No one else knows. How did you like the little 'swallow' visiting you last night?" Sergio, asked mischievously. "It was Nick's and mine welcome present to you."

In the beginning Michael could not understand what Sergio was talking about. Gradually, his face turned crimson as he replayed last night's events in his mind.

"I wish you asked me first, guys." Michael was able to say regaining his composure. "Before you went to all the trouble and expense."

"Well!...How was it?" Sergio asked with childlike curiosity.

"Man this is hard to admit, but here it goes. I got wind of the custom with the guards from my homies. Two of them after all were getting ready for the experience. Jerking off in the shower before hand, so the guards would work for it for a bit. I knew it was supposed to happen after the ten o'clock count and I had the best seat in the house. My lower bed bunky was one and the lower bed across the room from mine was the other. There was all sorts of merry-man flying off in the room in anticipation. I was picturing the guards, back to back, on their knees, their heads bobbing or praying. I don't know in the semi-darkness I was getting visions of a catholic church, praying nuns on their knees. Don't ask. It's a long story and I may tell you one day. It was these childhood memories that were giving me a hard on. I was awake during the count, because I wanted to get a good look at the faces of the two guards. But I must have gone out like a light as soon as the count cleared and the blue lights were turned off.  Next thing I know, I am in the middle of an erotic dream.  I don't remember the details, but the sensation was tugging at my spine. I came fully awake, because my knees were shaking so much. The sweet dream would not leave my senses though, even as I was getting more conscious and aware.  I sensed a milking machine or a giant vacuum cleaner got ahold of my joint and was sucking my insides for all that was worth.  I looked down and made out this head buried in my boxer shorts, making sucking sounds.  I immediately realized what was happening and I started pushing the head away.  At which point I saw the round face of Petunia looking up at me as she was straining to regain her balance, hanging on to my shorts and mattress as the upside down waste basket she had climbed on to reach my bed started tilting at a precarious angle."

Sergio was holding his stomach and sides laughing so hard.

"Stop it.  Stop it.  You are killing me."  He blurted  amidst the laugher, tears streaming from his eyes.  "I wish I was a fly on the wall to see that. Wouldn't it be funny if she brought charges against you for assault."

"I don't know about assault.  I got ahold of her shoulders and was pulling her up, because she lost her footing, kicked the trash can against the locker, and started kicking my bunky bellow trying to get a foothold on his mattress, while I was trying to tell her at the same time that she had made a mistake.  She was supposed to service the bed bellow mine. Petunia at this point, having woken up the entire room, didn't know whether to cry or start laughing."

Sergio fell from the bench on his back rolling on the grass, laughing uncontrollably and sobbing at the same time.

"Maki.  I got to hand it to you.  In the seven years I've been inside the BOP system, nothing made me laugh like that.  No movie, book or person.  I forgot I was in prison.  I became a kid again.  Thank you my friend."

He got up and started to walk away.

"Don't you want to know how it ended?" Michael called after him.

"I do.  But you will be late for your eight o'clock meeting.  Let's save it for next time.  All we have here is time on our hands."  He said sadly as he walked away towards the Mess Hall.

# CHAPTER 8

## The Legal System

"How did your meeting with Lee go?" Michael heard the throaty cigarette laden voice behind him rasping in Greek.

Michael new before he even turned in acknowledgement that it was the same fellow who spoke to him in the Mess Hall line. He could have been deaf and blind and still know from the nicotine smell that permeated the speaker's clothes announcing him twenty yards in advance.

"Hi there!" Michael greeted him like an old friend. "You must be Nick."

"You get around fast." Nick said, relighting a new cigarette from the stub of the old one, a procedure he repeated countless times throughout the day. "My name is Nikos Spiliotis." He added extending his hand.

"Michael Matrozos." He replied shaking the proffered hand.

"I saw you talking to Sergio earlier. I was going to join you guys, but I knew you had an eight o'clock appointment with Lee about a teaching job. How did that go?"

"I don't know. Lee liked me alright but he told me that he had too many people already in the Department of Education for the allotted budget. He is supposed to get rid of some of them, according to the Warden's orders. However, he told me that he does not plan to get rid of them and the Warden doesn't expect him to; but at the present time he cannot go hiring another body, so soon, on the heels of the Warden's admonition. He said he would keep me in mind for a future GED daytime teaching position. He wants me though to teach a night class in Construction

Management. I guess there is pressure from the GAO to teach vocational training to the inmates. The BOP wants me to teach prisoners, particularly blacks, how to read blueprints, perform project cost estimates and implement construction management techniques. The Warden wants the course to be mandatory prior to the release, so the prisoner can acquire skills that would result in employment on the outside. Additionally the Warden and the General at the Air Force Base got together and they want me to teach a ten working day course on the Base, attended by hopeful Contracting Officers from all over the United States and the US Bases around the World. The General wants to advertise it and charge $2,500.00 per head. I told Lee that the class should be limited to twenty students at the time. Lee is promoting the project so he could get credit and thinks they would have a waiting list. His reasoning being, who would not want to spend two weeks in Las Vegas at government's expense and get a Contracting Officer's Certificate in the process. I expressed enthusiasm and willingness but politely refused to commit."

"I bet he will go back to the Warden and lay out the proposition as two blacks talk among themselves. 'He will teach the niggers if you talk to him and give him what he wants.'" Nick added with a forced laugh which ended in a coughing fit.

He took a deep drag from his cigarette to settle his cough and continued.

"Have you filed an Appeal on your case yet?"

"What do you mean? With the Circuit Court of Appeals?"

"Yeah! That's it."

"I did with the 9th and they turned me down."

"Did you ask for a re-hearing?"

"I did. I requested a re-hearing 'en banc'.

"What happened?"

"My petition was rejected."

"Man, I heard you had a good case.  The word around here is that you were set up."

"It makes sense, because I don't believe the ninth circuit read my Appeal."

"It sounds like it.  This falls in line with the latest.  Have you seen it in the paper?"

"I don't know what you are talking about."

"The 9th asked to be split, because they could not handle all the Appeals they've been receiving."

"I believe it.  Before I filed my petition for re-hearing, I had filed a Motion for the government to produce the transcripts from the Grand Jury hearings.  I mean, it was not my idea.  The federal judge ordered the prosecutor to produce them during the last day day of my trial.  It was right there in the transcripts which I quoted to the ninth chapter and verse, because the government never complied with the Court's order."

"That's a little unusual."  Nick said, furrowing his brows.

"I realize this, but this was an unusual case.  It came up the last day of the trial, during the government's rebuttal stage.  The government put this Naval Intelligence Service witness on the stand and had to produce his prior testimony in front of the Grand Jury.  The Agent was scheduled to testify for months now, but the government gave his 'Jenks' material to us a few minutes before the witness was to testify.  My attorney did not protest because he was shortlisted by the government for a vacancy on the federal bench, which he did not disclose to me.  Basically, the government bought my attorney without my knowledge.  According to my attorney, the government had also promised the presiding federal judge on my case, promotion to the 9th Circuit Court of Appeals if he got a conviction in my case."

"Did your lawyer get to be a federal judge and did your judge ended up in the Appeals Court?"

"You know what the Ancient Greeks used to say. 'Everyone loves the treason, but everyone despises the traitor'. Anyway, it came out from the portion of the the Grand Jury transcripts the government produced, that this Agent testified in front of the Grand Jury representing himself as an Agent of the first Grand Jury. What first Grand Jury we ask? Well...the one which failed to issue an indictment. So, the government convened a second Grand Jury and did not call the witnesses who testified during the first; only this NIS Agent who tells this second Grand Jury, that he was the Agent of the first one, and proceeded to say to this second Grand Jury what the witnesses testimony was during the first Grand Jury. He lied about being an Agent of the first Grand Jury, such a title does not exist. He also lied about his interpretation of the Davis-Bacon Act and finally what the witnesses stated during the first Grand Jury.

"The judge became very suspicious of the NIS Agent's testimony in front of the Grand Jury, which the government omitted from the papers they had just submitted in Court and what actually the witness said to the Grand Jury, who when asked in open Court to state; the NIS Agent could not recall. The judge ordered the prosecutor to produce all the Grand Jury's proceedings to determine whether the indictment was tainted. The fact that it was tainted became rather obvious when the NIS Agent under direct questioning by one of the Grand Jury jurors, went ahead and interpreted the Davis-Bacon Act. This was not his role. It was that of the prosecutor, who was present in the same room, saying nothing. And to add insult to injury, the NIS Agent's interpretation was wrong. He stated that the Davis-Bacon Act stipulated that the employee was entitled to prevailing hourly wage rate regardless of what he was doing or where he was at the time , as long as he was employed. He said that the employee should be paid at the Davis-Bacon wage rate for merely breathing. The judge repeatedly asked the prosecutor for the Grand Jury transcripts.

"He should have suspended the trial until the prosecutor produced the Grand Jury transcripts. But he didn't. The government was dragging their feet in producing the transcripts. The trial was on going. My attorney did not file a motion to suspend the proceedings. The Guilty Verdict came in. The government felt that there was no need to produce transcripts any more. The ninth circuit sided with the government. I called a 9th Circuit clerk when I got their denial to my Motion and explained the situation. The clerk told me that it must have been some kind of mistake and she would look into it. She called me back and told me that the ninth had scheduled to grant my motion. It was put in a pile to be answered, because it had to be answered within fourteen days from the date of filing. On the fourteenth day the clerk who was supposed to write the order compelling the government to produce the transcript, did not show up for work. Another clerk came in a panic, grabbed everything slated to be answered that day, and slapped a form letter to each with a single sentence denying the motion. You see the Circuit Court of Appeals is not required to give explanations for what they do, unless requested by the Supreme Court."

"Man, what a raw deal. Didn't you complain or something?"

"Yeah! Or something. You know what she told me. They get fifty new cases per day. They cannot get to all of them. They claim that the Congress cut their budget and they did not have enough clerks for the workload. She told me to write to my congressman and complain."

"Wow! Cold man!"

"No! She was actually very matter of fact about it. They grade the Appeals in the order of the consequences to the Appellant. Capital crimes take precedence and so on down the line. A couple of years in a federal Camp as the downside, doesn't rate with them a hell of a lot;

even though it may represent a devastating alteration of circumstances for the accused."

"Mike, Mike, haven't you figured it out by now?"

"Figure what Nick?"

"You just stumbled on the tip of the iceberg.  It's all about money and a way to make more of it.  It's a government pyramid scheme.  We are at the bottom of the pyramid producing for the people at the top."

"I don't understand what you are talking about, Nick.  Aren't all the people here, inside, because they broke the law?  Now, we can debate the particular law in each case, but bottom line is that the government was able to convince a jury and obtain a Guilty Verdict for the individual."

"Michael,  do you really think the government wants their man made laws to be observed?"  Nick said lighting yet another cigarette from the stub of the one he finished smoking to the filter.  "They want them broken.  You heard me right the first time.  They want them broken. You'd better get it straight that it's not a bunch of boy scouts you are up against. The government is after Power and they mean it. They've been in the business a long time and they know all the tricks.  They intend to stay in power and you'd better get wise to it.  There is no way to rule innocent men.  The only Power any government has is the Power to crack down on criminals.  When there aren't enough criminals, one creates them.  The government declares so many things to be a crime, that it becomes impossible for anyone to live without breaking laws. Who wants a nation of law-abiding citizens?  But just pass the kind of laws that can be neither observed nor enforced, nor objectively interpreted and you create a nation of law breakers and then you cash in on the guilt. Now, that's the system Michael, that's the game and once you understand it, you will have a much easier time dealing with it."

"What did you do?" Michael asked, more as a reaction to the bombardment of all these alien concepts that were haunting his thoughts like harpies.

"It's a long story." Nick said, flicking his cigarette stub in the ashtray. "It boils down to a five year sentence for aiding and abetting the enemy. I am now down to the last year of serving."

"Were you in the military..." Michael asked. Nick looked older than him by at least ten years. He had a bad posture and favoring his left side, dragging down his right arm at the shoulder. His clavicle looked like it mended on its own after a fracture, giving him a lopsided look, particularly apparent when he was using his hands to make a point.

"No. No. It was nothing like this." Nick jumped in before Michael had a chance to finish his sentence. "I had my own company in Los Angeles. I was a CEO like yourself. The company was in the computer business. We were not in the home computer market. We sold systems and computers to large companies, the government and governments of foreign nations. When you play ball in our league, there are certain rules that everyone must observe. The two most important of these, are that you are limited on the size and capability of the unit you are selling overseas and for that matter domestically. You are also limited on the selection of your customers. The government has categorized the Nations of the world as friendlies, neutral and adversaries. The government publishes reams of paperwork which supposedly tell you to whom you are allowed to sell and what you are allowed to sell. The publications are not clear, however, in that they are in conflict with each other and many times within the same document. They are trying to specify generic characteristics of the computer and are not succeeding. Also they are hopelessly behind the times, so they publish, trying to tie into the previous publication by means of revisions and addenda, in many cases retroactively. The government has realized they are in a losing battle of ridding a bicycle, trying to keep up with the computer technology which is riding the super train at the speed of light. By the time the government publication hits the street, it is already outdated, thus obsolete by several months. The government has, more or less, abandoned their efforts now and instead they have concentrated to control the computer market by allowing and granting monopoly privileges to a few select software innovators and manufacturers. I on the other hand fell victim of trusting a supposed friend and relying on the floundering policies of the late eighties."

"I don't mean to interrupt you Nick, but do you suspect that you were set up?"

"I don't suspect it. I know it. I was the victim of a government 'sting' operation that rolled up three computer distributors in Los Angeles alone."

"I heard on the news in the early eighties that computer technology was leaking to the Chinese and Eastern Europeans at an alarming rate." Offered Michael. "Don't you think that the government 'sting' operation had anything to do with that little nugget of information?"

"You mean disinformation." Countered Nick. "The bankruptcy of the Communists was a foregone conclusion since the Carter era in the mid seventies. No I think the government's reaction was aimed to satisfy the peoples false sense of security that they were on top of the situation and that they were doing something about it."

"Nick hold on." Michael interrupted. "In order to have entrapment, you must have two parties. If you are not willing to go along, how can the government force you. It's the old 'You can't cheat an honest man'."

"Don't get me wrong Mike. I don't want to come across like the reluctant virgin who was raped on her wedding night. The government is too clever to fall for such obvious ploys, that can backfire on them. You should have realized by now that the government, when they go after you, they are on a win-win situation. Their favorite modus operandi is to trap a weak individual, catch him red handed, threaten him with Armageddon, turn him so he becomes a 'Confidential Witness' and they make him 'Rat' on his friends or become the Judas sheep in their ploys of entrapment."

Michael, took out his pipe and was packing it with tobacco, paying attention to Nick's monolog and thinking of the parallel issues and protagonists involved in his own case.

"In my case," Nick shook Michael out of his reverie, "the Judas was a friend of mine, from Belgium.  He was a freelance salesman who expedited Contracts or he acted as a catalyst amongst the interested parties to close the deal.  He called me up one day and he suggested we go out to lunch.  During lunch, for which he treated me by the way, he told me that a Belgian company was looking for a couple of computers that had such and such capability.  Now that was Spring of eighty nine and sales were dragging.  I took down the particulars from the advertisement and got to work.  I made a cursory review of the company, it was not really necessary, since Belgium was classified as a friendly nation. I started putting together the system and developing a preliminary proposal.  Price, I was told by my friend, was not an issue, so I was looking forward to a handsome profit and   my Belgian friend to a nice cut of the top as soon as the money arrived.  I compared the system with the government publications.  Memory was a little borderline. Speed was pushing the envelope.  But a new breed of computers was coming out in August, so by the time the transaction was complete, I would be within acceptable limits.  Like a law abiding citizen I sent the whole ball of wax back to the government, the Department of Commerce to be exact, for their approval and got back the approval in record time.  I had never had any problems with the export division because we were after the same thing. Me to maximize the profit. Them to balance the trade deficit.  We were both on the same team.

"So, Fourth of July came, around and with the computers crated for export shipping, with all my t's crossed and the i's dotted, I got us two first class tickets for Miami with the units on board in cargo.  The company buyer representatives were coming from Belgium with a cashiers check and I was going to hand them over the computers and pay my friend his cut of the transaction. Sweet deal all around. I was not planning on staying in Miami long. As a matter of fact I was not expecting to leave the red carpet room, so I only had a carryon with me. We landed late afternoon and we got arrested by the FBI the minute we made it through the arrivals gate. I mean these guys were ready. One minute they serve me with the indictment. The next minute they got me in handcuffs. They put me in a holding cell with twenty other prisoners; like murderers, bank robbers, rapists and drug dealers. There was old me in a suit and tie. I didn't sleep a wink all night hearing jokes about what they would do to me. My friend was not with me and the indictment was making him out to be the Benedict Arnold of modern times. In the morning, during the arraignment, the government appointed a temporary public defender who told me the government's version, which led to my indictment and arrest. Apparently, the Belgian company, hand picked by the government, was a front for Saddam Hussein. The computers were not bound for a friendly nation. I should have checked more thoroughly before making the deal. The government acted like they caught me in the nick of time, as I was getting ready to hand over the computers to Saddam Hussein to guide his Scud missiles that were aimed to kill our boys in the Desert Shield battle. My friend took the stand and testified that he was the Confidential Informant who realized his duty, overcame his greed and went to the FBI. I was in shock. By the time they were done telling their story to the jury, they had me believing it too. The Confidential Informant got off and was given a bonus of fifty thousand dollars for turning me in. I got no bail and was marched right back to jail. This time I was allowed to call my wife and tell her what happened to me."

"Hold on Nick." Michael jumped in. "Didn't you tell the judge that the government signed the paperwork for the computers to leave the country?"

"They were ready for that one too. They had an Agent from the Department of Commerce testifying that I had filed statements, representing the Belgian company to be on the up and up. They believed me. Only to find out that the Belgian company had been a front for Saddam Hussein since its inception. If they could find that out, why couldn't I? Then they pointed out a Disclaimer in fine print on the export documents they signed, stating that it was the shipper's responsibility to certify under oath that the statements were accurate. So they added false statements and perjury to my charges. I tell you Mike. These guys had the case pat. They had done it several times before me and they had developed a blueprint. The Confidential Witness, my alleged friend, had rolled in four other businessmen on the same charge. I met one of them in Jail and it made me feel real stupid for not checking out my 'friend' before. He left right after my trial for Belgium two hundred fifty thousand dollars richer and I got five years. My trial was in January. If you remember, that was the time when the Desert Storm bombing runs started. The prosecution kept reminding the jury with every new air casualty reported that it was illegal computers, same as the ones in my case, which were guiding the antiaircraft missiles killing our boys. I thought the courtroom audience was going to carry the Assistant U. S. Attorney on their shoulders at the end of each day. The judge sentenced me to the maximum jail sentence. A fine, which I cannot pay even if I worked the rest of my life for the government, and banned me from computers for the rest of my life.

"To make things worse, the judge sentenced me to a medium security facility, an FCI, where I had to dodge knives every day, trying to stay alive and healthy for two years with a clean record to be able to apply and come down to a Camp. I lost my business, my wife divorced me after two years and got everything. On top of it, I have to pay clild support of two hundred dollars a month as soon as I get out. What do you have to say about that? You think you got problems? The government treated you better than the Secretary of the Navy we had here for a couple of years. He left the week before you came here."

"No kidding?  What was he in for?"

"I am not exactly sure.  Something to do with using his job as Secretary of the Navy to secure a job in the defense industry after he got out.  I think they tied him to a defense contract award with him getting a job with that particular contractor.  The government claimed that the hundred thousand dollar sign in bonus   he got was nothing more than payoff for past services while holding the office of Secretary of the Navy."

"You got to be kidding." Michael said with genuine surprise.  "I know half a dozen high placed officials in the government that got a job with the private industry upon retiring from the government service.  I know a Navy Captain in particular.  He was the OICC, the Officer in Charge of Construction in Hawaii.  He was giving practically all the engineering work to this particular engineering firm for years.  One day he was working for the government.  The next day he was working for the engineering firm.  They were in the same building with our company.  I saw him in the hallway all the time.  He was really friendly, until I reminded him of the government regulation which forbids government personnel to seek and obtain employment with private firms they've been doing business with, for at least two years after they get out."

"The guy you are talking about was probably a real 'team player'." Nick piped in ironically.

"You don't know half of it."  Michael said.  "He was the one who covered up the SARGO Incident."

"I'd like to hear about this SARGO Incident someday." Nick said.  "While the Secretary of the Navy had made too many enemies in his job.  Probably, other government employees on the payroll of rival defense contractors."

"I know what you mean Nick." Michael said thoughtfully.  "Friends Come and Go; Enemies Accumulate."

"It sounds like you are talking from personal experience my friend." Nick said. "By the way, do you have a cigarette?"

"I don'y smoke cigarettes." Michael replied. "I smoke a pipe or cigars. Here, if you are desperate you can roll your own." Michael said, offering Nick his tobacco pouch.

"That's all I need." Nick said with an attempt at a raspy, throaty laugh. "The hacks see me rolling my own. Do you know what happens next? Piss test for sure. You know Mike, anytime time you have to take a UA, Urine Analysis, you are running a fifty-fifty chance for it to come back positive. This is not the result  of malice, more of incompetence on the part of the cheap lab the BOP is using. Then you get that added to your jacket and it will follow you out to your Parole Officer for the supervised release portion of your sentence. You will find then that you are guilty until you can prove you are innocent."

"I don't know about that Nick. That may be true of others. But from what I hear it does not apply to you. Somehow you got it made..."

"Where did you hear that? What did you hear? Who told you?" Nick kept firing questions, alarmed, looking around suspiciously and rolling his eyes.

"Don't worry about it." Michael assured him in a steady tone. "I heard around, more accurately I was warned, that you were a 'Rat' and was cautioned to watch what I tell you, because you go straight to the authorities with it. I didn't pay any attention, because I got nothing to hide. What you see, is what you get. But rest assured, I got to the bottom of the reason of that reputation of yours and it seemed to me you got a raw deal from the inmates."

Michael went on to recount his conversation with his homies on his first day at Camp, in the dinning room.

"Thanks Mike; but you don't understand these guys. They got the I.Q. of an amoeba. Next time they get together with their friends and are unable to repeat your reasoning, their friends will laugh at them and accuse them that were taken in for fools.  They will still keep calling me a 'Rat' and now they will be mad at you for convincing them otherwise.  You got to lose those guys.  Look around.  You will meet people with similar background. Stay loose. Keep your eyes open. You will see, they will come to you.  In the meantime watch yourself.  Every time you want to get close to someone, ask yourself the question.  If I was on the outside, is this the type of person I would hang around with?  On the other hand, don't make enemies.  You did good there in the Mess Hall.  Stay out of trouble and be your own man at the same time, so no one group claims you.  It's a balancing act all the way.  Set a routine for yourself and a program.  Pick a project you would have liked to do on the outside, but never had the time.  A lot of people here, myself included wanted to write a book.  We all talk about it.  No one does it.  Writing a book is work. You have to set time every day and write.  No one has done it, that I know."

Michael felt that he had found in Nick a friend, a kindred spirit, an older brother from whom he could learn and test ideas.

"How long have you left to serve?"  He asked Nick.

"Probably another six months here; at which time I am eligible for a halfway house."

"What's that?"  Michael asked.

"Well, for guys like you and me, it's nothing.  Just another scheme of the BOP to hit us for more money.  But for the majority of the people here it is the means by which to re-enter society.  You probably have noticed that a lot of the inmates here have come from other institutions of greater security. They have been serving long sentences, over ten years. The last two, they customarily serve at Camps where they have made it progressively.  A year prior to their release date, they must declare where they want to be released.  The BOP finds them a home in that city of their choice, run by the BOP, where they are free to go out and find a job and check in with the BOP. They are also required to pay twenty five per cent of their earnings for room and board. Now for hard cases involving drugs, bank robberies and other violent crimes, there are all sorts of restrictions, such as breathalyzer and drug tests. But for white collar type criminals the BOP has different rules. You remember what I told you. It's all a matter of money and risk. If you do not represent a threat to society, why should they waste the space and meals for you? So, they release you to society and you just go home. However, you still got to give them twenty five percent of the money you earn for six months. You cannot get out of that."

"Where are you going?"

"Probably to Long Beach, California."

"What are you going to do?"

"This I don't know. I will probably try my hand at teaching somewhere. But you know, your life will be different. They got you anytime they want you. Three to five years when you are under probation and beyond. I will try to leave the country. Start somewhere else fresh. After all, I am only forty nine years old."

Michael tried to hide his shock at that revelation about Nick's age. He looked well over sixty. Is this what four years in prison does to a man?

"It's too early for you to be thinking about halfway houses and what not." Nick continued. "Concentrate in doing good time, easy time. The first thing you do is get yourself a good job. By good job I mean an easy job, preferably here at Camp. You will hear all sorts of stories on this issue. A lot of people refuse to work for twelve cents an hour. Now you cannot come straight out and tell them that you refuse to work, because they will send you to an FCI which is a step higher than here. You are locked up in an FCI. You noticed here you are not. You are free to go wherever you want. Even escape. There was this guy who escaped yesterday from the other dormitory. He called a taxi from downtown Las Vegas. It came to his dorm. Picked him up and drove him to the airport. No one tried to stop him. The guy was Lebanese. I bet by now, he is halfway there already."

"Do they make you work at the FCI?" Michael drew back Nick to the main topic of discussion.

"Of course they do." Nick replied. "Haven't you figured the government scheme by now? It's all about money. Why do you think they give people such long sentences? Where else can you get workers at twelve cents an hour? In China, at least they are up front with it. They have labor camps and put their inmates to work under slave conditions. Here in the good old USA we don't want to admit it. But it is true. The federal prison inmate population is under slave conditions also. They started slowly by making making furniture and wood products for the BOP use and dairy products for internal consumption. Today, this cottage industry has grown to the point that everything used by the prison system and the federal government at large is made by the prisoners themselves, in effect robbing jobs out of the private sector. They expanded the scheme to all government agencies. They all have to buy from the BOP. No manufacturer can compete with someone who pays its labor force twelve cents an hour, while they are made to pay minimum wage at over five dollars per hour. Now in all fairness, not everybody makes twelve cents an hour. After a year at it, they give you a raise to skilled worker level at seventeen cents an hour. If you are a skilled worker that they have a need of, say a plumber or an electrician they pay you grade three pay at twenty five cents an hour. And last but not least there is the four grade where the bid bucks are made at forty cents an hour. I don't know of any grade four personally. These guys, whoever they are, rumor has it that they get a monthly bonus on top of their pay and other benefits depending of the productivity of their division and how irreplaceable they happen to be. Capitalism at work. It's a different world down here. Run by a very secretive organization called UNI-COR; cranking out work and earning profits like no other business in this country."

"Hold on Nick, how can they get away with it for so long? Doesn't word get to the outside? What about the news? Now I heard, not long ago, a segment in Sixty Minutes devoted entirely on slave labor conditions in China and the fact that the product, I think they were generators, have been banned in this country."

"Probably, because they were in competition with the ones manufactured by the prison system in this country. What do you think four hundred inmates are doing in Boron FPC in the middle of the Mojave desert? Generators. As I told you before, up until the end of the eighties, the BOP was using the products manufactured by the inmates for the federal prison system. Like all the metal lockers and cabinets we are using, are being made at Terminal Island. The mattresses, at Sheraton, Oregon. The beds, at Fort Dix, Texas. I can go on for hours. Bottom line is we are all working for UNI-COR corporation. They are our employer. Their last financial statement showed that they were turning a profit of 71%. Unheard of in the business world. They are listed in the stock exchange as a publicly traded corporation. You would think with that kind of profit margin, investors would be clamoring to buy their stock. Unfortunately, their stock is not available for purchase. UNI-COR is big business and growing. In the nineties they started selling their products to the State Prison System, the Armed Forces, Federal Hospitals and other government and state facilities with no end in sight."

"Nick lets go back a little. All these years and no one ever complained from the inmates? What about lawsuits and the like?"

"They've been able to weather adversity by hitting hard and in many directions simultaneously. The inmate who is brave enough to file a Complaint, is never heard of again."

"What do you mean? They kill him?"

"No! No! They are too clever for that. They simply send him for diesel therapy and an attitude adjustment cruise."

"What are you talking about?"

Nick smiled wryly. "Mike you are a babe in the woods, but I like you. All these questions. They are so refreshing. Let me tell you what the BOP does to the wise guys who give them trouble either in court or in prison, by resisting them or serving as an example for others in civil disobedience. They make examples out  of them. At three o'clock in the morning, two guards wake you up and and tell you are moving out. You got fifteen minutes to report to the Administration Building with all your belongings. You barely have time to grab your personal stuff and run there in the middle of the night. They tell you to strip. They catalog everything and put it in your presence in a cardboard box with your name, your inmate number and your new destination, usually clear across the country. This is the first time you find out where you are going. After a thorough strip search, they give you to put on a tee shirt, underpants, socks, canvas slip on shoes, a khaki shirt and pants and they load you on a bus in handcuffs, leg irons and shackles and tie you inside the bus cage so you cannot move more than six inches in any direction. The bus service is operated by the Marshals and it already has inmates inside  from who knows where, heading to who knows where, having committed any crime imaginable. The Marshals ferry service does not discriminate.  A president of a Bank who is convicted of money laundering in for six months, can be tied next to a rapist and serial killer for life.  The bus starts in the middle of the night for destinations unknown to pick up and drop prisoners. Stop at some warehouse type facility after a few days, where you are given a day's rest to take a shower and get a new change of clothes and off you go. Finally, after several weeks arriving at your destination, only to find that en route you've been assigned to another facility at the other end of the country. I don't need to go on. It's a journey without end. Its duration being determined solely by your physical and mental stamina. They say that the treatment reduces the most hardened  and determined individual into a gibbering, crying creature in a matter of a couple of months. It is my understanding that the record to date is one week shy of three months. What do you say Mike, care to tempt fate and break the record?"

Michael was stunned at all these revelations. It was difficult for him to comprehend that his adopted country of the free and the brave would treat its citizens in such an inhuman way merely for speaking out. "What happens with the impending law suit in the meantime?"

"The courts in the past decided that the wage rate paid was fair based on the minimum wage law  and taking into account taxes, room and board, medical and dental treatment and other services provided by the prison system. So after you deduct for these, what's left is paid to the inmate. They got it down pat, over the years. They beat all the minimum wage lawsuits to the point that the courts are now dismissing them without having to ring up the calculations."

Michael wondered how successful the government would be to prove that the wages paid against the Davis-Bacon hourly wages of thirty five dollars an hour are adequate, when they have already established what they are for the same inmate in their minimum wage cases. He bet someone one day will start a Class Action law suit for all the construction workers on Base and at the Camp working on federally funded projects.

'You make it sound like a racket." Michael said thoughtfully. "And you say this whole slave market is owned and run by UNI-COR?"

"That's right."

"Well, who owns UNI-COR?"

"That's the sixty four thousand dollar question. On the face of it, it sounds like a government enterprise, doesn't it?  It is however, independent, owned by a series of trusts; but both the Justice Department and the Bureau of Prisons are listed as its subsidiaries. It is listed in the New York Stock Exchange, but the stock is not available to the public.  I was able to crack their computer codes and find out the trust beneficiaries..."

"Get to the point Nick.  The suspense is killing me.  Who owns UNI-COR?"

"Mike, Mike, I thought by now you would have guessed it.  The Federal Judges, primarily, who else?"

"No!"  Cried Michael.  "The same people who passed out sentences?  It can't be.  That would be a conflict of interest to the max in the first place and give rise to miscarriage of justice."

"Let's go for a walk." Nick suggested. "We've been talking too long in the same spot and people will start wondering.  I will show you the track which would do you good to walk a few laps every day."

# CHAPTER 9

## Hawaii Blues Redux

Nick and Michael turned right at the end of the Education Building and followed the path that led North, towards the perimeter of the compound.

"Of course you know the building to the left, the Mess Hall." Nick broke in as the impromptu guide. "The building behind it and to the left is the Exchange. You may shop there once a week on the day predetermined by the last digit of your account card. What's yours for example?"

"Nine." Michael replied.

"You are ...let's see..." And Nick started counting on his fingers. "Thursday. I think. Right. Thursday."

"Are you sure?" Michael chuckled. "For a while there I thought you would be taking off your shoes."

"Mike, Mike, now don't be so vicious. I was only a history major in College. What little math I learned in High School I forgot with the Computer Age. On the outside, I used to have a calculator in a small case that I kept my business cards. The darn thing was the size of a credit card. I am lost without it."

"Don't worry Nick. You are not the only one. We are graduating a whole generation of math students that are calculator dependent. I taught high school math for a year, in the Hawaii High School system. If what I saw was indicative of the math education in all the states, High School students nowadays are incapable of adding, subtracting, multiplying and dividing without using their calculators. Talk about more complex functions such as percentage, interest and other basic everyday life math problems; they are totally in the dark.  Somewhere along the way, the system forgot how to truly educate the students.  They show them 'how', without bothering to explain to them the 'why'.  My daughter went for two semesters to a High School in Europe and among other courses, she took, was Geometry.  When she came back to her old High School in Hawaii she discovered she was ahead of her class.  Also the theorems that her teacher was telling the students to memorize, she did not have to, because she knew how to derive and  prove.  Something that she was taught in Europe.  Her Hawaii teacher never learned how to do that.  So, she had my daughter on the board each time showing the class how it was done.  It's the old saying Nick, give someone a fish a day and you've got someone depended on you for life.  Teach someone how to fish and you've got someone independent from you, for life."

They reached the main road that was snaking to the right and hooking to the left, disappearing around the tennis courts.  The road was going straight for quarter of a mile to the left, coming around the dormitories and disappearing towards the Las Vegas skyline in the distance.

"The building across the street is the warehouse where you can get clothes, shoes and personal items.  The building next to it is the gymnasium.  They have indoor basketball courts, racquetball courts, saunas and all the other amenities you would find in a private club."

"No kidding, Nick, all that for the inmates?"

"It used to be better." Replied Nick. "We could get the shuttle and go on Base.  The PX, we had an indoor swimming pool and we could play golf.  They tightened up a bit, you know as a result of the Barbara Walters interview.  Did you hear?"

"No.  What happened?"

"Well, Barbara Walters came here to interview the Secretary of the Navy and an inmate involved in some scam she was covering in that news segment.  She came during the weekend and at that time there was no Visitors Center.  The visitors came inside the compound and were free to go everywhere.  The prisoners were not required to wear khaki uniforms.  They were dressed in civilian clothes.  So, old Ba-Ba comes in, sees kids running around, couples laying on the grass in bathing suits sun bathing, men carrying golf bags going to catch the Base shuttle, couples dressed in tennis outfits swinging rackets on their way to the tennis courts, she turned around and said to her cameraman and assistants:

"What kind of prison is that?  This is a Country Club for the rich and famous - at that time the Camp was admitting only politicians and CEO type white collar criminals - all that at tax payers expense."

"So she went and did a second segment geared to inflame the hardworking masses, with footage of people swimming, playing tennis, golf, barbecuing steaks, and she commented that these people were supposed to be in prison paying for their crimes of shafting the people. She said that the taxpayers were getting screwed twice by these fat cats and the government was helping them do it.  So the government slowly took away the gourmet dinning, golf, swimming, junkets to town and sorties on Base.  We still got the tennis courts as you can see on your right. The baseball field is right behind them. To your left are the soccer and football fields.  The pre-fabricated metal buildings behind the chain link fence to are used store nuclear bombs and warheads for the airplanes.  Every three months or so, the Air Force sends a convoy to transport a load of live ammo and bombs for exercises and then bring them back for storage.  When they do that, they isolate the inmates and post off limit signs all over the place.  You haven't seen that level of security anywhere I bet. MP's cruising around yelling and screaming at the closest human target they can find.  The commotion is such that it becomes a dead giveaway of the ammunition transfer which is supposed to be conducted in secrecy.  I remember last time, some General decided on a three AM alert. So the Air Force rousted us out of bed at two thirty AM, herded us, still in our pajamas into an airfield hanger where we stayed for twelve hours  with a sack lunch.  We got back right before dinner the following day to find our rooms in a mess. You see the hacks used the opportunity to go through our belongings in search for contraband and they summarily dumped everything in the middle of the room."

"What happened to the contraband?" Michael asked.

"Well, that's another interesting story.  If they were found in front of witnesses, the contraband was confiscated and the inmate was punished.  If they were found without witnesses, usually the hack who found them kept them.  What is the inmate going to do?  Complain that the hack stole paper money from him that he was not supposed to have to begin with?  Don't be silly.  The matter was settled equitably.  If the money was too much, the hack returned  some back to the inmate.  If he didn't, the hack better transfer."

The two prisoners rounded the corner gazing in the distance at the desert spreading from the chain link fence line, warning the passers that this was government property, to the foothills.  Shot gun fire could be heard from the trap and skeet shooting range up ahead.

"This will be the future weight lifting and exercise equipment building site.  Next to the basketball court, volley ball courts, horse shoe pit and bocci courts.  This completes the outer perimeter tour." Nick said.  "The track ends by the Indian tepees used by the the Native American prisoners for religious ceremonies.  When you have crossed the mark in line with the tepee entrance, you have completed one mile.  Try to do four or five laps a day to keep in shape.  Let's do another one before lunch to work up an appetite."

"You are on."  Michael said.  "While you are on a health kick, did you notice the new fountain outside our dorm?"

"Yeah!  What about it?"

"Well, they activated it yesterday and I noticed that they tied into the same water line that feeds the water sprinklers on the lawn, without using a back-flow preventer."

"Oh yeah?" Nick replied amused. "What is a back-flow what's macall it?"

"It is a plumbing device made out of two check valves in line, sandwiched between two gate valves, some people add a filter to the system. The plumbing Code and OSHA requires installation of one of these devises wherever one ties into a potable service water line. The check valves allow flow only in one direction. In our case, fertilizer can conceivably get back into the potable water service and contaminate the drinking water."

"Now you tell me that they have polluted our drinking water on the heels of polluting the air we breath."

"What do you mean?" Michael asked, pretending he was surprised.

"Don't tell me you haven't noticed, Chemical Engineer and all." Nick replied. "The buildings here have roofing and siding made out of Asbestos. The heating and air conditioning ducts are lined inside with Asbestos insulation which is constantly breaking up in chunks and ends up blowing 'snow', I mean Asbestos fibers, in our rooms through the registers. You could shut them down, but then you die of the heat in the summer and freeze in the winter. Now concerning the drinking water problem, you could buy bottled water at the commissary, I suppose at a dollar a litter. The daily consumption, so that you don't dehydrate is a little over a litter per day. So a prisoner needs to spend thirty five to forty dollars  a month in drinking water alone to survive. The government pays inmates for working twelve cents an hour. That means that the average prisoner makes between fourteen and seventeen dollars per month. Not even enough to buy water to survive. We are all slowly dying here Mike and the government has given up, because it is not cost effective to hire an outside contractor to do the work. Instead they try to do it with with inmate labor. Yes, they save money that way, but the work is done at glacial speed with dubious results, because the hacks they hired to run the engineering and construction don't know any better. You will see for yourself when you end up running the show here."

"What do you mean? I don't have a job yet and no one talked to me about running the Engineering and Construction here."

"Hey! Are you Michael Matrozos?" An accented voice echoed behind the two inmates.

"Who are you looking for?" Replied Michael suspiciously, as he slowed his pace looking backwards. His eyes met a perspiring middle age Japanese fellow, dressed in black and white jump suit type sweats made of nylon.

"The guy from Hawaii; president of Akamai Engineering."

"That's me." Said Michael, stopping altogether and turning around. Nick stopped with him, tapping his foot impatiently.

"I heard that you were coming here, and been trying to look you up for days now." The Japanese fellow continued. "I am Rodney Iida." He said taking a small bow.

"I am Michael Matrozos." He said extending his right hand. "Pleased to make your acquaintance." He continued crushing the delicate hand of Rodney in his own. "Are you from Hawaii also?"

"Yes. You probably heard the name Iida Construction, we've been competitors for the past ten years."

"Well! Well!" Michael exclaimed. "It's a small world after all. What are you doing in here?"

"I was convicted for the same thing you are in for." Rodney replied digging the ground with his toe embarrassed.

"Don't tell me." Michael retorted. "The government has now patented my case and are going after other undesirables by converting an administrative law, like the Davis-Bacon Act, into a criminal offense?"

"Yes that's what they have done." Rodney replied. "They have gone after and convicted six contractors, so far, in Hawaii and it's my understanding that they have indicted two more. You were the first one. After you lost your trial and got convicted, they came to me and threatened me with ten years in prison, like you got, if I didn't plead guilty. So, what could I do. I pleaded guilty and got only five years."

"But, Rodney," Michael interrupted him. "I did not get ten years. I only got thirty three months after I took them to Court and lost at trial. They were offering me a twenty five thousand dollar fine and no jail time if I pled guilty. I am hopeful that I will be exonerated and would not have to serve that much if I win my Appeal or the congress repeals the Davis-Bacon Act as they are scheduled to do towards the end of October."

"You mean, you did not get a ten year sentence?" Rodney was able to whisper. "They lied to me."

"What else is new?" Nick broke in. "Welcome to the club."

Rodney turned in Nick's direction with a vacant stare. He was clearly in shock.

"Oh!" Michael interrupted. "This is Nick Spiliotis, a fellow I met here at Camp." Rodney smiled politely and took a small bow in Nick's direction.

"Anyhow." Michael continued. "The government obviously lied to you. Originally, they offered me a thirty five thousand dollar fine and a one count admission of guilt with no jail time. I turned them down. They came back with a twenty five thousand dollar fine and admitting guilt of gross negligence. At the time, I felt the government was blackmailing me into admission of guilty in order to collect some sort of fine to justify the money they had spent investigating me for two years and going through two Grand Juries. I was not guilty. Why should I admit I was?

So I took the government to Trial. My attorney advised me that the trial was rigged. The government had promised the presiding federal judge, Ezra, a promotion to the 9th Circuit Court of Appeals, if I was found guilty. I found out, shortly after the trial, that the government had also approached my attorney with an offer as well   for a position of Federal Judge and shortlisted him with two others during my trial. I had my interpretation of the Davis-Bacon labor law which I had followed and based all my Change Orders on the same interpretation. The government had their own, which if I had followed I would have been indicted for overcharging the government on Change Orders. If I applied the government's interpretation of the law, the government owed me over seven million dollars on the Contracts under indictment alone. These are the facts Rodney. Whatever else the government has told you, is not consistent with the facts as I know them."

Rodney followed my narrative with interest and seemed to come out of his initial shock.

"I wanted to contact you in Honolulu to verify the government's story and claims, but I didn't know you personally and my attorney advised me against it. Are you fighting them through the Appeals process?" He asked shyly.

"Yes I am. Although, currently I am ready to petition for a Writ of Certiorari. This is an appeal to the Supreme Court to hear my case. They get around ten thousand of them a year and they grant to hear around eighty five. So, as you can see, I have a better chance of winning the lottery than obtaining a Writ of Certiorari which they give to about five hundred cases a year shortlisted for review. However, it's been my life long ambition to argue a case in front of the Supreme Court and win. People tell me, fat chance. But one can always dream. Also, think about it, most of the cases that attorneys use as precedent to argue their point and win are based on a Writ of Certiorari or on a Habeas Corpus."

"What is that last one?" Rodney ventured.

"It's the next step in the appeals process if the Supreme Court refuses to hear your case. It is filed with the district court of appeals, in my case the ninth, and it is simply a request for retrial on the basis of inadequate counsel during the trial. If you win, you get a new trial, if the government wants to have a new trial, otherwise the case is dismissed. If the 9th Circuit Court of Appeals affirms the lower court decision, then you apply to the Supreme Court. If they refuse to hear your case, you are done as far as the criminal Justice System in the US is concerned."

"What that means." Nick cut in. "You are Finito. Caput. Asta la vista baby?"

"Not so fast Loui." Michael interrupted him. "That's what I thought also until recently. If you can show lack of jurisdiction, you can counter sue the government under the Uniform Commercial Code. The argument for jurisdiction is done in front of a UCC judge who is not on the federal payroll like the Criminal Court, with the Federal Judge. The playing field is a little more level. The government is known to lose and lose big. So, if you can show a jurisdictional dispute the government does a turn around and does not want to go to trial. Instead the government is ready to play let's make a deal. You drop your suit, we will expunge your record and pay damages. Now, jailhouse attorneys who have seen my case, tell me that in a UCC Court, the government will have a heck of a time to prove Mail Fraud, if the mailing was not an integral part to furthering the scheme, as I believe my case is. It would have made no difference whether I mailed or handed over the Certified Payrolls. As a matter of fact it appears that I had handed all of them each week for three years, the time in the indictment, except for two that I mailed and those were solely for government ordered corrections. Also the checks the government mailed me. They could have handed them to me. The U.S. Mails had nothing to do with furthering the alleged scheme. In addition, in Mail Fraud cases, under the UCC, the injured party, in this case the government, has to prove financial loss. How are they going to do that when I have them in the trial transcripts admitting that they benefited and in fact saved taxpayers money. Additionally, in my first Appeal to the Ninth Circuit they rejected my Appeal on the basis that the government need not show loss or damage to indict. Wrong. They do. So, to answer your question Rodney, I think I will prevail, but it may be after I have served my sentence here. The gears of justice move very slowly."

"At least you got a gleamer of hope." Rodney added resentfully. "I am truly done for, since I pleaded guilty. Same goes for the other contractors from Hawaii."

"What other contractors?" Michael interrupted. "What's the story with these other contractors?"

"After your case, that got a lot of publicity, the government quietly went after just about every other major non union contractor in Hawaii. They have split us up so we don't communicate with each other. There are two in Boron, two at Sheraton and two at Lompoc, besides the two of us at Nellis."

"What is he talking about, Mike?" Nick interrupted. "Did the feds just declare open season on the Hawaii contractors? What's going on here?"

"The open season, Nick, was declared five years ago by the Feds." Michael added thoughtfully. "The Federal government sued the Hawaii contractors collectively for violating the anti-trust laws. In effect the government accused us of Price Fixing."

"Any truth to it?" Nick asked slyly.

"Not really. What I mean is, not intentionally. If there was opportunity to cultivate any, it was only as a result of the way the government been doing business in Hawaii."

"How is that?" Asked Nick.

"The government in Hawaii, particularly the Department of Defense, has a yearly budget for construction that runs into several hundred million dollars.  Their fiscal year starts the first of October and ends at the end of September.  The Department of Defense has several projects slated for a given fiscal year.  They are supposed to put them out to Bid and be awarded to the successful low bidder  through out the year.  However, this is not what is taking place.  The government military employees who are transferred to Hawaii, are assigned to remain in Hawaii for a two year tour of duty.  They view the transfer as a just reward for services rendered in shit hole locations they've been and spend their time in Hawaii as if they were on an extended vacation.

"So, the work that is supposed to get done the first quarter of the fiscal year, is not.  Then you've got the Holidays that start from Thanksgiving and end with Presidents Day during which everybody takes a leave to the mainland to see relatives or have more fun in Hawaii and the neighboring islands or visit the Far East and Australia.  Then you have the rainy season during Spring which is spent on travel and meetings, mostly in the mainland. So, now you've got most of the fiscal year gone and they have not started putting jobs out for Bid.  At this point they start, say around June, to put jobs out on the street for Bid and the number of jobs increases as the summer goes into full swing.  By August panic sets in, that they will not be able to spend all the money on the budget.  This is a Cardinal sin, according to the headquarters in Washington DC, because whatever money is left at the end of the fiscal year, the Congress takes back and allocates next year's budget by deducting the left over amount from the previous allocation, since the Department of Defense can function with less.  So, if the government runs out of slated projects, they invent more, many times totally unnecessary, so that they may spend their allocation and can show even a little shortage of money, so that next year they can get more.

"Now look what this government modus operandi causes. In Hawaii you have a finite number of contractors, all of which have a set Bonding Capacity limit, since all government jobs require a Payment and Performance Bond.  However, when each day the number of jobs bidding outnumbers the contractors available, naturally each contractor will concentrate estimating one or two jobs and throw in a Bid number for a few others. The Bids become conservative, meaning they have a high margin of profit for the contractor. This margin becomes progressively higher as the number of jobs available for Bid increases and the Bonding Capacity of each contractor decreases. The loser in this format is naturally the government; ultimately of course the tax payers.

"The government refuses to admit wrongdoing and is blaming collusion on the part of the contractors, which is non existent, because it is totally unnecessary. It gives that impression, however, because primarily of the bid deposit and the common clearing house concept.

"The contractors formed an Association for collective bargaining with labor. This Association also serves as the clearing house for sub-bids from Specialty Contractors and Suppliers. The day before the Prime Bid is due, the Association receives sub-bids from vendors and forwards same to the General Contractors. Accordingly, the day before the General Bid is due, every prospective bidder knows the costs associated with the project and they are aware that their competitors have the same knowledge. Accordingly, on the day of the Bid, every competitor is playing on an even playing field. The only question being how much margin, overhead and profit, it could be made and still be the low bidder and end up with the job. Historically, since the same procedure is repeated year after year, the General Contractors have accumulated empirical knowledge of what is the percentage margin that would be the winning bid. For example in June it would be 30 to 32 percent. That is you multiply the bid deposit numbers by 1.30 to 1.32. This percentage gets higher as the summer heats up, to the point that in September it is safe to double and sometimes triple the cost and still end up with the winning bid. Many times, the bid requests are so many, that a number of them do not receive bids and go out for re-bid. It is safe to say that virtually all the Bids are in excess of the government estimate. The government officials at the GAO in Washington DC, which is the watchdog of the Congress, see that and conclude that the Department of Defense in Hawaii is the victim of Price Fixing. The local officials don't bother to set them straight, because they   would in effect be admitting that they were not doing their job; so, they keep quiet or actively support that notion of collusion.  So, the government convened a Grand Jury to indict the Hawaii General Contractors and their Association for violating the anti-trust laws, by inhibiting competitive sub-bidding and price fixing.

"They came to me and offered me immunity to testify against the others.  I explained to them the reason for the high bids and refused to lie in front of the Grand Jury.  The Naval Investigative Service, NIS, Agent who was conducting the interview told me how the government was disappointed in me to find that I was not a 'team player'.  Well I found out soon enough that if you are not a 'team player', you are a 'target'.  Then it is only a matter of time until you get indicted for something.   It is the government's way of paying you back for insubordination. So, here I am.  What do you have to say to this lida, ma man?"

"I see you picked up on the beep-bop lingo of your bunky." Interjected Nick.  "You talk like them, pretty soon you'll walk like them.  I hear you like to eat with them.  Bravo..."

"Hey! Hey! Nick. Cut the shit. This is serious talk here."

"Well Mike, do you want to hear the rest of the story, so to speak?" Rodney interrupted.

Nick and Michael stopped their bickering and turned their collective undivided attention towards Rodney.

"The government pretty much broke up the 'old boy' network in Hawaii. In their place they brought in mainland contractors, same ones they used in Viet Nam, twenty years ago.  I understand these guys are heavy political contributors."

"Did they get any jobs?  I don't see how they could compete with the local boys."

"They don't need to compete. This is the strange thing. The government no longer opens the bids in public.  Let me go back and explain.  Shortly after you got convicted, Mike, the government revamped the bidding process. When you submitted the Bid, in addition to the bid amount, the government required the prospective bidders to submit their company qualifications to perform the work under bid.  The government was reserving the right to award the job not necessarily to the apparent low bidder, but to the 'responsible low bidder'.  What qualified someone as 'responsible' was anybody's guess and the government was   opening the bids behind closed doors without outside witnesses and they were not announcing the 'responsible low bidder' until several days after the Bid opening date.

"The plot thickens further.  Listen to that.  The government opens the bids.  They see what are the numbers.  Then they call the one they decided to give the job to and ask him to submit another bid, post date it, and most important they tell him the number he got to beat.  If the guy doesn't go for it, they call their second choice, and so on.  I know this because I was party to the scheme in the beginning.  Then they were not calling me any more, because I refused 'to contribute' and threatened to expose them.  They indicted me for Mail Fraud due to DavisBacon Act violations."

"Why didn't you expose them during trial?"  Michael jumped indignant.

"For one, the judge told my attorney he would not allow it in Court, because it had nothing to do with the issues of the indictment and for another, remember, I never  got the chance to go to trial because, at my attorney's advice, I pleaded guilty."

Silence followed Rodney's revelations as the three inmates were lost in their own thoughts.  The silence was intermittently broken by the shot gun blasts from the nearby skeet and trap shooting range.

"I get depressed every time I am talking about it." Added Rodney. "Take care Mike, we will talk. One thing you should know though. I run the cabinet shop here at Camp and the other day I heard from my BOP boss that finally the guy they were waiting to run their Engineering and Construction expansion program, came on board. I think he was talking about you."

With these parting words, Rodney made his way toward the picnic area. The misting machines were on and blasting cool mist. He sat on one of the benches underneath them, closed his eyes and vicariously transported himself to Hawaii.

"What do you make of that, Nick?" Michael asked.

"I have not heard." Nick replied. "But again I am only in education. I don't hang around the powers to be. I will tell you one thing though. I've read in the September 13, Reform Act that Congress allocated to the Department of Justice for building new prisons and renovating existing, 175 million dollars for the year. For the next year, which started a few days ago, the figure became 750 million dol lars. The year after it will be over a billion and so on until the year 2000 when the appropriation tops 2 billion. Does this answer your question? I am sure the government, in its eminent wisdom, will make every effort to put a man in charge of the program, being an inmate having the appropriate qualifications and experience for a successful program of Federal Prison facilities construction. Does this answer your question?"

# CHAPTER 10

## The Housing Assignment

**B**eep! Beep! BEEP! BEEP!

"All right already motherfucker!" Lew yelled across the room. "Shut the fuck up!"

Michael woke up with a start. He rolled to his left and almost fell five feet down, butt first. Shit he thought. I will never get used to these bunk beds after sleeping on a king size bed for thirty years. He grabbed the iron headboard and lifted himself in a sitting position, trying to isolate the beeping sound in the semidarkness. That was another thing. No more hugging and kissing to get up in the morning, from his wife. She was five thousand miles away, hopefully tossing and turning in their king size bed, missing him. What time was it anyway. He located the alarm clock on top of the metal locker and pressed the stop button, which illuminated the clock face in the process.

Five o'clock in the morning. Shit. When was the last time he got up at five o'clock in the morning unless it was to go out sailing or for an early tee time at a golf course. Two o'clock in the morning Honolulu time. His wife was probably sleeping the sleep of the just or the just after. Shit. I better quit thinking that way or I will never make it. The home boys, the ones at least destined to slave the day at Base, started stirring, stretching and one of them was tentatively testing the floor with his toe.

First day on the job. God he hated the unknown. The call out said 'Housing', whatever the fuck that meant. He was told to catch the bus at six thirty. That's all he knew. The events would take cake care of the rest. Another thing he hated, not being in control, but for the events to take over and control his destiny.  He had better get his ass down to the showers, because there were only two showers, three sinks, two crappers and one urinal for twenty four inmates.  From the way people smelled around here, he was not worried of overcrowding.

True to his thinking the bathroom was deserted.  He did the three S's - shit, shower and shave - and returned to the room as the hallway was getting crowded with waking inmates streaming towards the end of the hall where he came from.  He made his way down the long corridor in his robe and flip flops carrying  a purse with his toiletries while his institutionalized neighbors in their dirty underwear stopped and stared at the vision of what the outside world must look like.

He made his bed - last time he had to do that was in college thirty years ago - and made his way to the Mess Hall where breakfast was being served.  Michael hurried up the steps to join the line.  Eggs, bacon, hash browns, english muffins, milk, fresh squeezed orange juice, butter, strawberry jam and a banana rounded up his hearty breakfast.  Not even BOP could screw up the All American breakfast, he thought.  He made his way behind the warehouse towards the picnic area where five Air Force busses were lined up.

A guard started calling roll call precisely at six thirty AM by job assignment and Michael found himself in a window seat in the middle of the third bus.  A tired looking black man plopped next to him. Instinctively Michael squeezed tighter, closer to the window.  The full bus lurched forward as the sun was breaking out of the mountains up ahead.  The ride lasted twenty minutes on a solitary perimeter road around the airfield before joining the steady stream of traffic at the Nellis AFB thoroughfare.  Ten more minutes of stop and go, the bus breaks hissed and the doors whooshed open.

The place looked like a shopping center parking lot, but without the shops.  The previous two busses had unloaded, so, the place was swimming in khaki uniforms.  A solitary guard was stationed under a gazebo with four picnic tables and was slowly taking inventory of the new inmates as they were coming down the bus steps.

The sun had cleared the mountain range by now and was bathing everyone in rose petal colors. Air Force mini vans bearing the insignia of the job assignment started making their way inside the parking lot surrounding the prisoners. The knowledgeable were drifting towards the van of their assignment, while each military driver armed with photo I.D.'s was taking human inventory, looking out for stragglers who were trying to hide unobtrusively among the uncollected. By seven thirty there were fifteen to twenty prisoners left milling around the gazebo area. The last of the Air Force vans had left. Michael found himself in the middle of the crowd. He was on the lookout for a van with a 'Housing' sticker on, but to no avail. The driver must have overslept, he thought. He looked around. The group of inmates was an even mix of white, black and Mexican looking, of all ages and description. A solitary Air Force bus; the last one was idling nearby filling the morning air with diesel exhaust.

"Listen up!" The voice of the BOP guard brought Michael out of his reverie. "Line up. Be quiet and speak only when you are spoken to."

The inmates shuffled forward as they were told amongst yawns, clearing of throats and phlegm on the pavement.

"If you are still standing there by eight o'clock;" the guard continued, "you are to board the bus and go back to the Camp. Once there, you are to go to the bubble and report to Custody. Is that clear?"

As if on cue, a line of civilian cars and station wagons started making their way inside the parking lot. The prisoners followed their progress with vacant eyes except Michael, because the suspense of what was to happen next was killing him. The civilian cars, a little over a dozen of them, parked by the gazebo. The drivers, civilian ladies, ranging in age from early twenties to late fifties surrounded the picnic table where the BOP guard was siting, browsing through the inmate cards and picture

I.D.'s on the table.  Half a dozen more cars parked on the other side of the gazebo and a new wave of civilian ladies joined the quay.  These newcomers made a bee line for the inmates stopping in front of one, circling another, going close by a third one making sniffing noises.

"Now you know what the slaves must have felt like in the markets." The black man whispered to Michael.

Michael turned and he realized that the person who spoke to him, was the same fellow who sat next to him on the bus.

"She can have me any time." A young fellow said on his other side leering at a twenty two year old who drifted towards the trio, eyeing Michael.

"What is this all about?" Asked Michael addressing his neighbors. "I feel like I am on display in a meat market."

"You are not wide off the mark." An unknown voice whispered behind him.

The young lady strolled by the picnic table fingering several of the cards; stopping on one, lifted it and handed it to the guard.  The guard pointed towards the young fellow to the right of Michael to come forward.

"Man, I will fuck her till the cows come home."  The young man whispered to his companions under his breath, followed by stares of admiration by the majority of the inmates.  He joined the lady who had selected him and together, they boarded a little Japanese tin can of a car.

"Mr. M, could you come here a moment please?"  The guard's voice brought Michael back to the present.  He tentatively made his way towards the guard who was surrounded by a foursome of middle age ladies.  They reminded him of a bowling team ranging from Roseanne to Peggy Bundy of Married with Children fame.  Dressed similarly in Las Vegas vulgarila, smoking cigarettes and flicking the ashes behind them eying Michael, approaching with a grin.

What am I getting myself into, Michael was thinking as he was closing the distance gingerly.

"Please go to the blue Volvo there." The guard pointed towards the end of the line. "Report to the driver inside."

The foursome parted to let Michael through.

"Nice buns; don't you think Flo?" He heard a voice behind him as he cleared the bowling team. "I wouldn't have minded giving him a workout."

What the hell was this 'Housing' assignment Michael was thinking as he leaned over the driver's side of the blue Volvo. Before he could have a look through the heavily tinted windows, the door opened and a tennis shoe appeared followed by a Nike sock, freckled leg, hefty butt cheek, 'D' cup and a blond mane that shook itself loose from the confines of the vehicle. She lowered her tinted glasses, eyed him for a long ten seconds, smiled and extended her hand.

"Hi! I am Trish Harris. You must be Michael." Her grip was cool, firm. Her hand was tan, slightly wrinkled with the start of liver spots. Michael held her stare, studying the crows feet at the corner of her eyes. Sliding on the back side of forty  he thought. However, well preserved for her age.

"Get in. It's open." She said nodding towards the front passenger side getting herself back inside on the driver's side.

Michael crossed the front of the car, opened the front door and got in the passenger side. Memories flooded from his subconscious. His daughter had a   similar car all through High School, he thought closing his eyes and letting the distinct Volvo head rest hit him at the back of his head. He tightened his eyes fighting back the tears that were trying to squeeze their way, trying to give away his emotions.

"Are you all right?" Trish asked with a slightly alarmed edge in her voice.

"I am alright now." Replied Michael trying to overcome the lump in his throat.

They continued the drive in silence towards the foothills that was the family housing quarters for Air Force officers. All the houses looked the same. Fifties vintage of California ranch style homes. Lawns front and back. A small patio with privacy shrubs overlooking the Base. They pulled into the driveway of 1352 Vanderberg at the end of a cull de sac.

Trish got out of the car, opened the single car garage door and wheeled out a rusting push type gasoline driven lawn mower.

Michael got out of the car and followed her as she made her way to the back yard along a path at the side of the house.

"You know how to start one of these?" She asked pointing to the non descript pile of rust she was wheeling. "This one is old and temperamental at best."

Without saying a word, Michael leaned over and got ahold of the bar from her hands and rocked the lawnmower back and forth listening to the sloshing of the gasoline inside. He lifted the chock halfway. Stepped gingerly on top of the machine and yanked the cord. The engine sputtered and coughed. He opened the chock some more and gave it a little gas. The engine sputtered for some time, started dying, changed its mind at the last minute and caught, sending a billow of black smoke in Trish's direction. He adjusted the chock halfway and let the engine warm up on idle.

"I say!" Exclaimed Trish, after quieting down from a coughing fit. "You have a way with engines. Someone must have been very lucky to have you at her house."

Michael grinned sadly, taking in the Air Force Base and the flatness of view in front of him.

"You don't say much." Trish said in a changed tone of voice. "Look, I realize your present situation, but you must realize also that I was not the one who put you in.  OK?  Say something.  I want to be your friend. Is this your first time on Base?" Michael nodded in the affirmative.

"All right have it your way." Trish replied letting off a slight tantrum of pursed lips.  She turned around and disappeared behind the hedges towards the house.

Michael looked at the lawn mower that was purring like a kitten by now. He closed the choke and engaged the throttle.  The machine jumped forward a couple of feet cutting a two foot wide swatch from the grass, throwing the clippings every which way out of the side opening where the catcher ought to be.  Startled, he pulled the bar instinctively backwards, forcing the machine to go over the same real estate down to bare ground.  This time he held on, but the damage was done.

"Look what you've done." Trish's voice sounded behind him, while she wrestled the lawnmower bar away from him, getting tangled, in an awkward embrace in the process.

Michael had the forethought of disengaging the machine by releasing the lever, seconds before finding himself face to face with the lady, their lips inches apart in each other's arms.

"You want to dance?" Trish exploded in an infectious laughter.

Michael, followed suit as he tried to disengage himself from Trish and the machine.

"I am so sorry." He was able to mumble.

"No sweat!" Trish said still laughing.  "It will grow back.  What I'd like to know is how many lawns have you mowed in your life?"

"None." Michael replied embarrassed.

"I don't believe you." Trish added with a chuckle. "Didn't you have a lawn in your house?"

"We did, but it was taken care of by five Philippine gardeners." Michael replied, looking down trying to cover the damaged spot by shifting grass clippings with his toe.

"Well!" Trish said obviously impressed. "That would be nice. I bet you lived in a mansion too. Well! I would like to live like that; but my husband is only a grunt working at the Red Flag."

"Now who is getting defensive?" Michael threw her a disarming smile.

"Touché. I guess I will mow the damn grass. I was hoping though you would keep me company. After all I won your company in bingo."

"What are you talking about?" Michael asked with peaked curiosity as he matched his stride with hers on the side opposite from where the grass catcher ought to have been.

"You must be new here. Every weekend at bingo, the prisoners assigned to 'Housing' are raffled. I mean winning one is equivalent to winning at least fifty bucks."

"How do you figure that?"

"The Base pays the Camp eight dollars an hour for every inmate hour spent here. They do all the janitorial and groundskeeping services on Base. I understand the Base utilizes four hundred inmates each day. This comes up to a pretty tidy sum. How much of that do they pay you per hour?"

"I don't know." Michael answered. "It's my first day on the job."

"Where do you come from? If you don't mind telling me."

"Honolulu, Hawaii."

"Oh! All my life I've been dreaming of someday to make it there. My husband is getting out in five years. We are hopping for a posting at Hickam Air Force Base to end his career. Do you know where it is? Of course you do. I mean in which island is the Base?"

"Oahu.  That's the same island that Honolulu is on."

"I am dreaming of course, but you never know.  The Air Force may send us there.  How is it over there?"

"I don't know how to answer this Mrs. Harris... However, whatever you do; don't drink the water at the Officer's Club... "

"Call me Trish please.  What's wrong with the water in Hawaii?"

"There is nothing wrong with the water in Hawaii. It is artesian. I believe it is the best water of all fifty states.  As I said though, you should avoid the water at the Officer's Club at Hickam Air Force Base.  The reason for this is that the water pipes to the club water meter are lined with coal tar epoxy.  I know this because the company I was working for installed them under orders by the Air Force, although the EPA banned the compound as causing cancer."

"Why would the Air Force insist on installing this compound which causes cancer?"

"Because they wrote the Contract Specifications before the EPA banned coal tar epoxy and they considered the specifications written in stone.  If I was to designate cancer in chemical form, it would be a mixture of coal tar epoxy and carbon tetrachloride."

"How do you know so much?  What was your profession on the outside?"

"Chemical Engineer."

"If I ever happen to be at Hickam Air Force Base Officer's Club, I would demand bottled water, because the Club tap water causes cancer.  I will tell them that I know so from the horse's mouth. The man who installed the water pipes. Is this all right with you?"

"It's a fact.  I have no problem with that."

"How old are you? If you don't mind me asking."

"Forty eight."

"Boy, you don't look it. I am thirty nine. I wish I would look as good when I get closer to the big five O."

"Well, I tell you Trish, if you get a posting in Hawaii, your skin for one will be rejuvenated. The air is humid. It feeds moisture to the skin, so wrinkles disappear. The sun is also hotter than here, somehow, so you get a deep tan. There are always fifteen knot trade winds blowing, so, the temperature stays in the eighties." "Oh! Michael. It sounds wonderful. How is the University situation there?"

"We have several Universities, but I don't think they are very good with the exception of the Law School at the University of Hawaii and their Hotel Management program. Other than that, I guess the Universities are comparable to the UNLV; they are in the same conference after all. But not in the same league as the PAC-10 schools. I don't know it's difficult to be more specific. What do you have in mind?"

"One of our daughters just started at UNLV and the other would be finishing High School in a couple of years. They are both at that crazy age right now. They don't know what they want; other than boys and parties."

"I know what you mean." Michael said sadly.

"Do you have kids of your own? How many? How old are they? Were they brought up in Hawaii?"

"Slow down." Michael said smiling. "We've got two. A boy and a girl. The boy is twenty five years old. He graduated three years ago from Boston University. He is an entrepreneur, has his own businesses and lives in Hawaii. As a matter of fact he lives right on the water at Black Point which is one of the exclusive neighborhoods in Honolulu where all the movie stars live. My daughter is twenty two years old. She is a senior at the University of Georgia. She is a Fine Arts major. She loves the South and will probably settle there. She already is a renown painter, famous worldwide.  As a matter of fact she got married on September 3, just before I came here."

"It sounds like you got two wonderful children Michael.  Is there a little woman in your life?"

"Oh yes!  My wife of twenty seven years.  A truly good person.  What about your husband?  What is the Red Flag?  Isn't it where he works out of?"

"It's no big deal.  Have you seen the movie Top Gun?"

"Yeah!  Ten years ago or so."

"That's the one.  Well, the Red Flag is the Air Force equivalent of the navy Top Gun.  It's a boy's club.  They go out in hot F-16 airplanes and simulate dog fights with adversary forces.  Then they go in and watch it on a big screen TV and drink beer, patting each other on the ass.  No different from when they were kids, except the size of their toys.  Each time they take one of them baby's for a spin, it's quarter of a million dollars of taxpayers money down the drain.  If they break something hot Roding on vertical lifts, the taxpayers' bill goes way up."

"I don't know Trish. It sounds exciting." Michael said with a dreamy look on his face.

"Well, it's not from where I am sitting.  He zips in half hour to San Diego at Mach 3 to go with the boys down to Mexico and I am stuck home with the kids, looking forward to the weekend to go and play bingo with the other women on Base."

"Why don't you go out on the town.  You are living after all only half an hour from the Las Vegas strip."

"That would be nice.  But who can afford that on a government salary?"

"I don't know what to say Trish.  I found myself taking my wife for granted, after twenty seven years.  This prison experience has opened my eyes.  All I want is to be with her, hold her and talk to her.  Maybe I was not communicating enough with her. Didn't tell her how much I loved her and most important, show her. I tell you, things are going to be different when I get out."

Trish stopped the lawnmower and killed the engine. She turned towards Michael and drew him in her arms. She squeezed him tight and whispered in his ear.

"You are a sweet man. If I was married to you, I would give you all the loving you wanted and never let you go."

Michael didn't know what to do or think. Trish's reaction was that instantaneous and unprovoked. It had been so long since he hugged another human being that his first thoughts were overtaken by emotion. The emotion gave away to feelings of attraction and desire; at which point the thinking process took over. He dropped his arms and stiffened his posture as soon as he realized where the encounter was heading.

Trish must have sensed the change also, because she broke contact and whispered slightly breathless.

"Enough mowing for today. How about a drink?"

"You go right ahead Trish." Michael replied. "I am afraid I cannot join you. See my khaki uniform. I am a prisoner. I am not allowed drinking."

"Come on be a sport. Not even a little one? No one will find out. I'll never tell. It's still early. By the time you get back, you'll beat the breathalyzer. They never take blood tests."

"No!" Michael added with emphasis. "You don't know me. Even if there were no checks, I wouldn't drink, because it was against the rules. That's the way I am."

"Well, I am going in to take a shower and change, because all this exercise of cutting grass, made me sweaty. If you change your mind about that drink, help yourself. The bar is at the back deck, I will bring us a pitcher of lemonade when I come out.  You must be thirsty by now in this hot, dry weather."

Michael looked up making his way to the back porch.  The sun had come up fast, the past couple of hours.  It was midmorning, rapidly sliding into the noon hour.  The back porch looked like the only shady spot in the whole back yard.  He pulled out one of the four lawn chairs around the table and sat down with his back towards the house looking towards the Air Force Base, shimmering in the heat.  Trish pulled the chase lounge, adjusted it facing Michael and fluffed the pillows.  She grabbed the arms of the lounge chair as if steadying herself to sit down; changed her mind in mid motion and straddled the chair, bending forward, exposing a sculpted ass of tempting shape before she got up and disappeared behind the sliding door curtains.

Michael was left alone with his thoughts.  Something that he was getting used to, lately.  He wondered how the other fellows were doing with their 'dates'.  Particularly that young guy who left with that twenty something year old good looking woman.  If Trish was indicative of the Air Force housewives, that young guy must be on his  just after cigarette, thinking if he could squeeze in a double header.  'What do I do now when she comes back?'  It's been a while anyway, he thought as he checked his Cartier watch.  He stood up and looked inside the sliding door. Nothing. The curtains were drawn.  He trained his ears to pick up a tell tale sound inside. Strike out there also. Well, I am not going to lose any sleep over it, he thought as he sat down again.

He was taping softly on the plexiglass table when the smell of Poison perfume assaulted his nostrils and his senses.  He would have recognized the scent everywhere.  His wife's favorite perfume.  Trish appeared a few seconds later, fresh out of the shower, barefoot, wearing a white terrycloth robe and sporting a white towel on her head that wrapped her hair like a turban.  Her face looked clean and wholesome without make-up. Michael stood up.

"Oh darn! I forgot the lemonade on the kitchen counter. Be a dear and go get it." She smiled at Michael, but her voice carried the undertone of an order. "Right through the sliding doors. You can't miss it. The glasses are in the first cabinet on the left."

Michael, went through the sliding door curtains and found himself in the middle of the sitting room. Something like a family room with a nineteen inch color TV, stereo and well used rattan type furniture with human sweat stained cushions. A couple of framed posters from Germany and a vase of dried flowers completed the pitiful decor. The pitcher of lemonade was on the kitchen counter as promised. He dipped his index finger, setting the ice cubes in motion. He licked the finger and opened the cabinet. The glasses were in neat rows. He picked two plastic looking water glasses with daisies painted on them. He swept the pitcher in one motion with the other hand and backed out of the billowing curtains. He set the pitcher and glasses on the plexiglass table. Trish was reclining on the chase lounge, her robe arranged tightly around her body. He poured equal measures in the daisy glasses and sat down holding one and sliding the other towards the table edge, in the direction of Trish. She lifted herself in a half sitting position, setting the right foot down on the cement and extending the left hand towards the table. The front of the robe dropped following the motion, exposing a plump right breast with an engorged pink nipple. She returned in the original position taking a sip and setting the glass down on the cement floor by her left side.

Michael held his breath, avoiding eye contact by concentrating on her left foot with the blood red painted toes that remained anchored to the floor. She had pretty feet and shapely legs. He noticed the latter the first time she got out of her car. His eyes traced the swell of the calf up to her knee, which was peeking out of her robe. On cue, the robe slid exposing her inner thigh, up, higher till the shape lost its contour in the shadows.

Michael's heart was pounding and he felt his blood rushing to his face. He raised his gaze and looked at her face. She was laying on a pillow with half closed eyes. A Gioconda smile on her face taking it all in, not adjusting her robe to cover herself. She dropped her left hand. Her fingers trailing the contour of the cement surface, stretching towards the edge where the grass was starting. Michael followed the movement aware that the stretching arm muscles were pulling the top of her robe apart striving her breasts to revolt, until her left breast broke loose from its restraints.

Michael jumped up from his seat. Trish followed his every move with half closed eyes, moistening her lips with the tip of her tongue. He passed her lounge chair slowly. The bulge in his pants at eye level and made his way on the grass towards the back fence. He sat his arms on the top beam and gazed into the distance. He sat in that position silently for almost five minutes. He felt calm now. He was ready to turn around and go back to his chair. The throbbing in his pants subsided, so he could straighten up now, when he felt two arms circling his waist. Before he could react, a hand started caressing his hair and he felt her lips nuzzling, kissing and nibbling at the back of his neck, sending shivers up and down his spine. He leaned back in ecstasy and she responded by squeezing tighter. Her robe came loose. Her breasts were squeezed tightly on his back. He felt her nipples like bullets through the flimsy material of his khaki shirt. Her scent was intoxicating and at the same time it stirred feelings of longing for his wife back home. He closed his eyes trying to settle his feelings. Decision time. He turned around and looked Trish deeply in her eyes. He made the extra effort to concentrate and speak in an even voice.

"It's very tempting, but I cannot betray my wife. I will be unable to rationalize it afterwards. She has supported me throughout this ordeal and been there for me all the way in my hour of need. It would be, how should I say this, so low class of me to betray her."

"Michael, honey, no one will know."

"Trish, you are not listening to me. I would know. This show of unbridled emotion and reaction strictly by instinct is not symptomatic with me. It is so out of character that I would be unable to reconcile it tomorrow. You are a very attractive woman. You have a very lively personality. I like you very much. Isn't that enough?

"Having a spouse in prison is a dramatic experience in any relationship. The feeling is the same as if your partner for life had temporarily passed away. It's up to you to make the temporary, permanent. At some point in time you will be given a reprieve. A miracle of sorts. The spouse is resurrected and you are allowed to resume the relationship. It will be different this time, because you've both changed. That's the only constant. For a lot of people, that over the years have taken each other for granted and their relationship has settled into a routine of cohabitation, the forced separation serves as a wake up call. These are the people that after a death in the family become inconsolable mussing 'what if' and 'if I had had to do it all over again'. For these people, when the spouse finishes his sentence, either by winning or by attrition, get their second chance. They may not always succeed to bring about the change born out of fantasy and lonely hours in an empty bed, but they will always have the experience to consider: things could be worse. Unfortunately, these people are scarce and far between. The majority, eighty five percent by government statistics, end up in divorce.

"Wives who all their lives been chained in an abusive relationship. They now see the incarceration of the spouse as a ticket to freedom. The abuse can also, in addition to physical, be mental or emotional. The results are invariably the same. The majority of the victims fall in the category I call, paraphrasing Thoreau: Most women lead lives of noisy desperation. They make a lot of noise, up to a point, regulated by their spouse, while he exerts domination, manifested in most cases as economic duress. Now all of a sudden, these women find themselves independent. Both emotionally and financially. Following the law of physics which states that where there is action, there exists equal reaction, they react to years of perceived subjugation. Invariably, they lack knowledge and experience to channel this newly found feeling of independence productively. They will learn in the long run by trial and error, the school of hard knocks; but in the short run, the spouse is run over, more likely bulldozed over, an early victim of the revolution.

"Finally, the curse of the young and restless or the young at heart, who view their relationship strictly from its physical aspects, this forced separation is the kiss of death. And it does not necessarily take two to bring about unravelling of the relationship. Jealousy, the green eyed monster, feeds and preys on the minds of the  people on the inside. The behavior and talk pushes the partner on the outside to find refuge and solace in the arms of willing surrogates, specializing in taking advantage of the situation, the ever present Santso. Santso who many times takes form only in the imagination of the captive, the one inside, who is convinced all the same and does exactly what he claims the government had done to him and put him in captivity. He acts as the judge and jury, selectively looking at the evidence.  In most cases reaching a predetermined conclusion."

He pulled himself free of her embrace and started walking slowly towards the patio with Trish in tow. Trish went through the sliding door curtain and disappeared inside. She came out seconds later wearing a pair of white shorts and a red tee shirt. Her pubic hair was a visible shadow against the white shorts. She stood in front of Michael, who was trying to avert his eyes from her crotch.

"The offer still stands. Your control and self determination is admirable, but I wonder how you will feel when I pick you up three months from now. That was a nice speech back there, but the little woman has barely left the parking lot. Give it time. I am patient...and equally determined. I go after what I want and usually get it. We'll call it a draw today." She took a couple of steps and turned. "By the way, are you ready for lunch? Have you fired a barbecue before? Or you had servants doing that also?

I got to ask you from now on ahead of time. I don't want you burning the house. It is government property after all."

Michael was slow in responding. Still amazed at the transformation. The little kitten, turned bengal tiger, pacing before her prey.

"I'd love to have lunch with you, and yes I know how to start a barbecue, but I cannot eat your food."

"What's the matter? Are you afraid I am going to poison you or something? Oh! I get it. You are afraid I am going to slip you something with your food to weaken your resolve. Don't worry. I fight fair and square. We got time. Your ass is mine..."

"No! You misunderstand me." Michael said. "It's not my decision. The Bureau of Prisons prepares my lunch. Someone will be bringing it to me at 11:00 AM."

As if on cue, a white van drove in front of the house. An inmate dressed in khaki's got out carrying a sack and silently handed it to Michael, eying Trish on the sly, trying to decipher the scene.

"What's happening man?" The inmate said finally. "Working hard or hardly working?"

"A little of both." Michael replied politely.

The van horn tooted twice and the BOP guard's head leaned over the passenger side.

"Get back on the double!" She yelled at the inmate who brought Michael the sack lunch. "We haven't got all day. Quit socializing and get your ass back here."

The inmate's pleasant demeanor changed as if a curtain fell across his face. You could see the hate for the hack on his face and you could feel it by looking at his clenched hands closing into fists and opening again. He turned without a word and made his way back to the van slowly.

"See what kind of low lives we have to put up with." Trish chimed after the inmate was out of ear shot. "This place used to be respectable. They kept it under one hundred inmates. All white collar. No druggies. No violent individuals. So the government would give them a slap on the wrist type fines. Nellis Camp was the best hunting ground for a rich husband. It still is to an extent." She said coyly eying Michael. "But it is like hunting diamonds amongst coal lumps. We have to thank that Barbara Walters bitch for turning a gold mine to shit."

"What do you mean? What does Barbara Walters have to do with Camp Regulations?" Michael asked innocently; although he already had found out.

"More than you can imagine. A few years back Barbara Walters came to interview the Secretary of the Navy who was a guest at the Camp. She came on a Saturday. Visiting weekend. The inmates were wearing civilian clothes, bathing suits, sunning by the pool, swimming. Wives, kids running around and playing. Barbecues blazing with steaks cooking. Mixed doubles on the tennis courts. People getting ready to board the shuttle to the Base carrying bags with golf clubs. No hack in sight...To make a long story short, Ba-Ba changed the focus of the interview and made it Life in a Federal Country Club. She ended up saying that the prisoners lived better than the great majority of the United States population. She said she would not have minded being incarcerated herself under those conditions. So the Camp, under pressure from the BOP, increased the  inmate population from one hundred to five hundred, by importing real criminals from maximum security facilities and cutting on the fringe benefits. After a while, of course, they brought some of the benefits back; but it never became like it was."

Michael opened his lunch bag. Always the same pressed turkey meat, two slices of bread, a small bag of peanuts, a can of generic soda and a piece of fruit. Today was an apple. This was interchanged with an orange or a pear. He started eating the fruit, taking large chunks.

"Well, it's the proper lunch if you wanted to lose weight." Trish smiled at him. "I feel guilty fixing lunch for me. Is this what you people have for lunch every day?" Michael nodded in the affirmative, staring at the bag.

"It's the shits." She said back. "How boring. What do you guys do all day after work?"

"It varies with the individual." Replied Michael. "Most of the inmates eat, watch TV and sleep. I eat, walk for an hour around the track, go to the library and write for three hours, play a game of tennis and go to bed reading until I fall asleep. Sometimes on weekends, there is a chess tournament in our room and I get caught in the excitement staying up most of the night playing against other rooms."

"If you are looking at me for sympathy, you won't find any. My life, I mean all of the military wives' lives are no better. You guys are limited to what you can do by the BOP. We are equally limited by money. You are a prisoner of the Camp. I am a prisoner of the Base. When we girls get together and have a few, late at night, we always talk about driving up at the Camp and see what's shaking. We are prevented from going up there by our own Air Force guards at the gate. You on the other hand can leave any time you want, on assignment."

"Trish, you are talking a lot of Bull. Our circumstances are not even close. You are free to go anywhere you want. Do anything you wish. You are limited solely by your ability to do so. Me on the other hand must ask for permission for everything. Take weekends for example, that you seem to be taking exception to. We have to eat breakfast between seven and eight thirty. Period. You sleep late, you are S.O.L., that's Simply Out of Luck, for your gentle ears. Then, in reality, we can't do anything because we have a ten o'clock count for which we must be in our rooms for it. By the time the blue light goes out, giving us permission to leave the building, it is time for lunch. We have a three hour period, from 12:30 PM to 3:30 PM to do whatever we want. Most people go for sports. Personally, I play soccer or tennis. These activities make me forget that I am in prison.  We have four quality, lighted tennis courts with club chairs and tables.  We play hard.  Then we sit and chat, having soft drinks and smoking cigars while watching and commenting on the play of others.  Yes, moments like these will stay in my memory.  Good friends, good cigars, lively conversation..."

"What's the other?" Trish interrupted.

"What's the other, what?" Michael replied puzzled and trying to get his thoughts in order.

"You mentioned one activity that takes you out of the prison environment.  What's the other?"

"Oh!"  Michael replied smiling good naturally.  "The other is writing.  There may be mayhem all around me and it would go over my head.  When I write, I leave the prison fences.  I enter a fourth dimension.  I hover above the pedestrian and see with the eyes of my soul and feel with my heart.  Time stops, or goes backwards or accelerates forward with the speed of light.  When I write, I am in control of my thoughts and emotions and the pace by which I deliver them on paper.  But I am diverging from the original topic of discussion.  All good things must end, so our tennis court chats end promptly at 3:45 PM in time to go back to our rooms for the four o'clock stand-up count.  Again by the time the blue light is out allowing movement outside the building, it is time for dinner, which again ends promptly at 5:45 PM.  After dinner, we have free time until the 10:00 PM count.  During the free time is when I do my writing.  After 10:00 o'clock we are confined to our building until six o' clock the following morning.  At any rate, you get the idea.  During the week is the same routine with the exception that we have to work between 7:30 AM and 3:30 PM in jobs assigned to us by the BOP.  So you see, by comparison, your life here on Base is ideal.  You have a much larger library here.  If I were you, I would spend a large part of my time reading and educating myself in all sorts of subjects.  This is something I used to do a lot all my life before I even came here."

"And your wife puts up with it?"

"What do you mean puts up with it?  I read while waiting to be called by the starter on the golf course.  I read in our back lanai while watching a spectacular sunset.  I read on the beach while my wife is catching a few rays and splashing in the water.  I read myself to sleep every night."

"Well, if you were married to me, every time I saw you with a book, I would be on your lap getting your mind away from reading.  The last thing I would put up with is loosing my man to a book."

"You don't have to view it in exclusive terms.  No one is losing here.  See it as a common bond.  Sharing an experience, where both parties gain.  What I am trying to say is don't feel that you are in competition with everything.  I believe a relationship is more healthy when the parties have their own interests while at the same time they share their experiences."

"I agree.  The important thing is sharing.  My husband does not share.  There I said it."

"Do you share with him?"

"No!  Of course not!  What do you expect after he treats me that way."

"Do you believe that two wrongs make a right?"

"What do you mean?"

"I don't know you very well, and certainly don't know your husband, but it seems to me that for some time now you guys got into a pissing match of one up-manship that is leading you towards diverging points.  One of these days you or he will say or do something which that person cannot take back or undo.  It's when, as my mom used to say 'le vaze brizze'."

"What language is that?  What does it mean?"

"It's French and it means that the flower pot or vase is cracked.  If you have a beautiful vase and you dropped it once too many times, it will break. Afterwards you may try to repair it and glue the pieces together, but you will always be able to see the cracks. It will never be the same."

"What's your answer Michael for someone who doesn't give a shit anymore whether the vase is cracked or not?"

"That's a problem. Do you think that both parties feel the same way?"

"I am sure of that. He...How do I put this politely. He has not touched me in six months now. He is hardly home anymore. One more year and our youngest will fly the nest. Then what do I do? I just have High School education, I haven't done a damn thing in my life except be a wife and a mother. I don't have any money to go out and meet people. Here on Base in the Officer's Club all the single guys are looking at the young stuff. There is nothing else to do except go play bingo with the other lonesome women, get loaded and talk about sex."

"Is this a widespread phenomenon around here?"

"Yeah! Most of the wives are like me. They put four of five of you guys each week in the prizes. We all fantasize what we will do if we get lucky."

"Well, Trish, I am afraid you selected the wrong guy." Michael said. "Maybe next time you will get what you wished for."

"But I don't want someone else. With you I feel so comfortable. I can talk to you like a friend. You are smart, obviously well educated, intelligent, you understand me. I can go on and on. What started as an opportunity for a quick roll in the hay, it has turned into something else. I am falling for you."

"What can I say Trish. I am flattered and vulnerable at the same time. But I already told you how I feel about this. I am already married. I cannot betray my wife, now more than ever after she has stood by me through thick and thin."

"Where is she now?  Back in Hawaii?"  Trish asked with renewed curiosity. "Does she write to you everyday?  Does she visit you every chance she gets?"

"She writes." Michael replied embarrassed.  "Not as often as I would have liked her to write and she visits me once a month."

"What does she do with her spare time?" Trish pressed.

"She has a quarter horse, mare, and she spends most of her free time riding and taking care of her horse.  We also have an awful lot of friends, I am sure they  invite her and include her in their activities.  She is also involved big time in our church and various philanthropic activities associated with the church.  I am sure she keeps busy."

"Are you sure she is faithful?" Trish asked with a sly smile.

"To the extent that someone can be, I'd have to say yes.  You know, because of circumstances in my childhood and the times during which I grew up, I don't trust people in general.  I trust, however, my wife.  She has handled all our money since we got married. I don't even know how much money we have or where it is.  For that matter, my wife could divorce me right now and run away with everything we have.  I am not worried though, because I know she won't."

"But what if she does?" Trish insisted.

"I don't see how?"

"Suppose she gets lonesome and she finds someone else."

"I suppose that could happen.  I don't know, loneliness plays many a dangerous games with human beings.  In that case, the fellow must be pretty special though.  I know that much. You will think I am conceited, but to find someone like me, will be very difficult.  People my caliber, would not be around and available.  While if the person is otherwise taken, would not betray his relationship.  You see my wife would not settle for anything less."

"I don't know what to say," Trish said with tears in her eyes, "other than I am jealous of her."

Michael looked at Trish in silence. He reached slowly and took his lunch bag. He opened it and looked inside. He closed his lunch bag, squeezed it into a ball and tossed it in the waste can in the corner.

"Two points." He said quietly. "I need to loose a few pounds anyway. Do you have any other job you need done?" Michael kept talking to lighten the mood and change the topic of discussion. She was probing close to his midnight nightmare that his wife somehow will not be around when he got out. He heard stories from a number of other inmates about the divorce rate for the men in prison. The letters from home came less often. They became impersonal, business like. Until one day the Dear John letter arrived. Or worse. Out of the blue  divorce papers were served. The worse yet made the rounds the other day. Old Greenbaum. The poor guy was married to a young wife and serving a ten year sentence. His wife divorced him barely three months down; but she told the Department of Justice that her husband had a weak ticker and would not take the news well. So, they did not tell him. Being a felon, the divorce can be one way.

No problem. All the time, the now ex-wife visited him, less and less, she put an appearance every other month. She wrote him often, sweet as ever. A few weeks before the day of old Greenbaum's release, the authorities told him that he cannot go home and served him with a restraining order forbidding him to see his wife. They gave him the divorce papers and told him the whole story. The poor bastard got as a reward early release. He got out in a coffin. Michael looked at his watch.

"Trish, you need to drive me back so that I can catch my 1:30 PM bus back to the Camp."

They got into the car and backed out of the driveway. They drove in silence each absorbed in their own thoughts. The Air Force bus was parked in place and already almost full with inmates.

"Till next time lover." Trish said in a throaty voice.

Michael looked at her.  She was wearing her face in a coquettish mask pushing her lips in a silent kiss.  He got out of the car without saying a word and made his way towards the gazebo to report.  He got his I.D. card back from the federal officer.  The cop looked at him.

"How did it go?" He asked.

"I don't know." Michael replied.  "I am not very good at cutting grass and trimming bushes."

"I think she was looking for you to water her bush, bud."  The guard replied in a lewd manner.

Michael felt his face going crimson.

"You are new here.  Give it time.  You will learn.  They all want to fuck a CEO.  It's the craze nowadays."

Michael made it towards the bus without looking back at the guard who was having a hearty laugh as if he finally got the punch line of their private joke. He stumbled on the first step.  Got ahold of the bus railing and pulled himself up without missing a beat.  The bus door closed behind him and he looked at the inmates for a familiar face to sit next to. He spotted the kid who got to go with the pretty lady in the morning. He was disheveled, sweaty, his shirt half out of his pants, his head leaning against the glass of the window.  He looked beat.

"How did it go?" Michael asked sitting down.

"Don't ask."  Replied the kid.  "All I want is to take a shower and take a nap."

"She work you out that much?  Eh?"  Michael winked.

"I wish."  The kid replied.

"What happened man? You look like she put you through your paces big time."

"She did alright; but not the paces you are thinking and I was anticipating when I got into her car."

"What happened?" Michael asked with genuine interest.

"I got in the car. She showed me lots of leg. The hem of her skirt was even with her crotch. Man I thought I would lean over and finger her right there and then."

"What happened next?" Michael asked encouraging.

"What happened? Nothing happened. We got home. Her husband was waiting there in front of an opened garage with all their furniture piled inside. They had just moved over the weekend and I spent the rest of the day hauling sofas and dressers with her husband. Bummer man. How was your day?"

"I was cutting grass all day and trimming shrubs and bushes." Michael replied diplomatically. "I had never done that in my life." He added so that he would not be lying entirely.

"That sounds shitty man." The kid said. "What do they think we are, fucking slaves?"

"I got news for you." Michael added. "At twelve cents an hour, we are fucking slaves."

They looked at each other and simultaneously broke into a laugh.

The bus made it into the camp and came to a stop in front of the bubble. That was the building that housed the BOP central control and monitoring room for all the hacks on duty. It got its name because it was surrounded by bullet proof glass with two guards at all times at the controls. Half a dozen female guards came out of the building and lined up. Six inmates came out of the bus, turned around, spread their legs and extended their hands. The guards patted them down and signaled for the next six to come out of the bus, while they dismissed the ones who got frisked to go on to the Camp.

Michael got the lieutenant herself. Wide Glide. Her skin was like leather close up due to many hours laying by the pool in the desert sun. She smiled at him mischievously and told him to turn around. He spread his legs and extended his hands. He waited. Nothing happened for the next twenty seconds. Then he imperceptibly felt the tips of her fingers at each side of his hair making their way down. Her nails grazed the side of his neck sending shivers through his spine and goose bumps on his extended hands. He felt a couple of squeezes on his shoulders and before he could recover, the palms were busy along the front of his chest. While he was trying to decide whether the squeeze of his right nipple was real or imagined, she quickly started rubbing him along the sides, One set of fingers worked their way along his trouser waist, while the other reached underneath his shorts and cupped his balls and dick getting a firm hold.

"I see you didn't use it all up." He heard her whisper and felt her hot breath in his ear.

He tried to say something in protest but the hand that was holding his lower anatomy told him otherwise. She released him and told him he was cleared to enter the Camp. Michael lowered his head trying to choke the tears welling in his eyes.

# CHAPTER 11

## Mia Fatsa, Mia Ratsa

"Hey Maki, what are you doing back already?" Nick bumped into Michael behind the theater building under construction.

The Air Force transportation bus hissed as it started to make the turn around the loop.

"No one picked me up today." Michael said. "So they shipped me back to the Camp."

"What do you mean 'you didn't get picked up'. You got a reputation to protect. You don't want to be a flash in the pan, three days on the job and you can't get it up no more."

Michael smiled trying to hide his embarrassment.

"I don't know how these rumors get started Nick. Nothing doing. There were twenty inmates out there today and only two customers. The supply greatly exceeded the demand. I did not get picked up. End of story. That's how prison stories get started. There you go. Make a story out of that."

"That's not what Jimmy is saying." Nick came back.

"Who is Jimmy?" Michael asked perplexed.

"The lunch delivery boy. He practically caught you in the act, or he would if he brought you lunch five minutes earlier. You guys were lighting a cigarette the way he is talking."

"Nothing happened." Michael said. "I don't care if the little weasel was there all day. I repeat nothing happened."

"OK. Have it your way." Nick shrugged disappointed. "What happened yesterday? I understand that a delectable piece of tail picked you up in jogging shorts. I always said a little dark meat once in a while does wonders for the diet."

"Where do you get your news?" Michael exclaimed in amazement. "Yes, a young black lady picked me up the second day on the job, wearing a jogging outfit; but nothing happened. That Jimmy better not make stories because the hack would corroborate the fact that they picked me up at eleven o'clock and I made the twelve o'clock buss back to the Camp."

"What happened?" Nick asked with renewed interest.

"We got home. She took off her jogging outfit. I thought oh! OH! NO! Not again. But she had a bikini bathing suit underneath and she only wanted to wash her car and asked for my help. I was inside her car wiping the dust, when she climbed on top of the hood and started soaping the wind shield. Her bathing suit top had a front snap which snapped and I ended up reliving the famous scene from Cool Hand Luke. We finished, I mean the washing and drying of her car. She left me outside and went back in her house. She came out dressed in a different outfit. Got into her car and drove off, leaving me alone outside her house. The lunch wagon drove up. I recounted what took place and the hack told me to climb aboard. And finally today's fiasco. I think today would be my last day on this job assignment."

"How come? Usually they keep you on the same assignment three or four months before they reassign you."

"Let's put it this way. After I came back that first day, I made a bee line for the BOP work assignment office and I asked them to be reassigned or I would be forced to make a formal request and then I would have to list my reasons for doing so."

"Ouch! What did the hack say?" Nick asked expectantly.

"No problem the hack on duty said. He would do it immediately, but it could take a couple of days to become official. The hack understood and he even thanked me for my discretion. I was heading towards the bulletin just now to read the call-out and changes sheet. I bet you, I would be on it."

"Don't bother. I can even tell you what your new assignment will be. You will be assigned to Custody."

"What is that?" Michael asked fearing the worst.

"Oh! Nothing. Usually you get lucky and literally do nothing. Provided they have given plenty of shots that day."

"Do you mind speaking English, so I can understand?" Asked Michael.

"Sorry! I've been down, meaning I already served, four years and keep forgetting that the people on the outside don't understand prison lingo. Every time an inmate does an infraction that is seen by a guard, he gets punished, period. No favors, because they are bad for morale and discipline and people start asking 'why him and not me'. Ergo, the guy must be a 'Rat', locked up in the cheese factory; that again is the special sector under constant surveillance where the known 'Rats' live. So, when an inmate gets caught, depending on the severity of the infraction, he is given a 'shot'. He is written up and it goes on his record. That costs him fur-lows down the road, special programs like 'CADRE' and finally he is denied a half way house for early release. If the infraction is serious, you get rolled up. Meaning you are forcibly removed from the population and you go to the Las Vegas County Jail for a few days or to a higher security institution. But for the small everyday type 'shots', like missing a call out, being late for work, being out of uniform etc. you get to do Camp community service like emptying trash cans and picking up cigarette butts. If there are not enough people doing 'shot time', then the Custody crew does the Camp community service work. If there are enough people who have taken a 'shot' the previous day, there is no work for the regular Custody crew and they take it easy. So, it could go either way."

"What do I do today though?" Michael asked.

"Nothing." Nick replied. "Just don't go to your room or rather don't get caught at it until after 2:00 PM. Go to the library. You can't go wrong there. Have you been to the library?"

"Yes." Michael replied. "I've been to the Leisure Library. But what I really need to do is go to the Legal Library and start working on my Appeal."

"In the Legal Library you need to talk to the clerks. You know we have here over a dozen attorneys. We even have a prosecutor who was caught on the take. Come on let's go. I will introduce you to the boys. They will do all the work. Did you bring the paperwork with you?"

"I have it in my room." Michael said. "However, before we bombard them with transcripts and briefs and frighten them off, why don't we go on a reconnaissance mission and feel them out. Are they any good?"

"Oh yeah! They are all good."

"That needs to be seen Nick, if they are so damn great, what are they doing here in prison?"

They turned left and started making their way towards the Education Building which housed the Law Library.

"Have you moved yet?" Nick asked out of the blue.

"Move? I just got here." Michael asked surprised.

"You never accept the room they assign you. Look at your homies. Are they the type of people you would associate on the outside? If the answers no. Move out of there. You are a businessman. You only associate with white collar criminals your age or older. Then everyone will leave you alone.  Otherwise, your room and your belongings will be shaken every week by the guards."

"I don't care." Michael replied.  "I got nothing illegal with me."

"It doesn't matter." Nick answered getting angry. "You are in prison. The rules you have been playing by on the outside have changed.  People may plant things in your locker.  Or the hacks may find contraband in the room.  Whose is it?  No one confesses and even if you knew, you could not say; so the whole room gets punished.  What are you going to do if they find drugs or a weapon?  Are you ready to do another five years on another charge?  In an FCI this time.  Listen to me and write a 'cop-out' which is nothing but a form requesting to move out of that room you are in as soon as possible.  Don't wait to find a reason to; because by then it will be too late.  You don't have to give a reason for wanting to switch rooms.  Keep your eyes open and get to know the good guys here who will keep you out of trouble."

They reached the worn out steps of the Education Building.  Inmates were sitting on the steps, banister and entrance stoop under the non smoking sign; smoking.  They made their way inside.  Michael almost tripping on the loose carpet that was exposing Asbestos tiles underneath."

"They will fix the carpeting one of these days;" Nick said,  "as soon as someone trips, falls down, gets hurt and ends up suing the BOP."

The Law Library was on the first floor across the hall from the Leisure Library.  It was a rectangular room twelve and a half feet by thirty one feet.  Nick opened the door and walked in like he owned the place. Michael trailing in his wake.

"Michael, let me introduce you to Joe Cohen the Chief Law Library Clerk. Joe, this is Michael.  He is new here.  He is in the middle of filing an Appeal or something, I am not entirely sure.  Anyway, I brought him to you to see if you can help him.  He got a raw deal from the government and the Department of Justice.  I am going to leave the two of you alone now to discuss the matter."

He started leaving the room and as an afterthought, he turned to Michael and told him in Greek.

"Let me know if this Jew will be of any help.  He thinks he is the prince of the synagogue or something.  Don't be taken back by his manners, because they tell me, he is a pretty good lawyer."

"Sit down Mike…that's your name, isn't it?"  Said Joe pointing at a chair by his desk that had a sign stenciled on it saying 'Law Clerk'.  "What can I do for you?"

"Well, I am trying to write my Appeal."  Michael said hesitantly.

"Where are you from?"  Joe interrupted.

"Hawaii."

'That's the 9th Circuit Court of Appeals."  He talked almost to himself.  "When were you sentenced?"

"This past July."

"Well, you are passed the deadline.  I can't do anything for you."

"But, this is not the Appeal I am talking about."  Michael said.  "I already filed my Appeal to the 9th Circuit in San Francisco and was turned down by them.  I  applied for a re-hearing  and a re-hearing en banc, that's a request to review the Appeal by ten different judges…"

"I am well aware of the terminology."  Joe interrupted.  "I am extremely busy.  So get to the point quickly.  The 9th turned you down.  There is nothing more you can do.  You are done in.  Do your time and go home."

"That's not true; that I am done in I mean."  Michael cut in indignantly.  "I can file a request for a Writ of Certiorari directly to the Supreme Court of the United States…"

"Yeah! You can win the lottery also." Joe interrupted.

"You don't have to be so negative Joe." Michael said quietly. "If you look at all the Landmark Decisions and the cases which are used most often as having established a precedence, they have been decided by the Supreme Court. If you believe you are innocent, you should fight and not quit. I believe..."

"Yeah! Yeah! Next you will tell me that you believe in Santa Claus and the Tooth Ferry. Let me tell you the facts. Every year, there are close to ten thousand cases referred to the Supreme Court all requesting a Writ of Certiorari. Only eighty five are granted each year. What makes you think that yours will be one of them?"

"For one, I am innocent..."

"Next." Joe broke in. "The prisons are filled with innocent people. Some, more innocent than you. If you are banking on Innocence or Justice or the American Way, you are wasting both my time and yours."

"Joe." Michael said quietly. "I'd appreciate it if you let me finish talking first. You've been interrupting me ever since I came here. I believe my case is one that the Supreme Court would be interested in, because it deals with issues that will effect a lot of people and it is based on the Constitution. It raises the question 'why is the government's interpretation of the law more valid than that of the individual?' Particularly when down the road, the government's interpretation of the law and the Judge's instructions to the jury are proven wrong by a later Supreme Court decision. Also the fact that the government criminalized a matter that Contractually, is an Administrative issue. The government made my case criminal, by misapplying the McNally vs the United States case. In other words  they accused me of Mail Fraud and having defrauded the United States. This fact had to be proven during the trial. However, during the trial the government failed to prove their case. Instead of proving that they were defrauded and/or lost money, they admitted that they were not defrauded and in fact they saved money.  Also, that the mails were not germane in furthering the scheme they were alleging.  Still the judge, did not dismiss the case, instead he verbally changed the indictment and advised the jury to disregard the written indictment.  His instructions to the jury, in addition to differing from the indictment, they misstated the DavisBacon Act.  By the way, the government had previously also misstated the same law in front of the Grand Jury, in order to obtain an indictment."

"I still think you have a better chance of winning the lottery;" Joe said, "than winning the Appeal for a Writ of Certiorari.  But everyone is entitled to try.  So I tell you what you do.  You sound like an intelligent man.  Write for me the points that you think the Supreme Court ought to rule upon.  Write a paragraph or so for each one.  Try to narrow the points to around five.  So, what I am asking for would not take more than a couple of pages.  This would also be helpful for you.  Right now you are angry and all the issues are jumbled up together.  Sit down and list everything.  Then prioritize.  Then combine the ones that could be addressed under the same issue. Then write a concise paragraph posing the question to the Supreme Court to make a ruling.  Let me see this and I will show it to a few lawyers we have here and get their opinion on your chances.  The Writ that you will end up writing, will address these five points in some detail.  You noticed that I said that you will end up writing the Writ.  This is because we don't have time to read the transcripts of your case.  You are more knowledgeable of the facts and talking to you here, you seem capable of articulating your thoughts.  You don't need us.  You can do a better job in writing the Appeal.  We can read it and correct it.  But our job is mainly for the poor and uneducated inmates who cannot afford an attorney and are incapable of representing themselves.  Most of them have not finished High School; a lot don't know how to read and write.  In my book, these are priority over someone like yourself who can do a better job on your own case than most of the attorneys we have around here."

Michael got up to leave without saying another word.

"Eh! Listen Mike. Don't take it the wrong way. It's just my way of saying that I don't really have the time to write your Appeal.  I will read it though, after you write it, and I will correct it.  That's the best I can do. Talk to the other attorneys here.  Maybe someone else has more time to help you."

"I don't know anyone here Joe." Michael said after a pause during which he scanned the room for a familiar face.

"Don't fret." Replied Joe.  "We will see if we can remedy this."

With that he singled at a balding middle age man with the beginning of a paunch. "Hey George.  You got a minute here."  He called out.

George looked up from his typewriter and tried to focus on Michael and Joe over his reading glasses.

"I am in the middle of something." George said.  ""Why don't you guys come here if you want to talk to me."

Michael started walking towards George's direction when Joe's shrill voice froze him in mid step.

"George, if you want to keep working at the Law Library, you get your ass here this minute."

George, pushed his secretary stool, back and got up to his feet, slowly, making his way towards the front desk where Michael and Joe were standing.  As he got closer, Michael could see that he was having a difficult time to contain his anger.  His face was beet red and his mouth was contorting trying to speak.  Michael was standing in place embarrassed, while George and Joe stood facing each other.  Joe was the first one to speak in a pleasant manner as if nothing happened.

"George, I would like to introduce you to Michael.  He is new here, a friend of Nick's and he is looking for someone to write his Appeal to the Supreme Court. Michael, meet George.  He was the prosecutor for the City of Los Angeles."

George extended a stiff hand which Michael shook.

"Joe, you know I am in the middle of writing my own Habeas Corpus and I don't have time. Why are you doing this to me?"

"Well George, you know the rules. You cannot work on personal stuff during working hours. So I suggest you take Mike here and start working on his Appeal  unless you can show to me that you are backlogged with cases for other inmates."

"What do you think all these other folders are on my desk?"  George replied in protest.

"I bet the ones on the floor are also cases pending." Joe added.

Michael followed Joe's gaze and saw maybe fifty files exploding with documents, leaning in stacks every which way against the wall.

"Are all these Appeals?"  He was able to whisper.

"What do you think?" George replied in anger. "Of course they are. The BOP assigned two lawyers to the Law Library to help inmates with their cases. Joe, like myself, have our own cases to fight also.

"What about the other attorneys in Camp?" Michael asked.

"What about them?"  Joe said. "Go and find them. They don't want to volunteer their services for free, you know like us dummies, and since the BOP will not allow payment, they refuse to work on legal stuff. Let me correct that. They refuse to work for free."

"How can I pay them?"  Michael asked. "The BOP only let's me have two ten dollar rolls in quarters, maximum..."

"Come on, you can't be so dumb as you pretend to be."  Joe said. "Tell your wife to deposit money on a specific inmate's account we tell you and then you will see how fast your Appeal gets done."

"What about the poor inmates who are unable to pay?"  Michael quoted back to Joe.

"Well, they go to George and get filed to the bottom of the pile." Joe and George looked at each other and smiled.

"What about deadlines?" Michael asked. "Papers have to be filed. Others need to be answered. Appeals must be submitted. All the paperwork needs to be  done within a certain timetable, otherwise it will not be considered because simply it was not filed timely."

"Look," Joe cut in gruffly, "we know all that. What can we do? Go to the BOP and demand that they assign more attorneys? Find a Public Defender."

"You are a businessman." George added. "Do you work for nothing? Why should the attorneys in prison work for nothing?"

"But what you are asking me to do is illegal." Michael insisted. "If we get caught, we will both go to an FCI."

"How will they know?" Joe asked. "We certainly will not say anything. You will not. If someone does, we have ways of finding out and he will wake up in the middle of the night with someone playing the drums on his body with lead pipes for drumsticks."

"I don't know. Let me think about it." Michael said thoughtfully. I will let you know. What's the going price for an Appeal to the Supreme Court these days."

Joe and George looked at each other.

"Well now, this is something you got to discuss with your agent." Joe said.

"My agent?" Michael exclaimed. "What agent? I don't have an agent."

"OK. You don't have an agent." George said. "Go discuss it with your countryman, Nick the 'Rat'."

Michael jumped as if a whip hit him, stinging him on the inside. He turned slowly and got to the door. He felt old and vulnerable. Who to trust in this joint? His supposedly friend, just turned out to be his friend for the money. He may turn out to be a 'Rat' after all he thought. Lost in thought he tripped on the torn carpet by the education building exit. He stumbled and bumped on a huddled shadow by the door, smoking. Nick extended his hand and steadied Michael.

"Protecting your investment?" Michael said sarcastically.

"Come here!" Nick commanded, flicking his cigarette and leading Michael by the gazebo. "What did the Jew boys tell you?" He demanded.

"A point here and a point there and a whole bunch of bull in between. Bottom line; money talks, bull shit walks. The question is what's the price?"

"Oh! These sons of a bitches; it wasn't supposed go down like that." Nick said avoiding to make eye contact with Michael.

"Nick let me tell you something. I wouldn't succumb to blackmail or be forced to do something I don't want to, even if it was the difference between walking out of here or spending my entire sentence in this place. The government offered me a $25,000 fine, a slap on the wrist and no jail time if I admitted I was guilty. I refused their offer. I was not guilty. I would refuse their offer today, again, even with all the things I know that can happen to me. You are Greek. You should know. There are no more independent minded people on earth than the Greeks. I am fortunate to posses average intelligence, so that I can read the Rules and Regulations pertaining to Appeals to the Supreme Court. I believe to be capable of putting down on paper the reasons for which my Appeal should be heard and granted. However, I feel for all these faceless, countless innocent who have put all their hopes and expectations on the jailhouse lawyers and aren't even smart enough to realize that their case is going nowhere, fast."

"Mike, people here are not like you. You got money. The government has taken everything they own. Their wives divorced them. They got no one on the outside. All they got to sell is their skill. The inmates buy that skill. They don't ask for the moon, like the lawyers on the outside. Couple of hundred bucks would do it. Say five hundred tops. Plus legal expenses like typing, another $50 to $75, copying twenty bucks and the mailings. That's reasonable. What do you think?"

"What about your cut Nick?"

"Don't worry about me. I am taken care of by them. I just gave you the worst case scenario. Maybe your case would be a little less. We wouldn't know that until we get a look at the issues involved. Maybe yours is a sure winner and they give you a real special price. After all, we could use a winner right now. We just got shot down on all of our requests for a Writ of Certiorari by the Supreme Court. All three cases shot down during their first meeting. So your case would be the only one we would have going. Maybe the issues involved would be something the Supreme Court would be interested in dealing. Our guys would do a selling job for you."

"Let me think about it Nick." Michael said thoughtfully. "It is certainly tempting. I will get back to you. In the meantime, I've got to organize the issues I believe the Supreme Court would feel compelled to address and come up with the whys. I mean, why should they be interested in reviewing my case. I need to do some reading in the Law Library, because some of the points I got to raise deal with questions of law rather than fact."

"OK. Take your time." Nick said agreeably. "But not too long. I need to know by the end of the week one way or another."

"Sounds like a plan." Michael replied and started walking away towards the direction of the dormitory.

Nick, flicked his cigarette on the grass and ducked back into the education building.

Michael took his pipe out of his side pocket and his tobacco pouch out of his back pocket and started filling his pipe mechanically while walking lost in thought. He tamped the tobacco and stopped under the building gazebo to light up. He turned his back towards the apparent wind which he could feel on his cheeks.

"Hey, this smells good." A voice startled him out of his concentration. He turned and saw that he was not alone. The tables under the gazebo were filled with inmates playing cards, reading magazines or otherwise having a quiet conversation while smoking cigarettes. He noticed a couple of cigar smokers. He was the only pipe smoker, for the moment. He tried to identify the person who talked to him, by recreating the voice and trying to determine its direction.

"You give up?" He heard the same voice, coming from the direction he'd been looking.

He was a slight balding fellow in his sixties with white hair wearing awful mismatched red sweats. The top and bottom must have been washed at different times because the bottoms looked new, bright red, while the top had faded into a red tile shade with pink splaces. The result of bleach and hot water. Michael took two steps to reach him and stood in front of him.

"Hi. My name is Michael." He said extending his hand. "What can I do for you?"

"I know who you are." The stranger said grasping the proffered hand in a surprising firm grip. "I am Dino, and to answer your question, you can give me a pipeful of tobacco, as I've forgotten mine in the room."

Michael reached in his back pocket and extracted a beat up plaid tobacco pouch and offered it to Dino. He doubted that Dino in fact forgot his tobacco in his room, from the way he was greedily filling an oversized pipe. He handed back the pouch to Michael, lit his pipe and drew on it. Dino sat back on the bench stretching his legs and puffed away with the pleasure of a man who had missed smoking for a long time.

"Well, what do you think of our legal eagles?" He said after a while.

Michael took a seat on the bench opposite him, crossed his legs and took his measure, while quietly puffing on his pipe.

"News travels fast around here." He commented.

"It's a small Camp and overcrowded for the real estate available. After you've been here a while, you will be able to read the signs."

"Well, being new and all here, you certainly have the advantage over me. How about if you level the playing field a little and tell me about Dino."

"Dino is a retired old man who is trying to reach level four…"

"I was not asking about Dino the philosopher." Michael interrupted. "I am more interested about Dino the inmate. What were you on the outside, for example.

"I was a student of Law and Justice. I practiced modestly, for exclusive clients. My practice was primarily in New York."

"Who were these exclusive clients?" Michael asked with interest.

"Members of the Gambino family. They were not necessarily named Gambino all of them, but my retainer was with old man Gambino himself."

"No shit!" Escaped from Michael. "Is that the New York crime family?"

"Not so fast." Dino said in a measured way. "I feel the playing field tilting dangerously in your direction. And talking about the mob, what do you think of our own Jewish mafia?"

"Jewish mafia? I don't think I had the pleasure of meeting them yet." Michael added thoughtfully."

"You've already been shaken by them." Dino said amused. "And by their Greek errand boy, also."

"Oh!  These guys." Michael said, the light suddenly dawning on him.

"You look like an intelligent young man."  Dino continued in the same amused tone of voice.  "You tell me.  What makes them different from the mob?  They have found a need, a product if you please, 'Hope', and they are selling it to the captive population.  They do so with exclusive rights.  I grant you that they offer a choice of doing your time quietly and obediently, but they bank on the human nature that defies convention.  Few people will allow themselves to be stepped on indefinitely.  They have capitalized on that and they have marketed their services accordingly, using the prison scale of equity.  They have scaled down their payment schedule and adjusted their services accordingly."

"What are you getting at, Dino?" Michael said slightly impatient. "Quit talking in circles and get to the point. Do you represent the competition by any chance?"

"No!  No!  Far from it my boy.  If you believe this, you have misunderstood my intentions.  I can no longer, officially speaking, give legal advise.  The government in its wisdom has seen to that by removing my license to practice law."

"Well, what are your intentions?"  Michael interrupted him again showing impatience. "I am not clairvoyant, you know.  It is evident that you have sought me out.  I don't have time to play games.  Speak up. What's on your mind?"

"Don't be impetuous." Dino cut in. "If there is a lesson prison will teach you, it is that: Patience and Caution.  You seem to have the analytical mind of an engineer.  So, I wouldn't worry too much about the second thing. If you learn patience, caution is not far down the line. As for me, I am not by nature on the same level as you intellectually, so, I have to take things more slowly.  For example, I've seen you hanging around Nick since you came here.  So, I have to think, is the attraction a sign of kinship being, how should I say in my own and your language, a case of 'Una fatsa, Una ratsa' or does it go deeper, say development of a habit for the taste of cheese."

"You can put that in your notebook counselor." Michael said adjusting to Dino's way of speaking. "It is a case of 'Mia fatsa, Mia ratsa' and I am not a 'Rat', if that is what you are wondering. For that matter, neither is Nick, based on what I have seen first hand."

"I am so relieved to hear that. However, do me a favor and say goodbye to Nick for me next time you see him. From the expression on your face, I can guess that you don't know what I am talking about. Well, your friend Nick will be leaving us next week, Wednesday...Oh!  You didn't know..."

"Leaving us?" Michael said a little too loudly. "Leaving us for where? Is he being transferred? How do you know?"

"Basta! Basta! My young friend. Slow down. One question at a time. I gather you know what a fur-low is by now?"

Michael nodded negatively. Although he knew.

"It's a reward for being a good boy in jail. It is usually for a day to three days maximum. Also, are you familiar with the halfway house concept?"

Michael again nodded that he was not familiar. Although he knew.

"It is another gift offered by the BOP and it is usually the last six months of your sentence to spent in a house in the City of your pending release where you have to pay twenty five percent of your earnings for your keep. You understand?" Michael nodded affirmative.

"Well then explain me why is Nick leaving us when he has another full year to serve on his sentence. And adding insult to injury, he is being released to his girlfriend's custody because the halfway house in Long Beach is full. Nick got a six month fur-low and a six month halfway house.  Why do you think the BOP is so generous?  What did Nick do to earn the privilege.  I will let you figure it out for yourself."

Michael tried to recall what he told Nick.  What was bothering him was that Nick disclosed more damaging information to him than the other way around.

"I know what you are thinking."  Dino said.  "Speaking with a mutual friend, I gather that old Nick once he secured his exit papers, decided to do the right thing for once in his life and tried to help you.  You are lucky. You could have equally been the last straw that bought him his freedom. The only thing is that Nick has been feeling good lately and has been blabbing to anyone who offered him a free smoke.  You need our protection, because we don't know who knows, what he knows and what they intend to do about it."

How far does the conspiracy go?  Michael was thinking.  Why should I trust this fucking Italian?  What is the price of the mob's protection?  He was so absorbed in his own thoughts that he did not notice the shadow that approached him from behind, until he felt the pinch on his rib cage. He reacted like he was hit by an electric current anticipating the cold steel of the ice pick as it was going to start ripping at his insides.  Instead, he heard the familiar.

"Patriotaki - from the same country.  Listen to the man.  You would be dead now."

Michael turned his head in bewilderment and found himself face to face with a smiling Sergio.  Michael leaned in his direction and whispered in Greek.  "Is this macaroni eater on the level?"

"You have no choice."  Sergio whispered back in Greek.  "Listen to him. He is an honorable man.  I've known him for twenty years."

"OK."  Michael said at last.  "I am in.  What's the deal?"

"I've been talking to Sergio."  Dino started.  "I've been very interested in your theory of UNI-COR and their obligations under the Davis-Bacon

Act. Have you heard of the term 'Class Action'. Well," he continued without waiting for Michael's response, "it is a lawsuit filed on behalf of one person, but the subject matter of the lawsuit covers a number of other plaintiffs that have been damaged under identical circumstances. Once the complaint has been filed and certified as a 'Class Action' suit by the Court, other plaintiffs may join and the damages multiply."

"What are you looking for out of the deal?" Michael cut in.

"Money of course." Dino said. "I will prepare the complaint. Give it to you to sign it as John Doe and file it as such, because of consequential damages due to reprisals by the BOP. I will run it and do all the work. At the end we split the spoils. I understand that you are in the process of writing a book. That's fine with me. Except we must agree that it will not be published until after the day we file the complaint. I believe the timing will provide excellent advertisement and the success of the book will enhance the public's focus on the trial. It's a win-win situation all around."

"What about Sergio?" Michael asked. "Where does he fit in, in all that?"

"Don't worry about Sergio. I will take care of him, out of my own cut." Dino said.

Michael sat quietly contemplating the situation. His wife was right. He brought confrontation and controversy wherever he went. Prison was no exception. The mob needed his knowledge and experience with the Davis-Bacon Act. After all the alleged violations he had been accused of which brought about his conviction. The government was doing the same thing on a gigantic scale with UNICOR reaping the profits at a rate of 71% per year. He needed the mob for protection and they his availability and supply of information. His short stay in prison had taught him that much at least. Knowledge was power."

"How do I know that I would be protected?" Michael broke the silence.

"Do you see these two guys standing next to the wall?"

Michael turned and looked.  He recognized one of the two, Pauli, one of Sergio's co-conspirators from Brindisi, Italy.  He did not recognize the other one.

"That's Pauli and his cousin Tony."  Dino continued.  "They will shadow you with others around the clock.  Within a day this will be known to both the inmates and the BOP.  No hack will fuck with you, because they will be afraid of you.  Same goes with the inmates.  Do we have a deal?"

Michael shook the extended hand without hesitation.

"You did the right thing."  Sergio whispered.  "You had no other choice. You knew too much."  He added with hidden menace to his voice.

Tony left the wall as soon as Michael and Dino shook hands and Pauli came to the next picnic table and sat on it with his feet on the bench, looking around at the other inmates for signs of someone paying a little too much attention at Michael.

"What now?"  Michael asked.  "When do I get rolled up?"

"Why do you say this?"  Dino said.  "The government has been drooling for someone like you.  Look at this Camp.  It is obvious under construction.  The pace is glacial because the hacks in charge did not finish High School and have no experience.  The inmates produce to the extent they get paid by building out of sequence and tearing it down. The Movie Theater has started two years ago and the progress is the same as if they started last month.  Next year Congress will give the Department of Justice seven hundred million dollars for construction. Four times what they gave them this year.  The Warden built the population to over five hundred inmates, so that he can qualify for fifteen thousand dollars more per year and up his retirement package by twenty percent.  Michael, they know your capabilities.  They know you ran an Engineering and Construction company on the outside doing the exactly same type of work they want you to do here.  Same goes for the Air Force Base.  You will be the most powerful inmate in the joint, because you will be an 'Essential Institutional Need'.  You will be it.  If you want, you can bring all the construction activities at Camp and on Base, to a standstill.  They are all waiting for you to ask them to place you in a job suited with your qualifications.  Keep them guessing for a little while longer.  You are doing a great job at being the model inmate with no aspirations, ready to do what you are told.  Tomorrow you will end up in Custody.  Don't let the word Custody worry you.  It is a detail of rejects that empty the trash cans in the Camp and pick cigarette butts.  They are Camp custodians.  Don't do any work.  No hack will talk to you and they will see that your work is being done by volunteers. This is only being done for a 'Man of Respect', which you have become as soon as you shook my hand.  Stay at the first gazebo and smoke your pipe.  At 8:30 AM a fellow will approach you and he will sit on the same picnic table with you."

"How will I be able to recognize him?" Michael asked.  "Do I know him? What if he is the wrong fellow?"

"You worry too much." Dino said with a smile.  "What do you think Pauli and Tony will be doing?  You forget.  If someone comes near you, he will not get very close.  Starting this afternoon you will see.  No one will speak to you until you   spoke to him first.  No one will come near you until you summon them.  You will get used to it after a while and you will like it.  I do."

With that, Michael turned his head concentrating on the swarthy types, trying to spot Dino's guardian angels.

"Don't waste your energy." Dino said.  "James, the fellow we are talking about, is a wise old man.  He will educate you on trusts and how to get money out of the country and back in, tax free and legally to boot way. You will enjoy it."

"Why do I have to learn about money laundering?" Michael asked.

"It's not you, we had in mind, although it never hurts to know.  We were thinking more along the lines of how the UNI-COR is set up.  We know for example that the profits are made and those are distributed to the shareholders.  Now, if the shareholders were known, how soon do you think they would make front page news?  Hence, the stockholders are not known to the public.  The only way someone can legally achieve this, is by means of blind trusts.  The payments are made to a trust whose beneficiaries remain unknown."

"If the beneficiaries are unknown, how do you know that they are the Federal Judges?" Michael asked.

"I believe Nick told you about this.  You can ask him how he knows.  As for myself, I got the information by way of second hand at Lompoc.  That's another Camp in California by Santa Barbara.  I got to be close to a Senator from Massachusetts over there.  He was in for bringing in a container load of Mary Jane.  He was set up because, as he told me, Senators and Congressmen would go together on container loads of dope.  He was making two million dollars a month in dope money while he was in the Senate.  Evidently, he voted the wrong way on a couple of issues and he was set up.  Anyway, back to the problem.  This same Senator told me that UNI-COR was owned by the Federal Judges through these blind trusts.  You should learn about them, because it will help you in your book and ultimately we need to know whom we will end up against.  Remember, these trusts represent the deep pocket of UNI-COR, should we prevail in our Class Action suit."

Dino contemplated for a few minutes and said.

"What are you going to end up doing with your Appeal?

"I will end up writing it myself.  Then I will send it out to my wife for typing.  I have not made plans past this point."

"What are the points of your Appeal?  Remember now that they must be applicable to a wide range of the population, otherwise the Supreme Court will not even read your Appeal past the 'Questions Presented' portion on page 1."

"I am aware of this Dino, but don't you think the Supreme Court would be interested whether a person is guilty or innocent?"

"Mike, they don't give a shit if you spend time in jail or not, even if you are innocent. Now if you had a death sentence hanging over your head, they may examine you as a person. Your crime and your sentence work against you in this case. The only thing that will make them review your case, are the issues presented..."

"And even then, what you are telling me;" Michael cut in, "they will review my case like pigeons review a statue."

"Now you got it my friend." Dino said with a hearty laugh. "Like pigeons review a statue. That's a good one. I am going to use it and quote you. Seriously though have you given any thought on the issues you intend to address? And remember, don't pick any more than five, tops or they will think you are on a fishing expedition."

"The Davis-Bacon Act states that an employee is to be paid prevailing wages for the time he spent doing laborers and mechanics work on the site of a federal or federally funded project. The law does not cover hourly rates for time spent off site or on site not working as a laborer and mechanic. My long standing position has been that the Davis-Bacon coverage was limited to those employed at the physical location, site, of the public project. The government asserted that an employee was due Davis-Bacon for merely breathing. As long as he worked one hour under Davis-Bacon, he was always a Davis-Bacon wage worker, regardless if he was on site, off site, standing around or working on a job not subjected to the Davis-Bacon Act. Since the majority of my projects were done as a Change Order or on a cost plus basis, if I applied the government's interpretation I would be indicted as overcharging the government. They were planning to go after me in the beginning on that basis, overcharging the government, that' s why they were videotaping eight hours a day all my jobs. However, when they saw that the reported hours closely tracked the actual hours spent on the job, they switched tactics, lost the video tapes and accused me of underpaying my employees. The government in that instance being the Navy via the NIS which is part of the Department of Defense and represents part of the Executive Branch. On the strength that the government's interpretation of the labor law was correct and mine was not, the federal judge sided with the government and asserted that my submitted payrolls were not in compliance with the Davis-Bacon Act, the way the government interpret it, and they indicted me for Mail Fraud. How they've come up with Mail Fraud is another issue, but at the time of my indictment, trial and conviction, there was no legal precedence justifying the government's or my position and interpretation of the law. Since then, there have been two cases that were decided in the Supreme Court which justify my interpretation of the Davis-Bacon Act. But that's beside the point. My first issue asks the question, which by the way has constitutional implications: Does the Executive Branch have the authority to interpret the Davis-Bacon Act and then act upon this interpretation to indict an individual who has a difference of opinion concerning the same law?"

"Hey! That's a good one to start." Dino said. "You and I know very well that the Executive Branch has as much right as you and me and every other citizen to interpret the law. It's the Judicial Branch's interpretation that counts. This will certainly get the Supreme Court interested. They are pompous asses all of them to begin with and if they sense that another government agency is stepping in their turf, they get mighty pissed off. Good start. What is the second issue?"

"Well, the federal judge accepted the government's interpretation as gospel and instructed the jury on the definition of the Davis-Bacon Act which was proven to be wrong on subsequent cases. That means that the instructions to the jury were erroneous. Also my interpretation of the law, caused the government to save money. The government admitted this during the trial. The indictment states that the government was defrauded.  It was not.  It saved money instead.  The federal judge's instructions to the jury misstated the law of Mail Fraud."

"That's another good one Mike." Dino said.  The government has been trying to expand the Mail Fraud statutes; while the Supreme Court has been trying to narrow them.  An example is the McNally case, the Supreme Court reversed the decision finding that the government did not experience a loss.  Same with the Gaudin case later.  This case was another opportunity for the Supreme Court to step forth once again and tell the government that they cannot lock up people for Mail Fraud if no fraud occurred, which is a fact necessary to constitute a crime.

"Your case Mike sounds very interesting.  I'd like to read your Appeal after you finish it and point out to you certain things to make it better.  Any other issues?"

"The other points are personal so to speak.  They have limited application, except the issue of 'stand-by time'.  That is the time spent on site doing no work.  Does this time fall under the Davis-Bacon Act or under the Copeland Act?"

"Didn't the 9th Circuit Court of Appeals decide this already?"  Dino interrupted.

"No.  They were invited by both the District Court Federal Judge and myself in my Appeal to rule.  But they declined by their silence on the matter."

"What about Midway Excavators or Ball, Ball and Broshamer after your conviction.  Didn't they address the issue?"

"No.  Their cases deal with offsite time.  The Supreme Court was very clear on this.  They stated that the phrase of the Act "employed directly upon the site of work", means "employed directly upon the site of work; i.e. the actual geographic and physical site".  The District Court Judge in my case instructed the jury that workers running errants which were not on site, could be found to be subject to the Davis-Bacon Act if their work was "integral to the construction project". This instruction was clearly misstating the law…"

"Do you have the transcripts with you Michael?"

"Yes I do. In my room."

"Good! Take them out of your room and we will assign you a locker in the Legal Library. So no one can take them away. It's going to be fun."

Michael looked at him questionably.

"No! No! I don't mean the Appeal. I am thinking about the Class Action suit when we feed back to the government their own testimony in your trial."

"Dino, you get excited over nothing. No federal judge will allow testimony from another trial. I remember what happened during my trial. The government had accused me two years before for overcharging them on Change Orders on a particular Contract. They translated overcharging into overstating the Davis-Bacon hours. Two years later, the same government witness testified that I understated the Davis-Bacon hours on the same Contract."

"Michael, this is hard to believe. I wouldn't have believed it coming from anyone else. I bet it really happened. What was your attorney doing when all that was going on? Asleep at the switch?"

"That's another sore point with me Dino. Attorneys. Mine did nothing more than collect his fee which ended up being over four times more than originally quoted. Two weeks after my trial I found out that he was short listed for a federal judgeship. What do you think of them apples?"

"No shit! Your lawyer was shortlisted for federal judge in Hawaii? Come on. Is this what you heard through the grapevine or something or you got proof? Because if you have proof, it is a sure fire way to get a new trial. Just file a 2255 with the District Court."

"Dino, I heard it on television the day after my trial was over, during the CBS local news with the rest of the people. They announced three names shortlisted. One of them was my lawyer Lowenfield."

"Oh, shit! Another Jew. What was the judge doing? He should have approached you after the announcement and ask you whether you got adequate representation. That's how things are done; otherwise he is running the risk of getting reversed on Appeal to the 9th. Didn't your lawyer include that as part of the Appeal?"

"Slow down Dino. One question at the time. The federal judge, Ezra, another jew, had a room temperature I.Q. and was spacing out during the trial. So, at the end of the government's presentation, he had no idea what I was accused of. He only came awake during my testimony long enough to shake his head and roll his eyes to the jury urging them with non verbal communications to disregard everything I was saying. He was promised a promotion, according to my attorney, to the 9th Circuit Court of Appeals if he got a conviction in my case. So, he was gung-ho to please his masters. The federal government. You know how the criminal trials go? The prosecutor and the judge have the same employer. In my case they offered my attorney a lifetime position to eat out of the same tax payers trough.

"Concerning my appeal to the 9th, I changed attorneys, but that was also a mistake, because the attorney I went back to, was the same one who had recommended Lowenfield to begin with. So he discouraged me from including anything about defective counsel in my Appeal to the 9th. Given the limited page space allotted for the Appeal, you have to decide whether to take a shot gun approach or select a few key issues and go at it in detail. He decided on the latter approach. The Appeal concentrated on two issues. One, that the government both mathematically shown and proven during the trial, and by their own admission during the trial, did not incur any loss, quite opposite, they saved money. Two, during the trial the district court accepted a sentencing measure of loss under the sentencing guidelines, which it had previously rejected at trial.  The government and the district judge were so inconsistent with the law as determined by the Court, that the Court would not allow it to be heard by the jury.  So my sentence was above the maximum allowed under the guidelines because of the overblown dollar amount.   Three, the government's contention regarding my role in the offense as an organizer or leader.  The district court however, did not find that any of the alleged participants under my alleged leadership were criminally culpable.  So, how could I be a leader of non-criminals executing my commands and be a criminal myself, only.  If the other people did not do anything criminal of what I told them to do, no crime was committed.  Why was I then indicted?"

"What was the 9th's response?"

"One line and not for publication.  "Denied.  The government need not show loss, or sustain damages to indict under the Mail Fraud statutes."

"The 9th is wrong.  No wonder they did not want their decision publicized.  I hope you include these things in your Appeal to the Supreme Court." Dino said. "If nothing else, they may sway the reader of your Appeal to view favorably the main issues of community interest, knowing that he is setting an innocent man free."

"I hope you are right Dino. But I am not hopeful myself. My doubts stem from the sheer numbers.  There are ten thousand Appeals filed in front of the Supreme Court every year.  Out of which they pick 80 to 85 to hear.  On the face of it is tantamount of winning the lottery.  First your case must be read by a clerk.  He must be sufficiently impressed with the issues and your innocence to write a favorable paper to the judges. Other clerks, including your clerk are doing this same thing several times over.  So the judges are looking, say, a couple of thousand cases. Then they pick 500 and they assign them a docket number.  They send them back to the clerks.  Then they pick 80, if they have time 85 cases, a  year to rule.  Discount half of them, because the reason they picked them was through political pressure from the Senate which is the body of the federal legislature who elected them. So it leaves barely three dozen cases a year from the pile. Then you got to eliminate some cases because of truly controversial issues and death sentences, which make the total of available slots barely a dozen. I think you have a better chance of winning the lottery than your case getting selected to be heard by the Supreme Court."

"I know Mike; but you can't quit either. Look at all the landmark cases. Even in your case the issue of Mail Fraud. McNally was decided in the Supreme Court. Lew was decided in a Habeas Corpus proceeding which is after the Supreme Court. Where would McNally and Lew be had they given up? For that matter, where would the rest of us be? The majority of the cases you are referring in your Appeal, I bet they come out of the Supreme Court rulings or from subsequent proceedings. You cannot give up. If you believe you are innocent, you have to show perseverance and tenacity."

"Dino, you are looking at the man who invented and defined the words, perseverance and tenacity. I know what I got to do. Speaking of perseverance and tenacity though; what about your case?"

"My case Mike, was the perennial: I was stuck between a rock and a hard place. The government wanted me to 'Rat' on my clients which happened to be organized crime figures, otherwise they were going to charge me with Money Laundering. 'Ratting' on my clients was out of the question, because it was morally and constitutionally wrong, plus unhealthy. You do not 'Rat' on the mob and live to talk about it. I know the Witness Protection Program and all that bull. If they want you, they will find you, sooner or later. So, I did not, and here I am. My family is being taken care of, though and I believe with your help I am going to have the last laugh. As soon as we got all our ducks in a row, we will file a 'Class Action' suit under John Doe, citing fear of reprisals. As soon as the complaint is docketed, we will move onto the UNI-COR and Discovery them to death."

"How are you going to open up the blind trusts?"

"By requiring a good faith Bond from the beneficiaries. They will either end up coming out of the woodwork or most likely they will move for a settlement. Either way we got them beat and who knows, we may get lucky and get a glimpse of their inner-workings. If you time publication of your book with the filing of the Complaint, you will be in fat city regardless of the outcome of the legal  proceedings. The controversy will be publicity for your book. Just remember. From now on "Omerta". Capish?"

"What nationality are you Dino? You talk Italian but you think like a Greek Byzantine conspirator. What gives? What Dino stands for?"

"Constantino. My mother was Greek and my father Italian. My last name is Adriano."

"Even your last name is Greek. Andrianos in Greek and it means brave. It is not spelled quite the same as its Italian counterpart. But I am sure the root of the word is the same."

Michael looked at his watch suddenly.

"Oh, my! Time flies when you have fun." Michael said. "It's almost three thirty. We should mossy down to Building 201 gazebo for mail call."

"I won't be able to make it today." Dino said. "I got to go shopping at the Commissary. It's my day you know. Do you need anything?"

"That's all right Dino, I am going to the Commissary myself tomorrow. I shop on Thursdays because my inmate number ends in 9. I will wait at mail call and if I hear your name called, I will get your mail."

"Good bye my friend." Dino said getting up. "Tell me how you make out in Custody tomorrow."

# CHAPTER 12

## Stealing, The Government Way

Michael left his room at eight fifteen in the morning on the dot. No six thirty bus to the Base this morning. He got out of the building, looked up towards the blue sky and breathed deeply the crisp autumn air. The heat of the day was descending pretty fast, so he decided the last minute to forego his jacket that would become burdensome carry on baggage by nine. He turned right at the gate and hastened his walk towards Building 201 partly to compensate for the cool of the early morning and partly because he did not want to be late. He was told that the meeting place was a five minute walk from his dormitory. Passing the Administration Building, he could not help but notice the quiet of the Camp. The majority of the inmates were already at work on Base, while the others working on Camp, had to report to work by seven thirty. As he rounded the corner, he noticed a few strugglers on crutches limping towards the gazebo. The Camp rejects and the infirm on some kind of medical disability made up the bulk of the Custody detail. After his first day experience at Housing, he asked to be transferred to any other assignment. It usually took a couple of days to take place. In the meantime, between jobs so to speak, the Camp Employment Office assigned those in transit to Custody. They needed some bodies after all to pick-up the trash and clean-up the Camp grounds.

Michael arrived at the gazebo with ten minutes to spare. He looked at the waiting inmates, most of them older than himself and wondered which one was his contact. More inmates were joining the quay as the magic hour of eight thirty was approaching.  He finally gave up and sat on the first bench available and lit his pipe.

"Let the games begin."  He heard a voice coming from the direction of Building 201.  A person resembling a younger version of Elmer Fudd appeared from the side building exit and assumed a military type step, resembling the rolling walk of the English bulldog.  He had a crew cut and was as wide as tall.  He stumbled on a sidewalk crack and Michael formed a picture of Humpty Dumpty in his mind.  Officer Humpty Dumpty's antics brought smiles to the faces of the inmates.  Officer Petunia followed in close step behind officer Humpty Dumpty. Obscene pictures of mission impossible flashed in each inmate's mind.  Officer Petunia threw a smile of longing towards officer Humpty Dumpty who tried in vain to maintain a   cool exterior and expressionless face.  Over five hundred pounds of combined flesh, mentally, joined and parted, were leaving the inmates slightly nauseated, so soon after breakfast.

"Listen up."  Officer Elmer Fudd whined away on his high pitched voice. "You old hands know your job assignments, the new, pair up with the experienced and follow their lead.  Dismissed."

What kind of job assignment is this? Michael was thinking as he saw the crowd thinning out and disappearing in pairs. Who is new? Who is old? Remembering the old saying: When in doubt do nothing, he sat under the gazebo smoking his pipe.

"On a break already I see.  Well, young man, you truly understand the purpose of your assignment."  The voice came from a silver haired man who had been staring at him throughout the meeting.  Septuagenerian, six three, military posture which deteriorated to double chin and twin tire belly, on each side of a tightly cinched belt.  Images of the Michelin tire mascot flashed before Michael's eyes as he got up and faced the advancing lumbering figure.

"May I help you, pops?"  Michael spoke with a slight edge in his voice.

"Pops! Pops? Is this anyway to talk to your new partner? Well from the vacant stare on your face, I can tell that you don't know what I am talking about."

"I am Michael." He said extending his hand.

"I know who you are;" the Michelin man replied, "or I wouldn't be talking to you. I am James Dean. You are smiling. Yes it's spelled the same way. I am the rebel without a cause.."

"Or the rebel without a clue." Michael added quickly.

"We are vitriolic this morning for some reason…" James piped in. "But my skin is tough. I can take it. Water off duck's feathers."

"Let me ask you a couple of questions, there, James," Michael interrupted, "before we go too far with this gig. How did you know my name and how did we end up partners all of a sudden?"

"A mutual friend and I selected you." The old codger came back like a whip.

"Break it down for me a little old timer." Michael said. "What exactly do you mean?"

"Which part you did not understand? Our mutual friend or that I picked you?"

"Touché. Are you then James, 'the trust' man?"

"Yes I am." James replied with a smug smile on his face.

"In that case, lead on McDuff and demonstrate our job."

"It's really quite simple, we pretend to work, and the BOP pretends to pay us."

"What exactly is our job?" Michael asked curiously.

"Now, take your time and follow me. First I will get my trusty bags." With that he flipped a roll of plastic bags from underneath his jacket without significantly effecting the size of the upper tire.  He stopped in front of the garbage can next to the administration building.  He pulled the half full bag.  Expertly tied a knot on the loose top part.  In a smooth continuous motion he slipped out a fresh one, popped it open, inserted the ballooning bottom part inside the can and secured the top by rolling it over the can lips.

"Under ten seconds, for the whole operation."  He crowed proudly.  "Grab the full bag and follow me towards the Education Building.  Along the way, we will repeat the process I've just demonstrated, eight more times and we will be done for the day."

"You've got to be kidding."  Michael said.

"No I am not.  The longest I made the job last was 9:15 AM and that was because we got a half hour late start from the gazebo.  I believe I am giving them their money's worth.  What did you expect for twelve cents an hour?"

"I don't know James.  Don't you get bored?"

"Not at all.  I carry with me a book at all times.  I sit under the Education Building gazebo and read.  I read three or four books a week and enjoy it immensely.  What would you have me do instead?"

"Well, I don't know."  Michael hesitated, lost for words.  "Something useful, I guess."

"That's exactly what I am doing.  Something useful for me.  What did you expect me to do?  Something useful for the BOP?  If that's what you mean, you will be bitterly disappointed.  They will use you and when it is convenient for them they will dump on you.  You don't count for anything as far as they are concerned, except to make them look good."

"Is this your theory gained from personal experience, or just inmate talk?" Michael asked.

"Believe what you wish." James said. "Sooner or later you will find out for yourself. One always hopes sooner and at minimum loss, for the experience."

"Are you now James the Prophet?" Michael asked laughing.

"Oh! I like the sound of that 'James the Prophet'. It has a nice ring to it and it would also make the Bishop jealous."

"What Bishop are you talking about?" Michael asked.

"Oh! Nothing. He is one of my roommates. A fussy old misogynist of a gentleman who has taken upon himself to mother hen us all."

"What do you say rebel, let's go for broke and break your old record." Michael said nudging Alex. "That way we will have more time to discuss the business at hand, which is the reason after all for us getting together."

"Speaking of the latter;" James added, "I've got to tell you Michael how much I am enjoyed strolling the grounds with you. You are bright and your naiveté is charming and engaging. I will now ask you, kind of a personal question."

"What's that James?" Michael asked. He liked the old codger and he was hopping it did not turn out that he was playing for the other team.

"I've got a proposition for you."

Oh! Shit! Here it comes, Michael was thinking. Look at the twinkle in the old goat's eye.

"I understand you are in a rough room. Drug lords, killers and bank robbers. That's no place for a businessman like yourself. Why don't you come over to our room. We are four business type people. I am in insurance and trusts as you know. The fellow I mentioned as Bishop, is in real estate. The other two are a drywall contractor and a stockbroker. The last two work on Base every waking moment, in the vocational training program. What do you say?"

"Thank you for asking James." Michael replied. "It sounds like a great room. I will seriously consider it. How about if I drop by and meet all of you. Get to know all of you face to face, so to speak and then I will tell you my decision by the day's end."

"Good. You can drop in after lunch." James said; the impatience creeping in his voice.

"What's the hurry?" Michael replied apprehensively, feeling pushed into a commitment.

"Well," James continued with some hesitation. "it is just that they are bringing in so many new faces, you know...not compatible...let's say quite inappropriate for our quiet room that we are afraid they will move one or two maybe in the next few days and there you go..."

Michael, understood immediately what James was getting at, but he decided to have a little fun with him and his anxiety over the...race issue.

"What's the matter James? Don't you want to expand your horizon by learning new things? The right kind of roommate would make your life here how should I put it...a little more colorful."

"Well, our life is colorful enough, in stereo if you please, each side of our room." James replied catching on immediately.

"As I said James, I will let you know by the end of the day." Michael said, bringing the discussion to a close.

They were left with three full garbage bags by the time they reached the entrance to the Education Building, after James habit of stuffing one partially filled bag into another.

"Where do they go?" Michael asked, shaking two of the bags.

"Into the dumpsters behind the kitchen." James replied lifting the remaining bag.

"I think we broke your old record." Michael commented glancing at his watch. "What do we do now for the rest of the day?"

"We sit under the gazebo, sip a soda and see if I can educate you about trust funds, the greatest legal swindle our country has invented."

"Now, James, you've got to realize that I am 'tabula rasa' on the subject, so, you've got to define for me all the terms and kind of give me a brief history of how these trusts got started." Michael said plopping quarters into the vending machine and punching for a coke and a smile.

"The trust was originally a device," James started with a professorial demeanor, "by which several corporations, engaged in the same general line of business, might combine for their mutual advantage, in the direction of eliminating destructive competition, controlling the output of their commodity, regulating and maintaining its price, but at the same preserving their separate individual existence without any consolidation or merger.

"This device was the election of a central committee or board, composed, of presidents and general managers of different corporations and the transfer to them of the majority of the stock in each of the corporations, to be held 'in trust' for the several stockholders, so assigning their holdings. These stockholders received in return 'trust certificates' showing that they were entitled to receive the dividends on their assigned stock, though the voting power of it had passed to the trustees. This last feature enabled the trustees or committee to elect all the directors of all the corporations and through them, the officers, and thereby to exercise an absolute controlling influence over the policy and operations of each constituent company, to the ends and with the purpose mentioned above."

"What you are speaking of here is price fixing." Michael broke the monolog. "That's exactly what I am talking about." James replied in an elevated tone of voice. "Why do you think the government named all the laws to combat price fixing, anti trust laws?" James took a sip of his seven up and continued.

"If you understood the historical aspect of how the trusts got started, you will understand how the concept was transferred to the individual. Remember, a trust is a document that specifies how assets are to be administered. The requirements include a trustee, who holds a fiduciary responsibility to manage the trust assets, called the corpus, and the income generated, and does so for the economic benefit of all the beneficiaries. The trustee contracts with the grantor or settlor who places the initial assets or corpus into the trust organization for the trustee to administer. The beneficiaries are usually family members, and if a contract type trust is in effect, they hold certificates as personal property showing their rights to distributors of income or corpus from the trust organization. The trustee is the manager of the assets and who authorizes these distributions to the beneficiaries. Am I going too fast for you kid?" James said seeing Michael struggling to take notes.

"No. I will be all right." Michael replied.

"Say I want to start a trust. Who do I pick as a trustee?" James continued. "It can be anyone as long as he or she are not blood related to you or under your control. For example accountants who prepare financial statements for your company, any of your employees that depend upon you for their livelihood. This last extends to other service oriented professions, like your attorney. There can also be more than one trustee, thus constituting a Board of Trustees."

"What if I made a mistake;" Michael interrupted, "and I assigned for a trustee a person who…how should I put it…did not have my best interest in mind. What do I do then? Kiss my money goodbye?"

"I am glad you asked me that kid. It shows that you are paying attention and most important that you understand the process and the thinking." James said with a smile. "Most trusts use a party and a procedure to be able to replace a trustee at any time. The person holding this position is usually called 'the protector'. This protector should always have the power to look at management decisions of the trustee and also the financial position of the trust organization at any time, so that he can act to protect the position of the beneficiaries. The beneficiaries quite often do not have the authority to see the financial records, but the protector does have the right and is responsible to act on behalf of the beneficiaries. Any person, except the settlor, can be a protector of the beneficiaries and can include even a beneficiary in his team."

"What types of trusts exist?" Michael asked trying to keep up taking notes.

"There are basically two categories of trusts. A simple trust and a complex trust. The simple trust distributes taxable funds every year at least once. The complex trust can accumulate funds for ever or distribute them at will."

"So, let me summarize what I've learned so far." Michael said. "Say someone is party to proceeds coming from a source, in this case company 'x'. He sets up a devise, this trust, to give management of his investments  to an outside person over whom the beneficiary has no control. If the trust is a "blind trust", the individual need not disclose his name and the public cannot identify the individual. The 'x' company simply makes payments into this blind trust."

"By George he's got it!" James piped in a mocking tone.

"So the general rules governing domestic trusts;" Michael said, "are that the trust be simple, a non grantor type by which I mean the grantor cannot not be a trustee, it must have a United States source of income and the source must be some type of United States business organization. Now this trust must make at least one payment a year to somebody and this somebody must pay tax on that payment. Now my question is: Can this trust make a payment to someone without that someone having to report it to the Internal revenue Service?"

"No." James interjected. "That would be income tax evasion and that person would end up in jail."

"So. Uncle Sam will get his cut one way or another." Michael commented sadly.

"That's not what I said!" James said raising his voice. "What I said is not reporting the income is a tax evasion. That has nothing to do with actually paying tax."

"Time out here." Michael said stopping taking notes. "How can someone not pay tax, when the government knows who he is and how much he got?"

"Well, there is a way, known only to a handful of people in this country and it is perfectly legal." James said pausing for emphasis. "Now, you need to accomplish some intermediary steps, mind you. You remember the rules for a domestic  trust, you so nicely summarized earlier. Consider the yearly payment of that simple domestic trust was made not to an individual, but to another simple trust; only this time, this new trust is not domestic but foreign; set up in a country that does not levy taxes on money that comes into the country. What you've got now?"

"Let's see;" Michael said checking his notes, "you've got another simple trust, again non-grantor, with a United States source of income, that's the original domestic trust payment.  What about the fourth requirement though, the one about the source must be some type of United States business organization. The domestic trust is not.  How do you get around that?"

"Now, now, don't fret my friend, there is a loop hole specifically created by the Internal Revenue Service for the wise ones to get around that obstacle.  Their IRC 875 (2) written in 1913 which says that Domestic United States Trusts shall be treated as a business when Foreign Trusts are concerned, with the stipulation that the trust must file a K1 form informing the IRS of who got the money.  Remember now, just that, who got the money, no tax on that money."

"I see." Michael said. "However, the IRS still has the origin, the final destination and the trail. The money accumulates tax free, but you got no way of taking it out."

"Based on what we discussed so far, you've hit the nail on the head." James said. "But I was told you are a bright guy. Show me that by taking the problem one step further. How would you erase the trail and the final destination in one stroke."

Michael gave it some thought. Lit his pipe and said. "Setting up a second foreign trust."

"Bingo!" James yelled. "Only now you only have to meet two requirements. Simple trust and non-grantor trust. No requirement for reporting of a foreign trust, so the trail is erased and the latest foreign trust is unknown and secure."

"That still leaves the question of how does the individual recover his money." Michael said thoughtfully. "New foreign trusts won't help, because the moment the individual gets ahold of his money, the IRS would be right there."

"That's where you are wrong my friend. The individual can get his money tax free and legally. All he has to do is set up a third Grantor Foreign Trust organized under the guidelines of IRC paragraphs 661 to 663. My advise would be for that last trust to be a complex trust. You remember this is the one in which the trustees have discretion as to whether to distribute and discretion as to the amounts distributed."

"What about the IRS?" Michael interjected.

"Don't be in such a hurry." James said. "What about the IRS? They have a Ruling which is called 69-70 that in effect states that funds from a Grantor Foreign Trust distributed to a U.S. citizen are tax free. So, there you go. The money came back to the beneficiaries full circle, laundered and tax free."

"What a scam!" Exclaimed Michael. "Does the government know about it?"

"Know about it?  The government wrote the book for it.  Then diagramed it for the robber barons and all the others associated with the Federal Reserve so they and their descendants can beat the system. It is a legal license to steal, my friend."

"How much did Dino tell you?" Michael asked hesitantly.

"Enough to know that you are trying to figure out how UNI-COR is fueling the proceeds from the corporate profits into the federal judges pockets without the taxpayers being the wiser for it."

"Did he mention anything about a Class Action suit?" Michael inquired.

"He did; but I didn't understand the basis for it.  He mentioned the Davis-Bacon Act but I am not aware what the law says.  The judges I noticed hand out severe sentences, some greater than maximum guidelines.  The convicts keep doing more work for UNI-COR at slave wages.  The profits go to the UNI-COR shareholders, the federal judges themselves who feed the labor pools.  The budgets go up and up each year.  It seems to be a vicious circle without end.  A giant money generating machine going on ad infinitum. As the older prisoners die off, new ones become of age to fill their ranks.  The number of prisoners overall throughout the country keeps increasing at a rate of 17.5% per year.  If the domestic prisoners thin out, we import them from ready made markets like Mexico, Central and South America.  You see Michael, justice is still very much a public  perception of what is right and wrong, instead of what is legally and morally right."

"You know,"  Michael said, "before I came in here I've been a strong advocate of keeping the criminals off the street.  Increase the number of cases going forward to the prosecution stage.  Tighten the loops, so we have a greater percentage of convictions..."

"You can't get better than the federal courts," James interjected, "where the percentage of convictions is upwards, North of 97%."

"I was a firm believer in our justice system." Michael continued. "I believed the media and their coverage of every negative aspect in society..."

"Yes, but this never ending stream of negative news," James added, "makes it easy for law enforcement to broadcast their rallying cry to "go get the bad guys". As you are finding out though, being on the inside now looking out, it is not quite as simple as it looked on the outside. There are many brought into the prosecution stage who should never have gotten into the system."

"Well, the government pyramid scheme needs labor force in order to function profitably." Michael said sarcastically.

"Don't you think though that any business that derived profits from forced labor," James interrupted, "should not give the profits to the owners, if such were the persons responsible for the incarceration of those performing the labor at slave wages?"

"You don't have to convince me about this." Michael replied. "But the profits are certainly attractive. Even with the government inefficiency, last year UNI-COR showed a profit margin in excess of seventy percent. How could those federal judges sleep at night?"

"Very peacefully, thank you very much." James said. "They may be morally wrong; but they justify their actions under the guise that they are legally correct and collecting on the misery of other people they helped put in, is nothing more than legally subsidizing their own income. You see, Michael, by legal definition, in order to avoid the possibility of disqualification, a federal judge could utilize a blind trust with respect to his or her investments. This is right out of their code of Ethics book. These are very neat legal devices, as you have learned, that allow  the judge to legally say he or she does not know what the trust manager is doing by way of investment management of assets formerly owned by him or her.  To elaborate, the judge places his investment assets, as settlor, into a trust that has an independent trustee acting as manager of those assets and the judge, his wife, children and whomever else he may add as beneficiary reap the profits of the trust.  In this manner, the judge has taken a step away from his assets and can concentrate upon his job, earning convictions and sentencing people to lengthy sentences, without concern about conflict of interest situations.  The trustee manages the trust and signs as the principal party so that the investments are totally separated from the jurisdiction of the judge.  If these trusts are properly written, there is no probate of the estate upon the demise of the settlor and of the spouse, and more important, there is no federal estate tax assessed against the estate.  The children inherit or continue use of everything in the trust without the deductions for taxes."

"This is fascinating."  Michael exclaimed.  "How are these trusts proper Contracts?"

"For these trusts to be a proper Contract, there must be an exchange for full and adequate consideration.  This is accomplished by the trustee giving beneficial certificates in exchange for the asset placed in the trust organization.  There is no direct gift made to the beneficiaries.  Instead the certificates received by the settlor, are gifted to the beneficiaries and since there is no ascertainable value associated with this exchange and subsequent gift, they are not taxable."

"Very slick."  Michael said.  "It operates pretty much like a corporation with stock and stockholders."

"You are close my friend."  James said.  "It operates much like a corporation except that the certificates are personal property and hold no equitable title like stock certificates.  The trust is in effect an unincorporated business entity, with minutes, meetings and operations equivalent to a corporate entity. They usually are given a thirty year life. New trusts can be added for family estate planning purposes at any time they are appropriate.  These can be funded from other income producing trusts as either loans or as beneficiaries receiving distributions. Since these entities are Contracts, they have all the privacy afforded in private Contracts. They need not be registered with the state and they pay no corporate franchise taxes. I believe these trusts are being used to isolate federal judges from their trust ownership of UNI-COR stock. It is entirely possible that you have uncovered my friend the biggest scam operation ever in this country."

James let that last remark sink in and asked quietly leaning towards Michael.

"How are are you planning to bring this off?"

"Well, with Dino's help, file a Class Action suit against the Department of Justice and UNI-COR. Then hit them with Discovery like they have never been hit before."

"You realize of course, if you bring it off; the enormous profit potential from all these trusts that would be declared Trusts ex Maleficio."

"You lost me there, James." Michael said. "What is a Trust ex Maleficio?"

"Trust ex Maleficio, according to the law, is a trust which arises against one who, by fraud, actual or constructive, by duress or abuse of confidence, by commission of a wrong or by any form of unconscionable conduct, artifice, concealment or questionable means and against good conscience, either has obtained or holds right to property which he ought not, in equity and good conscience hold and enjoy. In simple words Mike, you file a successful Class Action lawsuit and you may be able to knock the whole trust pyramid scheme like a house of cards. What are your chances?"

"Well, you tell me James. You know the type of work the inmates do. It ranges from janitorial to manufacturing. Under these categories the Bureau of Prisons is obligated to pay in accordance with the Copland Act, because these job classifications are subject to that law. Accordingly, he BOP is obligated to pay minimum wage. They have claimed in numerous law suits, and records exist for those claims, that it costs them a little under four dollars an hour, based on forty working hours a week, for the inmate's upkeep.  So, they end up paying the difference only which amounts from 12 to 40 cents per hour.  In this case the suits brought against the BOP are summarily rejected and thrown out of court because the Department of Justice has established an arithmetic precedence.  Now, I believe that someone that is required to pay the Bureau of Prisons for his stay here and still ends up being paid 12 cents an hour for his work while incarcerated has a very good chance of recovering the entire minimum wage rate, because of double jeopardy."

"That's right," James interjected, "the government cannot punish someone twice for the same crime."

"Yes," Michael continued, "the government should not be allowed to take a second bite out of the same apple.  Plus the BOP is being already paid $25,000.00 a year by the GAO for each prisoner because that is what it costs them a year for the prisoner's upkeep.  Triple jeopardy."

"What about construction?  Isn't that subject to the same minimum wage act?" James asked.

"No. It is not." Michael replied.  There is another law called the Davis-Bacon Act that dictates the hourly wage rate for laborers and mechanics work performed on federal site and/or on federally funded projects."

"What is the hourly rate for these people?"  James asked.

"It varies depending on the type of work they perform from $25 to $35 dollars an hour." Michael replied.  "The prevailing wage rates are published by the Air Force. They know them or should know them, since they include them as part of every construction Contract they let out to the public for bid."

"How do you know that the prison labor is subject to the prevailing wage rates?"

"I told you Jim, because of the Davis-Bacon Act that applies to construction and Executive Order No. 11755 in the Bureau of Prisons Rules and Regulations."

"What is the last one again?" James asked.

"Executive Order No. 11755 signed into law effective January 1, 1974 by Richard Nixon. It deals exclusively with Prison Labor and sets forth the guidelines under which it shall be utilized. I will read it to you. It is not very long, but it will give you an idea of the gross way the BOP has stretched the Order and is violating both the letter and the spirit of the law. The law had intended to provide meaningful employment for the inmates to develop skills and acquire knowledge to utilize productively when they got out. It has turned out that the Bureau of Prisons is exploiting the prisoners, utilizes pre-existing skills and does not pay the prisoners a fair wage. Let me read you the Order and you judge for yourself.

"The development of the occupational and educational skills of prison inmates is essential to their rehabilitation and to their ability to make an effective return to free society. Meaningful employment serves to develop those skills. It is also true, however, that care must be exercised to avoid either exploitation of convict labor or any unfair competition between convict labor and free labor in the production of goods and services. Under section 4082 of title 18 of the United States Code (this section), the Attorney General is empowered to authorize Federal Prisoners to work at paid employment during their terms of imprisonment under conditions that protect against both the exploitation of convict labor and unfair competition with free labor.

Rules:

The worker is paid or is in an approved work training program on a voluntary basis;

1. Such paid employment will not result in the displacement of employed workers, or be applied in skills, crafts, or trades in which there is a surplus of available gainful labor in the locality, or impair existing Contracts for services; and
2. The rates of pay and other conditions of employment will not be less than those paid or provided for work of a similar nature in the locality in which the work is being performed."

"Well, well well!" James exclaimed. What do you know. They've broken every Rule of that Order. Let's take for starters the inmates, between 300 and 400 that go on base going janitorial and custodial functions. Who do you think was doing the work before them? Private contractors." James answered his own question. "Private contractors that are now out of work."

"I can tell you the construction jobs." Michael said. "At Camp and on Base, are supposed to go out to bid. Qualified low bidder is then selected to do the work. However, with a government estimate utilizing 12 cents an hour for labor rates, no contractor has a chance because he has to pay his workers $25 to $35 dollars an hour, because he has to comply with the Davis-Bacon Act which is part of the Contract. If the private contractor is required to comply with the law, why not the government? The Department of Justice through their arm UNI-COR why do they feel that they are not required to comply?"

"I agree." James said. "It seems to me the Department of Justice is exploiting the convict labor force and forces the free labor in an unfair competition with the convict labor, dictating labor rates that are unrealistic and illegal."

"Now calm down James." Michael said. "You've got to give them some credit for trying to get around the law. For example, I remember before I started work, the BOP had me sign a form stating that I volunteered for the work. Now that same form among other things had the range of 10 cents to 40 cents an hour rate I agreed to be paid and by signing the form I endorsed the pay scale. I was also told that if I refused to sign the form, I could not work and if I was not working, I was going to be shipped to a higher security facility. So my signing the form under that kind of Duress, makes my concurrence with the contents of the form null and void."

"I didn't know Duress vacates an agreement?" James said.

"You better believe it. Particularly, in a case where you are captive and do not have a choice."

"Well, I will be damned." James exclaimed, waiving at a prisoner across the sidewalk from the gazebo.

"Who is that?" Michael asked of the balding, white haired stooping inmate with an extraordinary nose, like a hook at the end of his face. "He looks Jewish."

"That's Alan Hirsh." James continued. "I didn't think he was going to show his face back here again."

"What did he do?"

"What he is in for, is not important. I think he was a New York lawyer who moved West and was doing some development out of LA when he got in trouble over some deal with the government. So, he came here about a year ago and was making the rounds every few days from room to room. He was in our room for a day or so, until we 'coped him out'. As a matter of fact he was sleeping in the same bed you will be sleeping. Anyway, we signed a piece of paper to get him out of our room and the BOP transferred him to a room upstairs. I guess his new roommates on the second floor must have been saints because he stayed with them for a long time."

"What happened then?" Michael asked impatiently.

"I am getting there," James said, "hold your horses. One Friday night, just before the ten o'clock count, he came to the bathroom. There were about 4 or 5   people in at the time.  He went to the utility sink, by-passing two vacant urinals on the way and pissed in it."

"What?" Michael yelled. "He pissed in the sink?"

"That's what I told you." James continued. "The people who witnessed the incident were speechless. Alan shakes it, zips up and he is on his way out as another young fellow 6'-3" two hundred fifty pounds with tattoos up and down his arms and torso is coming with a load of pots and dishes to wash in the utility sink after the dinner he had with his biker friends."

"Don't use that sink!" Everyone yells at him. "Allan just pissed in it."

"What's the big deal?" Alan says without thinking. "I've been pissing in that sink for over a month now."

"The biker drops his tapper ware on the floor and tears after Alan, who is running down the hallway for his life.  He gets out of the building through the emergency fire exit and heads for the lieutenant's office in the building next door.  There he explains to the lieutenant the purpose of his visit. The lieutenant does not give a shit whether Alan lives or dies, but she has to protect the BOP from a potential lawsuit, so she tells Alan that they will put him in protective custody and move him to another location.  Now remember, Alan had been in and out of just about every Camp in the country and believed he had found a home here and does not want to move.  Also his choices are slim because he is 'persona non grata' in all the other Camps he's been in and has run out of safe haven. So he refuses to submit to protective custody and refuses to sign a disclaimer releasing the BOP from the responsibility and liability if something unpleasant happens to him by irate inmates.  Alan goes back to his room under escort to lay low for a few days, only to find that his belongings were taken and dumped in the same sink he pissed in and they felt awfully damp. So, the hacks take him out of his room and give him a bed by himself in the orientation room.  But by early morning the BOP has determined it was too expensive to be guarding him around the clock, so they rolled him up at dawn's early light for the North Las Vegas County Jail, until things cooled off a bit at home."

"That's why every time they call Alan's name at mail call, someone pipes in that he left for a piss," Michael smiled, "or he is pissed off or all sorts of other piss jokes."

"I guess the BOP believes that the memory of the inmates is that of a flash bulb, so here he is back in town after a week's worth of vacation at the County Jail."

There was a big commotion as the lunch wagon appeared from the Mess Hall.  A possession of three inmates dressed in white were pushing the trolley with a guard in tow, followed by inmates heading towards the Education Building gazebo where Jim and Mike were sitting.

"We better get out of the way, before we get trampled."  James suggested as Michael on cue got up and was lining up for lunch.

Lunch consisted of pre-made sack type lunch.  Identical to the ones handed out on Base.  Every day the same.  Turkey meat, a piece of fruit, two slices of bread and a soda.  Some sacks had mayo, others mustard, most had neither.  Once in a while, some sacks had a small bag of potato chips.  More than not the lunches were missing items.  One thing someone could always count, they were the same every day.  Michael got his lunch bag.  Reached for the fruit and soda and tossed the rest in the trash can that was already overflowing with rejects.

"Come by the room during lunch so you can meet the rest of the gang." James said.

"I will be there in half an hour or so."  Michael replied.  "I want to eat lunch with my homies."

James headed back to the building using the entrance by the Mess Hall, while Michael stayed on the path by the park and headed to the same building by the A&O entrance.  His homies were busy cutting up jalopenios, dicing garlic and slicing fat slices from a Walla - Walla onion. The smell in the room was pungent.

"Hey, what's happening?" Michael said kicking the door shut. "Don't you guys like the Prison lunch fare?"

"We love it bud," Randy said, tears streaming from his face on account of the onion, "we just try to give it a little more kick and spice."

Michael wolfed down his apple, tossed the core in the trash can with a skyhook, popped open the soda and exited in one slow motion for Room 113 down the hall. He was getting into the bowels of the building down the long corridor walking slowly soaking the ambiance and squalor, reading the numbers outside the  rooms. He stopped in front of 113. Either side of it were rooms filled entirely with blacks. They were loud, but he could not make out whether they spoke English or some other language. He leaned towards English because each sentence was being punctuated alternatively by "fuck you" or "motherfucker". He knocked on the door and an old sounding voice asked him to come in. He knocked again just to make sure over the din of the stereo. The same voice, this time sounding like it came from a cellar, told him to come in. The door knob was broken, there was no latch and the knob was freewheeling.

"Hi!  You must be Michael." A bearded old man stopped fussing with a lower bunk and arranging his shoes in a row, long enough to shake his hand. "Sorry, James just stepped out." He continued darting glances towards the door and out the window, like a trapped animal. His behavior was making Michael nervous. The man was behaving like he got interrupted from doing something illegal and was trying to dispel the suspicions by hopping around making busy talk and superfluous movements. He projected negative non verbal communications, but again you can't judge a book by its cover, Michael thought.

"Oh! Silly me." The old man said. "I forgot to introduce myself. I am Ron. James roommate. I will be your bunky." He blushed. "Of course that is if you decide to join us. You've got to excuse the noise. It gets awful sometimes at lunch. You know these niggers try to win an argument by seeing who will be the loudest. I think it is some kind of a contest for them. Don't you find them appalling?"

"On the contrary." Michael said. "I find them very educational."

"Educational? I've heard them being called all sorts of names, but educational? How's that?"

"Well, I never imagined a simple word like 'motherfucker' has so many meanings." Michael said with as serious expression on his face as he could muster.

Mississippi one, Mississippi two, Mississippi three...

Ron broke out in a toothy grin and wheezing laughter. If I was director, Michael thought, I would cast him as Fagan on Oliver Twist, leading his band of merry little thieves in song and dance.

"I will come back later." Michael said looking at his watch. "I've got to take care of a few things before I head back to work."

A sigh of relief inaudibly came out of Ron's lips as his behavior and mannerisms were heading back to normal. Strange bird, Michael thought. I wonder what he is hiding or what was he doing just before I knocked. Whatever it was, it was hastily thrown under the pillow or the folded blanket at the foot of the bed. He made his way towards the central bathroom. What a shit hole he thought as he was passing by the bathroom open door. His nose was assaulted by combination smell of feces, urine, vomit and stale tuna fish from a can that had to have been spilled on the floor, several lunches ago.

"James!" He was able to barely able to shout to the charging figure outside a stall, making his way out the door hastily without bothering to wash his hands.

"Oh! High Mike. Long time no see." James continued in a playful tone of voice. "Boy, I wouldn't wish that on my worst enemy."

"What's that?" Michael asked full of curiosity.

"I try to take a dump after lunch. I go to the bathroom at the end of the hall. No go. All the stalls are taken. I dance around a bit. I look at the urinals longingly. I look at the sink. No way. Look what it got Allan. I am thinking; it got to be the central bathroom or I am going to shit my pants. Boy, when I first got in, I thought the smell alone would make my lunch come out. Besides I think I twisted my knee on a chunk of rotting tuna. I don't know Mike. I pride myself being an open minded man. But seeing how these blacks live, close up, I am afraid they have turned me into a prejudiced man. By the way, were you looking for me? Let's go for a minute to the washroom by the building wing, so I can wash up. Did you see our room? Meet any of the roommates?"

"I met Ron." Michael replied opening the bathroom door.

"Oh! Good. What did you think of him?"

"He seemed all right, but I don't know whether he liked me. I got the feeling I was making him nervous or something."

"Don't think nothing of it Mike. It was not you. It was this damn stock market of his."

"What stock market is that James?

"Oh! You know, a bunch of fools got together and they invest in the stock market and are going in and out of it. I don't know all the particulars, but one of them spends his time in front of the television watching the ticker tape. Another makes calls on the floor to someone. I believe Ron keeps track of the transactions and plots the market performance. They try to get out so they don't hold paper overnight. That way, they believe the BOP cannot trace them. Ron believes that he can track different market indicators, so he is able to predict whether the markets will go up or down or remain relatively unchanged. He is an old fool, but you know everyone got to have a hobby in jail to justify his time here. You are writing a book. Ron is playing the stock market. I read all the books I was too busy to read on the outside. In case you have not noticed, I read 3 or 4 books a week." James said beaming proudly at the accomplishment.  "You probably caught Ron in the middle of something and he was behaving like he was caught with his pants down by a busload of schoolgirls. What are your feelings, now that you know what he was doing?"

"Let me put this way James.  I wouldn't intentionally do things that are illegal or against the rules of the BOP.  At the same time, I don't criticize others who do, as long as they don't cause harm to other people and they don't involve me, in some way, in their schemes.  If I was asked to actively cover up for them, I would refuse and would resent the fact that they've placed me in harms way by asking.  Does this answer your question?"

"Perfectly."  James said.  "I like a man who has made up his mind over issues and is not squeamish to speak his mind.  I think we will get along fine.  It's actually up to you.  Bill and Harry will go along with everything we say.  They are a little younger and look up to us wise old men.  Anyway, they don't stay in the room that much.  They work on Base and spend most of their time on Base, including weekends."

"Why are they such working fools?"  Michael asked.

"I don't think it's work that keeps them away.  But I've already said more than I should.  After you get to know them, ask them.  They may tell you.  It will suffice for me to say that the reason they spend so much time on Base is on account of the fringe benefits."

"You are a total of four in the room."  Michael said quickly.  "What happened?  How come you guys have two vacancies?  Isn't this a bit unusual?

"I know." James said as he started walking towards the building gazebo.  That's what got us worried.  Next shipment of fresh meat and I am sure we will get our share.  As for the reason that we have two vacancies, it's a sad story, which also taught us a lesson.  And that is to take charge in deciding who comes to our room, rather than leaving it up to the BOP to decide."

"Well?" Michael said. "You started it. What's the sad story?"

"We had Victor. A fellow put in our room by the BOP. Things have not been quite the same ever since Victor came to our room. He was in for telemarketing. I think he was part of the gang that your bunky belonged. The "say no to drugs" outfit. Well Victor was a bit loud and he loved to play practical jokes. That's not necessary a bad thing; it breaks the monotony you know, and gives us an opportunity to laugh. But everything in moderation, like your Greek ancestors used to say. Well, Victor did not understand that word, moderation. Consequently, the frequency and the severity of the pranks started to get on our nerves. We tried talking to the guy, no go. We tried getting even and playing pranks on him, even ganging up on him, he loved it. We were only encouraging his delinquency."

"Come on." Michael interrupted. "You must be exaggerating. A joke here and there never hurts anyone. Like what was he doing, that was so terrible?"

"I will tell you. After Victor came, no one dared to be in the vicinity of the two closets. If you needed something, you first had to check Victor's location in relationship to yours. Better yet, it was prudent to wait until Victor left the room, in order to get something out of your closet. Because Victor would shove you in and lock the closet from the outside. He did that to Ron one time and had poor Ron in tears begging after the missed lunch and the stand up four o'clock count was approaching. If you had a visitor coming, watch out. Victor would steal your card and show up in your place, telling a frightened wife that you've been rolled up. I could go on and on, but you get the flavor. Our belongings were not safe. He would take your left sneaker and exchange it with another one of the same type and size, but right foot from a room down the hall. So, both inmates would be left with two left or two right shoes. And you found that out, just before you were set to go to play tennis. Speaking of the work clothes, that was where he really excelled in imagination. He would take work boots, that looked alike anyway, and pull tricks in exchanging size or left and right shoe.  Poor Ron, he woke  up each morning to go to work and there would be a different surprise waiting for him. He thought he was having an Alzheimer's episode, which Victor was fueling.  Anyway, back to our original story, before we got sidetracked. We had then one bed left, because Don at the Department of Education 'coped out' to leave.  Have you met Don?  We used to call him 'mad dog'."

"You mean the guy who looks like 'curly' of the three stooges?" Michael smiled.

"Yeah!  That's the one.  He left us because he got tired of being locked up in the closet too many times.  So, we had a bunk open for a long time. So, one day, this kid walks in with a bed roll.  Straight out of juvenile hall, scared to death after a long bus ride in shackles, curtesy of the BOP.  We introduce ourselves.  He introduces himself.  He settled a bit.  Victor was in his best behavior for a change.  So, the kid decides to take a quick shower before dinner, to wash the road grime.  Victor showed him the nigger showers from the bathroom I just got out of, you know no doors only plastic curtains.  So the kid starts taking a shower.  Victor gets in his prank mood.  Takes off his clothes and walks in on the kid in the shower saying: "Honey I am home".  The kid looks at him.  Falls on the shower floor.  Starts shaking and goes catatonic on Victor.  Victor shakes him. Pats him. Apologizes up and down. Starts crying...Nothing. The kid slips into a coma and thats how the hospital staff found him and got him out of there on a stretcher.  It appears that the poor kid was gang rapped in the Juvenile Home and they brought him into the Camp for his own protection.  He didn't know any better.  Who knows, all sorts of rumors circulate in these Juvenile Homes.  The poor kid thought he was going from the fry pan into the fire.  Seeing Victor like that brought back all things he was trying to forget and the mind mercifully disconnected."

"What happened to Victor?" Michael asked.

"Oh! He got rolled up that same night. He spent a few days and nights locked up in the North Las Vegas County jail where they put you in a room with thirty other guys. No beds, no clothes, no towels, just a roll of toilet paper every day that serves as your pillow at night when you sleep on the floor and whatever other uses that you feel are necessary. I've never heard what ultimately happened to Victor or the kid. Probably at some Camp in Texas for Victor and the nut house in St. Lewis for the kid. But this is only a guess on my part."

Michael looked at his watch. It was 11:55 AM.

"What do we do for an encore in the afternoon?" He asked James.

"Nothing." Replied James Dean. "We are done for the day. Except we cannot display idleness, because the cops will find something else for us to do. So, what we do, is start again from one end of the Camp and walk slowly towards each building gazebo. There we stop in each one. You smoke your pipe as you are allowed to do under the BOP regulations, and I watch you smoke, because we are involved in a two men job. No one expects me to do work by myself. Then when you finish, we go to the next gazebo and repeat the procedure. By the time we reach the Education Building gazebo, it will be close to 2:00 PM and we can go home for the day."

"Tough day." Sneered Michael.

"Remember what I told you." Repeated James. "We pretend to work and they pretend to pay us. It washes out in the long run. Anyway, it will work out well for you today. Isn't it your shopping day?"

"You know James, I haven't figured out yet how does it work with the shopping here?

"It used to be that we could walk in the Air Force PX anytime we wanted. Buy what we wanted. Present our card at the cashier and she would deduct the total of our purchases from our total. You know, I didn't need anything, but I went shopping anyway, because it reminded me of the outside. I felt human somehow. I guess the BOP did not like the system of the Air Force making a profit, so they changed it. We now shop at a different building called the Commissary, owned by the BOP. Since the BOP runs it, naturally they shrunk the inventory. They shortened the hours and raised the price of everything. We no longer are able to shop every day, but once a week on the day corresponding to the last number of your inmate number, you are allowed to shop 2:30 PM to 5:30 PM. We are no longer free to peruse the merchandise. They have a list of the inventory available. You mark your choices  and the number of each item desired and you give it to the clerk at the window. Then, you wait outside for an hour or so, until they call your name and hand you your purchases and have you sign a receipt so that it may be deducted from your account. They took the fun out of it."

"Well, I don't want to waste my money in groceries, candy and other junk food." Michael said. "Just the bare necessities of personal hygiene, stamps and maybe some soda."

"You couldn't buy any quantity you wanted, anyhow." James continued. "They have put a limit on the amount of money you can spend per month. I think they recently raised it to $165.00."

"I don't know James. This may be a good idea, in addition to being consistent with their guidelines of equality. Otherwise, you would have well to do prisoners buying their way into everything."

"Bull pucky. You can still buy yourself into everything here. Look at you. I believe you've hired a house boy to wash and iron your clothes so you don't have to hassle in line. You hired another to make your bed and clean your side of the room. So, don't give me the equality speech. When you decide to step up into construction you will be making 40 cents an hour and $400 dollars a month in bonus, under the table and all sorts of other fringe benefits like shopping at the PX instead of the Commissary, eating at the Officers clubs on Base instead of waiting in line here at the Camp, two boxes of Cuban cigars a month caught on the borders, and who knows what other freebies.  You will be the richest man on campus according to Dino and whenever you speak everyone will listen.  With the bodyguards provided by the mob, you are untouchable.  Have you seen anyone coming close to us all day?  The word is out. You are a 'Man of Respect'.  That's why we want you in our room.  Who is doing your laundry anyway?"

"Jason something...I don't know his last name..."

"What does he look like?"

"A little taller than me, young looking, slim, blond, blue eyes, crew cut.."

"You describe someone from those white supremacy groups here."

"Now that you mentioned it James, he looks a lot like Timothy McVeigh. You know the one arrested for the Oklahoma City bombing."

"I think I know who you are talking about.  He plays a lot of tennis.  Yeah! When he looses a point, he slams his racket to the ground."

Michael filed that last comment and vowed never to loan his tennis racket to Jason.

"I am glad you said arrested, and not guilty." James continued.  "You've been here a couple of weeks and you are learning already not to believe everything you read and hear."

"Well, I don't know about that James.  I will call it an unconscious 'lapsus linque', slip of the tongue, then anything else.  If McVeigh did not do it himself alone, he is somehow linked into it."

"How do you figure?"

"The truck rental.  He is tied into the vehicle that detonated and caused the blast which destroyed the building."

"OK. You are an engineer. Now tell me, how can a vehicle that is parked on the street next to the building can cause such structural damage. You've seen the pictures.  The whole face of the building, forty feet in, was gone.  The concrete floors were brought down like a stack of pancakes and disintegrated. How can that be?"

"It all depends on the size and direction of the blast.  I grant you, the vehicle was a Ryder truck van, so the blast was multidirectional. But you can pack an awful lot of explosive in the larger size truck vans."

"OK.  Let's assume you are correct.  They loaded the truck and caused the damage eight stories high?"  James asked.  "Now from the engineering stand point when you have an action, the blast upwards, you must have an equal reaction, the blast downwards.  How big of a crater did it create?  Think about it and compare it with the World Trade Center blast that travelled down the garage; how many concrete stories?  What do you say about that?  Was the crater deep enough to justify the upward force of destruction?"

Michael remained silent.  He had a problem justifying it in his mind.  The size of the crater and the upward damage were indeed inequitable.

"Let me give you some more food for thought.  The truck is parked on the street next to the federal building.  You got the width of the street which is open ground and another building across the street. Forgetting for a moment the crater size and concentrating on the upward blast force and destruction done to the federal building, what do you think should happen to the building across the street, that  by the way is constructed entirely of glass?  Don't you think that the explosion would take a few of their floors also?"

"I believe so."  Michael said thoughtfully.  "If it was steel and glass, it would have suffered equal or greater damage than the federal building.  What happened to that building?  Do you know?"

"Would it surprise you that the other building, other than a few broken windows, it sustained no structural damage.  Not a single bent beam or column, while the federal building structural members looked like pretzels."

Michael was stunned and stopped in his tracks.

"What are you getting at James?  Are you trying to tell me that the crater was consistent with an explosion magnitude suffered by the building across the street?  If that's the case, what caused the damage to the federal building?"

"A second explosion."  James interrupted.  "Just about every witness recalled a second explosion a second or two after the first one.  The government officials called it a reflective echo of the first explosion.  That's a bunch of bull.  The distance between the truck and the building was such that it precluded occurrence of this phenomenon."

"What do you think then?"  Michael said.  "A second bomb inside the building?"

"That's exactly what I am saying.  McVeigh and their friends were nothing more than convenient patsies.  Manipulated to do what they did by the government."

"Hold on, James."  Michael exploded.  "Are you telling me that the second bomb was set and detonated by the government?"

"Who else?"  James said.  "Look at the results.  None of the 168 people killed were government agents or real insiders of the government structure.  They were mostly civilians trying to cash their social security checks.  The FBI and the Tobacco and Fire Arms agencies, including the DEA, moved out of the building the day before.  How convenient, don't you think?  Also picking the date.  The WACO anniversary.  A masterstroke of misdirect."

"What did the government have to gain by doing this?" Michael asked.

"The passage of the Anti-Crime Bill which was stalled and going no where.  Tougher gun controls and greater police state.  The government wanted more control.  Terrorized the people, who gladly traded less freedom for greater sense of security.  Mike, Mike.  For a smart person like yourself, you are politically naive."

"I don't know James. All these things. They are very disturbing. In any case, I believe that I will watch the proceedings of the trial with a different prospective. You are a dangerous man, though. You played me like a fiddle. Instead of preaching to me, you asked the right questions and asked me to explain the inconsistencies." Michael said, slapping playfully James on his back. "I wonder what the jury will think. I don't know, but if I was on the jury, unless the government provided answers, I would not convict the fellow. You've raised more than reasonable doubt."

"That's why you are in jail, Mike." James said with a twinkle in his eye. "The government does not want people like you sitting on a jury and asking questions."

# CHAPTER 13

## Red Flag

Bip, Bip...BIP, BIP! Michael finally found the button, after several attempts of thrashing around and slapping at all directions, cautiously searching, instinctively drawn to the annoying BIPing noise from the alarm clock. He grabbed it and looked at it. Five o'clock in the morning. Sleep, snooze or get up. These were the choices. Am I working here at Camp or on Base? What day is it? He smiled wryly remembering a movie he'd seen a year or so ago called Groundhogs Day. Every day was a Groundhogs Day at the prison Camp. He shook the sleep and made his way down from the upper bunk. He used the ladder this time, hurting on the way down the bottom of his feet where they met the round metal rungs. Where did this ladder come from? He remembered moving from his old room to a new room with the older roommates. The gasping for breath, the snoring and the chocking noises were definitely different from the farting stereo sounds of his old room. Apnea, the scourge of the old and out of shape haunted him to the showers where he resolved to start walking around the track five miles a day starting today.

The weather started getting colder outside and darker each morning. The Air Force busses were parked in a row waiting to be loaded with four hundred inmates for the daily trip to the Base. Michael started recognizing a few faces, nodding hellos and good mornings. At 6:30 AM on the dot, a security officer arrived calling out job assignments alphabetically. The mass of inmates moved towards the BOP policeman listening, while others moved towards a waiting bus anticipating that it would correspond to the right job assignment.

The prisoners whose job assignment was called, boarded the first bus giving the cop their name at the bus entrance. He, in turn was checking it off the call out list  that he was holding.  As soon as the first bus was full, the security officer signaled the airman driver to close the door and the bus was set in motion for the twenty minute journey to the Base.

Michael positioned himself in front of the fourth bus anticipating the call from the officer.  He looked around at his fellow inmates trying to guess which ones were in the same job assignment.

"Red Flag!  Red Flag!"  The security officer yelled at the top of his lungs.

Six inmates moved towards the bus entrance.  Michael followed close behind.  He gave his name to the cop, he waited until his name was checked off on the call out sheet, went up the steps of the fifties vintage bus and walked towards the back to join his co-workers.  Their faces were glum; at least the ones who were awake.  A couple dozed off with their heads resting on the grimy bus windows.  He found an open window seat towards the middle of the bus and sat down looking outside at the remaining inmates.

"Transportation!  Transportation!"  The officer yelled next.

"Am I glad I am not assigned to that."  Someone whispered in the seat behind him, as a dozen or more inmates moved towards the bus entrance.

Michael turned in his seat and came face to face with a smiling oriental.

"Are you from Hawaii?"  Michael asked.

"Right on!"  The oriental answered.  "I've heard of you, you are from Hawaii also.  My name is Rodney Shido."

Michael told him his name and shook the proffered hand.  He released the handshake, got up and moved back sitting himself next to him.

"From which island are you bra?"  Rodney asked.

"Oahu. You?"

"Same, I lived in Kaimuki."

"No kidding!" Michael said startled. "Small world, so was I. Maunalani Heights." "Oh! The high rent district." Rodney smiled good naturally.

"So, you work at Red Flag." Michael said to keep the conversation going. "How is it?"

"You know…not good. But not as bad as transportation."

"Why is that?"

"From the name of it, you'd think it's driving vehicles. Well, I got news for you. It's actually washing the vehicles. These poor bastards would end up in a parking lot the size of Ala Moana and start washing military busses, and every other type of Air Force vehicle for on and off road use."

Michael looked at the bus entrance. It's been close to three minutes now and no new inmate had made it to the bus. The security officer was examining pink slips, marking something in his call out papers and handing the slip back to the inmate who was leaving the ranks on his way back to the Camp.

"What's happening out there?" He asked Rodney.

"Medical slips." Rodney said laughing. "As soon as an inmate finds his name on a job assignment that's the shits, he immediately equips himself with a medical pink slip excusing him. I wonder how many of the twenty will actually make it to the Base."

"Well, they pretend paying us;" Michael said, "and we pretend to be working."

"That's a good one." Rodney said with a toothy grin. "I haven't heard that before, and I've been here for sometime…"

"It's not an original." Michael corrected. "One of my roommates told me that the other day. How long you've been here already?"

"I've been here three months already, but I've been down for over a year." "Been down?" Michael repeated.

"Yeah man! I meant the total time I've served in the system already. 'Been down'. That's prison lingo for the same thing. See he said," pointing at the prisoners who had just entered the bus. "I told you, three out of twenty. Par for the course."

"Where were you before coming here?" Michael kept on the same topic.

"Lompoc."

"That's where I almost went." Michael said.

"Good thing you didn't." Rodney said. "I was sick while I was there most of the time. It's damp and cold. You wouldn't have liked it a bit. It rains all the time and the rain is not warm like in Hawaii. My clothes were damp, the bed sheets were damp, even the toilet paper was damp."

"What's Red Flag like?" Michael interrupted.

"It's a two story building, sprawled on a ten acre lot made up of hundreds of offices and cubicles. It also includes three hangers across the street. One for the U.S., one for the Allied Forces and the third for the Adversaries."

"Adversaries? What Adversaries?"

"The Russians, I think. Let me explain. Red Flag is like the...Have you seen the movie Top Gun?"

Michael nodded.

"See it's just like that. Red Flag is the Top Gun program for the Air Force. They come here from all over the world; all the hot shot pilots and have dog fights during the day. Watch themselves on film during the afternoon over pupu's and beer, pump each other up and go to town to gamble, pick-up women and party. It's the Air Force version of the ironman, the three F's."

"The three F's?"

"Fly, Fuck and Float away in booze. It only lasts for a week and it is good PR for the Air Force and the Allies, when they get invited."

The bus brakes hissed as it came to a stop by the old parking lot gazebo where inmates from the previous busses were milling around waiting for their ride to the work destination. Air Force task sergeants were circulating armed with inmate picture I.D. cards, trying to identify their wards and direct them to the right van that was idling nearby. It was a human zoo.

Michael saw immediately the van with the Red Flag insignia and decided to cut through the chase, by climbing on board. One by one the inmates were rounded up leaving in the parking lot the ones destined for the 'Housing' pickings. A black  man, clean cut with a crew cut and glasses was the last one on board, plopping himself next to Michael.

"How do ma man?" He slapped Michael's shoulder.

"What did you say?" Michael inquired.

"Shit motherfucker. You didn't eat pussy last night or something?"

Michael looked at him silently. One of those days, he thought, before I get out of jail, I will master all the meanings of the word 'motherfucker'. The black man smiled widely.

"You are fine, whitey. You all right. I am Otis. You shouldn't have any trouble remembering my name. You rode enough times in them up and down the fancy buildings."

"I am Michael." He said as he shook the proffered hand and then hit the fist and got hit by the black one. "Does this make me a bee-bop brother now?" Michael inquired with a smile.

"No. But it may get you a cushy job at the Red Flag." Otis said grinning, exposing an enormous set of gleaming white teeth.

"What did you do on the outside Otis ma man?  You look like a government employee to me."

"How did you know?" Otis asked.

"I was just fucking with you.  Shot in the dark."  Michael replied.  "No kidding though, government employee and all, what brings you here?"

"The Post Office...I was a mailman.  The Post Office accused me of stealing...no correction, of thinking and planning of stealing a $115.00 welfare check.  They took me to trial and by the time they were through, they had me convinced that I done it.  Shit, if I was on the jury and saw a sorry ass nigger like myself and heard the government, I would have voted to take that motherfucker and lock up his sorry ass away."

"Hold it Otis. Did you actually steal the welfare check?"

"No.  The government said I didn't, because they caught me just in time before I stole it."

"How can that be? Who was the damaged party? You cannot go around accusing people on intend."

"There you go, Mike.  That's what I thought before the trial.  That's why I didn't accept their plea bargain offer.  I thought. I didn't steal anything. I am not doing to admit something I didn't do.  Wrong.  The government can use two witnesses saying that they heard me telling them that I was planning to steal something and it is the same as if I stole it.  It's called 'Conspiracy with Intent'.  That was not hard to prove in court.  The government had a lot of witnesses to pick from.  You see in the Post Office we have got a program..."

"I know." Michael cut in. "Dollars for Collars."

"You know."  Otis looked at Michael thoughtfully smoothing his mustache.  "Well, this program, money for turning in your co-workers has turned the Post Offices into cheese factories. I feel like taking an M-16 when I get out of here and going on a 'Rat' shootout."

"Hold on there." Michael tried to calm Otis down because he got that certain faraway look on his face experiencing the taste of an upcoming massacre. "I heard of disgruntled postal employees before, Otis, but you are a time bomb ready to go off at any second. Calm down. Revenge is a cold dish, as they say in my country."

"Oh, yeah, I've been meaning to ask you Mike," Otis said coming back from the distant planet he was visiting, "where are you from? I detect an accent and was wondering."

"I come from Hawaii, but I was born in Greece. So, take your pick. Probably, Hawaiian with a Greek accent. Where are you from?"

"Phoenix. Born and raised there."

"What do you do at the Red Flag?"

"Emptying trash cans. But I am getting tired of it. You have to walk inside every office and every bathroom and empty the waste paper baskets. I think I like to get the job of sweeping the hallways. The guy who was doing the job got out the other day, so there is an opening. See, I like a job where no one can hassle you. If the trash cans get full of trash, they know you have not been doing your job. But corridors and sweeping...they look clean already. No one will know if I swept them or not. See, I can find myself a room with a TV and watch till it's time to catch the bus back. I see a great future in trash for you Mike."

The bus was passing at that moment in front of the Thunderbirds hanger. Home of the Air Force air acrobatics team. The sliding doors were open and the mechanics were crawling all over the F-16 type airplanes; white with colorful tails of the mythical Indian bird. The stars and stripes was fluttering on the pole in front of the main building in the morning breeze. The sun was coming up on the horizon bathing the hanger in red and purple light. The airplanes were gleaming getting ready for their morning workout. The scene would have brought goosebumps, Michael thought, in another time. Now in prison he saw everything as an outside observer. The excitement was gone. He closed his eyes and the picture disappeared. When he re-opened them the mini van had moved on. Now, the only thing he could see out the window was the stretch of runway pavement and an F-14 testing its afterburners prior to take off. The van slowed down and turned right into a huge parking lot that was dwarfed by a rectangular two story building that was taking the better part of the parking lot. The crosshairs of a yellow target were painted on the side of the building centered on a fluttering red flag. The van pulled up in front of the main entrance to the building. The door was opened from the outside by a uniformed Air Force MP guard.

"Everyone out!" He shouted. "Single file to the front desk to register and be issued your security clearance badges."

The prisoners filed out of the van, Michael bringing the rear. A scale model of an F-16 was on display on the lawn, towards his left. He stepped on the gigantic rubber mat bearing the target sights and the red flag symbol and as he passed the crosshairs, the entrance doors slid open revealing a long hallway entrance. The security desk was to the left maned by two security officers. On the wall, across the security counter, maybe one hundred feet or more, there were displays of modern warfare dogfights taken from past Red Flag competitions. Behind the security counter there was an impressive array of several dozen security monitors which were scanning every conceivable corridor and common areas of the complex. The inmates signed on the register and exchanged their identification cards for security badges allowing them access to the building. A task sergeant was waiting for them at the end of the counter.

"Listen up!" He shouted. "We lost two guys and we got two replacements. I am not going to stay on your case, as you know; so, the old guard show the new guard the ropes. At noon we will lose another fellow and I understand his replacement will arrive with your lunch. Any questions?"

The inmates looked at each other in silence.

"OK. Dismissed. There is coffee in your lounge." He tailed off as the inmates turned right down a hallway the length of a football field.

Michael was assaulted by the sights and sounds in a place like he never encountered before in his life, while trying to keep up with his partners turning left and right down the infinite long hallways, through offices and partitions on a shortcut mission to the lounge set aside for the inmates. They finally reached a dead end side corridor with the only door that had no name on it other than the number 077. At the door the inmates looked right and saluted 'Hi Inge' and then turned left. Michael came to the door looked right and stopped; the words 'Hi Inge' frozen in his throat like the landscape he was looking. It was gigantic poster of an Icelandic frozen wilderness. Four F-16 airplanes were streaking the bright cloudless sky in formation with the afterburners on. At the bottom a Nordic beauty was laying naked on a bearskin looking up at the sky, fingering herself and saying: "The boys of the 57th Air Wing make me hot".

"So that's Inge." Michael whispered as he turned left.

The inmate lounge was a comfortable room 12 feet by 20 feet with two library type tables, a couch, TV and a dozen desk type executive arm chairs on casters. There was a telephone on one table with a computer connected to a monitoring console that looked like a support column in the middle of the room. Its scanner monitoring all sorts of signals relaying them to the war room.

"We've been tempted to order an air strike giving the Camp coordinates." Otis said to Michael who was examining all these new toys in the room.

"What do you say?" Otis continued. "You want to work with me this morning?"

"It depends on what you are doing." Michael answered cautiously.

"Trash detail. It's an hour job in the morning and half hour in the afternoon. Only you will have to do the afternoon rounds with a new guy, because I got a call out at noon."

"A call out?" Michael repeated. "What's that?"

"Oh! Nothing really. I got to go to the hospital and take a UA; that's a piss test. No big deal. They select at random, but all the time I've been there so far, all I saw was only brothers."

"Where do we start?" Michael asked. "I am going to get lost in this place."

"No. sweat. We first drink our coffee and read our paper. Then we go on the second floor and get our gear together. Don't look so worried. If you miss some offices, big deal, you get them on your way back. If the shredding machines get full, they will come find you, because those dummies don't know how to open them.

The building was relatively quiet when they had come in. By eight o'clock, the building was buzzing with activity. Military personnel were virtually running from office to office down the long hallways carrying top secret documents, computer discs and huge landscape topographic maps that were unfurling like flags. Otis and Michael jostled their way to an elevator which started ascending at glacial speed towards the second floor. Michael looked at the bottom elevator rail as the door opened.

"It's not an Otis brand." He heard behind him.

He turned and waived to his partner to lead the way to the equipment room. Otis turned left, then right and left again. He stopped in front of a door that had an electrical lightning symbol and a no trespassing sign.

He opened the double door and led the way. Inside, the electrical room housed a transformer and several motor control centers. The buss bar service to each unit was six to eight inches thick. A lot of juice. The humming and crackling of electrical circuitry was palpable in the room. Behind the transformer, Otis rolled out a barrel size plastic can on casters and a second three foot by five foot plastic clothes hamper on casters.

"Let's go around the corner to the closet and get ourselves some trash bags." Otis said pushing the two carts forward. "The way we will do it is as follows." He continued. "I go in first and pick up the trash bags from the waste baskets. You follow with the replacement liners. I fill a large trash bag and when full, I tie the top and dump it in your cart. Your cart will hold six bags. When it gets full, we go outside and dump them outside in the shredder room. It's eight o'clock now." He said looking at his watch. "Let's work straight through and we should be done by 9:30 AM."

The second floor consisted primarily of the engineering and the various satellite and signal tracking stations. Michael was feeling guilty because Otis was doing all the work. The Air Force engineers were extremely friendly as soon as they found out that Michael was a Chemical Engineer. They told him to quit picking trash because they wanted to demonstrate for him their latest toys. The security sector had a twelve man CIA contingent who actually let him operate a satellite camera. It was early evening in Europe and he was able to zero in Paris. He operated the close up to its maximum range and discovered that he could recognize fascial characteristics of people in Plaz Pigalle.

"That's nothing." A female operative told him. "Watch this!"

She took over the controls and centered the focus of the camera on one particular person. Followed him walking, stopping at the intersection, lifting his arm to see the time. The screen became the wrist with the watch magnified ten times. Michael was able to read the time including the watch brand.

Holly shit!  He thought.  Here he was at Nellis Air Force Base in Las Vegas, Nevada and he could read the time off a Parisian's wrist watch. Amazing.  At almost night also.

"Look at that." The CIA woman said switching to infrared.

The walls of the building into which the man they were focused on had walked in, became green transparencies and the people inside the building became negative images on film.  She pushed a button and a machine that looked like a copier, spit out instantly a picture of what the screen was showing as negative film.  Only the picture was not a negative, but looked like a regular black and white picture of the building, only without walls, the people inside exposed to whatever they were doing.  Michael thought that it looked like a giant doll house all opened up on the inside.  Only inside there were not doll figures but actual, real, people.   He was frightened suddenly by what he'd seen.  If the government can use this technology with impunity throughout the globe, what's stopping them turning the camera on its own citizens when a satellite crosses the United States or for that matter they may have a stationary satellite in the U.S. like the ones they got in Europe. Has technology made the right of privacy a moot point?  He smiled to hide his fear of what he'd seen and moved on to join up with Otis down the hallway.

"Come on man.  You are holding up the parade." Otis said as soon as Michael came within hearing range. "If you let them, these government fuck-ups will talk your ear off all day. They get paid either way. They got nothing to do because there are ten of them to do the job of one.  You are stroking their ego like there is no tomorrow. What's with you. That ugly bitch you were talking to...you haven't been down here that long. What the fuck is the percentage talking to them?"

"You learn so many things, Otis." Michael replied. "Aren't you interested in expanding your mind and experiences?"

"The only thing I wanna expand is a tight pussy." Otis said with a leer. "I don't give a fuck about her mind."

"Oh! man. What is your wife going to think?"

"I don't have a wife." Otis said. "As a matter of fact, I've never been married."

"What do you mean..." Michael hesitated. "I thought I heard you talking about your daughter."

"I did so. But who says you got to be married to have a daughter? Do you marry every piece of ass you had? Of course not. So, once in a while you have a child."

"But...but...with what sense of family would that child be raised? You cannot go around grazing, so to speak, around available women."

"I graze and if the bitch gets knocked up, I move on. I'm a traveling man and I travel alone."

"I don't know what to say, Otis. I raised my children trying to provide for them and instill security in their upbringing and stability. If everyone behaved like you  do, then children would be brought up by single mothers; or are they also the grazing type?"

"Some are. It's a free country."

"Then the children would be raised by sporadic, temporary father figures, just passing through; uncertain whether they would be around the next day."

They passed in front of the freight elevator and Otis pushed the button. The doors opened immediately. The elevator had not been used since they had come up. They settled in for the long trip down to the first floor.

"We did the easy part first." Otis said pointing to the half full hamper. "Downstairs...it's a different story. Stay close, because you will get lost."

Michael nodded.

"We will turn right and go through the Allied Forces Sector, then we will complete the Adversary Forces Sector. By then, your hamper will be full and we will go to the shredder room to get rid of the bags."

Michael nodded again and held the 'open' elevator button as soon as the door slid open to give time to Otis to maneuver both hamper and barrel out of the elevator. He then released the button and followed Otis as the elevator doors started closing.

They established a convoy and headed towards an area that resembled an airlines ticketing complex someone would encounter at a commercial airport. Behind the 'ticketing counters' there were three dimensional plexiglass screens with polar coordinates. They did not carry any information. The computers were not in use and the screens were replaying a geometric ellipsoidal figure ad infinitum. The waste paper baskets were clean with the exception of a few candy bar wrappers from a crew that had the Spanish flag insignia on their lapels.

"A German crew will be here tomorrow staying for a couple of weeks." Otis said passing the Spanish crew. "Training for the upcoming meet, Code named 'Gunsmoke."

On the left, they passed into the 'Red Sector'. There was a red enamel panel having Russian writing and crowned by a red star. The personnel were in  Russian uniforms and every sign, newspaper and magazine were in Russian. The language heard all around was Russian. The computers even were in cyrilic characters. This was the famous Adversary Tactics Sector, which at that time was on Red Alert in preparation for the 'Gun-smoke' meet in which all NATO countries were scheduled to participate. The activity was frantic. Michael was backing mesmerized by the giant screens showing MIGS in action, when he felt colliding with someone.

"I am sorry." He said automatically. He turned extending his hands and found himself in the arms of a plump, busty lady, wearing a beret and showing an extraordinary amount of cleavage.  She was carrying a mug of some kind of drink; it looked like tea judging from the color of the stain on her left tit, spreading and accenting a nipple the size of a walnut.

"Are you having a good time?" She asked with a throaty voice.

Two drops of tea were caught at the top of the ravine of her cleavage. The tea must have been heavy on sugar, because the gravity could not overcome the friction aided by the viscosity.  Her tits were milky white, with faint blue veins. Starting to wrinkle at the roots. More wrinkles on her neck. Great cock sucking lips. Large expressive grey eyes. Carefully plucked eyebrows and tuffs of grey blond hair spouting out of her beret with a red star.  Michael let his eyes plunge once more down the Grand Canyon of her cleavage, checked the progress of the spreading tea stain and quickly settled on the grey eyes.

"I am sorry. It's my first day on the job. I got carried away gawking at the screens." He said trying to put sincerity in his voice.

"That's OK." She said with a smile. "Are you new at the Camp or new at the Red Flag?"

"Both." Michael replied. "I am just off the boat as you may say.  Are you Russian?  Because I'd swear you look right out of the pages of a Dostoyevsky novel."

"How do you know? Have you met other Russians?"

"As a matter of fact I have.  Last Christmas in Atlanta, Georgia we had Christmas with a Russian family.  I believe my daughter's best friend at the University of Georgia is a Russian girl, whose family immigrated recently."

"So...you're married." She smiled coquettishly. "Are you still married or has she dumped you? Or it hasn't been that long yet?"

Michael threw his hands up.

"That's it!" He said. "What's with you women? I am a forty eight year old man in jail. What is it about me that has changed since I was outside? It seems every woman I meet inside is hitting on me. What do you have to say about it Natasha?"

"My name is not Natasha. Has anybody told you have the soulful eyes of a Russian?"

"No. They've told me I've got the bedroom eyes of a Greek. Because I am one."

"Oh! I knew it, you were from someplace hot and romantic. I've always wanted to visit the Greek islands. Do you go to church here in town?"

"You've got to be kidding. Look at me. I wear khakis. I am a prisoner. How could I go to town?"

"Well, you can petition the Chaplain at Camp, to file a request with the Warden. The Warden cannot refuse. Freedom of religion and all. I will be your escort."

"Really?" Michael's eyes opened up. "Are you sure about that? I can get a furlow to town to go to church?"

"Absolutely. On the grounds that they do not offer Orthodox Services on Base or the Camp. I will take you to town. Then I will take you home and give you an old fashioned Russian…lunch," she said with a wink, "and then I will bring you back at the Camp in time for the four o'clock count."

"Wow! Nat…, or whatever your name is; I am going to look into it."

"My name is Tatiana. But you can call me Teta."

More likely Tita; Michael was thinking, staring at her enormous breasts.

"OK! It's a date then. Let me know as soon as your request is approved. Pick a Holiday weekend for the first time. Let me see. Thanksgiving weekend is awfully  close. But you never know unless you try. The

Sunday before Christmas though is a natural.  Who will refuse a religious fur-low on Christmas?"

"Slow down Teta.  Let me go see the Chaplain first and we will talk about it."

She brushed by him rubbing her boobs on his chest and blowing her hot breath in his ear.  She slowly turned walking away and blew him a silent kiss swinging her rear in an exaggerated motion.

"Are you meeting her later in the closet?"  Otis whispered in Michael's ear trying to hold his laughter.

"Where did you come from?"  Michael asked looking around in a panic.

"Don't worry old buddy.  Your secret is safe with me.  Them turkeys all they can think right now is war games and strategic planning.  All the while you slicked yourself in that old lady's panties.  You silver tongue devil you."

"No.  You got it all wrong Otis.  She is a kind Russian lady who wants to be my escort so that I may be given community custody to go to church.  She wants to be my sponsor."

"All she is thinking is how to sponsor you to her bedroom.  I saw how she was looking at you.  If you think you are going to church; forget it.  You will be coming in her bedroom until you are dry or time to make the four o'clock count, whatever comes first."

"You grazing animal you.  That's all you can think of."  Michael said with a chuckle.  "However, for the record, she is the fifth or sixth lady hitting on me since I came to Camp and this is my second week.  This has never happened to me on the outside.  What has changed since I reported at the Camp?"

"Shit!  Modest too.  That's what happened buddy.  You are in the Camp. You are of excellent health otherwise you would not be here. You are a Chemical Engineer who had his own company.  They cannot take that away from you.  Your knowledge and experience.  You scored in the I.Q. off the charts at Processing.  This became common knowledge in the Camp before you cleared Processing.  Old Dianne wanted to fuck your brains while you were still in Processing.  They are drooling to make you an offer to head the Engineering and Construction Division.  Every inmate wants to be your friend.  You are a 'Man of Respect'.  I bet  your reputation has proceeded you on Base.  You think you bumped on the Russian bitch by chance?  She was waiting for you and made her move. I bet her tee in her mug was stone cold when she bumped into you.  You will do well inside and when you get out, the fact that you were down will be no more than a bump on the road.  I envy you and I wish I was in your shoes. End of discussion."

They made their way out of the hustle and bustle of the 'Adversary Tactics' group, towards the 'Friendlies' sector.  All the walls were full of dedication pictures showing dogfights, aerial acrobatics, vertical take offs, reverse dives, in flight refueling and other magnificent feats and formations.   The pictures were signed by Red Flag competition participants, government agencies, defense contractors engaged in the manufacture of the airplanes, parts and all others associated with the industry all over the world.  The pictures were dated going back to 1975.  It appeared that this Red Flag program was not very old. Definitely post Vietnam era.  The number of pictures and awards on display was mind boggling. Michael found himself lagging behind trying to read the inscriptions and messages.  Every conceivable flying machine, from the Red Baron's Biplane to the latest bomber and attack plane were on display, in action.

"At this rate, they will run out of wall space pretty soon."  Michael said pointing to the pictures.

"Never fear.  They are planning a duplicate building across the street." Otis replied.

They were passing in front of the auditorium where the sound of vacuuming could be heard behind the closed door. Michael stuck his head inside. Jeffrey, a telemarketer from San Diego, was standing behind a stationary vacuum while John, another telemarketer from Las Vegas, was holding the cord.

"You guys look like a couple of government employees." Michael said with a chuckle. "Men, keep up the good work. Your display of teamwork is exemplary." He closed the door quickly, because Jefrey was searching frantically in the waste basket for a missile to hurl at him.

"What's up?" Otis asked. "What about the trash in the amphitheater?"

"We will catch them later, on the way back." Michael said. "I don't think it's safe to go in there right this minute."

They turned the corner outside the mail room. They made their way inside the sorting cubicles occupied by female Air persons. Pale blue shirts and dark blue skirts. Sheer stockings and dark blue low heal shoes. Each one was swinging around their stools to let the two trash men pick up the plastic liner from their waste basket and replace it with a new one. They were quite aware that the salt and pepper team were prisoners from the Camp and they were spreading their legs a little wider than necessary to give them a glimpse of the forbidden fruit. The room was dizzying with the live video and the overpowering battle of perfumes. None was wearing pantyhose. Instead they had on the skimpiest see through lace underpants and garter belts. The two prisoners came out bent, reeling from all the sights and smells in the room.

"One of these days I'm gonna grab one of them bitches..." Otis said, breathing heavily.

"Look but don't touch. That should be their motto and they ought to hang it on top of the mailroom door." Michael added. "Talk about sexual harassment..."

"Did you see all them garter belts and lace panties?" Otis continued not wanting to get off the subject.

"Quit thinking about it.  Otherwise they win.  They were dressed that way to tease us and say: 'You cant have it'.  I think they were doing it on purpose and are now discussing our reaction.  Chuck it up to another government psychological torture."

"God damn!  That's mental cruelty." Otis continued.  "It's criminal to get a case of blue balls everyday you go to work."

"You can always put a cop-out for change of job."  Michael said.  "If it really bothers you."

"It doesn't bother me.  It gives me wet dreams at night of all the things I want to do to them bitches.  Right there in the mail room."

They finished their rounds uneventfully and headed towards the shredding room for a third and final time in the morning.

"It's only nine thirty."  Michael said.  "What do we do the rest of the morning?"

"I don't know about you." Otis said. "But I am going to find myself a quiet room and read the newspaper till chow time.  Then I am done for the day.   Don't forget now after lunch to empty the trash from the bathrooms and gym rooms and lockers.  They fill up during lunch.  Then I want you to tell me all about it when I see you at Camp." Otis added with a mischievous smile.

"What do you mean?" Michael asked.  "You know I hate surprises."

"You won't hate this one 'Mr. look and don't touch'."

On the way back, they stopped by the Officer's lounge and armed themselves with newspapers and magazines to combat the hours till 11:00 AM when their lunch would arrive.  Michael after reading the newspaper, decided to go out for a walk and smoke his pipe. He saw the sergeant at arms behind the security counter and asked whether he was allowed to go outside the building and grounds.

"Sure the sergeant replied. You got a badge on you. You can go anywhere on Base. Just make sure you get back here by 1:30 PM when the bus leaves to take you back to camp. Between you and me and the fence post, I wouldn't stop you if you wanted to walk outside the Base either."

"Right." Michael said. "How am I supposed to get back?"

"Twenty bucks at the gate gets you back in. Fifty bucks, we provide shuttle service."

"What about the BOP?" Michael asked in amazement.

"Fuck the BOP." The sergeant replied. "You are in a secure area. If they try to get in here, we will arrest them. This won't be the first time we arrested one of those low life's anyway."

"I will think about it and let you know." Michael replied, still in shock.

"Remember, you can go shopping also. As long as it is not against the law. Pay attention to the Air Force law, not the BOP Camp law. We also deliver at your Camp for a 10% surcharge. You don't have to suffer because you are in prison. Not in this prison anyway. Just stay away from things that would give you away in a piss test or a breathalyzer."

Michael fingered his badge to make sure it was still on and started walking towards the door.

"Have fun now, you hear!" The sergeant's voice boomed behind him. "Don't do now anything I wouldn't do."

Michael stepped on the Red Flag sign in front of the double sliding door and the panels parted aside with a loud his. He looked up. The sky was bright blue without a cloud in sight. The morning chill gave way to the midmorning sun. He was glad he left his jacket in the lounge. The fresh air, the smell, reminded him of his childhood in Greece.  It felt like late Spring weather, although he knew it was the early part of Fall.

He crossed the main drag and visited the first hanger on his right.  Inside there were two F-14 airplanes taken literally apart by Air Force crews.  A fellow inmate was inside the hanger leaning on his broom, watching the commotion.  Michael waved at the inmate, who waved back.  He did not know his name; he saw him around Camp and remembered that he was a Mexican 'mule', caught on the wrong side of the border.

"Que pasa cholo?"  He yelled across the hanger.

"Bien, bien, Patron."  The Mexican answered respectfully.

Michael walked out of the hanger into the bright sun.  On his right, an F-16 was taxing for take off.  He started walking towards the airplane.  He could see the housing development across the airfield, climbing and sprawling on the foothills.  He thought of all the frustrated military wives on the backyards getting drunk out of boredom and frustration.  He was wondering what the inmates on the 'Housing' detail were doing right now.  He set his left foot on the low tarmac dividing wall and watched the line up of the fighting birds, slow moving, shimmering in the heat and exhaust.  Between the reflection of the runway and the slow dancing heat waves, he thought he was watching a mirage.

He looked to his left towards another hanger.  He saw a group of Airmen in flight suits coming out of a single door holding trays with hamburgers, french fries and sodas.  They moved towards the patio and settled among the plastic white patio tables and chairs.  He noticed a lone khaki clad figure sitting at one end of the lanai, amongst the steel grey and blue clad Airmen.  He walked stealthily keeping close to the hanger until he was almost on top of him.  His shadow announced his approach, followed by a coughing and chocking spell of the inmate who tried to stuff in his mouth the remainder of the evidence, consuming contraband food, a hamburger, in one bite.

"You almost killed me 'malaka'." The inmate said as he turned after his coughing spree subsided somewhat and took measure of Michael.

"Sergio!  What are you doing here.  I thought you were back at the Camp."

"I was and officially still am." He said smugly.  "The dummies have me taking classes for my GED. I told them that I got my High School diploma in Greece.  They said it did not count from another country.  So I had to go back to school.   They get their allowance from the federal government and I avoid working.  It works for both of us."

"What are you doing here then?  Shouldn't you be in school?"

"You know, there are so many inmates in the program, one less won't make much difference.  At any rate the BOP is only interested in getting our signature in the morning; so they can turn them in to the Department of Justice and get their $2,500.00 appropriation per inmate.  After that, they could care less what we do.  By the end of the day, there are no students around.  I leave with the 10:30 AM shuttle bus and go visiting.  Today it was Red Flag.  Tomorrow the golf course 19th Hole Lounge.  The next day, the NCO club."

Sergio put the remains from his meal carefully inside a clean BOP sack lunch paper bag and set it in the middle of the table.

"That's for later, in case I get hungry." He said winking at Michael.

"How convenient.  It looks like a BOP issue sack lunch."

At that instant, Sergio looked up over Michael's head.  Michael, instinctively turned his head and saw a latin looking repair crew sergeant making his way towards their table holding his lunch bag. He sat it on their table and pulled out a chair contemplating siting down, while scanning the rest of the tables for an available seat. He appeared to have spotted a familiar face, two tables down.  He picked his lunch bag and headed in that direction.  Started talking with a black Airman, changed his mind about seating down in the patio to eat his lunch and started heading back towards the hanger in which they were repairing the F-14's.  Michael stared at Sergio.

"What's in the bag Sergio?"  He said slowly.

It did not escape him the fact that the latin mechanic 'accidentally' took the wrong lunch bag from their table.

"My friend, what you don't know, won't hurt you."  Sergio said cooly.  He took the remaining lunch bag and headed towards the Red Flag Building with Michael at his heals.

"Wait a minute Sergio."  He said as soon as they were out of earshot of the lunching airmen.  "What was that all about?"

"Nothing. I am just taking my lunch back to the Camp to eat in my room."

Michael was getting ready to let him have it, when he noticed the sergeant at arms of the Red Flag building across the street, waving at him frantically.

"OK.  Have it your way for the time being."  He said to Sergio parting.  "We will talk about it later."  He crossed the street and met with the sergeant at arms.

"Man, am I glad to see you."  He said trying to catch his breath.  "Some asshole from the BOP is down here to see you.  I got him cooling his heels for twenty minutes now while we are trying to locate you in the building.  Come on, follow me.  We will use the side entrance and you will materialize coming down the hallway in front of the room we got him."

"What does he want with me?"  Michael asked feeling the color draining from his face.

"Well, you are not getting rolled up."  The sergeant replied.  "There would be two of them if you did.  You are not being taken by Marshall's. I checked the van he came in.  There is only one prisoner in there.  It beats me, buddy, why the fuck he is here, but he is. You are lucky you are working at the Red Flag where the BOP has no access."

They approached the side door, partially concealed by well groomed evergreen bushes. They entered a deserted hallway.

"Turn left at your first opportunity." The sergeant said pointing the way. "He is sitting in the room four doors down to your right. Good luck."

Before Michael could thank him, he turned the opposite direction and disappeared down the corridor. Michael followed the directional instructions to the letter and barged into the office making a bee line for the waste paper basket, checking its contents.

"Hey." The BOP guard said dropping the People's magazine he was reading. "Don't you knock before you come in?"

Michael turned and came face to face with a small hispanic guard who looked barely out of High School.

"I knew the room will be empty from this morning." He said with a steady voice. "They had a meeting in progress till 10:00 AM. So I didn't get a chance to empty the waste paper basket."

Michael was amazed at both the tone and context of his lengthy explanation, which left no room for a comeback from the BOP guard.

"Well, it took you some to come down." The guard replied sullenly. But Michael could tell from the tone of his voice that he had won the battle.

"I got a prisoner in custody; I need to turn over to you."

"What are you talking about?" Michael pretended he was not aware of what was going on.

"Aren't you Michael M..., I can't pronounce your last name, serial number 84119022?" The guard replied reading from a photo I.D. card and comparing the picture with the inmate in front of him.

"Yes, I am." Michael said. "But what that got to do with accepting a prisoner. I am a prisoner myself here doing what I have been told to do."

"Well," the guard looked down at his shoes embarrassed, "I was told by the Lieutenant that you were on the ball...What I mean, you were the man to see around here, as the rest of the inmates look up to you."

Michael blushed at the dubious recognition. He certainly wanted to cooperate, but he would have considered it a successful tour of duty when on the date he was leaving, the BOP guards were coming to him asking him for his name with the comforting words: "You are new around here, aren't you?" He followed the BOP guard towards the building exit. The BOP guard turned his 'Uncleared Visitor' badge to the sergeant at arms, who winked at Michael as soon as the BOP guard headed for the double door exit. The BOP van was parked outside with the windows rolled down. A middle aged inmate with dark slicked back hair was sitting in the middle seat sweating the proceedings. The BOP guard opened the sliding door and signaled the new arrival to step down. He gave Michael the inmate's I.D. and placed a clipboard in front of his face with a pen to sign the receipt, like the prisoner was a piece of merchandise.

Michael stopped, poised to sign. "It says here 'Sergeant in Charge.'" He said dropping his hands. "I am not the 'Sergeant in Charge', I cannot sign receipt of the prisoner."

"Oh! Tsinga tu Madre." The Mexican started muttering under his breath. "The sergeant went to lunch. There is no one to receive the prisoner. I can't take him back and I can't wait any longer. The sergeant before going to lunch left you in charge, I was told by that old fart at security. Come on be a pall and initial the damn thing."

So you can get paid by the Air Force, Michael was thinking, remembering that the Air Force paid the BOP $8.00 per hour for every prisoner on paper.

He grabbed the clipboard and scribbled an unintelligible initials only signature, like the sergeant was in a vehicle when signing going over bumps at forty miles per hour.

"Hey, you are a pall." The guard beamed with satisfaction. "You put it on the line for me. I owe you. This is your Boss, El Jefe." He turned and told the Mexican prisoner who was watching the on goings in disbelief. "Do what he tells you to do." And without delay, he hopped into the van, started the engine with the air conditioning at full blast and pealed out.

"Como esta usted?" Michael asked him in heavily accented Spanish.

"Bien, bien!" The inmate replied smiling. "Habla usted Español?"

"Yo estoy estudiando Español." Michael said muttering the few rudimental words he could recall in Spanish. "I hope though you understand English, because we will be in shit creek without a paddle, if we rely in my knowledge of the Spanish language."

"Hi. My name is Frank." The new inmate said without a trace of accent.

"Mine is Michael." He said as he shook the proffered hand. "Am I glad you speak English. How come you join us late and under escort at that."

"Oh! Maki it's a long story."

"No problem Frank. I got time. That's all we all got here, time. Have you had lunch, by the way?"

"No." Frank said. "As a matter of fact I haven't eaten since last night."

"Lat's go over to the security desk to get you checked in and get our lunch. There is a picnic area at the back which I favor, because it doubles also as the authorized smoking area; so, I can smoke my pipe afterwards uninterrupted." "This sounds like a plan. Lead the way 'Boss.'" Frank said laughing.

Michael leaned back on the bench drawing on his pipe and sending clouds of blue fragrant smoke.  Frank picked a little cigar out of his pocket and lit it joining him.

"Well, Frank.  What's your story.  The suspense is killing me."

"I am an immigration attorney out of LA.  I got in a little bit of trouble with the paperwork of some of my clients…"

"What kind of trouble?" Michael interrupted.

"Let's put it this way; some of the papers my clients gave me were of questionable authenticity.  The government's position was that I am an officer of the court first, while mine was that the paying client comes first.  Anyway, that's not the important issue here.  I got a year or so at Camp Nellis.  So, I came to Las Vegas a week early with my wife, my friends and their wives.  We had a ball and partied all week long.  So, my reporting date arrived.  I had to self surrender by noon.  Needless to say we didn't sleep all night.  Plenty of time to sleep in jail.  Morning comes and I got a major hangover.  They take me to brunch to sober me up.  During brunch, we start our goodbyes and someone orders a champagne for toasts.  Then another champagne and another.  Mid morning, we pile into three cars and head for the Camp gate.  We notify the guard at the gate that I am self surrendering.  He said they will be right over to pick me up.  We wait five minutes, fifteen minutes, half an hour, nothing.  My friends brought champagne for the road and kept toasting me, cracking jokes about my cellmate Bruno, you know the usual gags.  We are laughing and drinking, feeling no pain.  Two hours later Patterson, a black dude BOP guard shows up at the gate in a white Bronco.  By now, even my friends cannot help me stand up.  The Air Force guard and Patterson pour me into the Bronco, my stuff in a couple of garbage bags piled on top of me.  I get to Processing.  That fat broad there, what's her name, takes one look at me and tells Patterson to get the breathalyzer ready.  Next thing I know, I am in shackles and handcuffs hauled off to the North Las Vegas County Jail and I am thrown into their holding tank.  Mike you should see that.  A room twelve by twenty with sixteen guys in there and a shit hole in the middle of the room. They give me a roll of toilet paper. "What am I supposed to do with this?" I ask. "Whatever you want. Use it for a mattress, pillow, wipe your ass, whatever. You get one each day. That's all." I spent the most miserable twenty four hours of my life there. The next day, Patterson came back. Man, I was so happy to see him. I just about hugged him. "Get me out of here, I told him with tears in my eyes." After the North Las Vegas County Jail, Nellis seemed like Camp Snoopy. I just came over from there and here I am. First day on the job. So, what do we do, 'Boss'?"

"Well, Frank our job is not very glamorous. We provide janitorial services. I got a couple of guys cleaning the bathrooms. A couple of guys vacuuming. One is outside cutting grass. Another inside sweeping and polishing the hallways. What's left, is you and me emptying the waste paper baskets in all the offices and bathrooms. A lot of these people eat in their offices. If the leftovers stay overnight in the trash, the next day the whole building is infested with ants, roaches and worse."

"Lead the way, 'Patron'." Frank said.

Michael explained to him the procedure.

"It's noon now. I bet you before one o'clock we are done. However, done or not, we got to catch the 1:30 PM shuttle back to Camp. Stay close. The place inside is a maze of offices. If we get separated, stay put. I will find you."

They started upstairs and moved downstairs. Michael dreaded the Adversary Tactics Sector and Tatiana. In what mood would he find her? He felt a pair of fingers covering his eyes. He felt being pulled backwards almost to the point of no return, when his fall was cushioned by a set of soft pillows pressing on his back. He tried to struggle out of the hold.

"Guess, who? Lover." He heard a soft familiar whisper next to his ear.

Tatiana, released him and Michael turned to face her while Frank was watching the whole thing dumbfounded.

"Have you given some thought, you know...what we talked about? Tatiana said coquettishly, batting her eyelashes.

"No. How could I? I got to get back to Camp and put a cop-out with the Chaplain. He got to get it in turn signed by the Warden. It will take some time." I hope you forget it in the meantime he thought.

"Good!" Tatiana said. "We will keep in touch. Don't worry. I will not forget." She added almost reading his thoughts. "Sunday after next, I feel it's a date."

Michael, lifted his shoulders and moved out of the Venus trap sector, indicating that it was out of his hands.

"What was that all about?" Frank caught up with Michael down the corridor. "You dirty dog you. You are getting some on the side and you don't share with your friends. Eh?"

"No. It's not what you think Frank. She wants to be my sponsor and escort to the Greek Orthodox Church in town."

"Didn't I tell you, I am Greek Orthodox also." Frank replied. "Ask her if she has a sister." He added laughing.

"Now don't get excited Frank." Michael warned him. "We are about to enter the 'Pussy Galore' zone, otherwise known as the mail room."

They parked their hampers outside the mail room.

"Wait here a second." Michael told Frank, taking a large trash bag. "It will only take a minute. I got to empty the paper towel waste basket in the bathroom across the way."

He opened the door and disappeared inside.

"Fuck a duck." Frank thought. "This job is alright." He mumbled as Michael opened the bathroom door labeled 'Ladies'. Frank looked inside the mailroom and noticed all the Air Force women sorting the afternoon mail and flashing him the occasional thigh and a rarer crotch shot. "Darn, Michael been in the bathroom an eternity." He thought. "How long has he actually been in there I wonder; or is it just my impatience to get into the honey trap of the mail room and start picking the litter between the broads legs." Frank decided to check the bathroom and stepped forward as Michael was getting out all red in the face.

"Hey buddy." Frank said looking over Michael's shoulder towards the closing door. "What happened in there? Where is the trash bag?"

Michael took him silently by the arm and urged him forward, by-passing the mail room.

"Hey. Wait there." Frank stopped. "We skipped the mail room."

At this moment, the 'Ladies' bathroom door opened and an equally embarrassed knock out of an Air woman made her way out the door adjusting her skirt and stealing sly glances towards Michael.

"What the fuck?" Frank said looking from Michael to the retreating woman. "You get around, don't you. And don't give me this time any of that religious crap. You should be ashamed of yourself." He said laughing. "She is old enough to be... your daughter."

"We are done for the day." Michael said. "Let the vermin's eat the leftovers."

"We may be done, old buddy." Frank said. "But you are not getting away until you tell me what happened in the bathroom."

"Nothing really; call it an awkward scene."

"How awkward? Can you attest to the fact that she is a natural blond?"

Michael was tapping his foot impatiently, while remaining silent.

"Come on man." Frank continued. "Give us a thrill. What happened in there? You both came out like you were caught in frangrante dilecto."

"You are close Frank. It's one of those situations where both parties are at fault. Me for not knocking and her for not using the privacy of a stall."

"Holly shit man. You really know how to peak someone's curiosity and interest. What did she do out of the stall? She has a dick or something? Pissing in the sink?"

"No! No! I am afraid we did not have a replay of the 'Crying Game'. Something more pedestrian than that. She must have been in the stall to do her business. When she pulled down her panties. She must have noticed that it was that time of the month, which caught her unaware. So, after she finished her business, she decided to hop out of the stall, keeping her panties out of harms way, for the sanitary napkin dispenser next to the sinks, over the paper towel waste paper basket..."

"And that's when you came in!" Frank jumped in.

"Close. It was actually while she was inserting the tube."

"Oh boy! Sexy, in a sick sort of way."

"Very kinky." Michael added. "The problem is how do I avoid seeing her. It will never be the same. I am sure she must feel as uncomfortable and as I do myself, I don't know whether to blush or get a hard on. Shit! I liked this job. Now it looks like I will have to ask for a transfer. Anyway it's for the best. I get rid of that barracuda also in Adversary tactics. Two birds with one stone. It was bound to  happen at any rate, sooner or later. Tatiana didn't look like the quitting type and would not take 'No' for an answer.

They put away their equipment and sat under the Norfolk pines up front smoking and waiting for their shuttle van, enjoying the sunshine.

# CHAPTER 14

## Shrimp Scampi

The small van was trying to get itself untangled from the Friday traffic jam at the Base. Michael looked at his watch. Two o'clock.

"Government employees!" Michael said in general. "They leave earlier and earlier every day."

"Be cool Maki. Three day weekend coming up. Kick back ma man and let it all hang out." Frank said.

"What are you talking about? Monday is not a Holiday?"

"It is for the government motherfuckers." An inmate named Jeffrey shouted.

"Gold Day. They get one day off per month as a reward for reaching their goals. Of course they set the goals and they decide that they have reached them. No big deal. Just another day per month on the dole. No wonder the government is going broke."

"What this got to do with us?" Michael asked.

"No people in the buildings. No need for cleaning. No prisoners on forced labor."

"What about the guys working on the Camp? Do they get the day off, also?"

"They are not supposed to. But the guards take the day off. So, nobody works. Meal times and stuff is the same as a regular working day though."

"Is this an odd or even weekend?" Frank cut in.

"Even." Jeffrey said.

"Who is this guy?" Frank whispered to Michael.

"A telemarketer from San Diego. He is serving a sixty month sentence. He just came in last month. He was the General Manager in San Diego for the Andriolli brothers. The government wiped him out. Poor guy he is almost fifty years old and married to a young wife with small children. He keeps track of weekends, even though he knows his wife cannot afford to visit him."

"What weekend are you?" Frank asked.

"Odd." Michael answered. "My wife was here last weekend. She won't be coming back till next month. How about yourself?"

"Odd also. My wife would be coming from LA. Maybe we will see each other, one of these days, at the Visitors Center."

The van found an opening in traffic and lurched forward. It then cut left and right and again left, freeing itself from the main traffic jam. The passenger bodies in free motion following the gyrations of the van and resembled the crew of the submarine in the late sixties television show, 'Voyage to the Bottom of the Sea'. Michael remembered seeing every Sunday while in College.

The van turned right towards Area II which was the airfield perimeter road towards the Camp, instead of heading out the main gate towards Las Vegas. The regular blue Air Force busses could be seen in the distance approaching the Camp Control Station.

"They will either wave us through or they will strip search us." Rodney said trying to gauge the mood of the guards from a distance.

"Nah! Man, them fuckers are as anxious as a motherfucker to hit the road." A black inmate cut in. "They don't want to see your ass this afternoon. I bet they wave us through and hit the road into town in the opposite direction. Of course now, some bitch like double 'D' didn't get any cock for a month now and she is pissed at mankind in general and wants to punish every swinging dick here. Yea! She may strip search us alright and have her friend 'wide glide' give us a piss test to boot. Have you had a piss test yet, Mike?"

"I think so. When I first came in. I was at the Medical Center. The PA gave me a jar and I went to the bathroom and pissed in it."

"Man, that's no piss test. I mean it is, but not the kind I am talking about. The one you gave was for medical shit, diseases and crap. The one I am talking about is for drugs."

Michael shook his head in the negative.

"That's what I thought. Man wait till them two bitches wake you up at four o'clock in the morning. They haul you in your underwear in the bathroom and you all three squeeze into the stall. You are half wake and have a hard on and you can't piss. They stand with you in the stall. Your dick hanging out like a pole in front and they stare at it because they got to sign on the jar that they eye-witnessed it. And they take their job seriously."

"How long does it take?"

"They will sit with you for an hour. If you cannot piss by then, it goes down as a refusal, which equals testing positive. That goes on your record and you have now a drug charge on top of everything else. If they want to press it, it means another eighteen months. But they don't, because they don't want it to come out in the jury. But it fucks-up your record anyway. You are now a suspect when you get out and you have to do your paper. Your parole officer has you in every week to give blood and piss and surprises you at home and in general the parole board makes your life miserable. Just because you could not piss on demand with two bitches watching you."

"How often did they do that to you?"

"It depends, but at least once a year. If you get hauled, look at your name in their clip board. You have an 'R' next to it, you are safe. That means the computer spit out your name at random. But if your name has an 'S' next to it, you are fucked in a major way, because it means suspect. Your name was put on the list by some cop. They will keep after you for a while."

The entire van turned and looked at Michael intently, who felt his blood rising to his head.

"What are you looking at? I don't care if they test me every day. I don't use drugs. Never had." He said with conviction and felt his blood subsiding.

The van pulled in front of Building 201 behind the two parked Air Force blue busses. The inmates from these busses were filing out and were met by a contingent of security officers, mostly female. All of them were patted down. A few were told to go on the grass and remove their shoes and socks. Paper currency was slowly tumbling on the grass like tumble weeds. A cop was positioned down wind collecting them. Mostly fives, tens and twenties.

"Those motherfuckers will never learn." The black man whispered leaning against the window for a better look. "You never carry money on Friday. The cops need their weekend spending money and are on the look out."

"What do you mean?" Michael asked. "They keep the money?"

"No, they turn it over to the BOP like good boys and girls." He added mockingly. "You see Slim over there?" He said pointing at the black officer collecting the money. "This motherfucker belongs in jail with us. He is nothing more than an inmate with a badge. Watch him. You see that!"

Michael saw the black cop scratching his behind.

"What do you mean?" Michael asked. "The man got an itch."

"Itch my ass. You shake this fucker right now and you will find a fifty or a hundred in his back pocket. This motherfucker is so crooked, will make your head spin. He steals from the inmates. He steals from the other cops. You ever get a shot to do extra duty, you give this mother two bucks for each hour you are to work and he will square it. You want something from town, he will get it for you and charge you ten percent. He is cool. He understands inmates."

"Man, what you are telling me is hard to believe." Michael said in disbelief. "I am aware that inmates are limited to coin currency only, not to exceed at any time twenty dollars; but this...this is clear out theft."

"Call it whatever, but that's the way it is." Another inmate said. "Who is going to complain? The inmate will get rolled up if he does, because he was not supposed to have paper money. I hope they get enough out of the buses, because I am carrying."

"So am I man." Rodney said.

"I bet we are all carrying." The black man admitted. "Weekend coming up and all."

"Why do you need cash for the weekend?" Michael inquired.

The entire van turned and looked at him like he had two heads.

"Be cool now." The black man said to no one in particular addressing the entire van. "Man, you are a Bambi." He said to Michael. "For the same thing these motherfuckers need it." He said pointing at the guards. "Gambling. College games on Saturday. Pros on Sunday. You pick four games. You call the bookies in Las Vegas and give the money to the civilians at the Chow Hall."

"Which one?" Michael asked.

"Man, it makes no difference which one. The cooks, the bitches, anyone. They are all wired with the bookies. No cash on Friday, no bet on Saturday and Sunday. You beat the spread, you are a rich man Monday."

"How do they get the money back in the Camp?" Michael asked. "The dinning room people again?"

"No dip shit. The money gets deposited in your account in one of the Casinos'. Don't tell me you have not opened an account with a couple of them, before you came here?"

Michael looked bewildered.

"That's what I thought. Tell your wife to open an account for you. All you need is a couple of hundred bucks each. A rich man like you, that's probably cab fare."

At the moment the van door slid open from the outside. A black lieutenant with afro hair, stocky, with several gold chains around his neck, rings on every finger and an imitation gold Rolex with a fake diamond bezel stood at the door opening taking measure of the inmates with a frown. He held them looking each one over careful. The atmosphere was thick with intrigue. A few flies came into the cool of the van from the outside and were buzzing by the windows trying to get back outside. This was the only noise you could hear other than the hum of the air conditioner as it kicked into a higher gear. Suddenly, he broke into a grin.

"OK motherfuckers, out. Today is your lucky day. I know you are carrying. But I will let you live. Go to your rooms and have some fun this weekend."

Relief spread in the faces of the inmates.

"Why you look so worried?" He said addressing Michael. "I know you ain't carrying."

Michael got off the van and felt his knees shaking and he did not know why or how to make them stop. He limped slowly towards the dormitory in the distance.

A small Air Force pick-up braked suddenly in front of the dorm entrance. Michael heard the squeal of the brakes before he saw the dark blue blur. He jumped further in the sidewalk as the bed tarp rolled down and an inmate jumped out who was laying on the truck bed.

"Hey 'Big Dog'! You scared the living shit out of me." He heard a familiar voice behind him. Michael turned recognizing Bill, one of his homies. Bill slapped the truck bed twice and the Air Force sergeant, driving, gunned the engine heading back towards the Base.

"Babalui! It's you." Michael said punching Bill affectionately on the shoulder.

"Easy now." Bill pretended he was mortally wounded. "You don't want me to drop the mother load here." He said as he switched hands holding an overstuffed pillow case.

"What's you got there?" Michael asked looking over Bill's shoulder to check whether a straggler guard, from the buildings down the road, might have gotten suspicious of the commotion.

"Don't worry 'Big Dog'. We are in the clear. No chili-mac tonight." Bill said lifting the pillow case.

"How do you get away with it?" Michael asked. "Private chauffeur and all..."

"Part of the fringe benefits, my boy. Part of the fringe benefits. I work in the Base construction crew. The sergeant's house needed fixing. So, I fixed it. It was in the repair order anyway. I moved it up in the waiting list. I made it like it was a  favor, so Mrs. Sergeant showed me how grateful she was and loaded for me a pillow case with store bought groceries and told Mr. Sergeant to drive me over. Simple as that, and tonight we are dinning shrimp scampi over rice."

Bill was always a scourger. He was working on Base Vocational Training Construction and was always on the lookout for deals. The usual modus operandi was that the inmates would raid the warehouse and stash material in places that only they knew.  If a new shipment came over, one thing went to the warehouse, one thing went to various unused buildings, rooms, basements and attics.  Anyplace out of the way was a good hiding place.  Pretty soon the Air Force would need, say a new toilet, because one broke.  The warehouse just ran out.  No money in the appropriation, or the money was frozen, or the person responsible did not want the item on the record.  So they went to Bill and gave him a verbal request to come up with one.  Sure enough, Bill would go to his 'dogs', as he called all his co-workers and buddies, at work and next day one new toilet was produced, no questions asked, in exchange for...whatever the fancy struck him at the time.  Mostly food stuff from the officer's Club.

Michael got in the building and walked down the long corridor to his room.  The scent of onion hit him before he opened the door.  He found Hank and Don busy chopping two large Walla Walla sweets and five jalopenio peppers.  They had put a large formica clad piece of plywood over the metal waste paper basket and were at it using the pull up lids of tuna fish cans as chopping knives.

"Hi Mike." They said in unison.

"Grab yourself a chair and start chopping a head of garlic."  Don indicated pointing at the other free chair in the room.  "Have we a surprise dinner for you tonight..."

"I heard. I just met Bill on the outside. How did you guys know already?"

"Oh!  Lester came in with the early bus and told us all about it."

Lester was one of Bill's 'dogs'.  A trader on the outside who was indicted on insider trading charges and serving a year and a day sentence after he pled guilty and bargained a five year possibility if he went to trial and lost.  He was Bill's bunky and one of the homies of Room 113.

Michael stepped on the chair to reach the shelf hidden over the door, where the inmates kept all the questionable implements they used in the exhibitions of their culinary skills.  He let his hand roam, touching gingerly all the objects trying to decide by feel which one was the garlic slicer.  It was an old coke can that they had cut one end off, after they hammered into the can walls slots made with concrete nails, so that the can could be rolled over the cloves of garlic scraping thin slices of garlic. He finally found what he was looking for and got himself busy doing his part of the evening meal.

"What are we missing in the Mess Hall menu?"  Michael asked.  "Does anyone know?"

"Well, it's Friday.  So, it must be some kind of fish sticks thing." Hank said.

"What do you mean by fish thing?  Fish parts ground up and made into patties?"  Michael asked.

"Don't forget the gills, guts and ground up fish tails."  James Dean said as he opened the door coming in and catching the last part of the conversation.  "What time is dinner?"  He continued.

"James, all you think is your gut."  Don needled him.  "What are you going to contribute towards this community meal?"

"Other than eating...well as always I will do the dishes and the cleaning of all the pots and cooking implements afterwards."

"I don't know if you can be trusted James."  Michael said good naturally. "Weren't you pretty close with that fellow who pissed in the sink?"

The room roared with laughter and James was looking all around for a retort.  His eyes finally settled on the head of Don who was bald and his head was glistening with respiration.  James grabbed an old tee shirt and tossed it on Don's head.

"Here wipe yourself.  I don't want your sweat on my food.  I was going to recommend a hair net but in your condition there is nothing there to protect."

"Yeah!  Don." Bill said coming into the room with the washed shrimp which he went ahead and emptied in the middle of the chopping board. "Are they picking on you again Don?"

"Don't let your baldness bother you Don." Michael said. "Look at it this way.  You are not losing hair, you are getting more head."

The laughter exploded in the room.

"And this is the only kind of head you are going to get while you are locked up in here." James added.

"Hey, this place starts looking like a Benihana restaurant." Lester said coming in carrying something inside a brown paper bag.

"What's you got there 'dog'?" Bill yelled from his top bunk.

"Look here." Lester said extracting two perfectly ripe home grown tomatoes. "I snagged them across the hall from the boys in Da Barrio."

"Where do they get all those vegetables?" Michael asked the room in general.

"These boys got gardens going in every nook and cranny in the Base." James said. "Even here at Camp.  Go look behind the garage."

"I have." Michael said. "What garden?  That place is overgrown with weeds clear to the road. You can hardly see the garage."

"That's exactly how they want it." James continued. "No one would venture in, fighting the cactus and cholla, to see what's behind the weeds and the garage fence.  However, if you have a ladder and you climb the garage fence from the inside, you will see the most spectacular vegetable garden.  Why do you think the barrio boys all work in the garage fixing cars?  The fringe benefits, plus they learn the latest about auto-motives so they can get a job when they are finally released."

"What time should we say for dinner?" Don asked.

"Remember now." Lester jumped in. "Be considerate. I don't want to wait in line for ever. There are five microwave ovens for 250 inmates and Friday is a big pop corn night. If we don't go there early, we will never eat before midnight."

"Here is the plan." Michael said. "Go down just before the 4:00 PM stand up count and put the pot into the microwave. Everyone has to be in their room, so our food is safe. Then go down immediately after the clear and fire'er up. We will be eating before five o'clock."

"Great!" All the rest of the homies said in unison.

"That's the plan then." Michael said. "Lester you can go down anytime the food is ready to go and according toy watch it is three forty. Another five minutes and the blue light would go on. Meaning no inmate can be wandering outside his room."

Lester left and came back five minutes later.

"Everything per plan 'dog'?" Bill shouted. "Give me five now!"

Lester dropped on the floor and started doing push ups.

"Who's your daddy?" Bill yelled.

"You are, Bill." Lester replied red faced from the exertion and the humiliation.

The rest of the room was stunned, looking at the display.

"What was that all about?" James asked.

"Oh!" Lester said. "Nothing really. We had a bet over something and I lost. What I lost is 50 push ups anytime anyplace. Now Bill here is being an asshole and has divided the total into ten parts. He already had me do five push ups in the middle of the street on Base..."

"It stopped all the traffic though, didn't it 'dog'?" Bill interrupted.

The room door slammed open at that time. The inmates jumped to their feet and stood in front of their bunks. The blond lady lieutenant with the big butt, called 'wide glide', stepped into the room counting five heads.

"No one died in here?" She asked smiling. Suddenly she started sniffing the air and peering at each inmate in turn. "I hope your cooking is confined to ingredients available from the commissary." She said.

No one said a word. Michael felt his face reddening and lowered his eyes looking at 'wide glide's' cowboy boots made out of rattle snake skin. A second cop came in taking a head count, confirming 'wide glide's' count and writing the room number into his running total. 'Wide glide' confirmed the new total and they left the room closing the door behind them.

"Do you think she suspects anything?" Michael asked the room.

"Suspect?" James volunteered. "She already knows."

"One thing to know, and another to prove it, so she can roll us up." Hank added.

"Well, the shrimp smell in here is certainly overpowering." Lester commented.

"Yeah! 'Dog' tell them." Bill said. "Either that, or she will start looking for the girl we smuggled in the closet."

The room exploded again with laughter.

James stuck his head outside the door. "The blue light is off. All clear. Lester go and get us dinner."

Lester left the room while the rest of the inmates were busily getting out their tapper ware bowls, cups and plastic utensils.

"I will go get us ice from the ice machine downstairs." Bill volunteered.

"Hey Mike. What are you in for?" Hank asked from out of the blue. "I don't think I've ever heard you explaining why the government zeroed in on you like that."

"What are you in for Hank?" Michael asked a little protruded.

"My case is pretty much straight forward, I did not file a federal income tax return."

"No kidding?" Michael said. "That's pretty rebellious stuff Hank. Haven't you heard the old saying, you can't escape death and taxes? What did they get you for not filing one...two...years?"

"No. Twenty years."

"Holly shit; you are a rebel Hank. How did you decide...let's see that would be 1976. The two hundredth independence anniversary. What made you decide in 1976 to quit paying federal income tax?"

"Two things. One, I don't believe the federal income tax is legal. It was not part of the constitution. Two, I wrote to the IRS in 1976 and asked them to give me in writing an accounting of where my previous tax payments went."

"What did they say? Did they write you back?"

"Twenty years later, I am still waiting; although they are required by law to give any taxpayer, who requested in writing, an accounting of his payments and how they spent it. That's the reason we went to war with England to gain our independence. The individual federal income tax was instituted in 1913. This means that our government in a little over 100 years, has come full circle to advocate a position that was fought and became the battle cry in the War of Independence. Enough about me though. Why did you become a target?"

"Have you ever bought a mattress Hank?" Michael asked after a pregnant pause.

"Yeah! What about it?"

"Did you notice a little tag on the mattress that says: DO NOT REMOVE UNDER PENALTY..."

"OK. Where are you getting at?" Hank interrupted impatiently.

"Well, I removed it!" Michael said.

The entire room broke in giggles except Hank who was becoming angrier by the minute.

"Laugh it up! Here I am trying to be serious for a moment and you clown around; and don't give me the Davis-Bacon shit either. That's the excuse. I am looking for the reason."

"Seriously now Hank. I don't know for sure. They never told me in so many words. If I was in their shoes and had to deal with a guy like myself, I would have thrown his ass in jail long ago. I can't figure out why it took them so long to do it. I wouldn't negotiate with them. I demanded payment on the Change Orders on my terms. If they refused or stayed silent, thirty days later I would file a lawsuit against them with the Armed Services Board of Contract Appeals. I did that 183 times in twenty years and won every single time exposing in the process their lies and incompetence. As a result of my lawsuits several Military Officers saw their career stall or they were dismissed from the service altogether. My winnings were more than the original Contracts themselves. I think that's what did it finally. If a Contract goes over 100% of the original price, then the Contracting Agency has to write lengthy reports justifying the reason for this to the General Accounting Office (GAO) who gave them the money to begin with on behalf of Congress. How can they possibly explain it with the court case transcripts in the possession of the GAO already. They would either be caught lying or admit that they goofed or the contractor was better than the government. All these were reasons for their defense budget to be slashed and their activities closely monitored by the GAO the watch dog of Congress. Needless to say heads rolled in the effected agency. Pair this with my arrogance to a degree that is trying to eclipse that of

Vercingetorix himself and you got the reasons.  In one word Hubris, extreme conceit, the subject of every Greek tragedy."

"Mickey you are a true rebel.  I thought James Dean, my bunky, was the rebel, but he does not hold a candle to you." Hank concluded.

"Tell him about the thank you notes you sent to the government attorneys." Don piped in.

"Yeah!  I almost forgot." Michael added.  "The government tried to get me numerous times in the past twenty years.  Each time they lost and ended up paying me damages.  So, I would take a portion of my winning and treat myself to a new toy.  A Mercedes 300 SD Turbodiesel, a Porsche 911 Targa, a 41 foot sailboat or something really outrageous.  I would take a picture of it with me driving or sailing in it and mail it to the agency, their attorney and his boss with a thank you note."

"Wow!  That's cold.  Man you are lucky the government didn't put a hit on you to get rid of you once and for all.  It would probably have been cheaper all around for them." Hank said.

"The worst I saved for last.  As soon as I won a major claim with the Navy, I bought with the proceeds a 7 thousand square foot villa on a hill in the island of Oahu with a 180 degree view looking down in the Diamond Head crater, one of the ten best homes, at the time, in the Parade of Homes. Every Christmas we  would leave for Holidays in the mainland and leave our home to the Hawaii Boy Scouts to conduct tours by busload of our home together with the others in their list. This was their yearly most profitable fundraiser.  Anyway, the Navy Project Manager who was in charge of the project was retiring.  The navy was giving him a grand sendoff party.  A friend of mine in the Navy who did not particularly like the retiree, brought to me a picture of my house taken by the Parade of Homes and asked me to sign it with a thank you note to the retiree, onto which I did adding: 'Living well is the best revenge.'"

"Have you got enough reasons Hank?" Don cut in. "Mike is the sort who we call 'sore winner' in my part of the woods. He pisses you off so much, that you want to go after him personally."

Lester walked into the room. He opened the cooking pot and everyone in the room was overcome with the garlic shrimp smell. The delicious smell must have been spilling in the hallway because fists were pounding on the door accompanied with hunger cries and pleadings. Suddenly a hush came over the building as the murmur of "Recount, Recount", took over.

"Hey Maki, check out the hallway there." Bill shouted. "What's happening? I thought we cleared. The blue light had come off. What's this recount shit?"

Michael stuck his head outside the door only to see two guards and a lieutenant at the far end of the corridor, all poised ready for another stand up count.

"I am afraid the number of inmates has surpassed their collective number of fingers and toes." He said laughing.

"What are we going to do with the shrimp scampi casserole?" Lester said still holding it.

"For one thing, I would put the lid back on." Hank said. "We don't want to advertise our culinary skills."

"Right." Lester said, complying instantly.

"For another, I would open the window." James added. "Don, would you do the honors. Do it now man and quit looking at Mike. He will not freeze."

The door opened freezing all the inmates in motion. The familiar bulk of Tony from across the hall appeared, relaxing the inmates of Room 113.

"Hey bambinos." He said playfully. "The smell is...delicioso. We can smell it clear across the room. You got there minutes before the cops are on your ass. My boys ask if we can help eat your food in three minutes."

"Thanks Tony, but we will manage." Lester said unsure of himself.

Tony looked down the long corridor and one second he was framed in the doorway of Room 113 and the next he disappeared behind the closing door of Room 114.

"OK. What do we do now?" Lester addressed the room.

"I've always maintained, when the wind changes, don't blame the wind, adjust the sails." Michael said and sprang into action. He took the pot from Lester's hands and put it underneath Bill's overstuffed laundry bag. After he backed off and satisfied himself that the pot was invisible, he climbed on a chair and started the air fan above the door going. There was now air circulating but was not dissipating the shrimp scampi smell.

"We need some diversionary smell." He mumbled. He gazed from the laundry bag sacks finally deciding on a sheet of Bounce clothes softener. He placed it behind the air fan cage and let it get stuck on the bars.

Don started sniffing the air to locate the source of the new perfume odor that was permeating and overpowering the shrimp scampi smell.

"What's the matter Don?" Michael said. "You behave like one of your cheap dates just walked into the room."

At that instant, the room door slammed open and the security officer with the big boobs everyone called 'double D' stepped in the door frame while the inmates were trying to choke down the laughter. She looked around suspiciously, counted everyone and walked out, closing the door behind her.

"For a minute there I thought she would be looking in the closets to find the girl we are hiding." Bill said, raising the laughter level by a full octave.

Before he could finish his sentence, the door opened again and 'Petunia's' head appeared. She came into the room. Sniffed the air and opened the two closets. She took her time, shinning her flash light and looking into every nook and cranny and without closing any of the doors she had opened, left the room.

Bill from his side, kicked the doors shut as the whole room exploded in laughter. They saw the whole security crew leaving the building after a few minutes, indicating that the count had cleared and the inmates could now leave their rooms.

"Let me make sure this time." James said and left the room.

James came back in the room a few minutes later with a 'I know something, but you don't' look on his face.

"Let me guess." Don said. The ghetto or the barrio this time?"

"The ghetto." James replied laconically.

"The brothers got confused and mixed the rooms up." Don continued.

"Yep!" James replied.

"What are you guys talking about?" Michael asked. "Why are you speaking in code?"

"It's not code." Don volunteered. "We just know what happens here every weekend."

"Why don't you enlighten me." Michael insisted.

"Every Friday the blacks in the rooms either side of us exchange clothes with their cousins or friends at the Base. Someone who resembles them physically, anyway. These impostors come in and take the place of the real inmates who, dressed with their relatives' clothes are enjoying themselves in Las Vegas with their hoe's.  Then on Monday, they meet again on Base and exchange identities."

"Come on!" Michael said.  "I know they all look alike, but that's taking it to a whole new level.  All this time, and no one spotted them?"

"Look who's talking." Lester said.  "You've been here two weeks now and you couldn't tell."

"Amazing!"  Michael exclaimed.  "This is the perfect ploy.  Unless they fingerprint them and send their finger prints to the FBI for comparison with the ones taken when processed, no one is the wiser.  As long as they don't commit a crime on the outside, they are in the clear."

"Even when they are." Bill added.  "Take last weekend for example.  You know Johnny, the one they call 'the mouth'. "

"You know Mike."  Don jumped in.  "The big tall nigger who you said sounds like he speaks into a megaphone?"

Michael nodded understanding.

"Well," Bill continued, "last weekend he was arrested as a suspect because he rolled a drunk behind Circus-Circus and stole from him a couple hundred dollar bills.  He had a driver's license I.D. on him with his real name and even a picture.

But the drunk could not identify him on the line up.  So, the police let him go.  When they checked his whereabouts the next few days, they found that he was locked up at Nellis.  So, they concluded he could not have been the one who committed the robbery.  The SOB had the perfect alibi.  Only the Warden is hip on what's happening, after all he is one of the brothers, so, he is covering up for them big time.  Now the white cops know also what's happening and they are trying to nail the niggers without showing that they are hassling them, so they don't piss off the Warden.  It's a game of cat and mouse that's been going on for a long time.  Tonight they came close nailing one of them being out of bounds, in the wrong room.  They could have rolled him up at the North Las

Vegas County Jail and finger print him. But on the re-count the brothers realized their mistake and pulled him to the room that he belongs. So the re-count cleared."

"You can say that again." Hank expanded. "Can't you hear the noise in the ghetto?"

"I meant to ask about that." Michael said. "I asked a black fellow from next door, I know slightly, named Henderson. Everyone calls him Hen. Anyway, you know he adopted me somehow, so every time I see him I say "Sup Hen?" and he replies "Sup Mike?" and we shake fists. So, the other day I asked him how come his room is so noisy all the time. It sounds like they were fighting. He did not  answer me directly but he said they have the same concern about our room. They stop once in a while to listen, to hear something, to find out whether we are dead or alive in there. We ended up our conversation by him asking me: "Mike don't you feel, once in a while, in this place like closing the door and scream MOTHERFUCKER at the top of your lungs? Try it, you may feel good afterwards."

"I don't know about that." Hank continued. "But it seems that their standard operating procedure is to argue at the top of their voice, and the one who yells the loudest is declared the winner."

"It's a different race alright." James added condescendingly. "It's unfortunate we have them in each side of our room, so we can hear them stereophonically."

"Now, now, James you cannot stereotype all people. Look at the boys in the barrio across the hall. They are quiet, as mice." Bill said.

"More like they are stoned all the time." James corrected. "You keep hanging around their room and you are likely to fail your next piss test. Something about second hand smoke."

"So, that's what it was!" Bill added mockingly. "I was wondering why every time I was leaving their room feeling better than when I went in. Thanks James, I will make a note of it."

"Joke all you want. What are you going to do if you fail the piss test? Are you going to be a 'Rat' or are you going to get rolled up quietly to an FCI with another eighteen months added to your sentence?" Michael asked.

The question hung in the air unanswered as the inmates opened the pot of shrimp scampi over rice.

"Boys! Boys! It is still piping hot." Don declared. "The delay seems to have helped with the flavor. All the spices had a chance to steep and blend. I think this is the best thing I've tasted since I've been in here." He added taking a generous spoonful in his bowl.

For the next fifteen minutes there was silence in the room, reminiscent of the holy eucharist. The only sound was the grunting and lip smacking of the 'communicants'. The garlic smell was pungent and savored repeatedly in appreciative  burps. A few rice remnants were floating at the bottom of the pot in a sea of butter.

"I wish we had some Shirokiya french bread, hot, right out of their oven." Michael said wistfully. "We could make some ace garlic bread with the remnants."

As if on cue, the door opened and Tony's head appeared.

"If you guys are done with your feast, we would like to do the dishes for you." He said eyeing the pot with an inch of congealing butter at the bottom, heavily seasoned with spices and food flavoring.

The inmates silently acquiesced feeling guilty more than anything else. Tony with his 'dog' Pancho on his heels collected the bowls, eating utensils and cooking pot.

"They are a sad bunch." Bill said after they left. Mules at the border, ferrying dope from Mexico to El Norte and getting caught like flies on the wrong side."

"The government offered them a deal. They can leave the U.S. and serve their time in Mexico." Said Hank. "There they can serve their time in a Mexican jail or they can buy their sentence. I hear $20,000.00 can buy a ten year sentence."

"You are talking now about the kingpins." Bill answered vehemently. "These little fuckers don't have that kind of money. Have you served time in a Mexican jail? If you did, you would understand why these pendejos declined the US government's offer."

"Hey, guys. Did you hear the latest?" Don said suddenly.

"Shit happens every day." Michael said. "What's the latest that you've heard?"

"You know the black cop, 'Slim'?"

"How could I not? He is the dude that checked me in this place and earlier today he was collecting paper money from inmates coming on the busses from the Base. I was told he is an inmate with a badge."

"Well, Johnny is in to him big time."

"Who is Johnny?" Hank asked.

"You know, that retard who thinks he is a cop." Michael said. "He walks around with a crooked neck and smashed grill. I was told when I first came in to watch out for him, because he was known to be a "Rat'. It seems someone did a number on him with a pipe and they have not managed to put him back together the same way. I heard something from his roommates who are Korean from Hawaii. They are trying to cop him out of their room, because he is a fag. I didn't hear about the gambling deal though."

"Hey, Mike's story sounds better." Lester jumped in.

"No!  No!" Mike said.  "Let's hear from Don, he was after all, first."

"OK." Don said a little let down.  "Johnny kept betting on football games with Patterson the guard.  'Slim' found a patsy so it was really no contest with the odds he was offering him.  Before you know it, the cumulative total is $1,200.00 and 'slim' is no longer interested in carrying Johnny.  So, it's pay up or else time."

"That's why the 'Rat' is selling apple pies every chance he gets." James added.

"Well, at least he is trying to pay his debt, but the vigorish keeps adding up faster than he is able to pay it back." Don added.  "I heard 'Slim' is threatening to pay a visit to the kid's sister and collect.  He told Johnny that he will either collect the $1,200.00 or he will make her work it off on the strip."

"Who is 'Slim'?" Hank asked.  "I confuse him with 'Sly'.  I don't know, all niggers look alike to me."

"He is the one playing cards with the brothers after the twelve o'clock count." Don said.

"No!" Bill jumped in.  "That's rich.  You mean he comes in our building and plays cards for money?"

"Yes!"  Don confirmed.  "Practically every weekend after the 12:00 o'clock count.  You can go downstairs and see for yourself.  They set up in the basement room closest to Building 202.  You know the room below the A&O room."

"If you go to the A&O room right now, you will see Johnny is in there also." Michael said.  "Bed and baggage."

"What is he doing over there?" Don asked.

"The word is he got copped-out of the room by his roommates."

"I don't believe that!" Don said emphatically. "The guy is practically a cop himself. The BOP would never do it. They may cop-out the rest of his room, but not him."

"What if he broke a law that even the BOP cannot cover up." Michael said cryptically.

"He broke a law that he didn't get rolled-up, and he still lost the room?" Don asked.

"That's what I am talking about." Michael said.

"Enough the mystery already." James jumped in. "Go ahead and tell. The suspense is killing us."

"The word is that he is...how would I say that delicate subject politely;" Michael pondered, "a little light on his feet."

"Come on;" Don said exasperated, "that's standard inmate gossip. The BOP would never fall for it."

"What if an ensuing search uncovered bras and panties, enough to equip a platoon of females and all sorts of other gay hard core videos and assorted implements and paraphernalia."

"I'd say that someone planted them." Don said with conviction.

"That was Johnny's argument also." Michael said.

"See I told you so." Don smiled.

"Well, I said it was Johnny's argument. I didn't say it was a convincing one." "What do you mean?" Bill asked.

"Well, the argument was holding up, until his roommates convinced the Lieutenant in charge of the shakedown party to strip search dear old Johnny."

"No!" Lester broke in laughing. "Don't tell me the bastard was wearing women's underthings?"

Michael shook his head in the affirmative, trying to keep a straight face. "I am afraid Johnny was caught 'pretty in pink' and his argument that research has determined the color pink to have a calming effect upon violent type inmates, did not hold water."

The room exploded in laughter.

"Let's wait till the midnight count," Hank said, "and we will pay him a visit. Maybe we will check out the action in the card room while we are at it."

An almost imperceptible knock on the door, got the room quiet. Jim, a prematurely balding inmate from down the hall appeared at the door and proceeded to huddle by Bill and Lester's bunk. He appeared to be showing Bill and Lester some photographs from a stack and carrying on a conversation in whispers. Pretty soon Bill and Lester pulled a well used envelope from under their respective mattresses and made their way out the door with their visitor.

"Don't forget the ten o'clock count." Don said in their wake. "The blue light will come on in another five minutes. It's not worth a shot getting caught outside the room."

"Thanks man! Later." Bill threw hurriedly as he chased after his friends.

"What was that all about?" Michael inquired looking at Don.

"I don't know if you qualify yet to be told." Don said mischievously. "You haven't been in the system that long. So you will not understand."

"Don't tell me they went to a butt-fucking party." Michael said jumping into conclusion. The remaining homies joined in the laughter.

"I am going to tell Bill and Lester what you just said;" James said looking at Don, "as soon as they come back that you told Mike that they were nothing more than a couple of queens."

"No! No! I never said that." Don protested.

"Well, you said enough, so Mike concluded that they were going to a fraternity party."

"OK; here it goes."  Don said in desperation.  The other roommates stopped fussing around so that they can hear Don's explanation; although Michael had a good idea that they already knew the answer.

Don stopped, looked around and motioned Michael to join him outside in the hallway.

Catcalls and jeers ranging from 'unfair' to 'are you going the join the party' followed the two inmates out the door.

In the corridor, Don leaned close to Michael conspiratorially.  "What I tell you, you didn't hear it from me, now.  Here, like in every prison there is what's known a wife swapping club.  Now, it does not have to be a wife.  It can be a girlfriend, a daughter, any type of female.  Not your dog, however, for example."

"Where do they get together?"  Michael asked, trying to think in vain at all the places available in the Camp.

"No!  You misunderstand me."  Don said.  "The females are in the pictures.  They have pictures of them in provocative poses and they exchange them."

"That's disgusting." Michael reacted.

"I warned you that you had not been in the system long enough to understand. Prison dehumanizes you. You become an animal driven by deprivation and instinct. You end up doing things that you wouldn't do in the street."

"I don't care how long I stay in the system.  I know that I will not allow the system to institutionalize me." Michael said with conviction.

"I hope you are right." Don said shaking his shoulders. "Time does funny things to otherwise strong men."

"Not if you have a mission." Michael answered back. "The daily grind leaves you unaffected, because you live for the hours that you can call your own, untouchable by the mundane. You experience a spiritual communion, as your soul soars in the waves of creativity. At those moments, I don't care if I am in jail, at home, in a telephone booth for all I care, because I am living an out of body experience."

"It sounds like a trip." Don added skeptically. "What do you call your club and how may I join?"

"Now, who is misunderstanding whom!" Michael exclaimed. "The pure joy you are experiencing comes from within. You have to generate and create it. No one else. I am speaking of course of the mind creating a writing or a work of art."

"What happens to us less mortals who lack the necessary talents to create?" Don asked.

"Find a hobby or better yet join a religious club." Michael added quickly. "I've seen agnostics turn fervent christians. The key is to remain one, once on the outside with all the distractions and the choices. In prison, we are a captive audience. Outside we are given the opportunity to chose. Are we going to chose right? You know we complain about the lack of freedom here. When we were on the outside, we pissed on freedom. Now, we have no choice. Someone else has predetermined a program and we adhere to it. In some respects, it is a good program insofar as nourishing the body and teaching healthy habits. In other ways the spirit is left to subsist. If the inmate does not find a way to nourish the spirit, he will become institutionalized. That is his whole life and existence would rotate around a schedule determined by the government. The individual will experience a type of brainwashing where the thoughts and ideas would be fed to him by the system. There will be lack of individual thought and creativity. The inmate will truly become a number of the whole, unable to thinking and function individually."

Don gave Mike a 'I know I can trust you' look and said looking left and right to check whether the coast was clear. "You know there is a way to make some money while in jail."

"What do you have in mind Don?" Michael asked. "I know there are ways. All of them illegal at that. If they are illegal for everyone, including the people on the outside, I am not interested. If they are illegal because of some prison rule, I will listen, weigh the risk involved and let you know whether I am interested or not."

"It involves the stock market." Don said hesitantly. "I've been studying it for years and observed that there are several factors that make it go up or down. Also other phenomena such as it does not behave the same way more than three days in a row. To make a long story short, I've monitored and tabulated these behavioral patterns and can predict with 70% accuracy what the stock market will do the next day. I've capitalized on this and made some money over the past year. Nothing big. Couple of hundred dollars per day on the average. I get in during the morning and get out in the afternoon. Sometimes I am in only for a few minutes. There are some other guys in on it. Good guys. Mature. Businessmen like you and me. Say the word and I will introduce you to them." "Why do you need a whole gang to carry it off?" Michael asked.

"I wouldn't call it a gang." Don protested. "I have four others. We pool our resources and talents. There are several factors that need to be monitored. The stock market must be tracked on TV. Calling the orders. Making calculations. Believe me, Mike, it is a full time job for five people. We need to build some breathing space, because the other day someone was caught in a detail and there was no one to carry the load. What do you say? You don't need to answer me right away. Think about it."

"No, it's OK. I thought about it." Michael said. "I can tell you I am not interested. The risk does not justify the reward. Plus it's an area I know nothing about. I would have to go on trust and frankly my resources are limited at this point to allow me this luxury."

"You don't need to invest." Don pressed on. "In the beginning, until you feel comfortable and confident, just help out."

"It sounds tempting." Michael said. "But I am afraid not. I am surprised you kept at it so long without getting caught. The place here is a cheese factory. I've never seen so many 'Rats' around. The phones are tapped and the conversations are recorded. Are the hacks asleep at the switch or too stupid to understand Wall Street jargon…"

"Don't worry about it. No problem." Don cut Michael off, visibly disappointed. "I expected things to work out differently, but we will manage. Let's go back to the room and wait for the ten o'clock count."

"I am new here." Michael continued apologetically. "I don't want to give the BOP reason to keep me here one day longer from my wife. How do you feel about this Don?"

"I am not married. Maybe if I was, it would have been different."

"Have you been married?" Michael pried, anticipating the usual sob story of sentencing, followed by divorce, or wife meets Santso scenario.

"I was twenty years ago. But I got tired of her. So, one day I came home early and found her playing cards with the maid. As soon as the maid saw me, she started picking things up.

"Don't worry." I told her. "There is no hurry. You are on your own time as of now. You can leave when you like and don't come back."

I started going upstairs. Stopped at mid step, looked at my wife who was trying to console the maid by giving her 'understanding' looks and told her.

"Why don't you ask her to pack you up while you are at it. You are leaving right after her. I am going to take a shower and change. I don't want to find you downstairs when I come down. That's the last I saw her."

"Man, that's cold." Michael said. "Wouldn't it have been better if you talked to her? Communicate with her and tell her what was annoying you."

"Mike! Mike! It was a done deal. I was sick and tired of her. No conversation was going to change that."

"Well, that is a little selfish for me to understand. Were there any kids? What about their feelings?"

"I had a daughter. She was off to camp. I was tired of her also. I didn't care what happened to her. I wanted to live. I was looking time passing me by and I decided to jump off the Merry-go-Round. Don't look at me this way. You are not my mother!"

"What happened?" Michael asked. "Did you find what you were looking for?"

"I thought I did. Until some bitch ratted on me to the government and found myself in jail."

"What happened?" Michael asked concerned and acutely interested at the same time.

"It's a long story." Don said with a pained expression. "I will give you the short version. I was in business of buying large parcels of land breaking them up in 50 acre developed pieces of property and selling them as mini farms and ranches to city folks. It was for years a very profitable business. I needed a secretary, so I advertised for one. The femme fatale in question showed up at my doorstep. Her husband left her with two small children. Couldn't make ends meet, you know the old story. I fucked her. She moved in. Started pressing me, after a while, to become the new Mrs. When it reached the point of full court press, I showed her the door. That should have been the end of the story. But it was not. Three years ago, I bought from the government on an Agreement of Sale some land. Two years later I paid them and that was the end of it. But you know the old story, there is no fury like the one from a woman scorned. So, she ratted on me that the financial statement I submitted to the government to convince them to let me have the land on an Agreement of Sale, overstated my net worth. It didn't matter that I paid off the loan. The Department of Justice came after me. They offered me a settlement. Half a mil fine and three years in jail. I told them thanks, but no thanks. I went to trial and got 33 months and fifty thousand dollars fine. But the story does not end here. With the government's help, that broad has sued me and is trying to take me for everything I got. So don't give me any of that compassion of yours. Women are bitches."

"Don, women are nothing more than mirror images." Michael said. "They only reflect you and your behavior towards them. For people that their self fulfilled prophecy comes true, my only advise involves the three "F's".""

"The three "F's"?" Don replied searchingly. "What are the three "F's"?"

"Whatever Flies, Floats or Fucks." Michael continued. "Don't buy. Rent."

Don laughed. "How does that go again? I got to remember this, before I get into another "F" deal."

After the ten o'clock count cleared, Michael and Don went the A&O room. There was a single solitary bed and locker in the huge room of game tables.

"How embarrassing and annoying," Michael whispered to Don, "for someone to try to sleep while others are having fun."

"It couldn't have happened to a nicer guy." Don replied. "He got what he had coming. He is a fucking 'Rat' and a fag 'Rat' at that."

"I like to hear his side of the story." Michael said as a skeletal figure raised itself from behind the locker.

"Oh, high Johnny." Don said shyly.

Johnny looked mistrustfully at the two approaching inmates.

"I hear you are behind the eight ball with Patterson." Michael spoke. "Anything we can help with?"

"Patterson is a piece of shit!" Johnny said vindictively. "But I will fix his wagon." He looked at his ironman watch with all the buttons and dials. "If my watch is not lying to me. This fucker should be getting busted about...Now!"

"How can you be so sure?" Michael challenged him.

"The stupid shit had the verve to call my sister." Johnny continued. "He tried to shake her for money that I allegedly owed him. So she called the assistant Warden and told her the story. They put a tap on her phone. Next time Patterson called, they had him down cold. I did not know all this until they called me at the office to talk to me. I came clean and told them that Patterson 'borrows' money from inmates and participates in gambling. So, they are going to arrest him tonight and roll up the inmates that get caught with him."

Don and Michael at that point exchanged quick glances indicating an unspoken language that they must warn the inmates tonight. Johnny looked at them suspiciously.

"What are you doing here at the A&O room?" Michael asked breaking the ice. "I thought you were in Room 212."

"I was." Johnny said getting embarrassed. "But you know, I got sick and tired living with all these fags."

"What do you mean?" Don blurted. "I heard it the other way around."

"Who said that?" Johnny retorted indignantly. "These little Korean fags are giving massages to each other. I couldn't stand it any longer."

"Why is that Johnny?" Don teased him in a mocking tone of voice. "They wouldn't give you a rubdown? Is that it?"

"Get out of here!" Johnny screamed, a vein on his throat popping out to the point of exploding. "Not you Mike." He said somewhat calmer. "Just that old faggot you are with." He pointed at Don. He picked a number of rolled up sheets that Michael recognized as tomorrows call-out sheets and threw them at Don. The roll opened. The pages fanned out, breaking into the wind and hitting Don harmlessly on the chest.

"Thanks Johnny." Don continued mockingly. "I was looking for this all afternoon."

The two inmates backed up against the side door and with a smooth motion opened it and took the basement steps two at the time to reach the card game in time.

They opened the game room door only to witness the black guard, Patterson, being led away in handcuffs, followed by four other black inmates.

"Well, look at it this way." Don said. At least they were all 'hamsters'. The place will be a little quieter for that tonight."

Michael shook his head and started back up the stairs.

"By the way;" Don said, "did you know that your name is in the call-out for Tuesday?"

"No kidding?" Michael said reaching for the call-out sheets, while Don purposely jerked them back out of reach.

"What are you going Tuesday morning?" Don continued.

"I don't know. I suppose go where I went today. Red Flag."

"Wrong!" Don exclaimed. "You owe me a Cherry Garcia ice-cream next time you go to the Commissary."

"Quit dorking around and tell me what the fucking call-out says." Michael said losing his patience.

"Ultimately, Construction 4." Don said. "You are to report there at 9:30 Tuesday morning. Aren't you going to ask me where you are to report at 8:00 AM sharp?"

"Where?" Michael inquired disinterested. "But before this. What is Construction 4? Do you know anyone working there?"

"No. I don't. I heard this is the General Construction Branch for all Camp Construction. They are the guys building the new Movie Theater and all sorts of other projects. But you never asked me where you are supposed to be going before. At 8:00 AM sharp. This must be a first. In all my time here, I have not seen this before."

"Spit it out." Michael said disinterested. "The suspense is killing me." He said mockingly.

"The Warden." Don said.

"The Warden?" Michael repeated. "Why does he want to see me?"

"I believe it is time to see your Godfather." Don said. "I wish I was a fly on the wall during this weekend's conference of the 'Men of Respect'.

Michael did not respond but silently started walking down the corridor with Don close on his heels.

# CHAPTER 15

## Let's Make A Deal

He felt the start of perspiration beading along his hairline. The heat and humidity made his breathing come strained in short gasps. He inhaled deeply and held the humid air in, as long as he could stand it, letting it our slowly. He felt his muscles relax. He closed his eyes tightly and wiped his forehead with his forearms flexing his back muscles. He opened his eyes slowly taking in the nude figure of the woman laying in the bathtub.

The soap suds pooled between her breasts that floated on the surface. The nipples were erect like peaks of twin islands. Soap suds filled the water surface playing with the light, glimmering pinks and purples, faint underwater shadows, darker shades where her legs joined the body. A knee broke the surface, gently separating the soap bubbles and submerged ever so gently, the suds closing the space on the water surface. Her toes flexed on the bathtub wall, pushing the middle of the body upward in anticipation as he groped his way in search of the soap. He playfully massaged the floating hair of her pussy while he dragged the soap with his other hand between her legs.

"Is it over already?" She murmured half asleep.

He picked one of her hands and examined her crinkly fingers. She opened an eye lazily and looked at her hand.

"I guess." She moaned. "But it feels so good. I could go to sleep right here. I feel weightless, I don't think I can control my muscles to stand up."

He put one arm behind her back and the other under her knees and lifted her effortlessly. He stood her up, leaning her against the tile wall and turned the water on, adjusting the temperature warmer. He flicked the shower massager on and pulled the tub drain plug.

The pulsating water hit her on the chest sending shivers down her spine. He smiled and twitched lovingly her nipples who shrunk around the areoles protruding upward like bullets. He turned her around massaging her buttocks guiding the water stream between them. He moved her slightly so the pulsating water hit the small of her back and left her there in search of the robe and towel.

He pushed the shower knob to off, wrapped the towel expertly around her head and slipped her arms inside the robe sleeves, pulling it around her shoulders and crossing the front flaps around, securing them with the belt. He scooped her up from the bathtub, turned the bathroom door knob, carrying her to the bedroom. The cooler air hit her face and she opened her eyes. She nuzzled his neck and felt his forearm muscles.

He tossed her gently on the bed and pulled the the bed spread and covers. She rolled on her stomach and he pulled the covers clear from the bed. He kneeled on the mattress and started patting her back, drying and massaging in the process. He kneaded the shoulders and moved lower, then up again rubbing and stimulating her back muscles.

He dried between her buttocks and thighs. He concentrated on her buttocks massaging them through the robe and striking them rhythmically with the edge of his hands.

He loosened one robe belt end, and pulled it through the single loop. He peeled the robe from her shoulders slowly exposing her back that was red from the strenuous rubdown and ensuing massage. He pulled the robe clear off her body and deposited it in a heap on the floor by the foot of the bed.

He looked at her face. Her eyes were still closed, but he knew she was not asleep, because her body was covered by goosebumps and her buttocks were flexing with anticipation.

He lifted his arms and let his finger tips brush her neck, moving to her shoulder blades, moving downwards on her sides in a racking motion. Moving to the center and racking her skin again and again, then stopping at random sections of her back and scratching softly.

He moved to her buttocks which he started pinching lightly and massaging, spreading he cheeks and caressing the soft moss of hair. She moaned and spread her legs as he moved his fingertips slowly down between her thighs. He cupped the soft flesh between her thighs gently squeezing and moving higher spreading with his index and middle finger her labia from behind.

He lowered his head and rested his beard on her spread butt cheeks, his hot breath on the bed of hair moss. Her anus reacted by a trembling of the muscles around it. He directed his breath towards her open pussy massaging the labia with his finger tips. He brushed his beard on the inside of her thighs and watched the goosebumps travel in waves towards the back of her knees. He trailed their path with his lips from side to side and back up again, just short of her pussy.

He rested his head on her buttocks and started racking and scratching her back with his fingernails, feeling her skin reaction with his fingertips and reacting to her mute demands by moving higher, lower and side to side. He concentrated on her sides moving ever so gently on the side of her breasts. He eased his palms under them, cradling them tenderly, kissing the side of her neck. He felt the hairs on the back of her neck rise and goosebumps travel the side of her neck disappearing towards her shoulder blades.

He rocked her gently side to side and rolled her on her back. She opened her eyes as he lowered his face on hers, his lips breezily brushing her upper lip feeling the fuzz below her nostrils. He took her upper lip in his mouth, sucking, pulling it away from her gums and inserting his tongue, darting quickly side to side.  He released her upper lip and repeated the process with the lower lip forcing her mouth open, his tongue meeting hers, touching, groping and swirling inside her mouth.  He buried his face on her neck stretching it to its full length, taking his weight on his elbows.  She reached and locked her arms around his back, holding him captive, squeezing tight so that their breathing was synchronized.  His exhaling to her breathing in and opposite.  He sifted his weight and she released him.

He started kissing her neck moving under her chin and trailing his tongue to the opposite side underneath her ear lobe and back again to the near side.  She stretched her neck out feeling his beard tickling her neck and moving ever so slowly, ever so gently down the swell of her breasts. His lips brushing and releasing her nipples. The areoles sensing the beard and his mustache before they actually felt it, shrunk and wrinkled in anticipation.  The nipples tightened and became two little bullets.  He squeezed them with his lips, took one inside his mouth and started sucking with pleasure.  As soon as he felt the other one relaxing to the touch of his fingertips, he released the one he was sucking, taking the other nipple, keeping them both hard and pouting.

He moved his chin between the valley of the breasts, licking the underside. Circling the nipples and down the valley once again changing sides.  He carved a path with his mustache the length of her breastbone, down to her belly, circling with his tongue her belly buttoned finally burying his face full force on her bush.  He breathed deeply the musty smell moving the palms of his hands under her buttocks, lifting and pushing her fuzz deeper into his face.

He lifted his face, raised her knees and locked them in the raised position by planting his shoulders on her shins.  He looked up and saw her face resting on the pillow, her breasts rising and lowering softly with her breathing.  He looked at the pussy in front of him closed like an oyster shell.  He blew his hot breath on the hairs and rubbed his beard on the inside of her thighs all the way to her knees.  He started licking, kissing and biting gently the inside of her thighs from the knees up, stopping short of the labia.

He spread her pussy open, revealing the pink petals.  He brushed his beard softly on the open labia, kissing them all the way to the opening.  He stiffened his tongue and inserted it in the opening, rotating and thrusting as deep as he could reach.  He took his tongue out slowly rubbing the upper side, brushing her clit. This sent a jolt to her body and reflex tightened her thighs around his head.  He planted his wet tongue on the underside of her clit and rocked it gently while his lips brushed it gently, pushing, freeing it from its restraints.  Stroking, licking, brushing, sucking until she relaxed her grip on his head and started an uncontrollable thrusting and rolling of her hips.  He gripped her buttocks firmly and held her pined, motionless, helpless slave of the pleasure he was giving her.

As soon as he felt the tension easing out of her body, he used a hand to spread her labia and gently inserted a finger in her pussy.  He moved it in and out, in and around the walls while all the time stroking her clit with a strong tongue.  The blood collected on the clit making it three times its original size and the finger action was bringing a flood of juice out of her pussy.  He inserted his tongue again inside the hole and tasted her juices.  He touched her nipples gently with both hands, rotating them in his fingertips.  He gently caressed the slopes of her breasts.

He sensed her breasts tensing first before he felt her nails clawing his back.  He savagely gripped her breasts squeezing her nipples between thumb and fore finger.  He buried his tongue in her pussy, licking and thrusting furiously.  His lips sucking on her clit while his tongue rubbing on it, moaning, transmitting the humming vibration on his tongue, sending shivers up her clit, opening the flood gates of her pussy.  The bed was vibrating, shaking, both bodies locked in the throes of pleasure...The bed shaking, shaking...What the heck, he heard himself cussing as he woke with a start, his bed shaking.

"Time to get up." Don said with a smile. "You don't want to be late to your meeting with the Warden this morning. By the way, that must have been one hell of a sweet dream. We hated to wake you up. We gave you as long as we could. But we have to catch the bus for the Base and if we leave without waking you up, you will end up missing your appointment and possibly be late on your first day of work at Construction 4."

"What time is it?" Michael asked siting up and trying to cover up a tremendous hard on.

"Six thirty." Bill said standing next to Don. "You are going to miss breakfast if you don't get your butt out of bed. They are closing the Mess Hall in half an hour. Hank is already there."

"Screw breakfast." Michael said falling back in bed. "Leave a note for Hank to wake me up when he gets back."

"Now, Mike; get your ass out of bed, or we will pull you down bedding and all.", Lester said grabbing the the corner of the mattress by the foot of the bed and shaking it for emphasis.

"That's right!" Don added. "Today is your first day at your new job in Construction 4 and don't forget your meeting with the Warden at 8:00 AM sharp. He is going to make you an offer your can't refuse. Is this any way of creating a good first impression?"

"You are right." Michael said getting finally up and putting a tentative foot down in search of the first ladder rung on his way down.

"You are going no place buddy;" Bill said baring Michael's path, "until you tell us what were you dreaming, when we woke you up."

Michael felt his face getting red and tried to hide his face by rubbing his eyes fighting sleep. "I don't know if I am awake yet or where I am, to remember what I was dreaming of." Michael mumbled.

"I don't know about that." Bill continued stepping aside. "We've got to go ourselves, but don't you get the idea that you are getting a reprieve.

The interrogation will continue this afternoon, after work.  Is that the plan guys?"  He addressed his companions who were nodding eagerly.

"We will see about that."  Michael said cryptically.  "I've been known to have the attention span of a flash bulb when it comes to remembering dreams."  He grabbed his robe, towel and shaving kit making his way out the door towards the far bathroom down the hallway.

"Who is in charge again of Construction 4?"  He yelled back towards Bill who he knew was working for the Base Construction Crew and seemed to know all the hacks for the various Construction activities.

"A fellow by the name of Rolfs.  Phil Rolfs."  Bill replied.  "He is a pretty decent sort.  You will like him.  You are lucky you are not stuck working for Construction 2.  The hack in charge of that Division is a real piece of work."

"Where is this Rolfs working out of?"  Michael asked.

"Mess Hall basement."  Bill replied as he got out the door.

Michael looked at his watch and noticed the time.  If he hurried, he could make it for breakfast just before closing.  He trotted up the steps to the Mess Hall and made it inside with a couple of minutes to spare.  On second thought he reasoned this job may work out just fine.  He wouldn't have to get up until it was ordinary time to catch the bus for the work detail on Base.  He would be here at Camp all day long; hundred yards from his room and in the hub of all the activity.  He was not aware as yet of what the job entailed, but he had a good idea after his conversation with Dino and the rest of the 'Men of Respect'.  He seemed to recall noticing inmates working at the new Theater whose completion date was a joke and slipping, already two years behind schedule.  He certainly didn't want to be late for his meeting with the Warden.  He looked at his watch.  Plenty of time.

He decided to make a recon of Rolfs office as he was at the Mess Hall already.  He found the concrete steps to the basement.  It was the first time that he took the steps winding down to a basement door with the sign on the door: Construction Management Services (CMS) Division. He opened the door and saw two offices.  The rest of the basement appeared abandoned.  One of the doors, the one on the left, had the name 'Rolfs' engraved on it.  The one on the right next to it  had the name 'Krupp' engraved on it and above a custom made sign proclaiming that this was the entrance to an omnipotent being, God himself.  A big belly appeared around the corner down the end of the hallway.  The enormous belly was attached to an ape like figure, bald with ears something between Dumbo the elephant and Yoda of Star Wars.  The overall appearance of the cartoon character was that resembling 'Bluto' in the Popeye cartoons.  He waddled down the hallway, coming in Michael's direction.

"I hope that's not Rolfs." He thought. "I won't be able to keep a straight face looking at this laughable creature."

Mercifully, he stopped in front of the door engraved 'Krupp' and pulled out a huge chain that was attached to his belt and looped down his knees with an enormous key attached at the end of the chain. He threw Michael a look full of suspicion and hostility and kept it on him, which caused him to keep missing the key hole and cussing under his breath. Michael smiled and threw at him a cheerful good morning, which the barbarian answered with a belch and a most offensive wave of odor that ever assaulted Michael's nose.  He instinctively turned his face downwind trying to keep his hurriedly consumed breakfast down, while a new cascade of cussing got started from the direction of 'Bluto'. Finally, he managed to open the door, keeping his suspicious eye on Michael, which threw off his concentration and he stumbled over the raised threshold to his office.  Michael brought a palm to his face covering his mouth to suppress a wave of nervous laughter that was breaking out in uncontrollable giggles.

"What the fuck is so funny?" Krupp exploded, slamming his door shut in the process.

Michael knocked on the door in front of him, but as soon as his knuckle made contact with the wood, the door receded as someone opened it from the inside and Michael found himself face to face with a tall footballer type individual, passed his prime, all muscle gone to fat.

"What was that all about?" The ex footballer inquired. He seemed addressing no one in particular, although Michael was the only other soul standing there.

"The fellow next door slammed the door." Michael said hesitantly.

"What did you say to him?"

"Nothing!" Michael protested.

"He must not have liked you. Which is a plus in my book, because I like you already." The stranger said extending his hand. "By the way my name is Phil Rolfs."

Michael shook the proffered hand which gripped his like a vice and delivered a crushing squeeze. Michael returned the favor causing Rolfs to wince slightly as Michael unfairly used the oversize ring of Rolfs as leverage to crush his fingers against the ring side intricate carvings.

"OK! OK! You are strong. I get the message." Rolfs said disengaging. "Who are you and what are you doing here?"

"My name is Michael. I was directed to report to Construction 4 later on this morning. I was in the area eating breakfast and thought I would conduct a recon of the location of your office."

"You must be the Engineer. I fought for you. Everyone wanted to grab you. I pulled rank as Construction 4. Construction 4 is the General Contractor of the Construction Management Services. I read your PSI by the way and I could not figure out what you did wrong to be here. You were framed, I concluded. Let me show you around and hear your ideas."

"I would love to sir, but I would be late for a previous scheduled appointment…" "Cancel it."

"May I use your phone and call the Warden's office?"

"You have an appointment with the Warden?" Rolfs pronounced incredulous. "I've been in the system almost twenty years, and I have never encountered a Warden giving an inmate an audience. I guess there is always a first. Reading your PSI, you do not seem like the run of the mill inmate we usually get. Better move your ass to the Administration Building and then come straight back here. I want to know how the meeting with the Warden went…By the way from now on, I am Phil and you are Michael or Mike? Which do you prefer?"

"Michael."

"Good Luck. I hope the Warden's plans do not throw a monkey wrench to mine."

Michael went up the stairs to the Mess Hall and out the main door heading towards the Administration Building. He arrived there, ten to eight. He made his way to the second floor. The Warden's office door was closed but the receptionist's was open.

"My name is Michael and I have an appointment at 8:00 AM sharp according to the call-out, with the Warden. I realize I am a little early."

The receptionist looked up from her computer. "How did you get up here?"

"I took the stairs."

"No one stopped you?"

"No. I did not encounter anyone."

She shook her head and picked up the phone from her desk. "Your eight o'clock is here."

She directed Michael to sit at one of the chairs across her desk and wait.

Michael sat and studied the female across from him. She looked just out of High School. White, blond, impeccably groomed with minimal make-up and an impressive set of boobs. He was aware that the Warden was black. He must be an equal opportunity employer, he thought as the door to the Warden's office opened and an older black man started towards him.

"You must be Michael…I will not try your last name." He said offering his hand which Michael instinctively shook. "I am Luther. Please come to my office."

He led Michael in and closed the door. He pointed to a conference table which took a corner of the enormous office and Michael sat in a comfortable chair with his elbows on the table. Luther took the chair directly across from him.

"I read your PSI. It reads more like a bio of someone on Who's Who. I couldn't figure out what you did wrong to be our guest. What did you do?"

"I was convicted of Mail Fraud…"

"I read that in your PSI and I am still asking myself, what you did."

"The central issue in the indictment was the interpretation of the Davis-Bacon Act and how it applied to the prevailing wage. I interpreted the Law strictly as it is stated; i.e. the prevailing wage applied only for the hours that the employee was engaged in productive work on the actual worksite. I really had no other choice since the work my company was performing was on a cost plus basis and the government was videotaping the worksites and comparing the hours I had charged them, with the actual work shown on the video tapes. I was not paying my employees the prevailing wage rate for travel between jobs, eating donuts and drinking coffee in the morning for an hour, leaving the job site an hour early at the end of the day to lock up the tools at the shop, waiting around the job site for direction by the government because they encountered a Differing Site Condition. If I had paid them the prevailing wage for these hours, the government on the basis of the videos, would have indicted me for overcharging the government.

For years the government went along with my interpretation of the Davis -Bacon Act because they were saving money on the Change Orders which comprised the majority of our work. A few years went by and the government decided to reopen past Contracts and re-interpret the Davis-Bacon Act and state that all hours spent while at work on site or off site or standing idle or eating donuts and drinking coffee, were subject to prevailing wages. Ergo I underpaid my employees. They calculated the money that the employees were underpaid by applying the highest hourly rate the employees had ever worked, times all the hours they had been employed. On that basis, I filed a claim with the Armed Services Board of Contract Appeals applying the same logic as the government and asked for over seven million dollars which I was owed. The government's response was that I was trying to profit from my crime. The government short listed my attorney just before my trial was to take place, for a Federal Judge position that opened in Hawaii and promised the presiding federal judge of my trial a promotion to the 9th Circuit Court of Appeals if he got a conviction.

There were many issues for Appeal to the 9th Circuit Court of Appeals. My attorney chose one issue which was proven and admitted by the government, which was that the government did not incur a loss, as a matter of fact they admitted in court that the government profited. Accordingly, since there was no loss or damage, they could not ask for an indictment. The 9th responded with one sentence: 'The government need not have incurred a loss or damages to seek an indictment'. I was told by our lawyers here at the Camp that the Supreme Court had recently vacated a case that had the identical language. This means that if I had  filed my Appeal to the 9the Circuit Court of Appeals today, I would have prevailed."

"What you are saying is beyond belief. Do you have any proof?"

"I do and have filed for a Writ of Certiorari with the Supreme Court and am expecting a response any day now."

"You sound like a very responsible and well educated person with on the job experience far surpassing anything we have here at Camp and the Air Force on Base. It's time to play let's make a deal. The Camp and Nellis Air Force Base will receiver the next five years, more money than we could possibly spent in improvements, infrastructure and new construction. My question is what you can do for us and what are you asking in return. I realize that other institutions have already started and will continue to try to lure you away from here with all sorts of promises. You are my first draft choice so to speak and I want to know what will it take to keep you here. I have a poor memory, particularly for technical details and I would like to record your proposal for my own exclusive use." Without waiting for Michael's response, the Warden pulled a micro recorder from his pocket and passed the 'record' button.

"I believe that you have the capabilities, with me on board, to Design Build all future construction both here at Camp and on Base. We should redesign the CMS basement to include all the requirements to reach this objective. The Red Horse have their own engineering. I looked into their capabilities and all they do is subcontract their work to outside consulting engineering firms in Las Vegas. You could offer them to do the same thing for half the money they are currently spending. They will require my consulting engineering services on as need basis as they are currently contracting to check on the work of their in house engineers for half of what they are paying. The current consulting engineering hourly rate on the outside is roughly $150.00 per hour. You should offer them to do the same thing for less, and I am sure they will jump on your proposal. Same goes for the cost to design the projects. They are currently paying 6% to 10% of the cost of the project in design engineering expenses. You can charge them half of that and still make money because our cost will be less than 1% of the cost of the project; and I mean our cost, which would be a little over half of the cost a

General Contractor from the outside would charge.  I am very familiar with the federal appropriation procedures.  I will make my own detailed construction cost estimate, verified by actual bids we receive.  For example for the new 30,000 square foot dormitory at $100 per square foot, which is extremely reasonable, the  appropriation will be $3 million dollars.  The actual cost of the dormitory build with in house resources will be $1.7 million dollars, leaving a profit of $1.3 million dollars to be distributed as bonuses to the Camp personnel.  This is for a single project.  I have the capability to supervise concurrently twenty projects.  For the projects at the Air Force Base, you should use the same method in the FYI appropriation and come up with a formula to split the profits.  Additionally, the Air Force Base is planning to advertise a two-week course in Changes in Construction Contracts, say for no more than twenty aspiring Contracting Officers at a time at $2,500.00 each and I bet you they will have a waiting list.  I was asked numerous times to conduct a seminar in Washington, California and Hawaii by the Army, Navy and Air Force and I declined every time.  Include my Resume in the prospectus they will send to other military facilities and a codicil that the Government engaged in litigation183 times with this individual during a twenty year span and lost every single time.  If you don't like this, use whatever advertising you wish; bottom line is that they will get their moneys' worth.  I will teach the course in the afternoon 3 hours a day, Monday through Friday.  I could also teach a course for inmates called Construction Management once a week that will help them, particularly minorities, to get a job, even start their own construction company if they attend the course for twenty five weeks, and they will be able to successfully contract with the government."

Michael stopped talking and indicated that the Warden should pause the recording.

"Amazing."  Was the Warden's response.  "Better than I would have anticipated.  Not only you avail yourself, you propose and recommend a possible solution and a blue print upon which to base the implementation.  Another use that you did not propose is to loan you out and solve the problems of other government facilities, not to exceed the weekend.  That will be on weekends that you have not scheduled a Visit.  Is this OK with you?"

Michael nodded consent.

"We are in agreement with what you have to offer and I will accept your proposal.  What is all this going to cost me?"

"The highest hourly wage available, forty cents an hour, deposited in my prison  account.

"The highest monthly bonus available, up to four hundred dollars per month,  deposited in my prison account.


"Two boxes of 25 cuban cigars, each box, per month.


"A golf cart to get around on Camp and on Base.


"A special card to eat at any Officer's Club on Base with the BOP covering the tab.


"A special card so I may shop at the Base PX with my expenditures to be deducted form my prison account.


"Freedom from having to be here or there, because due to my job I may be required to be in places that are out of bounds for the ordinary prisoner.  I am sure that if you explain to the guards that their bonuses are dependent upon my performance, they will be understanding."

Michael stopped talking.  In response the Warden offered his hand and they shook on the agreement.

"I have to go and report to Construction 4, after I leave here.  I went on a recon mission early in the morning to locate the whereabouts of Construction 4 and Phil Rolfs, it's supervisor.  When I met him he didn't want me to leave.  When I told him I had a previously scheduled appointment, he asked me to cancel it.  Accordingly, I had to tell him that my appointment was with the Warden.  Reluctantly, he let me leave, but I was told to come right back after I was done with my meeting and give him a full report of what transpired during the meeting.  Am I allowed to report to him what transpired here?"

"No.  I will tell him what's what.  You tell him that the Warden forbade you to disclose the events and conversations that transpired this morning."

Michael got up to leave.  The Warden stopped him and went around his desk and opened a middle drawer.  He extracted a box of Cuban cigars, La Gloria Cubana Maduro which he handed to Michael.  It was more than half full.

"This does not count towards your monthly allotment.  Things will start happening starting this minute.  I will be keeping an eye on you as to how you will perform on your first task, which is the new Movie Theater.  Rolfs is under pressure from  me to deliver.  He is two years behind schedule on this project alone.  I hope now that you are on board, things will change for the better."

They shook hands and Michael left the Warden's office with the box of Cuban cigars under arm.  He stopped in his room to hide the cigars in his locker inside a self improvised humidor made with an oversized water cooler.  He then headed for the Chow Hall and went down the steps to the CMS and Phil Rolfs office.  It was a little after nine o'clock, however, still earlier than his scheduled reporting time of nine thirty.  He knocked on the door.  Once again Phil Rolfs opened the door and broke into a wide smile as soon as he saw who was at the door.

"Come in!  Come in!  How did the meeting with the Warden go?"

"Phil, I am here as ordered to report for work and are complying as I was directed.  My meeting with the Warden went well and I was told by him in no uncertain terms not to disclose any of my conversation with him to anyone.  I will say in brief that basically, I was told what was expected of me based on my education and experience."

"I appreciate your candor Michael and I will get right to it.  My immediate problem is the new Movie Theater.  It is two years behind schedule.  The Warden is putting pressure on me for a completion date and that date better be soon.  So what could I do.  I don't understand where we are and nobody will tell me.  So I tell the Warden what he wants to hear: at the end of the month, and hope he forgets it.  And next month I repeat again at the end of the month."

Michael was informed over the weekend by the 'Men of Respect' that this 'end of the month' business has been going on for a couple of years now, to the point that Phil no longer promised at the end of the month, because he was threatened by the Warden with a transfer to some God fore-shaken high security facility, like La Tuna and a demotion, back to Custody, and a pay cut.  So a few weeks ago Phil started splitting the difference.  The first of the month he would promise completion by the middle of the month.  The middle of the month, he would go back to the familiar end of the month projected completion date.

"So, what I want you to tell me Mr. Engineer is this: When is the Movie Theater gonna be finished.  And I mean finished, so inmates and staff can go and watch movies.  You got that?  Don't try to bull shit a bull shiter.  I want the bitter truth." Phil Rolfs, Michael found out, was a former 'goon squad' commander.  He got injured on the job clobbering the 'bad boys' at some high security institution.  He never finished High School.  The BOP hired him, but made him get his GED through their diploma mill.

He could not read blue prints and his previous construction experience was limited to driving a fork lift.

"Don't worry." Michael reassured him. "You will get an exact status of the project, together with a projected completion date. I will even do one better. I'll make a Construction Schedule so, not only you will know today, but you can track the job tomorrow and the next day, clear to completion. Do you happen to have a Construction Schedule already, by the way? I hate to re-invent the wheel, if you do."

"No. I do't. Nobody told me about a Schedule. I don't know how to make one nor read one. All I know it's something in writing. Shit no. I don't want a Schedule. Next thing I know the Warden will get ahold of it. And then what? No. I want no record."

"I think you got it all wrong." Michael said shaking his head at the bureaucratic mediocracy and incompetence in evidence. "What if you lived up to the promises. What if you hit the completion date on the button or even better, finished early. Then what? The Construction Schedule, the written record, becomes a milestone. A monument attesting to your ability. Undisputed proof that you deliver what you promise. Think of it this way. Why do you always assume that you would fail? If you have this defeatist attitude, then you will surely fail. It is a self fulfilled prophecy."

"That's all good and fine. But how do you establish this milestone you are talking about? That completion date."

"You don't establish it. It reveals itself at the conclusion of your thought process in establishing a realistic Construction Schedule. If you fail to meet the completion date, provided you've done everything in your power to do so, then the failure is not your fault. Something unforeseen has taken place. Of course there are techniques in taking into consideration such unforeseen conditions, by establishing some float time between activities. Particularly the ones that directly effect the "Critical Path…"

"It all sounds fine. You sound fine. I mean like… you know what you are talking about. But this is not the outside world. This is a prison. How do I know you won't set me up?  It's obvious you know more about the business than I do.  An  inmate running the show!  Unheard of and dangerous to boot.  I don't know…All my life I operated under the principle that I didn't want anyone watching me.  Not that they haven't tried mind you.  But I always been able to spot the spies in time and neutralize them."

"What did this get you?"  Michael asked.

"Well…I still got my job as you can see."  Rolfs smiled cagey.  "Eighteen years and counting.  Another two and I can retire."

"Have you gotten a promotion?  I mean other than putting your time. Did you get a raise? A bonus? Anything based on Merit?"

"No.  But the government doesn't work that way.  You put in your time and you keep your nose clean.  That's all that is expected of you…"

"Then why is the Warden pressing you for the completion of the Movie Theater?"

Rolfs looked at Michael and could not come up with an explanation consistent with the theory he was expanding of how the government thought and operated.

"I am a Professional Engineer."  Michael told him.  "I always try to the best of my ability.  My commitment is to excellence.  This work ethic does not change by the fact that the client this time is the BOP or that I am a prisoner.  I don't do the work to please anyone else but myself.  If I screw up, I don't care if no one else sees it.  I will see it and I will know it. That's enough of a deterrent…"

"You don't fit the mold of the typical inmate.  This is self-evident.  Your knowledge and experience makes you dangerous.  What if you change your mind? No one will know but you. Then what?"

"You finally hit the nail on the head.  It boils down to trust.  That's the bottom line.  The issue of whether I posses knowledge and ability, is documented in my PSI. The question is:  Do you trust me?  If you don't, I am unable to function in the position I've been assigned by the BOP. It's obvious you need an engineer.  But if you don't trust me to function within my job description, then I suggest you sign my cop-out so I may be reassigned.  Maybe I'd be better off with the 'neat team'. I think I can be trusted to pick trash..."

"You are right."  Rolfs interrupted Michael. "And I trust you.  You have a free hand to do as you please.  I will back your play.  You can count on it. If it is a Construction Schedule you want?  Go ahead and prepare one. Let me see it first though, before you give a copy to anyone else.  Fair enough?  And in the future give me an idea of what you are thinking and planning.  Not that I will ever stop you, but I'd like to have a heads up when someone asks me.  Do we have a deal?"  Michael gripped the extended hand and shook it.  "In the meantime, anything you need from me, just ask."

"There are actually couple of things I will need.  The first is 3 to 5 draftsmen.  Go to the PSI's of all inmates in the computer and enter the key words of 'drafting', 'contractor', 'technical drawing' and 'High School Drafting'.  Put the names that pop up on a call-out for tomorrow to report to Construction 4.  We are going to start as part of Construction 4, an Engineering Department.  We will do all the design work and the Drawings for the work at Camp and the work at the Base.  In addition, I bet you we will end up checking all the design work out of the Red Horse and stamp it 'Approved for Construction'. I also want some writing pads with a square grid of an eighth of an inch each square.  It's called engineering paper which I will need it to design preliminary sketches on one eighth of an inch to a foot scale."  On that note, Michael grabbed a clipboard and left Rolf's office.

Michael had never been near the new Movie Theater building under construction.  It was off limits to the inmate population, except to authorized inmates, presumably the workers, and the entire area was patrolled by BOP guards, anxious to give out of bounds citations, 'shots'. It was a good place for the hacks to lay in wait, for not very long, to meet their weekly quota of citations. It was also a popular place for the prisoners. Part curiosity, part due to the endless supply  of useful materials like discarded nails, wood scraps, concrete blocks to make shelve bases, tables and other ancillary furnishings to supplement the inmates meager living quarters. The Movie Theater construction site was a perpetual theater of capture and evasion maneuvers.

Michael was one of the inmates who read the rules, learned them and followed them to the letter; in wait for the BOP employees to breach their own rules and then use his writing skills to prepare an incident report, where the regulations, BOP's biggest ally, became their worst nightmare. He would't cheapen this skill, by making it an everyday affair. He collected data on BOP personnel, daily and had  a case ready against everyone to be used at a moment's notice. The formal reporting was, however, used sparingly. Only to correct a serious wrong and only if it affected him personally. He only went after those incidents where he had   immediate knowledge of the sequence of events. He did not rely on witness testimony and hearsay. He believed a witness was only as good as his signed affidavit. Hence, he was labeled by the BOP guards as someone to be avoided to tangle with at all costs. In addition he was, after all, a 'Man of Respect'.

This factoid, together with his new title as the Camp Engineer, he was now one of the 'authorized inmates' to enter any area, gave strut to his walk towards the new Movie Theater construction site. He approached it as if he owned it, to check on its status and progress.

"Hey 'paisan'!  What are you doing here?"  A familiar voice distracted him and slowed down his purposeful step.

Michael turned and spotted Joe, an inmate who he met once and knew slightly, getting up, from sitting in the shade of the nearby tress among a dozen inmates, smoking and sipping soft drinks from the cans. They were sitting on pieces of lumber and plywood, destined to become forms for the cast-in-place concrete. Joe took a couple of steps towards Michael. Stopped. Tilted his head backwards and took a long continuous swallow from the can of Dr. Pepper he was holding, bringing finally the upside down can in the vertical position. He tossed the empty on the ground and stepped on it with a heavy boot, turning it into a pancake. He slap kicked it, like a hockey puck, towards the pile of construction debris, burped loudly, causing the others to break into an instantaneous laughter and continued walking towards Michael. Michael followed his progress and turned the clipboard pad face up to show him that he carried a 'tabula rasa', a paper with nothing written on it.

"So?" He stared at Michael questioningly. "What are you doing in our neck of the woods? Slumming?" He added with a grin.

"I was going to ask you the same question." Michael responded, "But I can tell from all these tools laying around, that you guys are pretending to work."

"What are you going to do about it? They pretend to pay us, we pretend to work." He came back making Michael laugh. His wit and one liner comebacks was breaking Michael up. Michael remembered the prisoner's name from the last time they had met, Joe Scala. Joe had a knack to lift your spirit. His enthusiasm and lust for life was contagious.

"I came over to look at the new Movie Theater. Part of my new job assignment." Michael said getting serious for the moment. "Do you know anything about it?"

"Know anything? Are you kidding me? I practically built what you see, so far, with my own two hands." Joe said showing off his callous palms.

"Then, you are the man I want to talk to."

"Why?"

"I want to establish where the project stands.  Then I am going to develop a scope of the unfinished work and divide that work into manageable activities.  I will put these activities into a Bar Chart type Construction Schedule, in order to find out when this project will be completed.  I will go back to make sure that the materials to accomplish all these outstanding activities have been ordered and make sure that they will get on site, timely.  That's about the size of it."

"Heavy shit!" Joe said in pretend fright.  "But I can save you from all this trouble and extra work.  The MovieTheater ain't getting built.  You can take this to the bank for me, off the record of course."

"Why?"

"Because we are pissed."

"Who is we?"

"We, us."  He pointed to the others who sat with him and some more, over two dozen at least, who had appeared since Michael and Joe started talking, out of nowhere, watching them.

"Are you guys guys all Construction 4?"

"Yep."

"Why are you pissed, if I may ask?  And don't give me the canned reply, 'because we are in prison.'"

"No, that's not it.  We are pissed at the BOP for treating us the way they are." "How's that?"

"First they promised us a bonus in the beginning of the Summer.  Here is September and we have not seen it yet.  Most of the guys in construction live on the money they are getting paid by the BOP.  A hundred dollars a month bonus, may mean nothing on the outside, but here, it is the difference whether some inmates are going to survive or not.  'Capish'?"

"Is that it  The beef centers on money?"

"No. Not only money. But it is a good start."

"What else?"

"Furloughs is another. Inmates in Construction have been promised: 'Work hard and you get to go home to see your wife and kids for a visit'. Well, it has not happened yet. Another BOP empty promise."

"Are you sure there is no misunderstanding?" Michael asked.

"Fuck you Mike! Give me a little credit man!" Joe was showing signs that he was losing patience with Michael. "Here you act like a 'cop' to solve everything. You ain't a 'cop'. Your shirt is khaki. Same color as everyone else's." He pointed again at the inmate gathering.

"Well, not exactly." Michael managed to say smiling.

"What do you mean?"

"Mine is more brown than yours." Michael said pointing to his new shirt, which had not seen laundry detergent yet, nor the desert sun.

Joe broke out laughing hysterically, causing the rest of the inmates to laugh. Joe's mood and mannerisms were such that could elicit the crack of a smile from the lips of even the most 'unhappy Camper'. He was that kind of guy. Michael's last comment, overheard and repeated by a number of inmates, seemed to break the ice between them. They joined Joe and started telling Michael their own grievances and tales of woe. A recurring theme of unjust treatment at the hands of the BOP, appeared to be a story told in various versions by several inmates. The salient points however, sounded the same in each case. That alone, made it believable.

It seems, a couple of weeks ago, after repeated pleadings by the BOP supervisor, Phil Rolfs, who was getting rather desperate to complete the project or at the very least show some progress to that end; the inmates decided to give the BOP another chance. Mind you, the inmates got no direction or had any clue for that matter, as to how to proceed.  The only thing relayed to them by Phil Rolfs was that the Warden was putting pressure on him to get the Movie Theater in operating condition by the middle of the month, a couple of weeks away. Absent further direction as to how to accomplish this, the inmates fell into deep thought as to how to go about getting the job done.  As it usually is the case, when a group lacks leadership and knowhow at the top, the only way they understand to accomplish the task sooner, is by working harder. If they were already working hard.  In w that case work longer hours.  They believed that the job gets done by applying brute force.  They end up working hard, rather than working smart.  Working overtime is a hard proposition on the outside.  In jail, it is next to impossible.  The inmate's hours don't belong to him, but to the BOP.  No one is allowed outside the building before five AM.  Work starts at six thirty AM.  Work stops at two thirty PM, because that's when the Commissary opens.  At three o'clock there is mail call.  Accordingly, in order to lengthen the working hours, something had to be done at the start of the work day.  The Movie Theater construction inmates decided to start work two hours earlier or at four thirty AM.  This meant that the construction crew had to be put on an out-count, because between four o'clock and five, the inmates were counted.  If anyone left the building before five, he was reported missing.  The guys notified Rolfs of their intent to start work two hours earlier.  Rolf said he would report this at the Control Center and the crew would be put on the out-count.

The next morning the guys started work two hours earlier, some even as early as four AM.  At five o'clock officer Parker, otherwise known as 'double D' on account of the size of her tits, foaming at the mouth, confronted them.

"How come you are out of the building even though the blue light is still on?"

The question was really rhetorical.  She could give a shit.  The inmates were not on the out-count sheet.  That's an automatic 'shot'. 'Double D' is a hardened woman.  In her career, as a custody officer, she had heard it all and did not believe any of it.

Needless to say, everyone working ended up with a 'shot' for being out of bounds during count.  A serious infraction, which translates to no furloughs and a reduced halfway house stay.  A 'shot' like that would follow them on their 'jacket' to the parole officer on the outside.  Inmates who leave the building, wandering outside in the middle of the night are up to no good. Taking delivery of contraband or worse: money, booze, drugs.  These guys are in for a rough probation period.  Urine Analysis (UA) tests to start with twice a week and frequent personal appearances to the probation officer's office.  All that hassle, because Rolfs forgot to put them on the out-count.

That same day, they corralled Rolfs and told him what happened.  He told them that he did his duty, reporting them to the Lieutenant in charge of the out-count.  Rolfs' claim was checked with lieutenant Dutro.  He told the inmates that Rolfs had said nothing to him.  Back to Rolfs.  He stuck to his story: Custody screwed up.  Custody stuck by their story: CMS screwed up.  Ultimately the inmates got screwed, because no one from the government wanted to admit they had made a mistake.

The question, however, as to when the Movie Theater might get done, still remained unanswered; compounded by administrative ignorance and incompetence from one side and an uncooperative, to say the least, work force on the other side.  Everyone in the meantime, was still in the dark concerning where the project stood.

A challenging situation, nevertheless, not unlike others Michael had faced in his career on the outside.  The players may have been different, the root of the problem remained the same.  Only this time, he found himself in a situation of limited power to bring about change.  He would have to tread carefully, never losing sight of the fact that he was an inmate himself.

"Joe, I understand you are you an Architect.  How come you are not working in an office?  Is there an engineering office in this camp?"

The engineering office here is a joke, until you came in that is man."  Joe replied.  "The office is Krupp and an insurance salesman.  High School education both, they neither can produce nor read Drawings.  For example there are no Drawings for the Movie Theater, sans the sketches I made when I used to work with them in the beginning.  But I gave up on them people, a long time ago.  I quit and came in the field.  Krupp was a piece of shit and Construction 2 was a shit hole; so I transferred to work with Phil Rolfs and Construction 4."

Michael started walking away from the inmate pack as Joe was still talking, drawing him away also as he started following Michael to get his point across.  Michael kept walking as he started noticing that no one else was following them.  Joe seemed to have asserted himself into a leadership position among the inmate labor force.  Michael wanted him away from his constituency.  He would talk to Michael differently, when he did, not having to concern himself with grandstanding for his constituents.  Michael wanted Joe to concentrate on what was actually being said, rather than the way it was being said and how was it playing to the audience.  Ochlocracy tends to feed on itself and Michael did not wish to put his demagogic skills to the test, yet.  In front of an audience, success would be ephemeral and he felt it would bring him into a collision course with Joe, who would feel his influence diminished.

"Joe.", Michael said, when he was sure they were alone and could not be overheard.  "I am surprised at you.  Surprised and a little disappointed."

"What do you mean?"  Joe replied in a conspiratorial tone of vice.

Michael expected Joe to react violently or at least start yelling and found himself braced for that.  But it did not come and in that respect half the battle was already won.  Joe was curious.  Joe recognized talent when he saw it.  Joe was in awe of Michael.  Michael had the whammy on Joe.  Joe could be talked to and he in turn would deliver the message to his constituents. Joe must have sensed the confrontation coming. He appreciated the fact that Michael was tactful enough to do it in private. If they were on the outside, Michael would hire Joe, because Joe would work for him. Joe knew it and he knew that Michael also knew it.

"First of all you are an Architect. You are supposed to be a professional. Start acting like one."

"But…" He started, but Michael cut him off.

"There are no buts. I know what you would say. You are in prison now etc. etc. That's no excuse. In my book excuses are like assholes. Everybody's got one and they all stink. When did you decided to sabotage the project for personal gain? That's totally unprofessional and you should be ashamed of even entertaining the thought of doing such a thing. Not performing to the best of your ability, which I understand has been going on for some time. I realize also that the BOP has behaved in an unprofessional manner. However, by bringing about a slow down in the workplace, you are lowering your standards. You allow yourself to get down to the BOP level. You are no better than they are."

Joe was looking down. Shifting uncomfortably. Kicking the dirt once in a while as Michael continued.

"On top of that, the whole thing is dumb and short sighted on your part."

"What do you mean?" Joe managed to say, barely above a whisper.

"You've picked the wrong battleground to make your point. Plain and simple. The project is the new Movie Theater. Two years behind schedule. Who is going to benefit from it? The BOP? I don't think so. The inmates are of course. The inmates have been deprived for the past two years from watching movies on a theater screen with a multi stereophonic sound system and in air conditioned comfort. Not the BOP. Am I making sense to you? Do you want to test this on your people?" Michael offered.

"No. No." Joe said hurriedly. "You are right. We just reacted in frustration. That's all. In prison, you know, you don't have time to think things through. You just react. An eye for an eye."

"Joe, I understand an eye for an eye. But in this case, you pulled both your eyes out and are swinging blindly, while the opponent sits back laughing. The only redeeming feature out of all that is that your adversary, the BOP, is too dumb to realize their advantage and capitalize on the situation, by killing the whole project." "What do we do?" A different, eager Joe, chomping at the bit, emerged.

"I am new here." Michael started. "I've never stepped foot on the project. You on the other hand lived and breathed it for two years. Help me understand where we stand. Help me get a handle on the situation. We will develop a Scope of Work based on the activities yet to be completed. Then you tell me what kind of people we got. What is their skill level? From what you tell me I will develop activity duration. We will put down the activities by sequence into a Bar Chart and develop a Construction Schedule. Based on that we will make sure that the material and equipment are on hand or if they even have been ordered. Their delivery status or place orders for the ones that are missing. We will decide when the project is to be completed and we will tell the BOP. As for the money issue and the 'shots', I firmly believe that the progress on the project will take care of them. The bonus is something subjective. It should be viewed as such. Bonus is like a tip. If you make Rolfs look good to the Warden, I believe he would tip accordingly, in order to insure continuance of good service. Believe me, he is not dumb. He will know why the project was done and who was responsible. The 'shots' on the other hand, is a separate issue altogether and should be treated as such. There are remedies designed for exactly such eventualities."

"If you mean a cop-out? Joe said. "You can forget it. They won't even bother to answer it."

"How about a BP-9? Better yet a whole bunch of BP-9's? Every inmate effected should file one. I will help every single inmate write it and I will edit them. These must be answered, in accordance with the BOP regulations. The government loves paperwork. But the individual bureaucrat who will be designated to answer the BP-9's does not. It's much easier to erase the 'shots' and make the whole thing a moot point. Particularly, if the BOP is convinced that the matter will not stop there. It will go to the Regional and then to National level for determination. The inmates are basically right on this issue. The locals certainly don't wish to broadcast their ineptness nationwide."

Michael spent the rest of the morning going over with Joey, as he started calling him, the entire project. The materials which were not on hand; i.e. visible on site or in the warehouse, were pressured lost, stollen or never ordered. Next came the task of writing material and equipment requisition orders and giving them to the BOP Purchasing. They had written on the requisition the expected delivery date and left written word with the BOP Purchasing Agent to notify them immediately, if one of the dates could not be met. The anticipated delivery dates were realistic given the fact that nothing, with the exception of the handicapped plumbing fixtures, appeared out of the ordinary and were hopefully in stock. They did not expect to hear from the Purchasing Agent and they did not. Based on the Scope of the Work. The labor force available and the expected delivery date of the shortages, Michael came up with a Construction Schedule. Today it was September 10. The earliest the project could be completed was the first week of November. The Construction Schedule was tight, with no 'float time' between activities, no consideration for 'Murphy's Law'. Michael decided to add 'float time' days between activities and artificially make the completion date the Wednesday before the Thanksgiving weekend, by adding a week of testing.

# CHAPTER 16

## The Movie Theater Saga

"I hope the Construction Schedule shows completion in mid-September." Rolfs hinted the next day. "The Boss came by asking. I had to tell him something..."

"In that case, I am afraid I got some bad news for you." Michael said as he unrolled the original Bar Chart, 24" x 36" standard Drawing size, on Rolfs desk.

Rolfs sat there for a while staring at it. It became obvious that he could neither read it, nor understand it. Time was of the essence. A copy of the Schedule was given to Joey who was spearheading the on site activities. Michael started explaining the thinking behind the development of the Construction Schedule. Rolfs eyes were glazed pretending to follow Michaels narrative and he winced when he heard the day before Thanksgiving as the completion date. Everything Michael had said to that point passed over Rolfs head and fell in the void. Rolfs could not get passed the completion date and he started arguing with Michael. Michael refused to falsify the Construction Schedule to accommodate what Rolfs had already said to the Warden.

"I told the Warden that you were making a Construction Schedule. He got excited. He wants a copy immediately to hang on the wall in his office. He said it would make an excellent conversation piece when visitors or representatives from the Regional BOP happened to drop by. I have no other alternative but to hand him the one you prepared. I don't know how am I going to to explain myself."

Michael knew exactly what Rolfs wanted. He did not disagree with the Thanksgiving completion date per se. He just did not want to be blamed for the delay. He envisioned himself as the scape goat. Michael pulled him out of his predicament by pointing out that the problem of having to extend the completion date centered on the fact that the electrical, plumbing and HVAC departments had not kept up with the overall progress of the project. They were the primary cause of the delay.

Rolfs eyes lit up. Finally, someone else to blame. He didn't think it would sound convincing to blame all the other BOP foremen collectively. It sounded like whine or worse, blaming everyone else but himself. The Warden might not buy this. Michael heard that Rolfs and Lips, the BOP head of the plumbing shop had words in the past. So, he took the chance telling Rolfs that the handicapped accessible plumbing fixtures had not been ordered.

"I went to Purchasing and ordered them myself yesterday. The Purchasing Agent would not because I was Construction 4 and the items I was ordering were not in my division. I told him that the Warden had appointed me as the Camp Engineer yesterday and as the Camp Engineer, I had jurisdiction over all Divisions. He called the Warden's office to verify what I was telling him and he placed the order as soon as he hung up. So, of all the shortages, the Warden is only aware that I ordered the handicapped fixtures yesterday. Even if all the other items were done, the BOP still could not get an Occupancy Permit from the Air Force, because according to the government regulations, every public facility must have handicapped accessible bathrooms. As I told you I went ahead and ordered the fixtures yesterday, but they are coming from the factory and would not be in Las Vegas until after the middle of November."

"Fucking Lips!" Phil Rolfs seethed for Michael's benefit; a wide grin breaking on his face. "I bet he did it on purpose to make me look bad. You caught his mistake and bailed him and me out, by placing the order the same day you reported for work for the first time. I love it."

With that, he grabbed two rolled up copies in full color Michael had already made of the Construction Schedule and they both left his office, Michael with the original, Rolfs with the two copies, presumably to deliver them to the Warden.

*     *     *     *

The Movie Theater was completed on the third of November, like the Construction Schedule said, sans the handicapped fixtures which were on route from the factory.  It was formally announced that the Movie Theater would be open for the general inmate population on Wednesday before the Thanksgiving weekend.  The movie for the opening would be 'Apollo 13'.

From the third of November until the last Wednesday of November, however, if you were looking during the day for a Construction 4 worker or select invited Red Horse personnel, chances were you would find them in the new Movie Theater, participating in testing and reviewing for the issue of the Occupancy Permit.  The Red Horse personnel were young engineers, just out of college, who were  Michael's students taking the course Changes in Construction Contracts for their Contracting Officer's Certificate.  All their work at Red Horse had to be reviewed by Michael and stamped 'Approved for Construction'. Needless to say that the Certificate of Occupancy was scheduled be issued as soon as the handicapped plumbing fixtures were installed.

Testing amounted to watching videos all day on the big screen.  Michael selected a particular seat on the fifth row, to sit and watch with a running commentary by Joey, sitting next to him, to everyone's delight.

Kevin Lips got an official reprimand in his file.

The Construction 4 crew got one hundred dollars bonus each across the board for the month of November, just in time for the Christmas Holidays.

'Double D' was convinced to expunge the 'shot'. Not because she or any BOP member were in the wrong. Just as a sign of magnanimity for a job well done by the Construction 4 crew, delivering the new Movie Theater on the exact day they said they would.

On opening day, the Movie Theater was packed. Two hundred fifty sitting capacity with two nightly showings. Michael had designed it to accommodate the five hundred Camp population. But on the premier, for Michael the novelty had been worn off. That and the great demand for seating by the inmates were enough of a deterrent to make him stay away. Not for long. Joey found Michael in his room reading.

"You better come over." He said. "The movie is not starting without you."

Michael rarely became emotional, but in this instance he was touched. He followed Joey and as soon as he entered the Theater, he was given a standing ovation by the audience. The Warden among them. They even had his favorite seat empty, designated for him only. It was to remain empty and available at all times; even on the days, which were most of the time, when Michael wouldn't even bother going to the Movie Theater. A new inmate, once in a while would sit by mistake, only to be rudely tossed out with a loud smack in the back of his head by unknown hands as soon as the lights dimmed.

"You have not earned that seat!" A hoarse whisper would follow the slap.

Joey did not have a designated seat. But he would always sit next to Michael. Joey was running a commentary throughout the movie, cracking jokes and lewd comments over the physique of the female star and in general improving the plot of an otherwise mediocre movie. At times, Michael would forget he was in jail. Instead, particularly when a sexually explicit movie was showing, like 'Show Girls', he thought he was attending a bachelor party. Joey was witty, resourceful, original, a sewer of word games and language skills. Many times, Michael wished he had a tape recorder with him.  After Joey left the Camp, going to the movies was not quite the same.

*   *   *   *

Rolfs returned from his meeting with the Warden and found Michael rearranging what was left over of the existing furniture in a sixteen by twenty four feet room with the door missing.

"This will be my office." Michael said.  "If it's alright with you.  I have scoped out the room next door to my office that is three times as large and even has a door for the Drafting Department."

"Fine...Fine with me."  Rolfs said; preoccupied, his attention on something else.

"What's the matter?  Didn't your meeting with the Warden go well?"

"It went just fine."  Rolfs broke into a broad smile, reminiscing.  "It's just that I was handed another assignment with very little information to go with it.  I am afraid it may be a trap.  I was assured that the exact same direction was given to the Red Horse and Construction 2.  We may be in a race old buddy."

"What's the assignment?"

"We are supposed to build a concrete block fence around the Air Force Base. Twenty feet high, in accordance with the Code for the earthquake zone we are in and able to withstand hundred mile per hour wind.  The Air Force General divided the Base perimeter into three sections for each construction crew.  What do you think of them apples?"

"Challenging."  Michael replied.  "I will get on with the engineering and design right away."

"Be quick about it.  The others have already started work in the field. Oh, by the way; here are the keys to your chariot I picked up and drove from the Warden's office.  His personal gift to you so you can get around faster and in style."

Michael picked up the keys to the golf cart and left the Mess Hall basement for an inspection. It would be a cinch to spot. How many golf carts were at Camp? None. On Base, other than the ones on the golf course, there were none also. He saw it right away. Brand new, electrically driven, street legal with headlights and rear lights, painted crimson and grey, his alma matter colors; nice touch by the Warden, he thought. The back end where the golf bags ordinarily set, was modified with the addition of a trailer attached to the golf cart body to carry tools and equipment. He went back inside and told Rolfs that he was off to inspect the progress of the masonry fence by the other teams. He asked Rolfs to buy him a transit, tripod and a telescopic measuring stick.

"Where do I find this contraption?"

"Any Las Vegas survey shop. Look one up in the yellow pages of the telephone directory. Call them before you go and tell them we will accept one manufactured by Dietz or better. If they don't have one, call the next shop. I will need it here tomorrow morning to get started on the fence. Let your fingers do the walking…" Michael wrote everything out in capital letters and handed Rolfs the piece of paper.

He went up the steps and out of the Mess Hall to his new mode of transportation. He spotted the Construction 2 crew working on the North side of the Base. Hand digging a three foot wide trench for the base of the fence, following a stretched blue string line. "At least it will be straight." He thought. Next stop the Red Horse section of the fence. They were also digging a three foot wide trench, sans the blue string guideline, using a Bob Cat with a backhoe attachment. The digging was going a lot faster, more or less evenly dug and on a straight line. "They were planning to take the height slack setting the first row of concrete wall block." He thought. He was surprised that they were not laying reinforcing steel at the same time.

Michael knew that Las Vegas was in an earthquake four zone. As such the wall footing must be reinforced. Steel dowels must be protruding from the concrete base every thirty two inches to tie to the reinforcing steel of the wall fence hollow block tile; which were to be filled with concrete around the rebar.  Every fourth horizontal row, two rebars must be added for a bond beam, thus the overall   masonry wall forming a checkerboard pattern of reinforcement.  He pulled out his notepad and started doing some quick calculations for one hundred miles per hour wind load on a twenty foot high wall.  He checked his calculations again and again.  He was still coming with a minimum base of seven feet six inches to counteract the wind overturning moment.  The wall being constructed by Construction 2 and the Red Horse brigade was not in accordance with the design parameters issued by the Air Force General.  He returned double time back to The Mess Hall.  Down the concrete steps to the CMS offices and caught Rolfs leaving his office.

"I am on my way to buy you the contraption you requested.  I found you a Dietz whats ma call it, like you asked."

Michael told him his observations and reservations over the method of construction employed by the other crews.

"Fuck'em!"  Was Rolfs response.  "You are working for Construction 4; and don't you forget it.  On second thought, why don't you come with me to pickup your stuff, just to make sure it is what you wanted.  I don't want excuses afterwards that I picked up the wrong stuff."

They went up the stairs and out door of the Mess Hall to Rolfs pick-up. Out the gate, maned by an Air Force MP, with a wave not a second thought about an inmate riding shotgun.  Michael felt like a kid in a candy store inside the Survey Equipment store which had also drafting equipment and furnishings.  He picked for himself two top of the line mechanical pencils Kohinoor Rapidomatic all stainless steel; one white for number five lead and one blue for number seven.  He picked enough furnishings, drafting tables, drafting machines and drafting equipment for four draftsmen to be delivered that same day.  He picked a drafting table and a drafting machine for him also.  Rolfs did not blink when the storeowner added up the total, close, but not over the ten thousand dollar pre-signed check he was carrying.  They loaded Michael's transit, tripod and telescopic 'stick', together with his drafting table and drafting machine still in their carton containers on the bed of Rolfs pick up. Michael carried the two mechanical pencils in his pocket.

"Your draftsmen candidates should be waiting for you back at the office." Rolfs informed Michael. "There should be five of them waiting, at 1:00 PM according to the call-out."

"I think I am going to have Joey with me when I interview them.  He will be working with them after all.  I decided to make Joey my assistant if it's all right with you, and bump him up a pay grade."

"Michael, I've got to give it to you. You have moved in as if you were born for the position.  Have you given it any thought to make it a career here after you get out?"

"No.  I have not.  Right now all I can think of is how hungry I am."

"Let's go through a drive in; with all that equipment at the back of the truck, I would not risk eating and parking anywhere else.  I see a Burger King up ahead on the correct side of the road."

They ate and returned to the Camp.  Same Air Force MP guard, same cursory wave of the hand to go ahead.  They both carried the drafting table box around the corners of the stairway, followed by the rest of the equipment. After he set the drafting furnishings up, Michael went to the construction site of the Movie Theater in search of Joey.  He found him with no trouble sitting under the shade of a tree getting ready to open his BOP shack lunch.

"I would put that away." He told him.  "I got a better fare waiting for you at my office."

Joey got up not relinquishing the bird in the hand and followed Mike back at the Mess Hall down the stairs.  Michael showed him his new office with the drafting table and drafting machine all installed and ready to go. A stack of note pads were on top light green with the eighth of an inch squares on them.  A black padded drafting stool with a back to it was in front of the drafting table.   Michael handed Joey a Burger King sack that had the complete hamburger meal, french fries, onion rings and a chocolate milk shake.   Joey handed Michael his BOP prepared sack lunch.  The sign crew showed up installing on the right side of the door opening a letter sign spelling CAMP ENGINEER with a metal slot underneath to insert a name.  Michael and Joe went out of the office to supervise the installation, Joey munching on his cheeseburger in plain site.

"You have to write down your name because we will mangle the spelling so we may engrave it on a panel made of bakelite the right size to fit in the slot." The head of the sign crew said when they were done.

"Go over the name a second time." Joey spoke for the first time. "Make the letters unique like nothing else at the Camp."

The sign crew said they will give it the old College try and be back shortly with the results.

Michael informed Joey that he was being bumped up a pay grade and from now on he may consider himself as his assistant.  Michael told him that in twenty minutes five inmates will show up to interview for a four slot position of draftsman.

Joey finished his meal, balled up and tossed the evidence in the waste basket.  Michael told Joey that since his office was so big Joey may scrounge himself a desk and furnishings and make it his office also. Tomorrow they were going out together to survey the new Air Force Base CMU, masonry wall fence the Air Force General had dreamed of and decided to implement pronto. He explained to Joey his thinking and the fence construction to meet the general's specification parameters. They were going to stake the entire construction perimeter and mark the line every forty feet to establish the  expansion joint location. Michael looked at his watch.  It was 1:00 PM.  Where were the drafting candidates? Joey guessed Michael's concern.

"I will go for a walk on a search and rescue mission. I bet they are somewhere lost. CMS is a big facility."

Sure enough he was back, a few minutes later leading the group of five inmates. He introduced Michael as the Camp Engineer and the person in charge of all the construction activities.

"I will interview each one of you, one at a time." Michael said. "The ones that qualify will be given a piece of paper with my signature attesting to your new position which you are supposed to take to the bubble and give it to the Lieutenant there. Henceforth, starting tomorrow you are to report at 8:00 AM to the room next to this office. Are we clear?"

No one spoke.

"Age has its privileges." Michael said pointing to a black man in his fifties. "As for the rest of you, please wait outside. Joey, will come get you when your turn comes up."

Michael sat in his chair at his desk next to the drafting table, and pointed at the single guest chair on the right side of his desk for the black man to sit.

"What's your name?"

"Herb Holmes."

"Do you have any drafting experience?"

"I had my own construction company for twenty five years building homes. Nothing big. A couple of houses at a time. I did my own drafting. I had a drafting table and a drafting machine like the one you got. I would put a Dietdzken surface though before you start drafting. The Dietdzken surface bounces back when the pencil presses down unlike the wood in which the pencil leaves a permanent indentation."

Michael let Herb finish talking and passed him one of his pads and handed him one of his mechanical pencils.

"Free sketch for me a house foundation plan and write for me the size of the expansion bolts that would secure the framing base board to the stem wall of the foundation."

Michael went to his drafting table and started filling out one of the Job Change forms with Herb Holmes name on it and signed it. He returned to his desk and Herb Holmes handed him the pad with the foundation plan with the details he requested. The lettering was very good. Not as good as his, but it would be acceptable in any consulting engineering office. He handed Herb Holmes his acceptance certificate wordlessly.

"You already accepted me before you even saw my sketch?" Herd Holmes asked in amazement.

"I know an honest man when I see him." Michael replied. "I believed you when you said you did your own drafting. You did not ask me a single question when I described to you what you were supposed to draw. I only wanted to check your lettering quality, which did not matter as much in this environment and because I bought lettering machines. There are furnishings still in boxes in the room next door and the kind of surfacing you mentioned to install on your drafting table. You are the senior man. So I will call you the Chief Draftsman. Go to the room  next door and pick a corner of the room and you may wish to set up now or wait until tomorrow."

"Were you a PE on the outside?" Herb asked tears in his eyes.

"Yes. I was." Michael responded. "Still am. Why do you ask?"

"I will be honored working for you, sir." Was Herb's response as he made his way out the door opening.

"He recognizes talent when he sees it." Joey opened his mouth for the first time watching the proceedings intently. "I was never an employer. I was always on the other side like Herb. I am learning a lot being around you that will be of some use to me later on the outside. This is a first time since I enrolled in the prison system. You made Herb one of your 'dogs', for life and it only took you less than five minutes." Joey said getting up from his chair to fetch the next candidate.

He came back with a white kid in tow. He looked in his early thirties with a baby face which made him look just out of High School. Joey, following the previous scenario pointed for the new candidate to take the visitor seat next to Michael's desk.

"What's your name?", Michael started.

"Steve LaBrie."

"I should have asked 'coman tu ta pel'?, Michael said showing off.

"I don't speak French." Steve replied. "Although my family on my father's side is French."

"Why didn't you make an effort to learn? Although I was born in Greece, I speak not only Greek but several other languages."

"My parents divorced when I was little kid and I left home for College and never came home again."

"What was your major in College?" Michael asked bringing back the interview into focus.

"Mechanical Engineering."

"Did you graduate?"

"No. I left College to work full time in building Home Movie Theaters. When I started making the kind of money I was making, I had no illusions of continuing my education."

"Did you have your own company?"

"Yes I did."

"Here!" Michael tore off the top sheet that Herb had sketched on and passed the pad to Steve with a mechanical pencil. "Assume I am one of your prospective clients. Draw for me what my Home Movie Theater would look like. Make sure to label all the equipment installed."

He signaled Joey with a nod to go with him outside and leave Steve alone to create. Three biker inmates with tattoos all over were milling around outside the door opening.

"We are a team." One of them who presumable was their spokesman said as soon as he laid eyes on Joey and Michael. "We work together. I suggest you hire all of us, and let go of the nigger." He took a step towards Michael cutting off his path.

"Do you know who you are talking to?" Joey asked.

"The sign on the door says Camp Engineer. The name is Greek to me. You are both swarthy greasers, so I don't know who is in charge."

Michael studied all three of them. One had stepped side by side with the spokesman, glaring at him. The other was standing shuffling his feet looking down at his boots. Michael stared right at the duo.

"Thank you for coming over for the interview on time. Unfortunately, the positions have been filled. You may return to the bubble and tell the Lieutenant that you were not needed."

All three started heading towards the stairway leading up to the Mess Hall.

"Not you." Michael pointed to the third who had stayed in the background.

"You must not have heard me the first time." The spokesman stopped and turned piercing Michael with a look that spelled trouble. "We are all hired or none."

"I heard you the first time." Michael said. "I am making an offer to stay for this gentleman only. It is up to him to stay or leave."

The quiet one separated himself from the trio and assumed a waiting stance back at the door opening.

"You haven't heard the last…" The spokesman's speech was cut short by the appearance out of nowhere of Michael's two Sicilian bodyguards. The two biker inmates stopped in their tracks and balled their fists.

"Don't even try." Joey stepped forward. "Didn't you know that Michael is a 'Man of Respect'?"

The demeanor of the two Bikers changed instantly from fight to flight, as they quietly made their way to the stairway. Michael nodded to his bodyguards and one of them broke off trailing the biker inmates. Joey and Michael, the excitement over, made their way back to Michael's office. Steve had just finished his sketch. It was a three dimensional affair. Michael passed it to Joey for a look see. Joey signaled his appreciation and handed it back to Michael.

"Steve your sketch is an Architectural wonder. Your lettering is outstanding in accord with the Drawing. Unfortunately, your talent will be wasted in our lowly department. We do Drawings that are less Architectural wonders and more in line that will assist the builders to follow and construct what is depicted on the Drawing…"

"I understand." Steve replied. "I took Mechanical Drawing in College. I know what you are looking for. You asked me as a prospective client to draw for you. My prospective clients are rarely engineers who can read blue prints. They do not understand plan view or elevations. So I have to draw three dimensional…"

"You are hired." Michael said as he made for his drafting table to complete and sign the job application of Steve LaBrie. "Give this form to the Lieutenant at the bubble so he may put your name in the 'call-out' sheet tomorrow. However, be fore you go there, you may go next door if you want and join Herb Holmes in selecting your equipment and furnishings or you can wait till tomorrow morning. You are to report here for work at 8:00 AM sharp tomorrow."

Steve picked his completed and signed application and made his way out of Michael's office. He momentarily stopped at the door opening. After some hesitation, he turned right towards the stairway to the Mess Hall.

"I'd keep an eye on him." Joey said. "Not the eager beaver type."

"Well, we are not pretending to pay him, until tomorrow." Michael said. "I don't expect freebies."

Joey made his way outside Michael's office to check whether the last remaining candidate was still waiting. He came back with the biker inmate. Other than the tattoos decorating his arms he appeared normal. Joey led him to the visitor's seat. The inmate appeared nervous and excited at the same time.

"What's your name?" Michael started the interview.

"Garry Young." The inmate responded eagerly.

"Do you have any drafting experience?"

"I worked for a couple of years in an engineering firm." He answered hesitantly.

"You have?" Michael asked wondering, based on his appearance. "Do you have any College experience?"

"Community College." Came the answer, like pulling teeth.

"Listen Gary." Michael paused. "I don't like being lied. The test I will give you shortly will reveal if you are on the level or trying to blow smoke up my ass. I have interviewed hundreds of engineers and draftsmen. Somehow you don't fit the profile I am used to. However, time will tell." Michael said handing Gary the engineering pad and the mechanical pencil after he tore off Steve's isometric design. "Draw for me freehand something you recall from your experience in the engineering office."

Gary stared at the engineering pad. "I don't have any drafting equipment…"

"Fair enough. Go to my drafting table. I will give you my own. Have you ever used a drafting machine before?" Michael said after he saw Gary looking at the one on his desk and hesitating to even touch it. "No. I have only used a tee square and a parallel bar."

High School drafting, Michael thought immediately.

"I want to see your lettering skill." Michael said. "Why don't you write something in capital letters."

He watched Gary lean over the pad concentrating on every letter. The result was bad penmanship even at High School level.

"You want to revise your story Gary?" He asked.

Gary stopped writing and you could tell he was trying to make up his mind to come clean or walk out of there. Finally he decided that the truth would set him free.

"All right you got me. I only have a semester's worth of High School experience. What are you going to do about it?" He asked in an aggressive tone of voice.

"Imagine someone will build a table and you are drawing installation instructions. Put yourself in his shoes and imagine what you will need to accomplish the task."

Gary thought about it for a moment and started drawing and numbering the table and the four legs and lettering instructions underneath the completed image. The lettering identified the components and the instructions how to accomplish each step. Michael looked at the finished product. He completed and signed the job assignment form and told Gary to give it to the Lieutenant at the bubble. Tears appeared in the eyes of Gary and he started thanking Michael on bended knees.

"I was kicked all my life every time I tried to get a legitimate job. You are the first who was kind enough to give me a chance. I will not disappoint you. Thank you. Thank you. I am sick and tired working outside;

freezing in the Winter and frying in the Summer.  For once in my life I will have an office job.  Thank you."

"Make sure you are here tomorrow morning at 8:00 AM sharp." Michael said.  "Don't worry. You can set your watch on my arrival." He hesitated a minute.  "Be careful of the others.  We belonged to the same bike club on the outside.  They are vindictive."

This last remark was heard by the two Sicilians who were standing in the door opening.

That same night the two biker inmates had a rude awaking with an ice pick in their balls.

Earlier, Dino contacted Michael and asked him to arrange for a cop-out, out of his present room.  He was moving into their room.  There was a sudden opening and Michael's new job was making it hard to keep an eye on him during the night.

# CHAPTER 17

## The Red Horse Engineer

Joey liked noise and commotion around him. One of the first things he did was to scrounge around and cockroach a radio from somewhere for Michael's office. The inmates were allowed a personal radio with earphones. The radio, however, Joey came up with was an alarm clock type with speakers. It was constantly on during working hours. Michael didn't know where he got it. For that matter, he didn't want to know. The music playing loud, even classical for Michael's taste, was bound to attract the BOP guards. Michael thought the chances of the radio lasting a day, were nil. His office did not have a door. A hack would pass in front of his office all day long. That first day with the radio on, Michael tried to spend most of his time in the field. Construction 4 had several projects going on concurrently at the Camp. Michael did not want to have to explain when caught with the radio. His office had no door. As far as he was concerned, he had no idea how the radio found its way into his office. At the end of the day Michael returned to his office, being greeted by loud rock and roll music coming out of his office which he could hear coming down the steps from the Mess Hall. There was no doubt of its origin. His office had no door. Just an opening.

"Didn't anyone say something, all day?" Michael asked.

"Yeah!" Joey said rather bored. "A few hacks stopped by and had a look see."

"So…" Michael encouraged Joey to go on. "What happened?"

"I told them that you could not work without music."

"So…"

"So…nothing. They left."

"Didn't they take the radio?"  Michael heard himself asking.  Kind of dumb, Michael thought after the words came out of his mouth.  The radio was still in the same spot as this morning.

"Mike, you don't realize the juice you got around here.  Everything that is getting built around here, comes out of this office.  There are a ton of projects under construction making millions of dollars for them.  The Warden has spread the word and the hacks know that the bonuses they will receive this year are one of the benefits that will come to them, because of you.  You think some lowly custody hack will interfere with that?  Man if I were you, I'd throw a tantrum once a month to get their attention.  I've never seen nor met a nicer guy, not taking advantage of this situation…"

"Joe."  Michael cautioned him.  "You are thinking and talking again like an inmate.  You will be getting out in a few months.  Start thinking like a professional, an Architect."

"Yeah.  Yeah."  Joey muttered blushing.

Regardless of what Joey was saying to others and getting by, Michael could tell he was no practicing Architect.  At least no Architect with any amount of experience behind him.  Maybe he got a degree in architecture and worked as a draftsman or gofer in an architectural office at one time.  He certainly had acquired some knowledge by osmosis, but he lacked initiative, originality of thought and he never had the responsibility for the bottom line.

First time they were out to do a survey for the new masonry fence, Michael found out Joey did not know how to set up a transit.  Michael must have raised an eyebrow, but he did not say anything.  He showed Joey how to set-up, level and work a transit.  Joey picked up on it fast.  Michael never doubted his ability.  However, Joey did not want the responsibility of operating the transit.  He felt more comfortable following Michael's directions and holding the stick.  Michael tried to explain how the transit worked and the principles behind it.  But when Michael started talking about congruent triangles, Joey got lost.  He had no knowledge of trigonometry.  It was not that he knew it at one time and forgot because he had no opportunity use it, he was simply never taught trigonometry in High School nor in College.  It was simply virgin territory for Joey.  He could never do the calculations required to obtain results for a topographic map.

The masonry fence however, was progressing slowly but surely.  Rolfs was getting a ribbing by Krupp for the tortoise pace of Construction 4.  However, the fence erected by Construction 4 was looking much better than the sections erected by Construction 2 and the Air Force.  The ground irregularities were taken into account on the eight foot wide reinforced steel spread footing, a foot thick   with number five rebar dowels sticking out every thirty two inches as designed by Michael.  The fence was erected in forty foot sections with an expansion joint between sections.  The Construction 4 fence was level and a straight line on top, while the Air Force and Construction 2 fence was continuous at the bottom but the top was wavy in accordance with the contour of the land.  Michael was worried how were the two dissimilar fences to meet.

All Michael's worry was for naught, because October came around with its wind gusting at one hundred miles per hour and blew all night.  Come morning the Construction 4 masonry fence sections stood intact.  The masonry fence constructed by the Air Force Red Horse and Construction 2, was laying on the ground with the footing pulled out of the ground.  The ground around the Construction 4 fence was undisturbed.  Michael was busy surveying the ground getting ready for another forty foot section when a delegation consisting of the Air Force General, the Warden, accompanied by Rolfs, Krupp, and an unidentified Air Force overweight female major who was dogging the general, appeared.  She came by the transit and she introduced herself to Michael as Shirley Pierce the head of the Red Horse Engineering Department and asked him to join their group.

"This is my engineer for the project."  Rolfs took the initiative introducing Michael to the Air Force General.  "He can explain and answer your questions better than anyone I know.  He is a licensed Professional Engineer and he had his own engineering and construction company on the outside."

"Why is your fence still standing while the rest is on the ground?"  The General lost no time coming to the point.

"The reason is that we followed the design parameters you specified and the Air Force and Construction 2 did not."

"Do you care to elaborate?"  The General asked making a sour face.

"You specified a twenty foot tall fence which met the Building Code, the earthquake zone for the area and was able to withstand one hundred mile per hour wind.  That's what you are looking at."  Michael pointed at the forty foot masonry wall sections.  "A masonry wall over eight feet high is not a decorative wall any more.  It is structural.  The Las Vegas area is a Group 4 earthquake zone.  As such it requires a reinforced steel foundation and vertical rebar into the masonry wall every 32 inches.  The hollow block tile eight inch square that the rebar  comes through has to be filled with concrete.  Additionally, every fourth row of masonry block requires a bond beam.  This way the masonry wall has a checkerboard structural construction of 32 by 32 inch steel reinforced sections that meet the earthquake zone 4 requirements of the Region.

"The hundred mile per hour wind requirement is met by the eight foot wide foundation.  By my calculations you need seven feet six inches wide footing minimum to withstand the wind and not overturn as it happened with the rest of the fence.  Further, the Air Force and Construction 2 fence does not have rebar, so it is not a structural fence.

Additionally, it only has a two to three feet wide footing which is not adequate to withstand hundred mile per hour winds."

The General looked questioningly to his major who appeared to be tongue tied.

"I saw his golf cart driving by…" She finally said. "If we were building the fence wrong, why didn't he say something to me?"

"With all due respect…," Michael jumped in, "this is the first time I have laid eyes on you…"

"Do you expect an inmate to go looking for the Air Force Engineering Administration?" Rolfs came to Michael's rescue.

"Why didn't you say something to Construction 2?" The Warden asked.

'I asked Rolfs if I should tell them the error of their ways.' Michael thought looking at Rolfs who was fidgeting because he remembered the answer he gave Michael: 'Fuck them!'

"As a matter of fact I did." Michael replied to both surprise and relief on the face of Rolfs. "I explained all that I've just said, to Mr. Krupp's clerk. Since I am Construction 4 and he is Construction 2, I couldn't make them change their method of construction. I was hopping he would report my concerns to Mr. Krupp."

"Well why didn't you research the matter?" The Warden asked looking straight at Krupp.

"I was told…," Krupp mumbled, "that some inmate from Construction 4 said something or other…but I thought it was deliberate to slow us down because they were falling behind. I patterned my fence to the one the Air Force was build ing. I had more faith in their engineering department that the word of an inmate. I did not know Mike from a hole in the ground. Now that I have met him and have realized his knowledge and capabilities, I will be checking with his boss Rolfs as the case may require."

"You will do better than that!"  The warden cut him off.  "Henceforth, nothing is getting built at Camp without Michael's stamp of approval. Order a red stamp," he said addressing Rolfs, "that says APPROVED FOR CONSTRUCTION with space underneath to say BY THE CAMP ENGINEER and for Michael's signature."

"Order one for the Air Force also,"  The General addressed his major, "the only difference being that it says BY THE NELLIS AIR FORCE BASE ENGINEER."

The General signaled the Warden and they stepped away from the group visibly discussing something.

"I will set up an office for you at the Red Horse..."  The major tried to steer Michael away from the group by pulling on his arm.

"Just a God damn second here...,"  Rolfs grabbed Michael's other arm pulling in the opposite direction; "Michael works for me!  He is very busy.  You must go through me to request Michael's services..."

"What have we got here?" The General said. "I was anticipating a tug of war contest and the Warden knowing his people shared my concerns. Staring tomorrow, Michael, after you chase away the morning alligators and get Construction 4 going, you go to the Red Horse to drain that swamp.  Set up a time clock there," the General said addressing his major, "to punch in his time sheet when he reports in and when he is done with the Air Force business.  We have to reimburse the Camp for his time with Air Force projects."

'The ex parte meeting between the General and the Warden must have been to set the reimbursement hourly rate for my services.'  Michael thought remembering his meeting with the Warden.  'I bet the rate is at least $55.00 per hour.'

"Do you have drawings and specifications for the correct wall?"  The General asked Michael.

"I do back at the CMS office." Michael responded. "Each wall section must be no more than forty feet wide, before an expansion joint is installed. If not for the wind, the other wall sections were bound to be bowed out when the summer heat hit the monolithic masonry wall with no place to expand."

"You heard that major?" The General expanded. "Bring a set to her tomorrow morning." The General addressed Michael this time. "Provide her also with a signed time sheet of the number of hours you spent designing the masonry wall."

Krupp was whispering something to Rolfs who was beaming. It must have been a request for the same thing the General had just ordered.

"I see you get around Michael in your golf cart, have you noticed something in your wanderings throughout the Base that I should be made aware of? I mean something glaring that the rest of us have not picked up on. Something that presents a liability or an accident to happen." The General asked Michael.

"Now that you mentioned it, there is. I did not have a chance to discuss it with Mr. Rolfs, yet, because I have not come up with a method of remediation, yet.

When I was assigned an office in Construction 4, I had to clean it up first. There were numerous debris and boxes. One of the boxes had a 1988 Report made by a Consulting Engineering firm hired by the Air Force to evaluate the condition of the Camp as part of the consideration and transfer to the BOP. The 1988 Report among other deficiencies, it listed as the first and immediate liability the construction of all the buildings. Specifically, all the two story buildings with a below ground basement. In an emergency or fire, the first and second floors may be evacuated. There is no way to evacuate the basement. All personnel located below ground will perish, because there are no two emergency exits from the basement like the Uniform Building Code specifies. All the two story buildings at the Air Force Base are similarly constructed presenting a fire hazard to the personnel in the basement.  At the time they were built, the Code probably did not require two emergency exits from the basement.  However, over the years the Uniform Building Code was updated, but not the buildings to comply with the Code.  The existing situation is a Health and Safety hazard issue that needs to be addressed immediately.  If such a report listing that a hazard exists and I was able to locate it, so would a third party during Discovery in a litigation after a fire incident.  The fact that the Air Force knew, or should have known of this deficiency would make the damages under the category of Tort three fold and the punitive damages, should the jury decide to assess, of such magnitude that only the government could afford to pay.  Needles to say that if the fire occurs during your  watch General, let's say it would not be a stelar mark on your career.  Is this what you had in mind in you inquiry?"

"That's exactly what I had in mind Mike." The General expounded. "Now why didn't we think of this? Or better yet, did you know of the existence of this 1988 Report.  After all it was the Red Horse who hired the consulting engineering firm." He asked major Pierce. "Any ideas how to remedy the problem?" He turned back to Michael.

"It would require excavation on two sides of the building at a depth of ten feet to reach the bottom floor of the basement.  The depth is more than the four feet excavation limit set by OSHA, the Safety Code to have workers working.  There is no room between buildings for a crane to lift and place trench jacks.  So the walls of the emergency exit must be precast concrete panels carried by a flat bed with an articulated crane.  The precast panels would lock with each other with a keyway that would make them water proof from ground water leaking into the well finding its way to the basement.  The base of that concrete box would be a concrete slab slopped towards a drain on its center.  The drain would be connected to a dry well, which is nothing more than a hole on the ground below, ten feet deep filled with one inch gravel.  This would prevent the basement from flooding due to rain.  One end of the concrete box, the one away from the building would be slopped at 45 degrees for access and the construction of the stairway.  On top at ground level, there would be concrete block planters, railing and other features to beautify the emergency exit on the outside and at the same time prevent an unsuspecting pedestrian from falling in.  I gave the assignment for this last part to Joey, my assistant, who was an Architect on the outside…"

"It sounds like you have given the matter some serious thought and got the thing put together already.  I will assign this remediation project as the number one priority because we dealing with Health and Safety.  I will issue a Memorandum to all Departments on Base."  The General pronounced his decision.

"We can work on this together, Mike."  Shirley the major in charge of the Red Horse Engineering Department volunteered.  "I am an Architect also."

'That was part of the problem.' Michael thought. 'Who, in his right mind, would put an Architect in charge of an Engineering Department?'

"I will be by at Red Horse tomorrow midmorning."  Michael said.  "We will discuss it then after I get my bearings together, regarding the projects you are working  on.  I would also like to meet your staff.  I would like to evaluate what I am going to be working with…their knowledge and potential."

"They are young engineers.  Just out of school.  They joined up as a career with the Air Force. No one, including myself, have any experience on the outside other than observing construction activities designed by a Consulting Engineering Firm and getting build by an outside General Contractor."

"I bet you are getting reamed on Change Orders."  Michael blurted out without thinking of the makeup of his audience.  "I apologize for the use of the word 'reamed.'"  He added red faced avoiding to look at Shirley.

"No use of mincing words." Was Shirley's response. "You are correct. Any ideas of how to rectify that?"

"As a matter of fact I do." Michael said enthusiastically. "I have an idea for a series of lectures under the heading Changes in Construction Contracts. It would help to create the syllabus and organize the lectures, by utilizing your young staff of engineers, in such a way that the entire series may be delivered and the course completed within two weeks. It will require three hour lectures in the evening each day, five days a week. I guarantee that by the end of the symposium every attendant will be a qualified Contracting Officer. I will personally issue a signed Certificate to each one if you wish."

"Say no more." Shirley responded almost jumping with joy. "I will write a Memorandum to that effect for the General. We will keep track of your time and reimburse the BOP at the agreed price of $55.00 per hour. As a matter of fact, in my Memorandum I would recommend that we expand the course and advertise it to all the other bases in the US and abroad and charge each attendee $2,500.00 for the two week course and we will provide room and board free of charge. Who would not like to come to Fabulous Las Vegas for two weeks and get a Contracting Officer's Certificate in the process. Do you have a resume handy to bring tomorrow? Do you have any personal experience in Disputes and Change Orders with the government?"

"I will bring you a copy of my resume tomorrow." Michael confirmed. "As to experience, in a twenty year stretch of doing work for the Department of Defense, I had one hundred and eighty seven Disputes with the government that ended up in litigation in front of the Armed Services Board of Contract Appeals with me representing the company with no lawyer involvement..."

"What was the outcome? The final score?" Shirley interrupted no longer able to contain herself.

"I won all one hundred eighty seven of them but they ended up being Pyrian victories as you can see; the final score was that the government got me here."

If there were no other people standing around, Michael was sure that Shirley was getting ready to give him his consolation price right there and then. He started walking away from Shirley.

"Thanks buddy." Rolfs took Michael aside after the meeting started breaking up. "Not only we are in charge of all the other construction departments here at Camp...you heard the General...we are in charge of all the construction activities on Base. We came out of this fiasco smelling like a rose. I will owe you if this results in a promotion with extra pay."

"The General appears hot on the subject of emergency exits for all the basements on Base. There must be hundreds of them. I better get the drafting department started on developing drawings. I don't need the major's input on it's architectural aspects..."

"I wouldn't be so steadfast on this old buddy. I smell a ripe pussy on this. Did you see the way she was looking at you? It was obvious to everybody that she has the hots for you. By the way, she lives within fifty yards of the Red Horse building. I bet your meetings with her tomorrow morning, will lead and end up in a nooner at her condo next door to the Red Horse."

"I am not the type." Michael protested; but made a mental note of the location of the major's condo for the future.

The emergency exits from the building basements both at Camp and on Base together with the ongoing construction of the Movie Theater were the primary projects in Michael's plate. He did not feel comfortable being involved with more than two dozen projects taking place concurrently. He asked major Shirley to select twenty Air Force Base building at a time; grouping them in close proximity to each other so it would make supervision and inspection a manageable activity.

Krupp, after the drubbing he received in front of the Warden, took up the matter of the building basement emergency exits as a zealot. Construction 2 was far   ahead of everyone else.  They were the first to call for an inspection of the precast concrete box, constituting the basement emergency exit.  Michael slid down the 45 degree dirt slope and inspected the precast box with particular attention to the joints.

"Did you use SIKADUR epoxy like I specified?"  He asked in general pointing at the closest vertical precast concrete joint, just to say something, because it was obvious they did, from the surface bubbles of the epoxy at the precast concrete panels joints that they were not ground away yet.

"We did as directed, sir!"  Krupp volunteered with a military mock salute.

"What are those blue lines on the existing building basement wall?  Are they what I think they are.  The location of the six foot double wide emergency exit door?"

"We are getting ready to saw cut the opening as soon as we are done with the inspection." Krupp explained getting progressively angrier for having to answer to an inmate.

Michael made some quick calculations and notes on his pad.

"No you won't." He said with authority.  "If you do as it stands, the entire building will come down on your head.  You cannot remove a section of an existing masonry support wall before structurally bracing the opening."

The group of inmates assigned on this activity looked in unison towards Krupp.  He was in the meantime changing between red faced and a color resembling eggplant purple.

"What do you suggest we do?"  Krupp said after a pause, scratching his head.

"Make the opening two feet wider on each side and two feet higher on top. Then at the perimeter of the new opening, allowing room for the concrete saw, use an eight inch steel channel inside and outside the building bolted through with half inch bolts sandwiching the existing building masonry wall in between the steel channels. Make sure the columns have two by two foot plates at the bottom where they rest against the concrete slab. After you cut out the door opening and before you remove the steel shoring, form and pour cast-in-place concrete consisting of a two foot reinforced steel concrete column, with number five rebar  12 inch on center each way; add a two foot reinforced steel concrete beam, its ends resting on top of the columns of the opening. After twenty eight days, when the concrete has attained its maximum strength, you may remove the steel bracing and supports around the opening and patch the holes."

"May we have this building procedure in writing?" Krupp requested humbly. "You may want to distribute it to all the work force groups assigned to the basement emergency exits, both here at Camp and on Base. And if I were you, I would run over to the Base Bachelor Officers' Quarters building because the Air Force inmate work group is planning to do the same thing you caught us contemplating."

Michael scrambled up the emergency exit slope angry at himself for thinking that something was obvious to him and not putting it down on the drawing, because evidently it was not obvious to others. He hopped on his golf cart and raced towards the Red Horse building. He barged in major Shirley Pierce's office and physically dragged her out of the building and in his golf cart. He explained to her on the way, his concern over the encounter with the Construction 2 crew method of intending to cut a hole on the basement wall without shoring thus bringing the first and second floor on their head. He went over his conversation with Krupp.

"You don't think they would be that dumb?" Shirley exclaimed. Michael had a way of explaining and simplifying issues that made such obvious sense to the listener that would have never thought them the same way as before.

"One way to find out." Michael said putting the metal to the petal of the golf cart trying to achieve its maximum 25 MPH design parameter speed in spite of the overload.

They reached the BOQ building in no time. Babaloui, the foreman of the inmate crew at the bottom of the precast concrete emergency exit was pulling the cord out of the concrete saw trying to get it started.

"STOP!" Michael yelled.

"Sup 'Big Dog'?" Bill Jarvis looked up surprised.

Michael with Shirley hanging on his arm made their way down the 45 degree dirt incline.

"Where is Sergeant Dooling?" Major Shirley Pierce inquired.

"He went for a coffee break." Bill Jarvis answered winking at Michael.

"He is supposed to be on site at all times while construction activities are taking place." Major Shirley insisted.

The place looked like a duplicate of the construction site with Krupp which Michael had just left.

"Let me have the Drawings." Michael asked an inmate who was holding a set, all rolled up. "Do you see Note 3 in the Construction Notes on the first page?" Michael asked looking at Bill Jarvis. "You as the foreman of this construction detail should be intimate familiar with the Drawings and Specifications. Note 3 states specifically to request an inspection by the Base Engineer, that would be me, before saw cutting and removal of the wall section of the existing building. I saw you getting ready to start the concrete saw. Why hasn't Sergeant Dooling request an engineer's inspection, like the Drawings call for, through Major Pierce?"

"You have to ask him!" Bill Jarvis suddenly stiffened.

"If you can find him!" An unknown inmate shouted.

"Check in at his girl friend's house." Another unknown inmate was heard from.

"What's going on here Babalui?" Michael stared at Bill Jarvis.

"You just heard 'Big Dog'. We started a couple of weeks ago. He was here for a couple of days and have not been seen since. What do you want me to do? There are no provisions of reporting the absence of the Air Force personnel in charge, by inmates. We are going along as best we can. Now tell me what the fuck is wrong and why are you here, so we may move on."

Michael looked at Shirley who nodded that she would take care of the Air Force supervision problem. Michael explained to Bill Jarvis and the inmates the problem of them bringing down the building on them if they proceeded as they were contemplating, without shoring and support. He spelled out in detail the process by which they were to proceed.

"Thanks. That's why you make the big bucks 'Big Dog'." These were Bill Jarvis parting words.

Michael and Shirley got back in the golf cart for the trip back to the Red Horse.

"It's almost lunch time." Shirley said. "Why don't you drop me off at my home where I go everyday for lunch. As a matter of fact why don't you come in with me. The least I can do is offer you lunch after you saved my butt here and averted disaster."

Michael was looking straight ahead contemplating the situation and the ramifications. A prisoner caught in an Air Force officer's home. What if she claimed rape? What if she denied inviting him for lunch? Was he even allowed to be inside private residences? He realized the situation was complex with many variables beyond his control. If he did not find himself in his present circumstances, he might have accepted the invitation. At the same time he was smart enough to recognize that he was in a minefield from which he had to extricate himself with no harm done.

"I'd love to have lunch with you Shirley, but I don't know whether your home is out of bounds for me.  How about if I drive us to the nearest Officer's Club and have lunch there." Michael offered.

"Are you allowed at the Officer's Club?" Shirley asked in amazement.

Michael flipped his plastic pass from his back pocket and showed it to Shirley, signed by the Warden and the Base General allowing him free meals at all the Base Officer's Clubs.

"I am impressed." Shirley said. "I never go to the Officer's Club. It is too embarrassing being by myself and seeing everyone else having a good time."

"What are you talking about?" Michael said. "A beautiful woman like yourself?  I'd would think you would have a waiting list for your social life..."

"Unfortunately, this is not the case." Shirley said all red in the face. "Do you find me attractive?"

"I hardly know you Shirley, but physically yes. I find you attractive and pleasant to be around.  I believe we will get along, professionally speaking, and accomplish a lot during my time here."

"I have a lot to talk to you also. The General approved your proposal for teaching.  I have announced to my staff that they are required to take the course.  They were all excited.  As a matter of fact your first class is scheduled at the Red Horse at 8:00 AM the day after tomorrow.  An announcement was sent to other bases and we already got back positive responses and $2,500.00 checks from two hundred places and people.  In view of that get started on the syllabus of the course and use my staff as a ginny pig to streamline its contents and duration."

They never made it to the Officer's Club.  An MP Jeep pulled them over and directed Michael to return back to the Camp immediately, because the Supreme Court of the United States was on hold on the telephone to speak to him about his case in the Warden's office.

# CHAPTER 18

## Hubris Sends Deus Ex Machina Packing

The excitement and suspense was palpable the minute Michael entered the Administration Building. The guards on the first floor rushed him immediately up the stairs, the elevator was deemed too slow and unreliable, to the Warden's office on the second floor.

"The word is out." The black guard, they called 'Slim', said as soon as he saw Michael. It was the same guard who had admitted him and was now escorting him to the Warden's office. "We have never received a direct call from the Supreme Court before regarding a prisoner. Everybody believes you must have won your case. Do you remember, I was the one who processed you in here. I did not know why you were here, but from the way you looked and your demeanor, I never thought that you belonged in prison. I got so interested in you, I went and read your PSI. What a bunch of bull shit case. I read it and I was hitting my head trying to figure out what you've done wrong. The government made money off you on the outside as they keep using you to make more money on the inside." Slim said shaking his head. "You are the goose who lays the golden eggs. I'd sure hate to see you go. I may have to kiss my bonus at the end of the year, the Warden promised us for the first time, good bye."

Michael in turmoil remained silent. Afraid he may jinx the outcome by merely hoping it would be good news. He wished he had at least a day to prepare and consult with his 'godfather' Dino. Analyze the alternatives and come up with plausible solutions to all the anticipated scenarios. Why was the Supreme Court calling him? Was it the 'Deus ex Machina' he was hoping all along and spoke at length to his wife? The

Writ of Certiorari gave them no other choice, he thought, 'Hubris' creeping in. It was like playing chess without leaving the opponent any other choice, other than the move you dictated. He wrote the Writ himself. He typed it himself. He signed it. They did not reject it, as they do to thousand others. They had already given it a case number 7011. This meant that at least someone, a clerk most likely, had read it and thought it had Merit, because it was shortlisted. 'Don't get your hopes up.' He thought. 'Many have slipped between the bowl and the lip'. They reached the second floor landing with the Warden's secretary waiting for them all in a fluster.

'I will take over now." She addressed 'Slim', the guard, dismissing him back to his guard position on the first floor.

'Slim' turned around and started down the steps with no argument wishing he was a fly on the wall during the telephone conversation of the prisoner and the representative from the Supreme Court. The Warden's secretary took Michael by the arm and started leading him wordlessly down the corridor towards the Warden's office. Her excitement manifesting itself in the tightness of her grip on Michael's arm; her nails digging into the arm of the prisoner, who was not protesting.

The Warden was waiting for them standing in front of his open door.

"Big day for you pal." He said to Michael trying to curb his excitement. "It's not everyday that we receive a person to person call from the Supreme Court. We have set up a special office for you to receive the call and converse uninterrupted in total privacy. The set up is the same as lawyer client communication. Rest assured no one will be monitoring your conversation."

He led the way to an empty office at the end of the corridor. It had a desk but it was obvious it was one that no one was using, because it lacked a computer and its surface was bare, other than a telephone with a red light blinking. He pointed for Michael to sit at the desk chair and asked him if he would require anything else.

"A paper pad and a writing implement." Michael requested.

The Warden's secretary disappeared and reappeared with a pad and a pencil. The Warden and his secretary waved and departed closing the office door behind them. Michael lifted the telephone receiver to his ear and punched the button next to the blinking light.

"Hello." He said in a neutral voice.

"Is this Michael...I will not try to say your last name..." A male, young sounding voice answered. "Boy I've been waiting close to half an hour for the BOP to track you down. I understand you were on Base. What were you doing there if I may ask? Were you there with the knowledge and understanding of the BOP?"

"I was appointed as the Camp Engineer by the Warden and recently as the Nellis Air Force Base Engineer by the Base Commanding General. I was trying to avert a disaster at one of the construction sites with the head of the Red Horse, the Nellis Air Force Engineering and Construction Department. Specifically, I was at the BOQ, Bachelor Officers' Quarters, where they were in the process of removing a section of a structural wall and had failed to call me, prior, as the Drawings required. They had not shored nor structurally compensated the activity they were about to undertake, that would have resulted for the entire two story building collapsing on their heads."

"From your description it sounds like activities that would take place on the outside and not in a prison environment." The voice on the phone sounded amazed.

"Who are you? If I may ask." Michael inquired. He's been in conversation for five minutes already with a person unknown other than his word and presumably the telephone number identifying the caller as making the call from the Supreme Court of the United States.

"Oh!  I am sorry.  My name is Tom and I am a clerk at the US Supreme Court assigned to the Honorable Justice Sandra Day O'Connor."

"What can I do for you?" Michael asked.

"I have been reading your case, which we have shortlisted and assigned a docket number 7011.  I have prepared a one page brief for Justice O'Connor where I have listed the five issues you have brought up.  I have researched them and have found the first four to be factual…"

"If that's the case; i.e. the first four issues are de facto, what am I doing here?  Is this a telephone call from the Supreme Court ordering my immediate release?"

"No.  It is not.  Although I will not dispute the fact that ultimately this may be the case."

"What is the purpose of the telephone call then?"

"To review the issues in order to make sure we are on the same page and decide how to proceed henceforth."

"The first issue deals with my original Appeal to the 9th Circuit Court of Appeals where I argued that the government sustained neither loss nor damages to seek restitution.  Instead with my interpretation of the Davis-Bacon Act, the government saved money.  The decision came back from the 9th denying my Appeal on the grounds that "The government need not show loss or damages to bring about an indictment".  On another case recently the Supreme Court struct down that interpretation.  The current law dictates that the government must show and prove loss or damage before they commence indictment proceedings.  On the basis of this first issue alone, I am a free man."

"You are correct in your assessment.  However the Supreme Court has made the Ruling.  It is up to the lower court, in this case the 9th to implement the Ruling.  Have you filed with the 9th requesting your release?"

"No." Michael admitted. "I have not. The problem being that according to the recently passed by the Congress Patriot Act, there is a stipulation that all Appeals to a Higher Court must have a prior approval by the sentencing judge with no time limit for this approval. I have filed the request with the sentencing court and so far silence from judge Ezra."

"This is unfortunate. The stipulation in the Patriot Act was made to curb the plethora of frivolous Appeals filled with the Higher Courts to the point that they were causing a bottle neck based on the number of the Court of Appeals judges available."

"The second issue in my Writ of Certiorari was that my attorney, as soon as I hired him, he was approached by the government and was short listed for a position of Federal Judge in the State of Hawaii, which fact he failed to disclose. This alone has been decided on another case by the Supreme Court to require retrial."

"This is the case." The Supreme Court Clerk said. "But once again this is a matter for the 9th to adjudicate and implement. I am afraid you have to file a request with the sentencing court in Hawaii for permission to Appeal to the 9th."

"The third issue raised in my Writ of Certiorari was the fact that the government calculated the amount owed to the employees, by applying the highest earned hourly wage rate to all hours for the duration of their employment regardless of what they may be doing and regardless whether the project was under the DavisBacon Act jurisdiction. If I had done the same on all the Change Orders in the  same Contracts with the government, I was owed over seven million dollars and I would have been indicted for overcharging the government. When I appealed to the Armed Services Board of Contract Appeals the government response was that my claim was not timely since the Contracts were completed and closed. When I mentioned that the government re-opened them to indict me for underpaying my employees, the government responded that I was trying to profit from my crime. The

ASBCA accepted the government's version without argument and rejected my claim. The government's interpretation of the Davis-Bacon Act was used by the district judge in his instructions to the jury; which were wrong."

"Once again the decision lies with the 9th." The Supreme Court Clerk patiently commented.

"The fourth issue pertains to the Grand Jury proceedings. From the few pages of paperwork which the government produced to the defense a few minutes before they called for the first time the NIS agent to the stand during rebuttal, it appears that there were two Grand Juries involved in my case. The first refused to indict. On the second the government did not produce the same witnesses as on the first. Instead only the NIS employee, Dave Brown, who testified and introduced himself as the 'Agent of the first Grand Jury'. He testified as to what the witnesses of the first Grand Jury testified. His statements to this second Grand Jury were false and fabricated to serve the government's case. Then his own testimony was full of lies and so self serving that the district judge requested that the U.S. Attorney's office produce the entire transcript of the Grand Jury proceedings to determine whether the indictment was obtained under false pretenses. The government never produced the transcripts. My attorney let it go and did not insist that the government produce them. The judge proceeded with the trial as if nothing happened and ended up in my conviction. I brought this up with the 9th and they chose to ignore it."

"I hate doing this, but once again this has been argued and decided by the Supreme Court in numerous cases. The indictment should have been thrown out. It is up to the Higher Court and the District Court to implement the Supreme Court decisions."

"The fifth issue." Michael continued is really a question for which I have been unable to find a precedent. The government had its interpretation of the DavisBacon Act. I had my own. The law is the law. Shouldn't the jury decide whose interpretation is valid? Why did the judge decide that the government was right and I was wrong?  If that was the case, why did we need a jury?  The judge gave   his instructions to the jury favoring the government's position.  It was a fore gone conclusion that based on the judges instructions to the jury, I would be found guilty.  Why bother with the trial and expense if the judge had made up his mind to side with the government.  Particularly, since the governments interpretation and by extent the jury's instructions proved to be wrong according to the subsequent decision by the Supreme Court on another case.  Did it have to do that the District Judge was seeking a promotion to the 9th Circuit Court of Appeals, as my own attorney told me?"

"This is the only issue the Honorable Judge O'Connor wishes to pursue. Is the right of the individual less than that of the government?  She has discussed this with the other judges and they all want to see both parties arguments on the issue. It has never come up before. That's why you are unable to find a precedent. It is a very interesting constitutional question you have raised. I am sure at the end no matter how the matter is decided, the Supreme Court would advise the government advocate on the other four issues you have raised. I am certain the government would not wish for you to file a formal Complaint and would move immediately towards settlement talks."

"Where do we go from here then?"  Michael asked curious as to where the matter was going.  "Don't forget that I am already in prison, by all accounts an innocent man."

"I have tried to talk to the government on this. Unfortunately, Omar Pierre, the attorney of record apparently disgusted with the proceedings quit right after your trial.  The government has not assigned anyone else and they have requested a year's time extension for the new attorney to catch up and be brought up to speed for an equitable hearing..."

"But I will have served my sentence by then..."

"I didn't say that we granted the requested extension. We need to hear from your attorney first."

"I don't have an attorney." Michael protested.

"You don't? Who wrote your Writ of Certiorari?" The Clerk inquired.

"I wrote it long hand first. An attorney here at the Law Library advised me on the number of pages, letter size, spacing and other requirements and I typed it. I signed it and sent it Pro Se."

"I didn't realize that there was no attorney involved." The Clerk expanded in amazement. "It is so well written and succinct that we all thought it was written by an attorney. However, based on our conversation and on your grasp of the issues, I can see you writing it. Are you an attorney?"

"No I am not."

"What did you do on the outside, if you don't mind me asking?"

"I am a Chemical Engineer and a registered Professional Engineer with the National Society of Professional Engineers. I do now in prison what I have been doing all my life on the outside."

"What do you mean by that statement." Tom the Clerk asked surprised.

"I have an Engineering Department here at Camp and at the Red Horse where they have around twenty young sergeants recently graduated with no experience. We design and construct with a labor force of approximately a little over two hundred inmates and equal number of Air Force airmen all the projects at Camp and on the Base. I also teach two hours a day five days a week a course for future government Contracting Officers called Changes in Construction Contracts."

"You are certainly not the run of the mill prisoner I envisioned when I placed this call. Let's see...we first got to find and assign you a lawyer..."

"I don't need a lawyer." Was Michael's immediate response. "I had it with attorneys. Their motto is 'Bleed them and Plead them'. At any rate even if I wanted one, the government has run me dry. My wife has to work to support herself and she is slowly but surely sinking in debt which I have to rectify when I get out of here."

"I am sincerely sorry for your circumstances." Tom the Clerk announced. "Unfortunately, the wheels of justice move very slowly. It appears that the government may get their wish in their Motion. Your attorney and theirs will be on equal footing as far as knowledge of the case. However, I would rather be in your future attorney's shoes on this case. Five issues. A slum dunk on the first four issues with a liberal court bound and determined to limit the government's overreach, leaning towards your side on the fifth issue."

"I am very familiar with my case and the transcripts of the trial have been cast in stone in my memory bank. I am ready to start right now." Michael insisted.

"You may be." Tom responded sympathetically. "Your new attorney though, whomever you select, won't."

"I told you. I am prepared to argue my own case..."

"Michael...Michael... Unfortunately this is not how the system works. Only a select few of the hundreds of thousands of attorneys in the country are allowed to argue in front of the Supreme Court. Believe me they are the best of the best. It is an honor to argue a case in front of the Supreme Court. The government was given a copy of your Writ of Certiorari. They were told that it has been assigned docket, 7011. They have been told that of the issues one to four the Supreme Court has already decided in your favor due to precedent decisions. Do you think they will try to reverse the Supreme Court on four issues that have already been decided? They are not dumb. They see the writing on the wall. I will be surprised that as soon as you select an attorney, by the way at no cost to you, if someone from the Navy and NIS don't contact you and start settlement negotiations."

Michael stayed silent contemplating.

"Are you still there?" Tom broke in after a couple of minutes of dead pause.

"What happens if they don't? If I was in their place I wouldn't. I'd stay quiet and see what happens. I cannot go to the 9th Circuit Court of Appeals on the four issues you have decided in my favor. I need the permission of the sentencing judge to file. I have applied to do so. I am still waiting for an answer from his 'honor'. He does not have a deadline by which to respond. So he does nothing. If I hire an attorney from your select pool of lawyers allowed to argue in front of the Supreme Court, like you are asking me to do, he or she will only argue the fifth issue plus I will lose control of my case. The chosen attorney has no need to even talk to me in order to argue a purely intellectual and Constitutional issue of who has more right in interpreting the law: The Government or the Individual..." "You certainly will discuss all that with the prospective attorneys before you make your selection."

"And they will behave like a prospective Supreme Court Judge in front of the Senate during their confirmation hearing: Tell them what they would like to hear and once confirmed, all bets are off."

The clerk started chuckling. "Mike...Mike...Mike..."

"The Supreme Court is all powerful. Why don't they contact or better yet order the 9th Circuit Court of Appeals to abide by their Rulings on the four issues that you are in agreement. You do that and I will say 'YES' to your request to hire an attorney from your select pool."

"We can't do that because we would be circumventing the sentencing judge. This would also be defeating the Law that has recently passed, of which we were in favor, in order to control all the frivolous Appeals being filed and clogging the Justice System."

"How else am I going to bring the Government in the negotiating table? In my twenty years dealing with the government in Civil Litigation I dealt with the Armed Services Board of Contract Appeals, ASBCA. The fact that I could Appeal their decision to the Court of Claims; i.e. the feared General Accounting Office, GAO, kept them honest and impartial. In this case however, I do not have an 800 pound gorilla in the room to set things right. Look at what started all this. Mail Fraud. The eight counts were Payment and Performance Bonds mailed by the SBA to the Navy. I did no mailing. What do the Bonds have to do with labor rates?"

"Didn't your attorney file a Motion with the Court on this issue?

"Don't make me laugh. My attorney, unbeknown to me, was short listed for a position of Federal Judge. I found that out a week after the trial in the evening news on television. My attorney did not want to rock the boat with Motions."

"I am simply amazed hearing all that. Didn't the presiding federal judge approach you on this and discuss the issue of a mistrial?"

"I already told you that he was promised a promotion to the 9th if he brought in a conviction. Look at his instructions to the jury..."

"Mike, I feel sorry for you getting mangled in the gears of Justice. However, I still need your 'YES' to get started with the issue on hand and the reason for my phone call."

"In that case my answer is 'NO'. I do not wish legal representation at this point. I don't want to lose control of my case. I filed Pro Se and I will defend my position Pro Se. I am prepared to argue my case in front of the Supreme Court..."

"It has never happened before." Tom cut in.

"It is my understanding that the Supreme Court is the defender of the Constitution of the United States." Michael countered. "Accordingly, I believe that this elitist position of the Supreme Court is unconstitutional..."

"You are a very clever and dangerous man." Tom interrupted. "I will relay your position to the Honorable Justice O'Connor and the Court. They will get back to you."

*   *   *   *

"You dumb ass! You blew it." Dino said, after Michael relayed to him his conversation with the Supreme Court Clerk immediately after he hang up the phone. "How did you manage to wrestle defeat from the jaws of victory. You had victory in your grasp and you let it go. 'Deus ex Machina' appeared on stage and you spit on its face. Your conceit, your 'Hubris' has no limits. I am so mad at you, I want to punch you. All you had to do was say 'Yes' to the Clerk and you were on the road to freedom and restitution. He spelled it out for you. What made you think that you will change the system that has been in place for as long as there has been a United Staes and the institution of the Supreme Court. Yes. Probably the Supreme Court system requiring an elitist group of lawyers approved by them to argue cases, could be argued that is unconstitutional. But you don't say that out loud. The Judges at the Supreme Court think in their head that they are the Constitution! Who are you to challenge their thinking? You, saying 'No' to them after they reached out to you is a slap to their face. They consider themselves Gods or at the very least Godlike. There is no institution in this country that may challenge the Supreme Court's decision. You, saying 'No' to them is like slapping the face of God. That my friend is 'Hubris' to an unprecedented level."

Michael stood silent, absorbing the rage of his friend and mentor and going over in his mind the words he was hearing.

"Isn't it possible that they may follow up on the first four issues of my Writ of Certiorari since they are de facto valid and order the government to follow through?" Michael pondered.

"The Clerk told you that this was not within their jurisdiction since their decision on those issues was already made. The 9th would hate to admit it, if it was brought to them, that their one sentence decision on your Appeal that the government need not show loss or damage to bring about an indictment on Mail Fraud was wrong. The district judge of the sentencing court will seat on your request for Appeal until he retires; if he knows what's good for him, and believe me he does. He has no intention of pissing off the 9th Circuit court of Appeals. He has to work with them. There is no law that tells him how long he has to sit on your request. You are truly fucked, my friend. You will get one of these days a form letter from the Supreme Court saying that they ran out of time to take up your case. I can't believe you let this opportunity of having one of the judges in your corner pass you by."

"Dino think back." Michael said. "All the Supreme Court landmark decisions came out of controversy…"

"You are correct. But no one ever challenged the Supreme Court system. The fifth issue in your Appeal is controversial. The Supreme Court ate it up. I would have loved to have seen how the issue was decided and I don't believe you are the best legal mind to argue the issue of the right of the individual to be heard when his interpretation of the law differs from the one advocated by the government. The Clerk told you. This was the only argument they were going to take up. They were going to tell the government that the other four had already been decided in your favor. The government would have had no argument, unless they were willing to challenge all four of the Supreme Courts previous decisions. Think about it. The government would never undertake this route. You are not that important for them to take on that monumental task. Admit it. You let your pride take over and refused the hand offered by the Supreme Court. Your "No" will haunt you the rest of your life. But, I would be lying if I did not tell you that I admire you for it. You are, at some level, my Hero. You listened to the Supreme Court offer and spit in their face. Tell me what other individual has done that before, or will do in the future. They are not used to someone like yourself, as the Clerk told you on the phone."

"I did not intend to do that." Michael admitted. "I thought that the Supreme Court judges were the guardians of Justice. They all know, or should know, that in my case I have been denied Justice. Isn't this enough to motivate them to rectify the situation?"

"They offered to rectify it, but you refused to accept their offer."

"I never said that. I just refused to accept the legal representation they offered, as it is my right to do under the Constitution. Based on my previous experience with legal representation do you believe it's equitable to deny me this Constitutional Right?"

"You have a valid argument. Further reinforced by the timing. Immediate Justice, your way or Justice delayed by a couple of years, the Supreme Court's way. I hope the Supreme Court will think the same way you do and come up with a middle ground to decide the case based on the evidence in front of them. However, based on historical evidence, they simply will refuse to take up your case. No one will criticize them for their decision. Not taking up a case has happened before and it will happen again. No one but a Senator can make them take up a case. Even then, they have ways to make the Senator regret his decision. Once the Supreme Court judge has been appointed by the Senate, all bets are off and the slate has been wiped clean as far as the members of the Supreme Court are concerned. They are there for life. People may disagree with the Supreme Court decisions, but they can do nothing about it. They are the law of the land. I suppose the president may try to change the make up of the Supreme Court, but this will take years to accomplish provided there is a vacancy. Congress may try to increase the number of Supreme Court Justices, thus tilting the scale, but that would mean the president has an overwhelming majority of loyal supporters in both the House and the Senate. This will never happen because of the special interest groups, who through their lobbyists, buy the votes of the Representatives and the Senators alike. They in turn need the money in order to get re-elected. It's a vicious circle Mike and not you or anyone else will ever change. For practical purposes the Supreme Court Justices are there to stay and whatever they decide is the established Law."

"Somehow what you are saying seems unfair, Dino..."

"Who said life was fair? Who said Justice is fair and equitable? Justice is just blind stumbling along and inevitably once in a while finds its way. These are the   cases the media concentrates on to expound and the rest of the country believes that things are as reported by the media. You on the other hand is an aberration. You are 'sui generis', your own man, and refuses to conform to the main stream.  The government tries to eliminate people like you, or at the very least control by containment. I bet that's the real reason you are here today."

"How do you figure, Dino?"

"Well they offered you to pay them $25,000.00 towards their expenses in investigating you as justification to their superiors if your case came up, and you refused their offer..."

"Their offer was also contingent on admitting that I was guilty..."

"Technicalities, which could have been ironed out.  You could counter offered them a plea of 'nolle contendere' and they would have jumped on it."

"What's 'nolle contendere'?" Michael inquired.

"It literary means 'no contest'. In reality it is refusal of admission of quilt. For all practical purposes the contest is decided as a draw and the judge will readily sign it to get this complicated case off his docket."

"But I was not and still am not guilty.  I want this to be decided and posted as such."

"Mike...Mike...here again it's your 'Hubris' speaking.  The matter of guilty or innocent is highly debatable and the outcome swings like a pendulum.  Take for example the first issue or your Appeal.  The 9th rendered a guilty verdict because the government was not required to show loss or damages. This was the law at the time. The Supreme Court decided not so fast Lewis, and voted on another case the exact the opposite. The government must show loss or damage.  This became the new law.    Which means you are innocent since you proved mathematically and the government admitted during your trial that they saved a shitload of money.  See, it's like a pendulum, guilty swings to innocent to whatever the future may hold.  These are manmade laws and they get interpreted in accordance with the society modes and beliefs at the times.  Clinton wanted to appease the unions to get their votes and get elected, he expands the jurisdiction of the Davis-Bacon Act:  You are guilty.  He gets elected, sees his folly and he reverses himself: You are innocent.  Based on this example alone the term guilty or innocent are interchangeable and irrelevant at the same time."

"I don't agree with you, Dino.  Maybe on an intellectual level you are right.  For practical purposes though the guilty verdict carries along the stigma and personal damages in the form of curtailment of rights and liberties imposed by the government. Anyway that's the way I am. I will still say the great 'No' because I believe it is the right answer, even if it defeats me the whole of my life."

*    *    *    *

A month later Michael received a form letter from the Supreme Court stating in one sentence that, due to the overwhelming case load the Supreme Court would be unable to select his case.

# CHAPTER 19

## Internal Affairs

Michael had a General Arrangement Plot Plan on top of his drafting table of the entire Nellis Air Force Base, including the Camp.  He marked in red the location of each ongoing project with notations pertaining to each project status and anticipated completion date.  He marked in green the location of the next phase of upcoming projects, currently under design in both the Camp and the Base.  He noted the status of the engineering Drawings and Specifications and the projected design completion date which would transfer their status from green to red.  They were several other notations of upcoming projects, still at the funding level, for which he had prepared FYI requests to the General Accounting Office, GAO.

One bright day in late October he came in his office and the General Arrangement Drawing was no where to be seen. Although his office had no door, he couldn't fathom who was the culprit.  The crews had no use for it and they would never take something particularly a Drawing which clearly stated right on top OFFICE COPY.  DO NOT REMOVE. The guilty party must have had other, nefarious, uses such as drop off points for delivery and pick up of contraband.

He reported the loss immediately to the SIS office, as the Rules and Regulations required.  The BOP SIS office was like the Internal Affairs of the Police Department.  They conducted investigations and brought criminal charges.  Not only on prisoners, sometimes even against guards and other Bureau of Prisons employees.  SIS was hated and feared by everyone at the institution, including the guards and the Warden.  Their role, sans the 'I', was similar to another branch which had its origins in

Germany, over fifty years ago.  The SIS office at Camp Nellis, was run by a diminutive, in height only, woman in her mid forties, called by the guards and prisoners alike 'wide glide'.  Her actual name was Teresa Kyle, but because of her ability to glide in, so to speak, unnoticed, right into the thick of things, and her wide posterior, was never referred to, behind her back, by her real name.

The call came to Michael's BOP supervisor, Phil Rolfs, a week later from the date Michael had filed his missing Drawing report.  Michael happened to be in Rolfs office at the time.

"Control to Rolfs."

"Rolfs here, go."  He answered, increasing the volume of the intercom speaker.

"Send inmate Michael Mat...something...I can't pronounce his last name...you know the one we all call 'Big Dog', to the SIS office immediately.

"Will do, out."  Phil Rolfs said dutifully and replaced the inter come unit on his belt.

"What the fuck you've done now?"  He turned towards Michael with a look on his face indicating that chances were, this was the last time he would be seeing him again.

His look said it all.  A trip to the SIS office invariably meant automatic shipment, of the inmate in question for a serious alleged infraction.  Alleged or real, made no difference as far as the BOP was concerned.  If your name came up with the SIS, you were immediately transferred to the North Las Vegas County jail, pending further investigation of the allegations.  Ten percent of the cases made it back  to the Camp when the allegations proved to be without basis.  However, in the meantime, the suspects got to spend twelve to sixteen weeks, that was how long the investigation took, in a twenty by thirty foot holding cell, locked down twenty three hours a day, with twenty nine other prisoners, waiting trial or waiting to be transferred to commence their sentence. No bed. Sleeping on the concrete floor, on a plastic sheet which served as a mattress. You had to roll it up or fold it during the day. One blanket to cover yourself. No pillow. One roll of toilet paper per day, doubling as a pillow at night. No locker. No belongings, except what you had on. Each day on your way out, for your hour of being free to roam in the general population out of the cell and the lockdown, you were given a one time disposable toiletry kit. During that time out of the cell, you had to wait in line to take a shower, shave, use the phone, mail a letter and all the little things one took for granted at the Camp. If and when someone made it back to the Camp, no apology was given by the BOP for the hell he went through for no reason.

With these grave thoughts in mind and fear gnawing at the pit of Michael's stomach, he went back to his office and started packing his meager belongings in anticipation of having to come back under guard to collect them. Part of the procedure of getting 'rolled up'. He still did not know for what he was being accused of, punishing himself going back and and re-examining everything he had done or failed to do. He couldn't think of anything, no matter how critically he looked. He prided himself in being the world's toughest critic when it came to self evaluation. But then again, he had no way of gauging whether his compass was reading the same under his present circumstances. His head was trying to tell him that it was bound to have changed some, after the prison experience. He was trying to convince himself that it was now more fine tuned. His antenna was more sensitive. The prison experience broadened his horizon, made him more worldly, increased the angle of his peripheral vision.

If all that was well and good, why then was he unable to figure out what the summons to the SIS office was all about? Michael hated surprises. Particularly of this type. Walking into an ambush. Did he have a fighting chance? He was quick on his feet. What was the charge? Whom would he be facing?  A person or a pre set charge activated the moment he walked into the killing zone?

The officer in charge of SIS was a woman.  Known simply as Lieutenant Kyle.  Michael doubted she was even aware of his existence, until that is, his name came up.  Even then, he doubted whether she could put his name and face together.

In the past, he recalled he only had come in contact with her two other times.  It was an impersonal contact.  The first time he was returning to the Camp after his first day at work on Base.  She frisked him briefly and intimately.  The second time, he was also returning to Camp from the Base.  He was stopped and searched.  No names...but he could still feel her fingers on his crotch massaging his balls, running the length of his dick...lingering there.  It was the only female intimate touch he had felt since he reported at Nellis AFB Camp.  The experience tends to stay with someone under these circumstances.

That second time, he was returning from the Base.  He forgot the exact circumstances as to why he was on Base.  Probably inspecting one of the construction activities of the Air Force or invited to attend a meeting on Base or solving some problem encountered on site.  It did not matter. Upon their return from Base to the Camp, the inmates were searched. The search consisted, from a perfunctory pat down, to more involved procedures, depending on the demeanor of the prisoner and the mood of the federal officer.  Michael was never searched, because every guard knew who he was and the fact that he had authority to go everywhere on Base with his golf cart loaded with equipment he used on his job as the Camp and Base Engineer.  He nodded to the guard at the gate and continued on his way.

Suddenly, the Administration Building door opened and a blond female federal officer came out and motioned him to stop.  He got out of the golf cart and stood at attention next to it.  He was in his shorts wearing the regulation uniform shirt and construction steel toe boots.  She started coming towards him, with the sun behind her.  Her blond mane ended in a frieze of curls.  The light breeze, trailing behind her, had spread her hair like a halo.  She was a biblical vision.  She was Lieutenant Kyle, he realized.  On closer inspection, her skin appeared dried up, because of too much sun in the desert, highlighted by freckles down her neck, disappearing down the 'V' of her impeccably starched and ironed white short sleeve shirt, to the beginning of the valley created by her generous breasts.

She stopped in front of Michael.  His chin came to the top of her forehead and the mass of blond hair curls.  They were standing in the middle of the main street into the Camp.  She pointed a well turned crimson nail towards Michael, curling her index finger up and down towards her, indicating to follow her.  Michael followed he, unable to take his eyes away from the most magnificent behind he had ever seen, a few paces towards a cluster of dwarf cypress trees.  There she stopped.  So Michael stopped.  She turned facing him and said, in a husky, cigarette ravaged voice to lift his hands up and extend them on his side.

Michael did as she asked, and she left him in place suspended in anticipation of what it seemed almost a minute.  He lost sight of her, as she moved behind him, and for an insane second, he felt alone and ridiculous, standing behind the trees with his hands up in the air forming the sign of the cross, a victim of some bizarre hold-up in progress.  He didn't feel her presence until he sensed the fluttering of her nails behind his shirt collar, sending goosebumps down his spine.

By now, Michael was not a virgin at pat downs.  Done by female federal officers, particularly and unavoidably before and after each weekend visit.  But Lieutenant Kyle's touch was electric.  Her fingers screamed out loud that they were enjoying what they were doing. Michael sensed it had something to do with power.  She seemed to take delight in having a man, stand in front of her, helpless, with his hands up in the air and his legs spread wide.  She enjoyed the whole process and took her time to go through the preliminaries, the approach or the foreplay so to speak, before she actually laid a finger on her victim.

She stayed behind Michael.  The only thing visible were her arms and hands working in a downward motion, turning into a lingering circular motion in places, to throw off the 'suspect', as to what she was actually looking for.  Michael had been working out with a personal trainer the BOP under the Warden's suggestion   had hired to keep him healthy because he was an 'Institutional Need' and he had been working out two hours a day at the Air Force workout room.  This was in addition to the hourly work out at five o'clock in the morning with Milton and the tunnel rat with excruciating heavy weights.  This exercise program, plus a daily five mile walk around the track, caused Michael to lose eighty pounds since he had been processed in, and was sporting an impressive six pack on his stomach, for the first time since his boxing days in College.   His chest, shoulders, arms and legs were those of a serious body builder.

Lieutenant Kyle's proximity, her perfume, her fingers more massaging than patting, furtive contacts of her body with Michael's back, letting his imagination run wild, trying to guess which part of her anatomy protruded to achieve contact, all that had the effect of stirring long forgotten feelings of companionship, fast turning into lust, by the time her fingers reached the waist band of Michael's shorts.  By the time her hands went a couple of times around Michael's waist and her nails started scratching his stomach, she succeeded in giving him a hard on.

If the duration of the pat down search was divided into equal intervals, the time it took to search Michael's entire body, equaled the time it took Lieutenant Kyle to search his crotch.  By the time she was done with him, had he been braver, he would have asked her: "Was it as good for you?"  But instead, purple with embarrassment, he put his head down and scurried back to his golf cart, the memory and sensation of her fingers still burning on his shaft and balls.

That was Michael's only experiences with the SIS lady.  These memories and thoughts were swirling in the cauldron of Michael's brain as he was heading out the door of the Mess Hall where his office was located in the basement of the same building. He almost collided with a couple of inmates from his construction crews at the Camp coming in.  They jumped aside as soon as they saw Michael through the front entrance glass.  Michael greeted them in passing, registering their expression. They already knew.  The word was out.  He was dead meat.  Dead man walking.  As far as these two were concerned, Michael was out of there. Already history.  All that was left was to report to the SIS office and make it official.  Down the sidewalk, towards Building 10202, the Administration Building, Michael might as well been clanging a bell, announcing the approach of a leper.

The SIS office was located in the basement of Building 10202, appropriately called the dungeon. Michael had never been near it in the past.  Accordingly, it took some wandering down the silent hallways to find the SIS office.  The absence of people in the basement was eerie. The only facilities along the  deserted hallways were behind locked doors with the exception of the open door to a huge staff lounge.  It took the entire East wing of the basement, leading into an adjacent staff exercise room full of the latest Nautilus machines.  There was no one in the lounge, and the machines in the staff weight pile stood still.

In the middle of the corridor, stood a heavy steel door, painted dark blue with a peep hole.  A sign on the right of the door, told the visitor that he had reached his destination.  He timidly knocked on the door, only to hurt his knuckles.  Michael stood outside the door wondering what to do next. Knocking on the door, just hurt his knuckles. The door was that thick and massive.  The door was closed, locked, with no visible hardware. The door was a steel sheet, which looked painted on the wall. Just walking in was impossible.  The door was intimidating.  Michael started doubting whether the gleaming blue mass of steel, in front of him, was even a door.  He wished he had brought with him a hammer from the tool room to take a whack at it. But then he could see the headlines: 'Felon was caught outside the SIS office wielding a sledge hammer'. But then again he was going to be 'rolled up' anyway, for who knows what; he might as well add a charge for which he would be cognizant.

The door was not entirely free of blemishes. A foot from the bottom, it had a number of black scuff marks, Michael had not noticed at first glance because they were blending in to the dark blue color of the door and due to poor lighting of the hallway, having walked in from the bright sunshine of the outside. But now that his eyes had adjusted, to the semidarkness of the basement, he could make out details that eluded him in the beginning. Details of both sight and sound. Like, he became aware of the drone of machinery hidden behind by the wall in front of him. The vibration was palpable as soon as he leaned on the wall on either side of the SIS door. He could even make out that a bearing was out of alignment. The mystery compressor, pump or other mechanical device, did not have long for this world. On the verge of sounding like a garbage disposal, trying to spit out or grind a bone caught in its gear.

It dawned on him that the scuff marks were made by inmate steel toe boots, in the same predicament as he was, trying to get the attention of the keeper of the SIS gate, after having worn out their knuckles. He drop kicked the door gently, aware of the strength in the lower part of his anatomy, due to years of High School and College level varsity soccer. He waited, aware subconsciously that he was being watched. There was a peep hole lens in the center of the door. He was tempted to put an eye against it. However, if indeed he was being watched, he doubted whether the watcher would share his sense of humor.

A single click brought him out of his quandary, as the steel door swung out a few inches. Michael caught sight of Lieutenant Kyle, shoulder to the door, pushing with all her five foot frame and giving it all its worth, managing to swing the door quarter open. He was tempted to help pull, while she pushed, but thought better. Any woman working as a guard in a male federal prison, must have a certain size of balls. Figuratively speaking, of course. At any rate, she must be sufficiently liberated. Also any sudden tilt of power, given the angle she was leaning, would have resulted in loss of her balance, ending on the floor. By no means the best foot forward. So, he stood watching, trying his ten mile vacant stare. She stopped pushing and signaled him to enter. She turned as soon as Michael crossed the door frame and followed her, giving furtive looks at the door behind them, which was left open.

The SIS office was a single room twelve by thirty feet, with a ten foot ceiling. It was no better lit than the corridor, reeking of stale cigarette smoke; its source readily apparent due to the lit cigarette resting on the ashtray smack in the middle of Lieutenant Kyle's desk, on top of piles of paperwork. The far wall was taken by various recording devices, stacked floor to ceiling. Immediately below the sign, denoting an inmates dorm, a light in the telephone banks started flashing. The caller must have said a key word in his telephone conversation that must have triggered the computer and now his conversation was being monitored and recorded.

One entire wall was taken by four drawer steel file cabinets. Michael's guess was that every inmate must have had a file. Also folders with cases under investigation in various stages. A copier, FAX machine, various other audio and video equipment, cameras and gadgets he would have loved to play with. Lieutenant Kyle motioned Michael to sit on the only empty chair in front of her desk, while she started searching for something. Her measured movements turned frantic as Michael sat silently observing her. She finally plucked a single page from a paper pile, cleared a spot in front of her and placed the document face down.

"How do you pronounce your last name?" She asked.

These were the first words spoken so far by either of them. Michael cleared his thoughts and glanced back at the door, where he had come into the office. Disturbing thoughts has caused him to panic. By virtue of being seen, sitting across from the head of the SIS officer, by either a hack or a wandering inmate, was enough to label him a 'Rat'. The inmates whose universal cry was the unfair way they had been treated by the government, and the underhanded ways employed to obtain a conviction, were the first ones to place judgmental names on fellow inmates. On mere suspicion, so and so was labeled a 'Rat', a Snitch'.

Labels that stuck to the individual for the duration of his sentence. They were judged guilty. It was up to them to prove they were innocent, and absence of proof, it was their duty to take out the accuser. Thus dictated the unwritten law of the prison. An environment where viciousness was applauded and rewarded. Sneaky attacks and ambushes were an everyday occurrence, where your ability to keep your mouth shut was put to a test. If the attacker was punished, the victim was labeled a 'Rat'. The attacker was removed from the general population and sent to the Las Vegas County Jail which had the reputation as 'gladiator' heaven. Ultimately, after several weeks or months, depending on the severity of the beating, the attacher was moved to a higher security facility or brought back. In the latter case, he now enjoyed a reputation of someone not to be fucked with. The reputation, unfortunately, as all friendships and relationships in prison, was ephemeral. It also cut both ways. It invited fear and invited challenge.

A wiser choice was to stay out of the limelight all together. For that reason, Michael anxiously glanced at the door. His fear evaporated, just as it had come on. The door had, mysteriously, shut by itself. He distinctly remembered being left open, not having been touched by him, and he would vouch that Lieutenant Kyle never moved from her desk. It must be spring loaded, he thought. A button on the floor or under her desk. He was now locked in the SIS office with Ms Kyle, all five foot of her, one hundred and twenty five pounds, mostly butt.

It took a while, but finally he pronounced his name. She smiled, trying to put him at ease. If it had taken that long to get an answer out him, to a simple question, she must have been concerned, he thought, of how long it might take to get answers to more complex questions.

If the smile was designed to put him at ease. It was not succeeding. Her eyes were still those of the spider calling to the little fly: "Come closer my dear." Michael was keen on keeping his alertness, because her voice had siren qualities.

She moved to more innocuous questions, of which she already knew the answers, like how long he'd been there, was he self report, how much longer  had to serve on his sentence, what had he done to end up at the Camp.  His answers were laconic, all along he had been thinking: "Cut the shit lady.  You already know the answers to the questions you are asking.  I am sure you have read my PSI file. Cut through the chase and come to the point.  Why am I here in your office?"

Her next barrage of questions, threw him off.  They were getting progressively personal.  Michael felt himself blush, when she tested the fine line between inquisitor and prisoner, by asking him whether he was still happily married, after being placed in confinement.  She was probing, scraping an open wound, exploring the effect of a forced separation from a loved one.  Michael's antenna was up and buzzing.  If he was not aware of where he was at the moment, he'd swear she was flirting with him.  Her interest in him was unnerving.  If it was an interrogation technique to put him at ease, it was having the opposite effect.  Michael's answers were guarded, while he was stubbornly refusing to be drawn into a lengthy conversation.

"How long have you been married?" She asked.

"Twenty six years."

"I've never met or known somebody married to the same person that long.  What's your secret?"

Michael stared at her, trying to think of an answer.

"Don't worry.  You don't have to answer." She brought him out of his dilemma.  "If I was married to someone like you, I'd still be married today." She said, blushing.

Michael was stunned.  He could not trust his ears that he had heard right. The atmosphere had turned electric all of a sudden.  Her last comment had leveled the playing field.  Their relationship seemed to be no longer that of a jailer and a prisoner.  He kept thinking back to all the stories he'd heard when he first arrived.  About prisoners and female federal officers, while Lieutenant Kyle droned on about her unhappy relationships with men.

Michael hadn't been in prison fifteen minutes, still in processing, and the talk among the two female officers checking him in, was about the wedding that past weekend between a released inmate and a female guard.  The line of prisoners, he've seen on his first night at the Camp outside the duty officer's door, after the ten o'clock count.  Freshly showered with a roll of quarters on hand, eagerly waiting their turn. The rustling of sheets and moans in his room...

"What did you do with the Drawing?"  Lieutenant Kyle's words had the effect of a bucket of cold water thrown at Michael.

"What do you mean?"  Michael answered with a question, trying to compose himself and sharpen his focus.

"How many missing Drawings you know of?"

"I only had the one on my drafting table.  I kept notes on it regarding the construction projects in progress, the ones under design and the ones submitted for a GAO appropriation.  No one had access to the Drawing, that I know of.  But I don't know what happens after hours.  I leave around two PM, unless I have to go and teach.  On those days I leave at noon."

Michael was very candid with her, and thought at times that she liked him. She was shocked at the work he was doing, and horrified at the lack of security in his office.  When she asked him, why no one bothered to lock his office door at the end of the day, he told her that his office did not have a door.

"What was on the Drawing?"

"The General Arrangement of Nellis Air Force Base and the Camp."

"You had in your possession such a Drawing?" She exclaimed, shocked.

"I created the Drawing. I gave copies to the Red Horse because they did not have any of the entire layout and the tunnels. They pay the Camp for my time there…"

"Tunnels! Did I hear tunnels?"

"Yes. The entire Air Force Base and the Camp have an underground network of interconnecting tunnels."

"And you know of their location?"

"I walked all of them, with a couple of assistants from the Red Horse office, and incorporated their location and routes to the General Arrangement Plan."

"What you are telling me is invaluable. Is Phil Rolfs aware of your activities?"

"He does not want to know because he does not understand them. He has no education. Total ignorance of math. He knows how to operate a fork lift and I arrange assignments for him. He leaves the Engineering and Construction to me. The Warden is aware of the situation. I am not going to go into into details, because part of my work involves other bases that are secret, including Area 51, and I was told not to speak about it to anyone, including BOP personnel. That's where I go on non visiting weekends. Phil drives me to Mercury Air Force Base and he leaves. They take me from there to Area 51…Let's say my activities earn the Camp and the Air Force Base over ten million dollars a year profit, which they split fifty/fifty…This is where your bonus will come at the end of the year." Michael said with finality.

At the end of their meeting, she told Michael that he was not the run of the mill inmate the system was designed for.

"Your welfare is vital for both the BOP and the Air Force Base. Henceforth I will make your welfare my number one priority and I will personally take on the task to safeguard you."

Michael was tempted to tell her that this was not necessary as he was guarded already, being a 'Man of Respect'.  But then again he remembered: 'Omerta'.

"In my eighteen years in the system," she exclaimed, "I've never met anyone like you before, and never will."

The next morning, while Michael was taking his six thirty shower, there was a massive evacuation of the bathroom which had twelve of everything, shower stalls, urinals, toilets and lavatories.  What was the cause of the mass exodus of the inmates, Michael wondered, but not for very long as the figure of Lieutenant Kyle appeared in the entrance of his shower stall, holding a cup of coffee.  The first thing you loose in prison is your modesty.  Michael continued his shower, ignoring the presence of Lieutenant Kyle.

"Is this the time you shower everyday?" She asked.

"Yes." Michael answered laconically.

"Were you aware that most incidents occur, while a person is taking a shower?" She asked.

"This is a Camp." Michael replied. "Also I don't have any enemies, that I know of.  Everyone's job is dependent on me, and they know it.  Why would they want to hurt me?"

"I have no intention of finding out." She cut him off. "I will always be there for you.  I made a few calls after you left yesterday and found out that nothing gets built here or at the Air Force Base without your approval and signature.  I thought you were bragging to me yesterday.  Only to find out that you understated your importance, instead.  For example, you did not tell me that you were driven to other military bases and solved their problems.  You mentioned your work in Area 51 without going into details.  I understand that.  It's classified.  You said you were teaching.  You did not tell me, however, that you were teaching prospective Contracting Officers at the Base coming from all over the world twenty at a time for a ten day course at $2,500.00 a pop each and the BOP and the Air Force were splitting the proceeds of your labor."

"I did not know that myself."  Michael admitted.  "I knew that someone was raking in, fifty thousand dollars every couple of weeks.  I thought it was the Air Force only, because it was their program.  I was told by the Head of the Red Horse that the BOP was charging the Air Force $55.00 per hour for my time.  The fifty/fifty split is news to me."

Lieutenant Kyle became various shades of red.

"You just don't realize how powerful you are…"

"I know that I am busy from the time I get up, until I go to bed.  It takes my mind away from thinking how unfairly I was treated by the government before and during my trial…"

"In all my life, I've never met a man like you."

"That's because you have dealt with criminals, some of them even wearing badges…"

"Oh!  And what do you consider yourself?"

"A political prisoner?"

"You are right.  I read your PSI.  You do not belong in prison for administrative infractions, which are the opinion of someone and highly debatable at best.  Who did you piss off to become a target?  By the way be careful how you talk to other inmates.  You have a way of speaking…and the words you use…they will think you are looking and talking down to them.  This may cause you grief.  And I won't be there to protect you every time.  Unless you initiate a special request…"  She added as an afterthought.  Michael sensed that they were right back into the danger zone, as the bathroom temperature was rising…Maybe from all the steam he was creating showering.

"Friends come and go; enemies accumulate."  Michael said sagely, changing the subject.

"Is this an original?" Michael nodded.  "I love it.  I may borrow it and use it myself."

Michael got out of the shower, dried up and started shaving with Lieutenant Kyle as his sole audience.

"I can place under arrest everyone around here.  Including the Warden. I don't work for the BOP.  I work for the Department of Justice directly. Do you understand?"

Michael almost asked her to tell him what she knew about UNI-COR, but thought better, not to tempt the fates.

"If you feel threatened, or if someone, I don't care who he is, is being unfair to you, let me know.  I'll take care of it.  I understand it's bad enough for someone like you to find himself in a place like this.  I don't want you to suffer needlessly.

Is that clear?"

In lieu of an answer, Michael took Lieutenant Kyle in his arms and gave her a tight hug.  They stayed that way for over a minute.  Michael gave her the hug of her life, she had been missing.

"If I was not married," he told her, "I would have liked to get to know you better.  You have a good heart and an unwavering sense of justice." Were Michael's parting words that day.

*   *   *   *

Every morning at 6:30 AM the bathroom was empty.  Lieutenant Kyle, like a  guardian angel, always present waiting for Michael to take his shower, until the day he left the Camp.

*   *   *   *

A steel door, frame and cypher lock hardware were waiting for Michael as soon as he arrived at his office.  He assigned a crew immediately to install them, making his office a mini Fort Knox.  Only SIS and himself knew his office combination.  All his tools and equipment of his profession were now locked and secure.  A drafting drawing storage steel cabinet was delivered to his office mid morning and all the Drawings were stored there.  New locks were installed on all doors of the Engineering and Construction offices, including the drafting room.  All keyed to the same special key that could not be duplicated.  There were two keys made.  One for Michael and one for Lieutenant Kyle, the SIS officer in charge.  Michael added his key to the leather cord he had around his neck that already had a key to the tool and equipment room with the number '10' engraved on it.

# CHAPTER 20

## In Hot Water

All work away from the Camp was not top secret or taking place in non existing, at least on the map, Department of Defense facilities. One morning Phil Rolfs intercepted Michael as he was coming in and after he unlocked the Engineering Department he stopped him from turning the dial to unlock his own office.

"Leave it locked." He said. "You are going on a road trip today. I have already notified the bubble."

Michael looked at him concerned. "Am I being sent on a diesel therapy for rehabilitation...?"

Rolfs laughed. "Far from it. You are traveling in style my good friend. It will be just you and me. We will take my car."

"Oh!", Michael exclaimed. "Another one of those trips that I will be blindfolded... Don't you realize that as soon as we leave the Camp gate I take the blindfold off.

I already know how to get to China Lake and Area 51..."

"Don't let anyone else know about it, if you know what's good for you..."

"OK! I give up. Where are we going this time?"

"It's a Warden special. I have no idea what he is getting out of it. But it is an emergency. That's all I know. The entire Dublin Camp has been without hot water for three days now."

Michael started laughing. "It would make Spartans out of the inmates to shower in cold water. The Spartans never showered in anything but cold water..."

"How about their women?" Rolf inquired. "Did the Spartan women take cold showers also?"

"I don't know." Michael admitted. "Why are you asking?"

"Because Dublin is an all women Camp. Including their Warden and every guard there. We will be the only males there. I always fantasized to be kept locked up in an all women prison...Stay close to me when we get there. I don't want to have to explain to our Warden and your SIS girlfriend, if you end up kidnapped and held for ransom by these crazy women prisoners." Rolf added laughing. "Its a six hour drive. We will stop by your room so you may load up on cigars and way we go. We will stop for lunch somewhere on the way. They are expecting us around two in the afternoon."

"What's wrong with their hot water?" Michael asked.

"If they knew, they wouldn't be asking for you. Mr. boiler expert. At least that was the way the Warden sold you to them. All I know is that they had every boiler and HVAC contractor around to repair their boilers and they were all baffled. After three days of research and development, she, I mean the Dublin Camp Warden, called her old buddy, our Warden, for help. Just so you know they are both black and she may be playing for the other team."

Michael became instantly apprehensive. He had built, so far in his career, numerous power plants, which invariably had boilers involved, but he always viewed the forest rather than the individual trees. He was always involved with the process and the Flow Diagram, rarely involved himself with the individual components, the equipment, unless he was forced to; because it was effecting the process.

He filled his cigar case with five cigars putting one in his mouth immediately and started chewing it.

"You can smoke in my car." Rolf informed Michael. "I always do. Smoke, I mean, cigarettes that is for us mortals. You never told me. How do you get cigars in here and Cubans to boot..."

"The Warden provides me with two boxes a month." Michael answered laconically.

"Right!" Rolf replied equally. He always treated Michael's statements as speculative fiction.

The road trip was uneventful. Rolfs truck was only two years old with less than twenty five thousands miles on the odometer. He was being reimbursed thirty five cents per mile from the BOP. He was making money while driving and he loved driving. Heading West outside Las Vegas the advertising for 'Bunny Houses' started.

"Don't get any ideas." Rolfs admonished Michael. "We ain't stopping. Not on the way to Dublin...anyway."

Michael ignored him trying to decipher the meaning of 'Bunny Houses' unwilling to disclose his ignorance on the matter. The mystery was solved as they passed the first 'Bunny House' and he noticed the women on the balcony above the entrance lounging in see through gowns in their birthday suits underneath leaving nothing to the imagination.

"Look but do not touch." Phil Rolfs said slowing way down and stopping for a closer look. The women started dancing for the two potential clients, lifting overhead their nightgowns and jiggling their boobs for enticement. Rolfs started the truck rolling, to the boos of the women, for the next 'Bunny House'.

"Phil!" Michael exclaimed. "You better put the petal to the metal. The speed limit is fifty miles per hour. At the rate you are driving, we will never make it to Dublin before night fall."

"You are right old buddy.  It's no use anyway getting all hot and bothered. We don't want to arrive at Dublin with a hard on."

They decided to have an early lunch ending up during rush hour after several stop and go perusing the menus of several establishments and arguing over conventional, Michael's choice, versus Mexican, Phil Rolfs choice.

The decision was made when Michael announced.  "Phil I love Mexican. It's just that Mexican does not love me.  I don't want to show up at Dublin with a heart burn or worse, in urgent need for a restroom.  Don't you want the 'expert', the SOB from out of town, to make at least a good first impression?"

That did it.  Over two pastrami sandwiches fries and a Dr. Pepper for Michael and a beer for Phil, they tried for small talk as there were both in the dark about the upcoming 'lack of hot water' issue.  Phil complained that on his salary there was very little he could afford to do in Las Vegas.

"Here I am in a sea of yogurt and don't have a God damn spoon."  He complained to Michael.

"I think you will get a big bonus at the end of the year."  Michael corrected him.

"If I had found you.  You are probably right.  However, the Warden believes he has found you and all you are doing are his own ideas.  I was told by him to stay in the sidelines and let you blossom.  The rest of the people don't know this of course, and as a result my stock at Camp has risen considerably.  All I have to say is Michael thinks...and I get my way. But when the time comes to share the spoils, the Warden will get the lion's share and the rest of us will split the remains.  Not that twenty to twenty five Gees, which I think I will get, is something to sneeze at. That's an awful lot of golf games and taking the wife and family to eat out and enjoy a few shows.  But other than that and a few decent clothes, that's the extent of the bonus.  The Warden on the other hand will get enough to augment his nest egg for retirement."

Dublin was a sleepy little bedroom community with the women's camp as the only industry to provide employment for the female population of the town.  The Camp looked like a small college surrounded by a six foot chain link fence.  An unguarded sixteen foot gate with warning signs to keep out because it was federal government property with the penalty being prosecution and a five year sentence with a $250,000.00 fine was enough to keep the casual visitor at bay.

Phil Rolfs drove in and followed the signs to Administration.  He parked in a Visitors stall and they made their way to the one story building main entrance at precisely 2:00 PM.  The receptionist was all excited at their arrival.

"Are you fellows from the Nellis Air Force Base?"  She immediately inquired solicitously.

"We certainly are and just as promised, on time."  Phil Rolfs volunteered.

"Thank goodness."  She exclaimed.  "You cannot image the fix we are in.  The inmates refuse to take cold showers…and after three days without washing…you can smell them from afar…",  She wrinkled her nose for emphasis.  "I sure hope sir you can fix the problem."  She said addressing Michael.  "We were quoted hundreds of thousands to replace the piping and the control valves…here I go running at my mouth again.  I better ring the Warden that you have arrived."

She picked up her phone and punched a button presumably connecting her with the Warden.  After a brief conversation with her palm covering her mouth so the visitors would not hear her conversation, she hung up.

"The Warden will be out to meet you.  In the meantime do you want something to drink? You've come a long ways. Its a six, seven hour drive.  You must be thirsty."

Michael asked for water.  Phil nodded that he was fine.  She brought Michael a bottle of water which she retrieved under the reception counter from a small refrigerator, because the water bottle was very cold to the touch and introduced herself as Michelle.  It was obvious, her name emblazoned in huge letters on top of the reception counter beneath her enormous breasts which they both noted when they arrived.  The Warden chose to make her entrance at that moment.  If she was not in uniform, black pants, stiletto heels and white starched shirt, Michael would have taken her for a model.  He wondered what price old Luther, the Nellis Camp Warden had extracted from her.  Then again he remembered Phil Rolfs had mentioned that 'she played for the other team'.  Who to believe?

"Luther, I mean your Warden Faxed me your PSI and I have read it."  She said looking at Michael.  "You belong on 'Who's Who', not in prison."  She added.

"He is actually on Who's Who."  Phil Rolfs volunteered.

"I don't doubt it."  The Warden proclaimed.  "Shall we…"  She pointed at the door, "visit so to speak the scene of 'the crime'?"

She led Phil Rolfs and Michael out the Administration door along the sidewalk meandering through the Dublin Camp and ended in front of a one story building with a sign announcing it as the MECHANICAL & ELECTRICAL BUILDING.  Two heavily perfumed female prisoners and two female guards were standing in front of the building's six foot double wide door.  They led the way to the well lit building interior which housed two No. 2 oil fired hot water boilers with all their appurtenances such as feed water pumps, water softener et al.  Two chillers for the AC.  And a good size Motor Control Center.  Michael walked and stopped in front of the two boiler burners.  Looking expectantly.

"Let me introduce you to the two M & M's as we call them, Marilyn and Mary, they are our boiler operators.  Michael is on loan from the Nellis Air Force Camp."  He introduced Michael to the assembly.  "He is a

Chemical Engineer and a   Professional Engineer who has built power plants around the country for many years.  For him these…," She pointed at the offending boilers,  "are probably nothing more than 'a tempest in a tee kettle'…"

Michael looked at the Warden newly impressed with her for quoting Shakespeare.  "That may be the case, but the principles and the ignition system is the same as in a power plant."  He spoke for the first time.  He pointed for the others to back up and he started tracing the lines to the burner paying particular attention to the flame safety system twin shut off valves.

"Fire it up."  He commanded the two M & M's pointing at the boiler he was standing in front of.They did and immediately the two safety shut off valves tripped and stopped the flow of oil.

"Fire the other one." He said.

They did, and the exact same thing happened.

"This is what has been happening with the others who were here before you."  One of the M & M's volunteered.  "One contractor proposed to by pass the valves…"

"This would be suicidal."  Michael exclaimed.  "It would defeat the flame safety shut off system and it would be an accident waiting to happen. In that case the BOP would be liable and the insurance would not cover the accident as it occurred with a compromised FM system."

"What does FM stand for?"  The Warden inquired.

"It's the initials for Factory Mutual; an insurance company that has set standards for the safe operation of boiler burners." Michael responded.

He remaining silent tracing the electrical wiring from the safety shut off valves to the fire eye overlooking the burner flame through a circular window in front of the boiler.

"May I have a wet rag mixed with soap. Another wet rag with water only. And a clean dry rag." He asked the M & M's.

His wish was their command and the three rags were produced promptly. He used the soapy rag to thoroughly clean the window in front of each burner inside and out and the fire eye lens looking through the window. He then used the wet with water rag and finished with the dry on both boilers. He ordered the M & M's to fire both boilers and the safety shut off valves remained open allowing No. 2 fuel to ignite each burner. The look on all the women was priceless. Something similar to what a Las Vegas magician must experience every night on stage.

The Warden broke the silence with the boilers humming in the background. "Are you going to explain your magic Michael, or is it a professional secret?"

"No secret." Michael explained. "This little devise," he pointed at a small cylindrical piece an inch in diameter by three inches long, "is called the fire eye. It views the burner flame and sends a signal to the two safety shut off valves in front of the boiler to remain open and allow the fuel oil to flow. However, if the fire eye is unable to see the burner flame through the window, it immediately signals the two safety valves to shut and stop the flow of oil because without getting burned up, it will collect at the bottom of the boiler. The next time or if there was fire in the vicinity, the oil fumes would cause an explosion that could take half the Camp immediately and the ensuing fire would endanger the survivors. Over the years and due to poor maintenance, soot built up on both the surface of the fire eye lens and the window looking into the boiler. The fire eye could no longer view the burner flame through the soot. So it was sending a signal to the two safety shut off valves to close and prevent the oil from flowing so the burner. The flame was getting extinguished for lack of fuel. A vicious circle until I cleaned up the lens of the fire eye and the window looking into the burner flame. Everything will be fine in the foreseeable future. However, I suggest every month or so to repeat the procedure you have witnessed to render the system soot free."

"I could listen to you all day." The Warden gushed. "The way you explain everything and in such detail...it is so obvious and logical it makes us and all the others we had here to remediate the problem look like idiots and let me not get started at all the contractors and consulting engineer experts we had here..."

"He is my boy!" Phil Rolfs exclaimed. "He did it once again. You wouldn't believe the problems he has been solving...," Michael's severe look made Rolfs shut his mouth immediately. "They are classified..." Rolfs mumbled embarrassed and red in the face.

"No harm done." Michael winked at Rolfs in forgiveness. "There should be hot water in half an hour." Michael proclaimed. "In the mean time we better get a move on." He said addressing Rolfs.

"Its after three. We need daylight all the way for the return. The Warden, I mean our Warden," he said looking at the Dublin Warden, "told me to stay overnight so I don't endanger Michael here with me driving in the dark. He is worth his weight in gold as far as our Warden is concerned. The liability to the BOP is too great to endanger his well being. I will get a room in town. By Regulations Michael has to remain confined, not that he presents a danger to himself or others...he was ridding shot gun with me driving all the way here. He was self report. He has a golf cart and he can go anywhere on Base and off Base...But the Regulations you know are the Regulations."

"Don't worry." The Dublin Warden volunteered. "Michael will stay with us overnight. You two;" she pointed to the two female guards, "he is assigned to you as his protective custodians. You got that; all through dinner and while he is awake until ten o'clock at night when your shift ends and he is in a secure room locked for the night. Am I making myself clear? Michael may be a liability, but after what I witnessed here he will be our liability for the next fourteen hours or so.  Mr. Rolfs you will be here first thing tomorrow morning?"

"You bet yah!"  Rolfs emphasized.  "Seven o'clock at the latest...or... when do you open the gate?"

"Seven AM will be fine."  The Warden stated with finality.

Rolfs turned to leave with a parting shot at Michael.  "Don't do anything I wouldn't do."

"Michael please come to my office."  The Dublin Camp Warden said.  "I'd like to have a chat with you, before I turn you over to Jennifer and Audrey."  She introduced the two female guards to Michael.  "They will be waiting for you in the reception area."

The Warden and Michael got out of the MECHANICAL AND ELECTRICAL Building to retrace their steps back to the Administration. As soon as the Warden  opened the door she was greeted by several hundred of female inmates.  As soon as Michael appeared behind her they all broke in a spontaneous applause. "News travels fast around here."  Was the Warden's simple comment.  As soon as the applause quieted down she announced that the problem was fixed in less than fifteen minutes by Michael, on loan from the Nellis Air Force Base Camp, where he was both the Camp and Air Force Base Engineer.  He would be their guest for the night and will have dinner with them shortly.  She urged the women to behave like ladies and make Michael's stay uneventful.  Michael was beet red as he stood next to the Warden trying not to concentrate on any particular inmate, which was difficult to do as a large number of the women inmates were trying their damnedest to attract his attention by blowing kisses, making sucking noises with their mouths and worse.

The Warden started walking through the cordon of the women inmates who parted to let her through. Jennifer and Audrey each took Michael's each side for protection and dutifully followed.  Michael, although he made sure he stayed in the middle between them, nevertheless he felt numerous pats on his behind and a few gentle pinches which he tried to ignore looking straight ahead at the Warden's luscious butt.

"Tell me something about yourself that is not in your PSI." The Warden said as soon as she ushered Michael into her office. "I want to kill as much time as possible before your supper. Forget what I said for PR purposes. Some of the women here are very dangerous. The majority in here are for drugs, telemarketing, bank fraud and other non violent cases. However, like your Camp I believe, we have a number of cases that have come to us from high security institutions for murder and armed robbery as a way to re-enter society before their stay at a halfway house."

"What do you want to know?" Michael asked without expecting an answer. "I was born in Hydra, Greece which is one of several islands comprising the Saronic group. I was a civil war baby which raged throughout Greece at the time. My father was the Governor of the island together with the rest of the Saronic islands. I lived on the island until I was three and a half years old and I was very confused because my mother was teaching High School in the North part of Greece close to the Bulgarian border. The Bulgarians were supporting at the time the rebels in the Civil war. At three and a half I went to live with my mother in a town called Arnea where she taught in the town High School. The rebels occupied the mountains surrounding the town of Arnea and were shooting at the government troops who occupied the town. The town square was the place where all the children played. We were watching the fighting all day long like we were watching a video game, only this was live and for real. It was shortly after the Second World War and there were mines and unexploded ordinance. Playing with a dozen kids we found a can of soup, we thought at the time, with a wooden handle sticking at one end. It was a German hand grenade. We were tossing it in the air and chasing where it fell to do it all over again. The pin in a German grenade falls off if it is struck hard on a rock or hard ground. Evidently that's what must have happened because an explosion took the lives of all my playmates and spared mine. My mother took me to a nunnery, because she got the message that Arnea was not a safe place. It was run by catholic French nuns and they had with them two dozen French girls, all orphan children refugees from France as a result of the Second World War. They were novices because their ages were between fourteen and sixteen. The school was closed throughout the Civil War. I stayed there for three years and forgot my Greek, learning French instead and proper manners. I started grade school in Greece not knowing Greek and being left handed, which was considered tantamount to a disease at the time. I believe my PSI starts with my 'exclusive' High School in Greece."

"Fascinating life. As I have said previously, I could listen to you talk all day. You have also such a cute accent..." She looked at her watch. "I believe if you join Jennifer and Audrey just about now you will be at the start of the first serving."

Michael got up and shook the Warden's proffered hand.

"I will give Luther a call right now and tell him of your amazing performance here. You have saved me a great deal of money of having to replace the boiler burners and all their piping. I owe you. You have a friend here for life... Did you see the response of the women prisoners? I will have stories to tell all my friends during 'Happy Hour' this evening."

Michael met the two female guards waiting for him at reception. He could not remember who was Jennifer and who was Audrey. The Warden did not make that clear and Michael did not have time for socializing with then. He made time now by addressing each and inquiring as to who was who. The two guards were looking at him in awe and were very pleased that he took the time to get to know them. They were white little girls, just out of High School with very little worldly experience. They asked Michael if he would like to follow them to the Mess Hall. They walked for five minutes and the Mess Hall became apparent with the line of female prisoners forming already. Michael had a chance to survey the prisoners waiting in line and noticed that were split into distinct groups. The blacks were the dominant group, followed by the Latinas, the whites and very few orientals. The guards led Michael at the head of the line. He stopped, and instead joined the quay at the end of the line.

"You may miss the first seating." The two guards objected in unison.

"That's OK." Michael responded. "I am no different than they are. They were here before me."

"Are all the inmates at Nellis as nice as you?" Jennifer inquired.

"It is like every where else. In prison, Army, College or society alike, some are and some are not within varying degrees…"

"Where did you go to College?" Audrey interrupted.

"Washington State University." Michael replied. "Graduated before you were born, most likely." He added looking Audrey up and down. But she was too excited almost jumping out of her skin.

"I am from Pullman, Washington!" She exclaimed. "I was born there. I knew it. You look and behave like a WSU Alum…"

"GO COUGS!" Michael exclaimed. "Why didn't you go to school there?" Michael asked Audrey taking a guess at that, because she did not speak like a College graduate.

"I wanted to. But I got pregnant on my Senior year in High School. I graduated from High School, but my parents were not supportive and showed me the door. What could I do with just High School Education and a new born baby? BOP was hiring so here I am."

The line started moving and sure enough Michael and his escorts made it to the first seating. The Mess Hall was divided like the waiting line outside. Blacks, chicanos and whites, interspersed with half a dozen orientals. The food was better than the one at Nellis Camp, but not as good as at the Officer's Clubs, Michael replied, because this was the first thing he was asked by his escorts.

They were siting in a four person table in the middle of the dining room and Michael felt that he was the center of a Mercedes car symbol with all eyes studying his every move.  He adopted immediately the eating habits taught to him by the nuns when he was their guest for three years in the early fifties.  He knew he   was making an impression because his escorts had stopped eating and were gawking at him with their mouths open.  He was the only male in the room from the cooks, to the servers, to the inmates to the guards, who were eating at a special table that Michael refused to sit when was asked by his two escorts.  The meal finished, Michael fished a cigar from his case and rolled the tip in his mouth.

"Smoking is not allowed in the Mess Hall!"  Both guards said in unison, looking around at the astonished faces of the other dinners.  Michael unperturbed took a cigar cutter from his pocket and clipped the end of his cigar.  He looked at his escorts with the cigar in his mouth.

"I was under the impression, after I made the boilers to produce hot water that I could ask for just about anything and it would be granted to me." Michael said with a mischievous smile on his face and putting the unlit cigar in his shirt pocket.

"Is it allowed to have cigars at Nellis?" Jennifer asked astounded.

"I don't know about the rest…but I am allowed to…"

"I love your style." Audrey gushed. "I just wish I was older… and had met you while you were a student at WSU."

"Is there a place that is designated for smocking?"  Michael asked, ignoring Audrey's statement, as soon as one of the servers removed his tray.

"There are several."  Jennifer said. "Basically, all the gazebos in front of the dormitories are smoking areas.  Most of the inmates here smoke. We will go to the gazebo in front of the dorm you will be staying."

The gazebo was crowded.  Word must have leaked where Michael would be staying.  Not only every seat was taken, but there was a crowd standing already around the gazebo three rows deep.  No one was offering her seat.  Michael looked around and decided to sit on a rounded rock and light his cigar.  All the inmates turned around and were facing him.  The two guards stood each side of him and Michael noticed that several other guards had joined the perimeter of the inmates' circle.  The inmates, freshly showered and smelling fine in a cacophony of conflicting and over applied perfumes were busy talking among themselves; relaying the stories and gossip they heard about Michael and the return of hot water.  Michael felt uncomfortable, unwilling to either concentrate on any one conversation or in any way respond to provocative stares and sitting positions  exposing a plethora of inner thighs and beyond. He whispered to one of his escorts after a while whether they had a sports field with a walking track.  They led the way followed by groans and protests of the inmates who immediately emptied the gazebo and followed the trio to the track which was deserted.  There at the track ensued a happening similar to Plato's peripatetic school. Michael walking the track smoking his cigar, flanked by his two escorts and followed by a crowd of female inmates of all colors, ages and looks, bubbling with excitement.

"Do you know what would happen if we left you alone to fend for yourself?" Audrey asked after a while.

Michael looked at her confused because he was thinking what he would be doing next day.  Specifically, whether they would visit the 'Bunny Houses'  they had encountered in Nevada on their way to Dublin, California?

"Do you want to find out?" Jennifer teased from the other side.

"I believe this is the second time in my life I have felt sexually harassed." Michael said.

"Which was the first?" They both asked in unison.

"I was asked to lecture Chemistry in an auditorium in Hawaii, because of lack of Chemistry teachers.  When I arrived, I found out that the hopeful Chemistry teachers outnumbered the students and were all female.  After the lecture I was invited into the McKinley High School lounge for refreshments.  I walked in and there must have been over fifty women teachers already there staring at me and behaving...let's say not very lady like...I understood what women must feel when they have to walk through a construction site with all the workers starring at them and making...noises."

The two female guards started laughing and the female prisoner contingent were craning their necks to catch what was so funny.  After almost an hour of walking around the track, Michael saw that his two escorts were dragging.  He was used to walking a cigar's worth at the Nellis Camp, which calculated an hour and a half or five miles worth; so he was used to it.

"Lets go to the library."  He proposed to the delight of the two female guards.  "I will borrow a book to read before bed.  Take a shower under your watchful eyes   to make sure nothing happens to me.  Then you can tuck me in for the night so you can go home."

"Aren't you bothered that we will be watching you taking a shower?" Audrey asked.

"Not in the slightest."  Michael replied.  "I am used to it.  Every morning the head of the SIS who happens to be a female, approximately my age, watches over me from the moment I step into the bathroom, drinking her morning coffee."

"What do the other inmates do?"  They both asked, amazed.

"They know the ritual and during that time they become scarce."

"Why is she doing this?  Do you guys have a thing going?"

"That's what the rumor around Camp is.  But in actuality she is there for my protection.  I am considered an 'Institutional Need'.  Everything that is built at the Camp or the Air Force Base comes out of my office with my signature."

The room he would be staying for the night was ten by twelve feet with a steel door that locked from the inside. It had a sink and a toilet. It was only in use during the rare occasions when a guard had to be in situ because of rumors of an impending riot. In a female prison Camp this was something very rare.

"We will be here at six thirty tomorrow morning and knock on the door. Please keep the door locked at all times. I hope you get used to the noise and nonsense outside your door. Just remember, they can't get in. The door to your room is riot proof." Jennifer said.

"How would I know it's you two knocking?"

"What was your first car?" Audrey asked.

"A 1967 Triumph Spitfire."

"Never heard of it." Audrey said.

"That's because the company went out of the business of building cars sometime in the early seventies."

"No wonder!" Audrey exclaimed. "But that's good for our purpose. No one but us would know."

Michael locked himself in for the night with Christopher Buckley's book "Thank you for Smoking" as his sole company. He wished he had Henry Miller's trilogy "The Rosy Crucifixion" with him instead, but he was happy with his find in a Library full of Romance novels. The noise and harassment started almost immediately outside his door, with notes and explicit photographs and drawings being slid underneath his door. It was interesting in the beginning but like everything else the repetition dulled the subject matter. He made a note to collect the material in the morning for show and tell back at the Camp.

"Rise and shine Mr. Mustang convertible."  Was Michael's wake up call six thirty in the morning on the dot.

He got out of bed and started getting dressed.

"We are only joking Mr. Triumph Spitfire."  Came the same voice after a few minutes.  "We were only testing you before."

Michael unlocked the door.

"Phil Rolfs is already here to take you to breakfast."  Audrey said.  "I will remember yesterday and you for the rest of my life."

"Me too."  Jennifer added, but not with the same enthusiasm as Audrey.

Michael followed his escorts from the dorm to the Administration Building.

"You look AFO little buddy."  Was Phil Rolfs greeting.  "But other than that, you look OK.  No harm.  No foul."

"What's AFO?" Both the female guards inquired. Michael already knew, 'all fucked out', and was not interested to hear Rolfs explanation, so he made his way outdoors towards Phil Rolfs truck parked the the VISITOR designated parking spot.

"I want details little buddy."  Rolfs said as soon as he settled in on the driver's side.

Michael pulled out of the inside of his shirt the material he had collected under his door and hid there before he unlocked the door to his room for his escorts.  Phil Rolfs eyes looked like they were going to come out of their sockets.

"Quite a collection of love letters." Phil Rolfs was able to say after a while.  "I only imagined, but I never would have thought that women would be so... forward... so explicit...and the language...my God they ought to get a job writing pornography when they get on the outside." He said shoving the material in his glove compartment.  "I will need to review them later leisurely and attach them to my report to our Warden when we get back."

"In the meantime let's wash our hands thoroughly before we eat breakfast." Michael said sagely.

# CHAPTER 21

## A Man Of Respect Who Knew Too Much

There was mystery in the air when Michael opened the Camp engineering that Friday morning. Rolfs once again told Michael not to open his office. Michael looked at him questionably. He was not usually asked to travel on a weekend.

"Where are we going?" He asked instead.

"Is this a visiting weekend for you?" Phil Rolfs asked him instead.

"No. It's not." Michael replied.

"Good. I didn't think so."

"You still have not answered me. Where are we going?"

"I cannot tell you." Rolfs said, smiling like a cat who swallowed the canary.

"Oh! Another top secret facility that is not on the map." Michael said reminiscing his trip to China Lake. "This did not stop you, last time, telling me beforehand." He commented.

"I know. But this is different. If I tell you. I've got to blindfold you; so you can not find your way there. These are the rules. I am not even allowed there. I will drop you off somewhere and they will arrange transportation to your final destination. I am not kidding. Take your pick. Be surprised or be blindfolded? That's your only choice in the matter."

"What do I take with me? Do I need tools, equipment?

"Nothing.  They will provide everything."

"What about clothes?"

"They will provide everything."

"How do I get dressed?"

"What you are wearing is fine.  They will provide…"

"I know…'everything'.  How long will I be gone?"

"You will be back Sunday night and back to work at the Camp on Monday."

"How many cigars do I take with me?  We need to stop in my room first."

"No time.  You already have a cigar in your pocket to chew on the way there.  I am sure they will buy you a whole box of your choice of stogies once there." "I should inform my roommates that I will be away for the weekend."

"No.  Let them wonder.  The official word will be provided by others.  If it comes from you…that's how rumors get started around here.  Let the BOP worry what they will say.  It will be a lie anyway.  No one knows where you are going.  Very hush-hush.  I don't even know, and I am driving. I know where I have to deliver you.  Then I have to leave.  I was told to be back at precisely the same spot I dropped you off at five PM on Sunday."

"It sounds like an adventure.  Is there any danger involved?  What if something happens to me?"

"Your wife will be a rich and merry widow.  I am sure the government will pay her what she asks and give her a made up explanation of what happened."

Michael shut up after this somber explanation and put the cigar in his mouth for emphasis.  He got in the shot gun seat of Rolfs truck and headed out the Camp gate.  They proceeded North.  Nellis Air Force

Base was located on the North part of Las Vegas.  Heading further North would take them out of town.  There was nothing out there but the Nevada desert, until they reached Oregon which started hundreds of miles from Las Vegas. They drove in silence. The mystery destination weighing heavily between them.

An hour later they were crossing Indian Wells, a small town; if you wanted to call it that, because it was just two whore houses separated by a saloon.  That was the extent of the town.  There was no exit from the freeway.  However, the buildings did not look boarded up.  There were lights and loud music coming out of all  three buildings.  There were Air Force vehicles parked in front of the buildings.  There was no road visible passing the gravel parking lot that surrounded the three buildings.  There were no people visible anywhere.  The traffic going North on the freeway was non existent.  There were very few truckers on the Southbound lanes heading to Las Vegas.  Approximately, ten miles later going North, a freeway exit appeared with no previous warning.  No number on the exit.  No name.  Right at the side of the exit was an announcement 'THIS IS NOT AN EXIT'.

What the hell.  It is built like an exit.  It is an exit.  Michael was thinking as Phil Rolfs swerved his truck and took the exit ramp which was not an exit.  The exit ramp kept going straight and eventually would become a freeway entrance back on the same freeway from which the vehicle exited.  Halfway, there was a gravel road on each side of the paved exit ramp.  On the left, the gravel road was intersecting the exit from the other side of the freeway serving as an access point to the Southbound traffic who took the exit, presumably labeled the same way 'THIS IS NOT AN EXIT'.

On the right there was a Western style fence going forever in each direction, East and West.  From the freeway it looked no different than a standard cattle fence to keep the livestock inside the pasture.  That's why it did not make an impression to be noticed viewed from the freeway.  There was no cattle to be seen.  No pasture.  Just desert, as far as the eye could see.  There was a sixteen foot gate on the right.  Not a gate really.  Just two posts forming a sixteen foot opening to a gravel road with desert plants and thick chola cactus on either side of the gravel road stretching like a mine field in all directions.

Phil Rolfs stopped at the intersection of the exit ramp with the gravel road and turned right.  There were warning signs on each side of the gate posts with the usual boiler plate GOVERNMENT PROPERTY, NO TRESPASSING, NO UNAUTHORIZED VEHICLES BEYOND THIS POINT…Same kind of stuff you'd encounter on every Base.  They slowly proceeded East on the gravel road.  The road was going straight as the eye could see towards the notch of two mountains in the distance.  The sun was in their eyes blinding them, that's why they did not notice right away the two military armored vehicles closing in on them from the East and blocking the road with twin machine guns, their bore winking at them.  Rolfs stopped immediately.  An Air Force sergeant in fatigues jumped out of one of the military vehicles and approached their truck from the drivers side.

"Is the subject in your vehicle?"  He inquired of Rolfs, who pointed at Michael.

"I'd request that you turn your vehicle around at this point."  The sergeant asked politely.

Phil Rolfs maneuvered the truck back and forth until he complied with the request.

"I am afraid that's where you get off, little buddy."  Phil Rolfs said to Michael.  "I will see you in the same place this coming Sunday at 5:00 PM."

"Where am I going?  How do I get back here?  Why can't you come along?"  Michael asked these penned up questions not expecting real answers.

"I am not cleared…"

"And I am! A prisoner?"

"I know." Rolfs commiserated. "Like Red Flag. You are cleared, I am not…"

"Government logic…" Michael commented. "An oxymoron."

"I am not sure what this last comment means." Rolfs said. "What I am sure of though is that they have looked up your asshole with a microscope and talked to who knows whom before they decided to request your presence here. It must be some underground secret facility, because I could find nothing on the map. I was told to take this road and we would be met. Very hush-hush. Try to enjoy yourself and as always, don't do anything I wouldn't do."

Michael jumped down from the passenger seat of the truck and slammed the door on his way out. Phil Rolfs took off without delay looking in his rear view mirror at Michael and the Air Force sergeant on the ground, until he reached the gate and went through, presumably to catch the Southbound ramp of 'THIS IS NO EXIT' and get back on the freeway, Southbound this time for Las Vegas.

"Will you follow me, sir." The Air Force sergeant addressed Michael.

"What is this all about?" Michael asked.

"I wouldn't know, sir." The sergeant replied. "I'd be the last to know. I am just a guard…"

"Guard of what? What is this that you are guarding?"

"The perimeter of Mercury Air Force Base." The sergeant said after some hesitation.

"Mercury Air Force Base." Michael repeated. "I've never heard of it."

"We don't advertise." The sergeant said with a smile.

"What does Mercury Air Force Base do? I mean how does it justify its existence, in the eyes of the GAO?"

"We provide security.  A trespasser, if he made it that is further up the road evading our fifty caliber bullets, who still refused to stop, would get an RPG up his ass."

"What if he was just a lost traveller?" Michael's inquiry was met by a raised eyebrow by the sergeant, after the scenario he had just described.

"In that case, we kill them all, and let God sort them out."  Was the sergeant's brief reply.

"What do you guard?" Michael asked.

"The Base of course...and beyond."

"What's beyond?" Michael inquired.

"You ask too many questions, sir." The sergeant commented. "Too many questions." he repeated. "Which I don't know and I am not authorized to answer even if I knew.  You are about to enter from this point on, a highly secure area.  If I may offer the same advise as my superior officer told me in no uncertain terms when I first arrived 'Keep your mouth shut and do as you are told'.

Michael followed the sergeant back to the 'humvee'.  The sergeant opened the passenger door, flipped the seat forward and pointed to Michael to take the back seat.  Michael was now able to see out of the porthole size windows on either side, his forward view being partially blocked by the gunner's rear end. The 'humvee' followed the other after making a wide circle through desert cactus, as if  it was not there, eating its dust.  They moved side by side after a while until they reached the gate of the Mercury Air Force Base which appeared to be a tenth of Nellis Air Force Base, if someone was to judge it by size alone.  They drove to a one story building with a sign ADMINISTRATION above the door, where the sergeant told Michael to get out and report to the reception.  The two 'humvee's' departed in a cloud of dust as soon as Michael got out, before he even made it through the building door.

The building was a poor cousin of the ones at Nellis, by appearances alone. 'Don't judge a book by the cover.' He reminded himself. Two female sergeants were manning the reception counter with a small waiting area on its right comprised of a love seat, two arm chairs and a low coffee table in the middle. They appeared Motel 6 type of mass produced furniture. The sergeants seemed to be expecting Michael and merely pointed to sit himself in the waiting area. Michael felt under the seat cushion for a tag and confirmed his thoughts. The arm chair and presumably the rest of the waiting room furniture was made by UNI-COR in Portland, Oregon according to the tag.

He barely had time to settle when the closed door to the right, facing him, with a cypher lock on the wall next to its hidden hardware opened from the inside and the welcoming committee appeared. Two dressed as Air Force Colonels in uniform and two in civilian clothes. Even number of male and female. They marched to where he was sitting and one of them, a female Colonel, asked him to follow them. They led to a small conference room with a long table surrounded by eight comfortable looking chairs. All made by UNI-COR again he guessed, but had no way to verify without looking underneath, which would have been a poor way to start the ball rolling.

"They are by UNI-COR." The female Colonel confirmed with a smile, putting Michael in an inferior bargaining position from the start. He realized that he was under the microscope right from the start, as soon as he got off the 'humvee' or probably before, when he was selected for the assignment. He thought of saying something clever, but he changed his mind. What was the use? They held all the cards. He was only going to advertise the poor state he was in and remove all doubt they may have. He decided he was going to maintain his mystery man status to the mysterious committee.

"You are probably wandering where you are and what you are doing here." The female Colonel continued. "It's only human."

Michael kept his mouth shut.

"Speak your mind man!" The male Colonel encouraged him. "We are all on the same side here."

"Who or rather what is the Mercury Air Force guarding?" He asked forcing the rest of the meeting participants to look at each other, in surprise.

"We were warned, you were smart…" The female Colonel said. "You are also very observant."

"Let's cut through the chase." The male Colonel said impatiently. "We are all on the same team, he repeated."

"That's the reason I asked." Michael confirmed. "I am a prisoner and powerless to do anything on my own. Put yourself in my shoes. I was yanked this morning from the Nellis Air Force Base prison Camp. I was not told where I was going. Then, I was dumped on a gravel road in the middle of the Nevada desert. I've never been here before and was not aware that this Base even existed…"

"We get the picture." The male Colonel cut him short. "This is what we will do now. We will explain to you our problem and ask you for a possible solution. Are we on the same page so far?"

Michael remained silent. Not committing either way.

"We need your engineering and construction skills to accomplish what we have been directed to do by our superiors. We are hiring your expertise in this area. We have established that you are a trustworthy person, highly intelligent with experience in the area we are looking for." The female Colonel said continuing to maintain the 'good guy' position in the discussion.

"If you keep talking in circles, I will be unable to complete the task you are contemplating for me to do by 5:00 PM Sunday. We will still be here talking in riddles and trying to show how clever we all are. Spit it out. What is the problem and where is it located, if you know." Michael announced exasperated.

The look he got was stony silence and contemplation in turn by the group. Who was going to be first to break the ice?

"You are right." The female civilian spoke for the first time. She must be the head of the snake. Michael realized. "We have been ordered to downsize. This has been an ongoing issue for years and has finally come to a head. The order is: Do it now. A number of buildings have been abandoned and have not been in use since the Regan administration. They have now been classified obsolete and must be removed from the premises. A number of government facilities have showed an interest and we established a waiting list for the buildings to be transported there at a considerable savings to the government which is our desire as well..."

"How large buildings are we talking about?" Michael interrupted.

"That's the problem. You hit the nail on the head. The buildings are very large, some are three stories high..." The female civilian said.

"Where are the buildings?" Michael inquired with confidence. "From my brief observation though the porthole size window of the vehicle I was driven into the Base, I have only seen one story buildings..."

"You are right again!" The female Colonel said with conviction. "Nothing gets past you." She passed Michael a two page document. "Please read this and sign at the bottom. I will sign as the Witness. You must do this if we are to continue our discussion here. If you refuse to sign this document, as it is your prerogative to do under your constitutional rights, we will stop our discussion, put you in the Base brig for the duration until your ride shows up here on Sunday. Am I making myself clear?"

Michael was silent reading the Disclaimer and the consequences if he breached its confidentiality for the next twenty five years. He had signed numerous such documents in his career. Trident Submarine Base in Keyport, Washington; Mare Island Naval Shipyard in Vallejo, California; Eilson Air Force Base in Anchorage, Alaska; Pearl Harbor

Naval Shipyard on Oahu, Hawaii; Hickam Air Force Base on Oahu, Hawaii; and so on, and so on…

"Do you have a pen?"  Michael asked the female civilian.  She surprisingly, got up from her chair and came around the table like lightning to close the deal, before the customer had second thoughts.

"Here you go!"  She said pulling a warm ball point pen from the inside pocket of her jacket and handing it to Michael.  He was tempted to put the pen under his  nose and smell deeply, pretending he was handling a fine cigar; but he thought better and he simply signed at the bottom of the second page.  She took her pen from him and signed herself in a complete, legible  cursive signature Maria Rodriguez.  Michael realized for the first time, concentrating on the black hair under his nose, that Maria had maybe white features at first glance, but definitely Mexican blood was pulsing through the vein on top of her writing hand.

The moment the Non Disclosure document was signed all four started talking at once unloading all the penned up information.  Michael lifted his hands signaling a time out.  Everyone stopped talking.

"I figured you all are talking about a site called Area 51, because it was repeated numerous times.  All other information you provided talking all four at once was either not heard clearly or possibly misunderstood. I have one question for you.  What is this Area 51 and where is it located?"

"Just up the road."  Maria was the sole spokesperson.  "It is a top secret installation and the sole purpose of Mercury Air Force Base is to provide security for Area 51."

"Have you, all of you I mean, been to Area 51?" Michael asked the room in general.

No one responded.

"I cannot believe it!"  Michael exclaimed.

"We are not cleared for it." Maria said meekly. "No one from Mercury Base is allowed on the premises. The security is conducted remotely with sensors and cameras. They patrol the perimeter, however, 24/7!" She exclaimed proudly."

"Am I supposed to solve your problem remotely, also?" Michael asked.

"No. You have been cleared to be on the Area 51 property."

"But I am a prisoner. How did I get the clearance?"

They all lifted their shoulders and shook their heads, with no answer forthcoming. The federal government at work. Michael had heard of course of Area 51. It was the main topic at Camp when they ran out of subjects to talk about. Everyone  knew that it was located somewhere North of Las Vegas. The precise location was pure speculation. Michael could now speculate with some accuracy that it was located just beyond the notch of the two mountains to the East. There was only one road after all and one access in or out.

"There is a jeep parked outside for your use." Maria spoke once again. "I assume you know how to drive a stick shift.  You must remember, because your first car was..." she leaned over the table consulting a two inch thick file, "a Triumph Spitfire."

"You are correct on both counts." Michael said, dying to read the file in front of Maria. What other information did it contain? He was thinking.

"You are free to go and conduct a reconnaissance while the sun is still up." The male Colonel said.

"I will go to Area 51 first thing tomorrow morning." Michael said authoritative.

"Why wait till tomorrow?" Maria asked. "We have you here for a limited time..."

"I will need some equipment before I venture forth." Michael cut her off. "I don't know what I am getting into. I have heard all the Roswell stories about aliens and the like. You have not provide me with any useful information in that regard. As a result I will need a hazmat suit and a Geiger counter to start. Additionally, I will need a dosimeter to wear at all times and a laboratory on stand by to conduct tests after my visit. I will need accommodations for tonight and tomorrow night. I need several pads of engineering paper and two mechanical pencils, preferably Kohinoor brand, Rapidomatic. One No. 0.05 HB lead and the other No. 0.07 HB lead; one forty five degree drafting triangle and one ninety/thirty degree drafting triangle; finally an eraser. I have come here unprepared with just the clothes on my back. I will need, by the way, a one piece suit to wear under the hazmat suit to preserve the clothes I came in for the return trip and a toiletry kit."

"Did you get all that William?" Maria inquired of the other male civilian, who was busy the entire time writing on a legal pad. He must be Maria's assistant Michael concluded.

Michael was given a folded full size General Arrangement Drawing of Area 51. The obsolete buildings marked with a ball point red pen small 'X' and an eleven   inch by seventeen inch map of the Mercury Air Force Base Camp. He studied the map and asked relevant questions as to the location of the Commissary/PX, the Library, the BOQ building and the Officers Club. He told them that he needed a box of cigars, a book to read, a place to sleep and a place to eat; he answered Maria when she asked the significance of his itinerary. The Colonel passed him a temporary plastic card with his name and picture, to serve as his I.D. and Credit Card. Michael shook hands all around and he was assured that the material and equipment he requested would be delivered to his room at the Officer's BOQ at six o'clock tomorrow morning.

Michael got on the jeep, which was brand new with barely one hundred miles on the odometer and a full tank of gas. He limited his purchases at the PX to a box of Arturo Fuente, Hemingway series cigars and a six pack of diet Dr. Pepper bottles. At the Base Library he borrowed a First edition copies of Eric Ambler novels 'The Levander' and 'The Intercom

Conspiracy'. They were expecting him at the BOQ and gave him the 'red carpet' treatment. He found in his room, not only a toiletry kit, but two pairs of shorts and a pack of three underpants and tee shirts; all his size, together with a pair of flip flop shower slippers size eleven. He brushed his teethe and splashed water on his face. He needed a shave but what the hell the hunger pains gave away to the shave. He lit the Cuban cigar he had brought along, with a spare Hemingway in his shirt pocket. He consulted the Base map and headed towards the Officers Club.

The mercury Air Force Base Officers Club had that sixties charm, tacky for some, rekindling memories for Michael who had come to this country to study at WSU in 1965. It reminded him of the Cub, Student Union Building and the memories of his days there were flooding back. He ordered the Friday night surf and turf special without second thoughts, a Caesar's salad and a diet coke. He debated over ordering a beer, but he did not want to run afoul of a breathalyzer test or worse a DUI. For desert he ordered Spumoni ice cream, which they had on the menu. The club was half full, and he felt the center of attention with orders to be left alone. He did not initiate conversation and none was forthcoming. He retrieved the Arturo Fuente, Hemingway from his pocket and headed towards the BOQ on foot in a pleasant seventy degree evening.

He took a shower and shaved, so in the morning he would be good to go as soon as he got out of bed. He read until he fell asleep. A pounding on his door woke him up. He had worn a pair of shorts over his underwear before going to bed and with a tee shirt on he pronounced himself presentable. He looked at his  watch. Six o'clock on the dot. He opened the door. An Airman stood there holding a sealed cardboard box approximately three feet all around. He handed it to Michael and requested a signature on his clipboard. All it said on the clipboard was 'cardboard box', no mention of its contents; so Michael set the box on the floor and scribbled his signature. The Airman saluted and left. Michael opened the box by pealing the duct tape, which was hard on the nails, and wished he had ordered a pocket knife.  Everything he had requested was there and fit perfectly.

He left the hazmat suit unbuttoned, flapping over his coveralls, so he would not alarm the Airmen at reception of an impending disaster.  He collected the rest and put them in the sport bag, that was included without him having asked for it, the Assistant evidently had put some thought into it, and headed for the Jeep.  He drove this time to the Officers Club for breakfast and ordered a sack lunch with a six pack of water bottles to take along.  The attendant at the club was thoughtful to include a small styrofoam chest full of ice where he had placed the six water bottles.  He carried the chest to the jeep, tilted the drivers seat forward and placed the styrofoam chest in the well, behind the driver's seat.  The Jeep was the two door variety without a top or sides above the window line.

There was one main road on Base running East and West.  That made two access gates to the Mercury Air Force Base.  He pated the breast pocket of his coveralls to make sure he had his pass handy and gunned the Jeep heading East.  He passed the East gate without getting stopped, receiving a salute from the attending Airman and was out of the base with the sun in his eyes.  He tilted the Jeep's both windshield visors to minimize the glare and headed out following the sole road.  He checked the odometer to establish the exact distance between Mercury Air Force Base and Area 51.  Maria's directions 'Somewhere close by East' were not good enough for him.

There was a total absence of traffic to and from Area 51.  With him being the only vehicle on the road and no visible traffic speed limit, made him abandon the traffic rules and speeded up straddling the center line.  He pressed the brakes when he noticed a dot fast approaching him from the notch of the mountains at the speed of a bullet.  He realized it was a low flying airplane like nothing he had seen before.  It was not the 'Backbird', the infamous spy plane.  This one was triangular shape, rather than a bullet shape low profile.  It was making an almost vertical lift as it came within several hundred feet above the Jeep, which was at a stand still in the middle of the road, with Michael watching the spectacle. The forty five degree shadow passed him overhead. He thought the sound would be deafening. But there was no sound. Dust devils formed in the wake of the silent   airplane which was evidently using the road as a guide for its take off.   Michael turned around to see, but the airplane had disappeared from view. How fast was it going? He wondered. Did he experience a close encounter...of the fourth kind? He started doubting what he witnessed. The airplane was shaped like a glider, only with a supersonic speed and silent engine. Was it even visible on the radar screen at the Base? He wondered.

He stepped on the gas and the Jeep lurched forward. Forget about the strange airplane he thought. One never knew what other strange things he would see and witness in Area 51 before the day was over. With his mind still on the black glider he arrived at Area 51 in no time. There was no gate. No fence. It was just building after building in no particular order, rime or reason. He stopped at the first building he encountered and unfolded the General Arrangement Drawing he had set on the passenger seat weighted down with the sport bag, the Geiger Counter and the drafting material inside the bag. He located the buildings with the red 'X' mark in the distance. He got out of the Jeep and snapped every button of the hazmat suit in place making sure his boots were completely covered and the Velcro's secure underneath them. He put on his helmet and snapped the buttons to secure it on the suit. He got in the Jeep and headed to the closest building with an 'X' mark. He got out of the Jeep  as soon as he arrived. Activated the Geiger Counter in the on position and opened the door to the building, which was unlocked. The building had not been used for years. Cob webs were hanging all over making them the only hazardous condition present. He walked around confident that if a gamma ray could not enter his hazmat suit, neither could a spider. The Geiger Counter on his hand was silent. There was not a mark on his dosimeter card he had hanging from a lanyard around his neck. He visited every room and onward to the next building. There were eighteen 'X' marks on the Drawing he was holding. He marked the number of the building next to the 'X', together with identifying notes of the condition of the building, it's possible uses, the square feet of the footprint of the building, whether was single or two story or three. The construction was all the same. Prefabricated metal buildings. Slab on grade. No basements involved.

He stopped for lunch under the shade of some trees. He had not encountered a single human being all morning, neither of the terrestrial, nor the extraterrestrial variety. He was disappointed. He continued with the rest of the buildings during afternoon and returned to the first building; this time to make plan views and a few elevations to quarter inch to a foot scale utilizing the eighth of an inch squares of the engineering paper tablet. He was done a little after five o'clock. He unbuttoned and unsnapped every button of the hazmat suit. The overalls were glued to his body. He had never sweated as much since College training for three hours a day as a Welter Weight boxer for the varsity. His workout clothes were similarly wet as if he had just jumped into a swimming pool and had just got out. He had underestimated his water consumption. He had run out of water at four thirty, all six water bottles, and he was now thirsty. He headed for the main road and the trip back to Mercury Air Force Base. He returned in record time, petal to the metal straddling the center lane of the road. He did not encounter a single other car on the road, going or coming. He was not stopped at the Mercury AFB gate. He slowed down, but the Airman waved him in with a salute.

He parked in the BOQ parking lot and cleared the Jeep of all the equipment sans the styrofoam chest with the remnants of ice and six empty water bottles, to prove he was not a litter bug. In his room, he downed two bottles of Dr. Pepper and jumped in the shower. He dumped the hazmat suit and the wet overalls in the laundry bag made out of netting material that came with his room. He was wondering what the poor maid would think of her find. Probably scream for a hazmat team to arrive and remove the laundry bag.  He headed to the Officer's Club for an early supper.  He followed the flow deciding on the Saturday night special prime rib.  He returned to his room and started writing his Report with the sketches he had made as attachments.  He made little headway on 'The Levander' before Lethe claimed him.

He got up at six, snoozed until six thirty and took a shower and a shave.  He got dressed in his khakis and walked to the Officer's Club.  He smoked an after breakfast cigar on his way to the BOQ.  Other than the cigar box, his Report and the sketches he made, together with the remaining pad of engineering paper, he left everything else in the room, sans the mechanical pencils which he prominently clipped on his shirt pocket.

A little before eight, he drove to the Administration Building for his prearranged meeting with the four musketeers.  He found three stooges in lieu of the four musketeers.  The female Colonel was absent.  'This town is not big enough for both of us' was the scenario he imagined.  The civilian representative and assistant to keep notes, on the other hand seemed to be working and getting along, just fine.  Probably FBI or CIA Michael guessed.

He was exactly on time, but he found out they were already there, anxiously waiting for him.

"How did it go?"  Maria asked immediately.

"Are you done with the reconnaissance?"  The Colonel added, not to be outdone by the CIA.

"I am done and I have good news and bad news.  There are eighteen buildings.  Seven of them have some radioactive rooms."  He placed his lanyard with the dosimeter card in the middle of the table. "Not bad, but the EPA would not consider them for human habitation. The rooms are sealed though.  They do not represent a hazard in their present condition.  Whoever was working in them, must have used radioactive material and had worn a hazmat suit.  The other eleven buildings are fine."

Michael went on explaining how he would approach their relocation. He would be back in a couple of weeks with three draftsmen and make full size As Built Drawings.  He would then paint numbers on the building structural members which would match the numbers he would put on the As Built Drawings.  Then the building pieces would ship to their ultimate destination and put together using the As Built Drawing as a guide. All that was in his report and attached sketches. The building connections were bolted.  However, if the building was being shipped to a location next to salt water, when they were putting the building together they should use plastic washers between the metal parts to prevent galvanic action which would eat the bolts away over time.  It's best however, to utilize the steel columns and beams as reinforcing steel and cast them in concrete.  This will extend the life of the building because otherwise the salt water will oxidize and rust the steel members, weakening the overall integrity of the structure.  He brought as an example the Aloha Stadium in Hawaii where they used steel to save money, initially, only to have to spent millions of dollars annually, ever since, in maintenance and repairs.

"Everything I just said and more are in my report." Michael said. "I have two requests though.  One is make a copy of my report and sketches to safeguard my involvement and direction provided, should the need arise."

"I understand."  The Colonel expounded.  "It will be allowed.  You just want to cover your butt.  What's the second request?"

"The Building marked as number eleven, which is an eighty foot wide by one hundred sixty feet long, twenty feet high, at the eves, single story building; to be  earmarked for Nellis Air Force Base.  It will make an excellent Motor Pool, a gigantic garage."  Michael placed his request.

"How do you propose to accomplish the disassembly of the buildings?"

"Using inmate labor from the Nellis Camp, under my direction.  Twenty workers from Construction 4, which is the General Contractor at the Camp, would have all the buildings down and ready to ship in approximately two months time." Michael promised.  "Call the Warden and make the arrangements.  There are no security concerns.  The buildings are remotely located and I have not met or seen a soul all day yesterday."

"How long will you take to prepare the As Built Drawings?" Maria asked.

"Seven to ten days.  Depending on the 'worms' and mistakes we uncover.  The new buildings will be better rebuilt than the existing.  We will get started in two weeks…"

"Why wait that long?"  They all exclaimed.

"Why not get started next week, Monday?"  Maria added.

"Because next weekend is a visiting weekend for me, is the main reason; plus I have to clue in my assistants that I would be away for the next two weeks and make assignments for the working crews, both at Camp and on Base.  Otherwise all work will come to a stand still."

"What do we do with the seven contaminated buildings?"  The Colonel asked.

"That's a good question."  Michael said mechanically, thinking.  "You will see in my report that I recommend disposal as nuclear waste.  Fortunately they are isolated from the rest and they are all together in two rows of four each.  Whoever assigned the work involving radioactive materials was thinking ahead…"

"And your unofficial recommendation?"  The Colonel insisted.  "Just between us.  It will never leave this room."

"Well…based on the fact that there is a world wide shortage of steel, the raw material going for twenty five cents a pound and the fact that the contaminated rooms are made of 316 L stainless steel at a buck and a quarter a pound...I am  sure a third world contractor would buy them for ten cents on the dollar provided he demolishes and removes them from the site with his own people.  It is up to you to find him," He said staring at Maria, "which I am sure it would be no problem with your background and connections...It is up to you to decide whether to disclose the contamination.  Geiger Counters are not an everyday tool of the trade.  Plus when they get to the foundry and get mixed with other material there, the radioactivity would be diluted to the point that it no longer represents a hazard."

On that note, the meeting broke up.  Maria's assistant left the room with the report and the sketches and returned with ten copies all bound in spiral.  He gave each a copy and Maria the rest.  Michael leafed through his copy.  It was all there.  They decided to go to a late lunch as a group to the Officer's Club.

A few minutes before five in the afternoon, the same sergeant who drove Michael inside the Base appeared at the Officer's Club and took Michael away.  He had the same khaki's on, his box of cigars, the three mechanical pencils in his shirt pocket and a bound copy of his report.

Phil Rolfs was already there waiting in his truck, although they had arrived before five o'clock.  The sergeant got off the 'humvee' with Michael and handed Rolfs an envelope.  Rolfs opened it and peered inside resealing it.

"You look good and rested." Were his first comment as soon as Michael opened the passenger door to his truck.  "The Camp made ten thousand out of your visit.  The Warden upped your hourly rate to one hundred dollars an hour for every hour you've been away from the Camp.  It came to nine thousand something, but they rounded it off to ten grand.  He told me to make sure the check was for that amount, and if not to raise a stink...It was.  No harm; no foul.  Tell me about yourself and your adventures.  What the fuck is this place for starters."

Michael recited the pertinent information on the drive back to Camp. Phil pulled a miniature tape recorder and told Michael to speak into it. The Warden wanted a record to cover his ass, was Phil's explanation. There was no interruption in Michael's monolog. Phil Rolfs expressions were a sight to behold as Michael was staring at him. To his credit, he did not take his eyes away from the road. Michael informed him and made sure that he spoke clearly for the tape recorder's benefit that he had signed a non disclosure document, in effect for the next twenty five years, and every one listening to him, live, or in the recording was bound by the same document. He limited his narrative on the information included in his report and sketches. He said that he would keep his copy of the report himself to assist him in the engineering and design that was supposed to commence in a couple of weeks. He told Phil that he would take with him the three Philippine draftsmen for seven to ten days. He would leave the other three, Herb, Steve and the biker at Camp to work at the direction of his assistant Joey Scala. He told Rolfs that he recommended procurement of four portable drafting tables and drafting equipment chargeable and job costed to the project which would be implemented on a Cost Plus basis. He was sure that the draftsmen would end up signing non disclosure agreements also, but he recommended a two hundred fifty dollar bonus for each in their next month's paycheck.

"Only in America..." Were Rolfs first words after he made sure the tape recorder was shut off. "A prisoner would get involved in secret government dealings, visit non existent installations and dictate to the government what to do." Phil Rolfs was shaking his head as Michael got off the truck, to unlock the door to his office and store the General Arrangement Drawing of Area 51 with his notes that he had kept and the copy of the report in his locked desk drawer. Rolfs followed him.

"Anything you have to say to me; off the record..."

Michael told him about the deal he made with the powers to be at Mercury Air Force Base for Building number 7 at Area 51; to be dismantled with Construction 4 inmate crew and transported to Nellis Air Force Camp to be utilized as the new motor pool building. Phil Rolfs was beaming and thinking all along how to capitalize on this new information.

* * * *

Two weeks later Michael found himself in the same shot gun seat with Phil Rolfs doing the driving. In the back seat were the three Philippine draftsmen. Rolfs did all the talking and Michael pretended that all the information provided by Phil was news to him. They were given a duffel bag each and were allowed to take with them two extra khaki uniforms, two hats and anything else of personal nature they wanted; forewarned that their belongings will be searched and scrutinized. Michael took nothing else other than the two uniforms, a couple of hats, the General Arrangement Drawing of Area 51 with his notes and the report. He had his mechanical pencils in his shirt pocket and two spare cigars next to them and one in his mouth which he was planning to chew on during the ride to their destination. The portable drafting tables, drafting machines and drafting supplies, all still   in their boxes were in the bed of the truck covered with a tarp securely tied all around.

There was very little talk during the ride. Rolfs could not erase the smile on his face throughout the ride. Michael was chewing on his cigar and spitting occasionally in a plastic cup. The three Philippine draftsmen in the back seat were whispering among themselves in Tagalog.

They were met by three 'humvees' this time. One empty, to accommodate the supplies from the bed of Rolfs truck. The prisoners were whisked directly to the BOQ and Michael was handed a sealed envelope by the sergeant. He felt the Jeep keys inside and saw the same Jeep he drove before parked in the same spot he had left it two weeks ago. The prisoners were each given by the Airmen attending the reception of the BOQ a picture I.D., Michael's was also given a credit card, and a key with their room number. They unloaded the equipment and supplies and set them up in their rooms. The two books Michael had checked out of the Library two weeks ago were stacked on top of his night stand next to his bed.  He proposed lunch at the Officers Club. They all four rode in the Jeep with Michael driving.

The three draftsmen were in a daze; awe struct at the accommodations and their lunch at the Officers Club.  After lunch Michael explained to them in detail their assignment.  He drove them around the Base and showed them the Library where they could check out books, reading being the only entertainment available.  The three draftsmen being cigarette smokers, Michael took them to the PX where they loaded themselves with several cartons of cigarettes each and Michael two new boxes of cigars.  He picked a couple of boxes of Romeo and Juliette, Churchill's this time because he knew they were stored individually in aluminum tubes inside the cigar box as an added precaution for keeping fresh, absent an actual cigar humidor, in their battle with the desert dry heat.  That, and the fact that they were his father's favorite, when he got hooked on them during the second World War.

Next morning bright and early, after breakfast, they rode into Area 51. Michael did not request sack lunches this time, only a large styrofoam chest filled with ice and three dozen bottles of drinking water to be placed at the back of the Jeep.  He explained to the draftsmen that they would be working half days on site.

They would come back to Mercury Air Force Base, have lunch at the Officers Club and work all afternoon in their rooms where they were staying to create drawings of the building they were in the morning taking measurements and   the sketches they prepared on site.

Once again they were the only vehicle on the road.  He parked the Jeep equal distance between three buildings and dispatched the draftsmen. He told them to take with them three bottles of drinking water each and to keep hydrating themselves.  If they ran out of water, to come back to the Jeep and resupply.  He then drove the Jeep under a Jacaranda tree nearby and sat in the shade smoking a cigar.

Life was good, he contemplated.  He wished he had brought a book along to pass the time.  He had nothing to do until the draftsmen started producing Drawings for him to check and to figure out where the building connections should be by assigning assembly numbers.  He got out of the Jeep to stretch his legs.  He looked over towards the condemned buildings in the distance.  He thought he saw movement.  He wished he had with him his Zeiss binoculars from his sailboat.  Instead he hopped in the Jeep to drive closer and investigate.  He was right.  He was not seeing things.  Two dozen or more figures, clad in khakis, like the ones he was wearing were busy with cutting torches demolishing the condemned buildings.  What the hell he thought.  He could not detect a single hazmat suit among the khakis.  Nor any equipment, other than the cutting torches.  Simply manual labor.  Who were they and what they thought they were doing with no safety devices whatsoever?

The closer Michael got the more amazed and puzzled he became.  There were a lot more inmates on and inside the condemned building than he originally saw.  They resembled a swarm of ants virtually attacking and disassembling the buildings.  They must have just started that day, because they had not made any significant headway other than reducing a portion of a couple of buildings into a pile of structural steel and stacking the decking in layers. He stopped the Jeep fifty yards from the site and stared.  A number of workers closest to him stopped work, turned around and stared right back.  That was when he noticed for the first time that they and the rest of them were orientals.  He was used to it, being from Hawaii, but exclusive orientals in Area 51, must be a first, he thought.  The workers broke the staring contest after a while and got back to work.  These were not American prison labor Michael thought comparing their work habits with the Construction 4 crews.  These fellows did not take a break every fifteen minutes.  They were all asses and elbows.  Constantly working, with no one in charge.

He got out of the Jeep, contemplating a closer look on foot.  At the same time a single worker broke off the pack and started walking towards him.  Michael stopped and waited.  The worker sweaty and stinking of b.o. approached him and bowed.

"My name is Michael."  He said not returning the bow.

"I am Chen."  The oriental worker said.

At least he spoke and understood English Michael thought.  They were silently appraising each other.

"Are you an Air Force Officer?"  The oriental worker asked breaking the silence.

"Who are you and what are you doing here?"  Michael asked ignoring the question.  "Who is in charge?"

"We are Chinese prisoners."  The oriental said after some hesitation.  Michael tried to keep his mouth from gapping open at the disclosure.  "We have come from China on an assignment to demolish these eight buildings ready to be transported to Mare Island in Vallejo, California...Do you know where the location..."

"I do."  Michael responded.  "I built the power plant there in 1977-78. I am a Chemical Engineer.  I am also the Base Engineer at Nelis Air Force Base in Las Vegas Nevada."  Michael said, shading the truth slightly by the act of omission.

The Chinese prisoner whistled in amazement and reinforced his respect with a deeper bow.  'Maria, Maria...Michael was thinking.  You dirty rat. You sold the buildings to the Chinese government, and I bet not under full disclosure at that'.

"We will load the building steel at Mare Island Naval Shipyard on several old American Navy barges, which were bought by the Chinese government as scrap metal and they will be towed by a tugboat to Shanghai to be melted down for new pipes. We were told to separate the building steel members from the stainless steel. I have no idea what the Chinese government will do with the stainless steel, I am guessing railings for Navy ships."

The mothballed fleet at Mare Island Naval Shipyard immediately came to Michael's mind where he had paid a visit back when…

"You speak English very well." Michael observed. "Where did you learn the language?"

"I graduated from Berkeley University and have a PHD in communications."

"Are you an American citizen, then? What are you doing in prison in China?"

"I am a Chinese citizen. I returned to China after I completed my studies. As for the prison part…the government decided that I was a dissident. I am a political prisoner you may say."

Welcome to the club Michael thought.

"Where are the guards?" Michael inquired. "Surely you are not here on your own?"

"The guards are at the Officer's Club back at the Mercury Air Force Base. This trip is like a vacation for them. They brought us here in the morning. We and them all stay at one of the enlisted men's barracks. We eat at the enlisted men's Mess Hall. The guards eat at the Officers Club. They will bring us lunch at noon from there; or at least that is what they promised. We were told this place was abandoned. What are you doing here, if I may ask?"

"How do you manage for water?" Michael asked, ignoring the question and offering Chen a bottle of cold water from the styrofoam chest.

Chen accepted it gratefully, bowed and pointed at the location of three barrels in front of the buildings sitting on elevated tripod legs.  The barrel steel must have rendered the potable water to be good enough for shaving by now, he thought, if it lacked ice...

"Sorry Chen, but I got to go." Michael said suddenly, putting the Jeep in reverse; thinking...poor bastards like their forefathers brought in the U.S. to build the railroads...their descendants just  follow in their footsteps.

*   *   *   *

It took the Chinese prisoners till the close of business Friday to finish, pack up and disappear as swiftly as they had arrived.

A knock on his door surprised Michael that weekend.  He found Maria standing on the threshold.  She walked in.  Michael dispelled quickly any romantic interlude he may have imagined or thought at first glance.  She was all business.  "Chen escaped!"  She exclaimed.  Nothing went past her, Michael thought; in this case with the help of course of the Chinese 'Rats', amongst the Chinese prisoners.  His brief meeting with Chen on Monday morning was duly observed and reported to the proper authorities.  With so many 'Rats' around, no wonder the Chinese prisoners were left unattended.  "Do you know anything about it?"  She asked like she was suspecting that Michael organized and orchestrated Chen's escape.  Michael felt disgusted with her.

"Try locating his ex girlfriends while he was at Berkeley." Michael replied laconically.  Showing her the door.  You are no Teresa Kyle he thought, reminiscing and picturing in his mind the head of SIS at the Nellis Camp, drinking her coffee while he was taking his morning shower.  He wished Chen all the luck in the world, wherever he was.

*   *   *   *

It took Michael and the crew the full ten days he had promised to finish and provide the three stooges with the As Built Drawings of the ten buildings.  He kept the As Built Drawings of the building destined to be the New Motor Pool.

"Who is going to take the ten buildings apart?"  He asked Maria as he was leaving. "We have excellent crews at Nellis to do so in record time."

"You will be given a chance to bid on the work." Was her curt reply.

He never heard from her or the rest of the 'stooges' again.  He was the Man Who Knew Too Much, already.  Maria was probably reluctant to compound on his knowledge.

# CHAPTER 22

## The Team Of Transfer Payers

Michael had over two dozen ongoing construction projects simultaneously; while he had previously told the Warden that he only felt comfortable with twenty or less, when he got word from Phil Rolfs that he wanted Michael to file an FYI to the GAO to remodel a 30,000 square foot abandoned building at the Camp.

"But we already have over two dozen ongoing projects." Michael protested.

"You are right!" Rolfs exclaimed. "Construction 4 is too busy already. I will tell the Warden to give it to Construction 2. Krupp has hardly any work. However, you are still in charge." He said with a mischievous smile.

"We don't have the trades for such a project." Michael said taking another approach to the matter.

"What do we need?" Was Rolfs response.

"Concrete finishers, steelworkers, electricians, plumbers, sheetmetal workers, drywall installers, carpenters both rough and finish…"

"We will have them before construction starts. In the meantime get started with the financing and the design."

The word got out almost immediately on the upcoming project and Michael was besieged with requests for a meeting by the head of the education department, almost all the BOP councilors who wanted their own office, even the chaplain.

Mr. Lee the head of the eduction department was the first to arrive at Michael's office. He was a slight black man in both statute and intellect. He was accompanied by his secretary a statuette black lady who reminded Michael of a chorus girl, which she probably was in her salad days, a head taller than Lee. Michael had met her before when he first arrived at Camp trying to get an appointment with the head of the education department as a prospective GED teacher. She had given him a hard time, he recalled, and never got his appointment right  away. How the wheel has turned, he thought. After the introductions, during which neither Michael nor the secretary mentioned that they had met before; she probably did not remember; probably because all honkies looked the same to her. Lee got the sole guest chair and the secretary, Michael already had forgotten her name, the drafting stool. She wore a black mini skirt and a red blouse projecting her impressive cleavage to the maximum advantage. The mini had ridden to her crotch and she made no effort to cover herself. Instead she smiled seductively at Michael when his eyes travelled to her generous thighs. She switched her legs exposing her bikini briefs which were also red. Michael averted his eyes immediately thinking of his wife's habit of wearing red underpants on certain days of the month. Instead he concentrated starring at Lee.

"How may I be of help?" He inquired.

"We are here to discuss the Education Department arrangement in the new building you are designing." Lee said sounding like a white man. No jive.

"The total square footage will be within the guide lines of the BOP Rules." Michael explained. "The general arrangement will be up to you. However, I have the final say because of its effect on the structural support system. Otherwise you will end up with columns in the middle of the rooms."

"Have you given the design any thought yet?" Lee said timidly.

Michael got up and retrieved a stack of Drawings stapled together. He walked to the drafting table and unrolled the set with the plan view which showed the education department foot print and his proposed General Arrangement, which had already the Warden's blessing. He stood silently next to the secretary. Lee got off his chair and stared also. It became obvious that neither Lee nor the secretary could read blue prints, with Lee reluctant to admit it. Michael did not have all day so he kindly pointed the outline of the education department and started explaining its components. The Leisure Library occupied the lions share of the real estate, double its existing size. The Legal Library was half. The Jewish mafia would object, but they did most of their work in their rooms. They could use the Leisure Library for their interviews he rationalized. The GED classroom sizes remained the same. An extra room was added for lectures he explained to Lee at the request of the Warden. It would be used for the betterment of the inmates with lectures to assist them on the outside. He explained that he was directed by the Warden to develop a course in Estimating and Construction Management. The two hour lectures will be given one day a week. The inmates who attended the course for half a year, would have no problem getting, immediately upon release, a high paying job in the Construction Industry. The real go getters could even start their own companies with loans from the SBA. Michael underlined that he had given priority to the construction and finish of the lecture room so he could start the course as soon as possible. It was his understanding that the Warden's secretary was already hard at work in preparing a poster for Michael's approval before it was hung on all the bulletin boards announcing the course.

Mr. Lee's face stiffened at all that information.

"Why was not consulted?" He finally asked.

"I have no idea." Michael admitted. "Why don't you ask the Warden? It was his idea. I just did what I was told."

"It's just a funny way of finding out about the course from you, after the fact. Do you realize you will be working for me? Didn't you think you should have given me a heads up?"

"I tried two Fridays ago, but your secretary would not let me see you." Michael lied, compacting the time element.

Lee stared at his secretary. "What do you have to say about that Roxane?"

"I don't remember." She finally admitted.

"You were rearing blue jeans and a red football tee shirt." Michael recalled from their earlier meeting. "It had the UNLV logo in front and the number 10 on the back with a name I cannot recall."

"He is right." Lee said with venom. "That's what your uniform is on Fridays before the game Saturday. I am sorry for the misunderstanding." He said addressing Michael. "Let me know when you plan to start and I will personally be there to make your introduction to the class."

"Thank you." Michael said. The issue was put to bed, he thought. He was getting ready to pick up the Drawings to put them back in the drawer when Lee stopped him.

"Sorry but you didn't show my office." He said hesitantly. "I was going to ask you if you could squeeze a private bathroom with a shower..."

"Here you go." Michael pointed a room, a third the size of Lee's current office.

"What about my office?" Roxane exclaimed. "I don't see it."

"Right there." Michael pointed at a corner of Lee's office.

"You can't do that!" Lee exploded, forgetting the argument he was formulating regarding the size of his new office. "I need privacy. Now every Tom, Dick and Harry will have access to me..."

"Mr. Lee." Michael started with a placating tone of voice. "Be reasonable. I was only given a finite square footage of real estate. Do you want me to violate the BOP Rule book?"

Lee signaled his secretary, who vacated the drafting stool and abruptly they both stormed out of Michael's office.

The existing building had both asbestos and led paint contamination. Michael did not want to risk using inmates for its removal. They would have to buy hazmat suits and build a clean room. On top of that, the liability from lawsuits by the rest of the Camp inmates, claiming they breathed the stuff, was there for a Class Action suit waiting to happen. Michael recommended that they hire an independent hazardous material contractor to assume the responsibility and liability.

Michael sent a Bid request to every hazardous material contractor he could find in the Las Vegas telephone book yellow pages. He insisted that they attend a mandatory pre-bid meeting followed by an on site visit.

The Bids he received back were all over the spectrum. He selected the low bid which was ridiculously low. He made the selected Contractor to provide in addition to the Construction Payment and Performance Bond, a Consequential Damages Liability Bond from a triple AAA surety for the next twenty five years. The contractor agreed and signed the Contract.

Michael expected his first activity to be encapsulating the building. Followed by construction of the clean room.

None of the above took place. On commencement day a bunch of Mexican migrant looking workers showed up and started demolition and removal of the Asbestos and sand blasting to remove the led paint. Michael was shaking his head. At least he made them install fans along the side of the building blowing the sandblasting dust away from the Camp towards the open desert.

"Is this how it's done, little buddy?" Rolf inquired.

"Hardly." Michael replied. "The guy is 'a fly by night contractor'. He employs a bunch of Mexican migrant workers who don't know any better and gives them the ballon test…"

"What's the ballon test?" Phil inquired.

"At the end of the day he has them blow up a ballon. Whoever fails, he is fired, only to be replaced the next day by a fresh body. I bet they are not even listed as employees. I bet on his Davis-Bacon payroll form he lists them not as employees but as private contractors. It is not our job to argue with him. We just pass the information along. It's up to the IRS to spot them and raise a stink. If they do, down the line after several years from now, the contractor would just file for bankruptcy and start a new company under a different name. It's a racket Phil. I am just glad I thought to require a Liability Bond. No matter what happens, the Surety won't go away. They are liable for ten percent of the damages…"

"Only ten percent!" Rolf exclaimed. "Who covers the ninety percent?" He looked at Michael like he had screwed up.

"The Federal Government is the deep pocket. That's how it works for all the SBA type Contract Bonds. The Surety has to show to the Government that they have liquid assets to cover ten percent of the Bond, the government gives them a triple AAA rating and assumes ninety percent of the liability through the SBA."

"Good to know." Were Phil Rolfs final words before stepping away to go back to his new toy, a backhoe, front unloader combination.

The Chaplain wanted the entire first floor West wing to be the new chapel, he told Michael during their meeting. He was a Catholic priest.

"What do you do if you hear of an impending crime during confession?" Michael asked with curiosity. "Do you keep it to yourself or pass it on to the BOP?" "That's a tough one." The Chaplain admitted. "I'd probably try to convince the penitent to abort his plan. If that fails. I don't know what I'd do.  Thank God it has never happened to me.  The Catholic inmates believe that I would turn them in; so they are very selective as to what they tell me during Confession."

"What happens if you start the Liturgy on Sunday and the Blue Light comes on? The inmates have to go back to their rooms. You cannot stop the Liturgy.  How do you reconcile the situation?"

"This actually has happened.  The inmates leave to go to their rooms and I stay to continue and finish the Liturgy..."

"You cannot have Liturgy without an audience." Michael protested.

"You are right.  However, I had a full church when I started the Liturgy. I rationalize that what took place was an unanticipated event like a natural disaster or an act of war.  Under those circumstances the Church Rules provide for the Liturgy to continue without the audience, provided the Priest is able to do so."

"You will have a funny looking church if you insist on the location." Michael said.

"How do you define funny?"

"There is a cluster of four two by two feet concrete columns coming from the basement going through the fist floor and ending on the ceiling to support the second floor.  This, not only would cut visibility, but will effect the overall use of the chapel.  I assume the reason you want to move out of the existing one room set up is that you want to expand the capacity of the church."

"You are right.  Is there anything you can do to eliminate the obstruction posed by  the existing support columns?"

"The whole existing building structure is designed on the basis of fifty pounds per square foot.  This is good enough for houses only, under the current Uniform Building Code.  For commercial use, this design parameter jumps to one hundred pounds per square foot.  I plan to revise the building structure to one hundred fifty pounds per square foot, because its primary use will be a prison dormitory. I have to be able to justify the expense if someone questions it. Within the budget I have in mind, I will see what I can do with the chapel problem." Michael said with finality bringing the meeting to a close.

Michael designed and the Construction 2 crew constructed a new support structure to install before demolition of the interior to make room for the new chapel, so the second floor wouldn't be collapsing on top of the workers. He eliminated the columns on the first floor of the West wing, at the request of the chaplain, that were supporting the second floor, so that the first floor could be a free standing open chapel with no visual obstructions.

Michael concealed a pair of steel columns inside the end walls in the new chapel going all the way down to the basement. He had the Construction 2 crews saw cut and remove the basement slab at the four locations and build in their place four by four feet, two and a half feet thick, reinforced steel concrete footings to support the steel columns. At their end underneath the second floor he had them install two steel beams running the length of the chapel and welded them at the top of the four steel columns coming through the floor from the basement. The four steel columns and the two beams were sized to be able to carry, with less than an eighth of an inch deflection, the entire second floor dead load, the roof loads plus one hundred fifty pounds per square foot live load.

Everything was in place when Krupp, the Construction 2 foreman, came to Michael's office and asked him to come over and check things out. Krupp assured him that he believed they did everything in accordance with his design. Michael inspected the installation including the welding of the beams to the top of the columns. He then traced the columns to the basement all the way to their footings. The column base plates were seated right on top of the anchor bolt leveling nuts. He pointed this out to Krupp and showed him on the Drawing Notes that it called for the base plates to be grouted before the demolition of the four existing concrete columns. He explained to him that as it stood, the weight of the second floor would strip the anchor bolt threads. Krupp was pissed off that he had not noticed it before calling Michael for a final inspection and in his mind blamed the construction crews for not reading the Drawings. He ordered two of his workers to grout the column base plates as called for in the Drawing. The demolition of the existing columns had to be postponed for the following day to allow the grout to cure.

The next day, Michael went through the installation once more and pronounced it completed and in compliance with his design.

"They may start demolition of the existing columns and the walls." Michael told Krupp.

Krupp looked at his crew waiting with jackhammers, sledge hammers and crow bars. They were apprehensive. They doubted that these two beams would prevent the second floor from falling on top of them.

"You heard the man." Krupp barked. "Get on with it!"

A crew of a dozen inmates with sledge hammers and crow bars started, tentative at first and with gusto later on, as they were getting warmed up, gutting the interior. The interior walls were not structural walls; they were partition walls for offices. They were not load bearing walls. They were demolished and removed to the construction dumpsters outside the building. Only the four concrete columns were left standing in the middle of the West wing. Throughout the activity, Michael remained inside the West wing, watching the progress. He felt it would be a breach of faith to the integrity of his design to abandon the working crews now.

Krupp kept his eyes on Michael. Michael looked back at him. Krupp was silently conveying his apprehension. Did he want to give Michael a chance to back down? Michael was not sure what Krupp's game was. Did he expected Michael to say something? Michael just stood there silently starring alternatively at Krupp and at the four concrete columns.

"What are you waiting for?" Krupp finally yelled at his troops who had formed a circle around the last remaining, existing means of holding the second floor up.

The jackhammers started their pounding. Michael stayed put. Krupp stood beside him. One by one the concrete columns came down. Nothing else did. All eyes were on Michael. The Construction 2 crew broke in an applause directed at Michael and their opportunity to be part of such an event. Moments like those was the reason Michael had chosen to become an engineer. Flashes of the movie 'The Flight of the Phoenix' were flooding his brain.

"Pretty confident, eh!" Krupp cracked a rare smile.

"It's actually stronger than before." Michael ventured. "The existing structure was rated for fifty pounds per square foot. Well below the current Uniform Building Code requirements for commercial buildings which is one hundred pounds per square foot."

"You never gotten it through your head." Krupp barked. "You are in prison now. I am the Code around here now."

"Alright Mr. Code." Michael braved. "How are you going to hold up two hundred fifty inmates that you plan to warehouse on the second floor weighing five hundred pounds each?"

"Five hundred pounds?" Krupp grinned. "How do you figure? I know we have some animals here, but five hundred pounds? I dare you to name one right now who weighs that much."

"Mr. Krupp." Michael said smiling. "You are forgetting, each inmate has a steel bed which weighs at least one hundred pounds and two steel lockers which weigh, once again, at least one hundred fifty pounds, loaded. This leaves room for one hundred to two hundred pound inmate. I believe the entire Camp population fits under this category."

Krupp looked at Michael seething.

"You think you are pretty smart, hot shit engineer, don't yah!". He said turning on his heals and leaving the building.

"Hey Mike!" Dave Hill the Construction 2 lead man called after him as Michael turned to leave the building. "How are we going to support the rest of the building?"

"I have not given it much thought." Michael said. "No one asked me. I have no work order request on the subject. Remember, I am a prisoner here, same as you. It's not my problem until someone from the staff asks me about it in writing. Then it becomes my problem. Why don't you ask your boss, Mr. Code?"

The request for funds went without a hitch. No clarifications requested nor additional information. The package sent to GAO requesting three million dollars for the project included Michael's detailed cost estimate in the amount of $3,054,689.00 and three proposals from Las Vegas general contractors the low being $3,153,000.00. The three mil was approved by the GAO and sent right away to the Warden, undisputed.

"What do you figure the actual cost will come to." The Warden asked in one of his weekly visits to Michael's office.

"I have made a tentative cost estimate and I am working on the premise of a $1,700,000.00 budget. This includes the cost for the hazardous materials removal by an outside contractor and upgrading the building structure, which by the way is outside the scope of work, for remodeling. An outside Contractor would be asking for additional money and he would have prevailed if it came down to a Dispute. Plus the chaplain's pet project to recreate Notre Dame at the Camp."

The Warden smiled.

"This means I can count on a mil three left over?"

"Yes sir. You can count on it."

"My boys and gals will sure be happy with their bonus this year. I will make sure to spread the word as to who is responsible for their windfall."

Michael noticed the influx of additional inmates, all recent arrivals, all assigned to Construction 4, on temporary loan to Construction 2. Surprisingly, they represented every trade required to perform the activities associated with the new building. Where did they come from? There were no bums amongst them. They were all journeymen class or better, particularly the cement finisher whom Michael sought and befriended.

"Where are you from Dan?" He asked him.

"Right here in Las Vegas. Born and raised."

"How did you end up here?"

"I got caught in the deadly spiral of trying to keep up with the Jones. Rather my wife did and here I am..."

"I don't understand. Your job skills are exceptional. It would seem to me that you would have no problem whatsoever landing a premium job with lots of overtime, with the construction boom happening in Las Vegas. I had a heck of a time getting proposals for this building, for example. Had to wait forever and the bids came way high."

"I know what you mean. I had a good job with unlimited overtime. I hardly slept. I was always working and I became afraid that as I was so tired my attention at work was just not there like it used to. I was scared everyday that I would get hurt on the job. So, I asked a coworker who was matching my hours, how in the hell he was still so alert on the job. He gave me a little pink pill and let me tell you. I was a new man. I asked him where did he get the pills. He told me and I got my own which I kept in the glove compartment of my truck. I was not hooked or anything mind you. I only took one just before I started work. The boost it gave me lasted all day. I could work twelve hours a day, seven days a week.

My wife was delighted. I didn't feel I was doing anything wrong. People get the same pills by prescription from a doctor to lose weight. Everyone in the trades was using them. Life was good. Until the federal Marshals showed up one morning at the job site and opened the glove compartment of every truck parked on site. They rounded us up and offered us to plead guilty with a year and a day at Nellis as punishment with no fine or five years at an FCI with a horrendous fine if we took the government to trial and lost; which was a foregone conclusion we would lose. They had us cold on possession. We all plead guilty and here we are."

"The rest of the inmates working here were your co-workers on the outside?" Michael asked remembering his conversation with Phil Rolfs when he outlined their manpower needs to undertake a thirty thousand square foot remodeling project.

"You got that right." Dan responded. "Actually, I am not complaining. I will only be in here nine months, that is with good behavior and halfway house. The wife has plenty of money to last. I will be busy here with the same kind of work I was doing on the outside keeping up my skills. I will have my old job back as soon as I get out of here. I have no paper. To tell you the truth I may have become addicted to the damn pills and the feeling of alertness they gave me. I was aware and noticed things I was not aware they existed before. I was getting used to the pills. When I was caught, I was taking two or three instead of the one when I started. There is no overtime here. I will use the time to exercise, detox my system and rest. I consider my time here as a long overdue vacation, I never had for the past ten years."

He seemed like a happy man. The rest of the newcomers had carbon copy stories to tell and they were happy at Camp. So, why was Michael feeling guilty? He swore he will never open his big mouth ever again to talk about manpower requirements and shortages. He would play the game with the players he's got; no outside transfer players.

# CHAPTER 23

## The Myth Of Sisyphus

All the construction activities at the Camp produced debris. Not only dirt but rocks also and old chunks of cement. It was accumulating at an alarming rate.

"You better call in some Air Force trucks, pronto." Michael suggested to Phil Rolfs.

"No can do little buddy." Was Rolfs reply. "The mess is ours to clean up. We are not allowed to export it."

"The Air Force has the same problem, then." Michael said. "Only they have a larger area to dump unwanted construction debris. But they must be running out of room to dump."

"Right you are little buddy. Can you think of some use?" Rolfs said scratching his balding head.

"Not unless you have a highway project in the works." Michael said. "The construction debris and rocks, crushed, would make excellent sub-base material."

"Nothing like that that I know of. Anyway you are better informed on that front than I am. You prepare all the FYI appropriation requests for both the Camp and the Air Force Base after all. I tell you what. You think of something to do with all that debris and go ahead and do it. I will back you up all the way."

"I will need to borrow a 'hop two' from the Air Force. The biggest they got." Michael requested after a pause.

"What the fuck is a 'hop two'?" Rolf exclaimed.

"I am sorry. I used the Hawaiian term for it. It is a backhoe, front unloader combination." Michael explained. "I will also need a driver. How about you volunteering. You are an expert fork lift operator and you practiced with the little 'hop two'. With a little more practice you can add the larger backhoe, front unloader in your resume..."

"You may have something little buddy. How soon do you need the 'hop two'? Damn, I like calling it that, instead of the boring name we call it." Phil Rolfs said enthusiastically.

"Yesterday." Was Michael's laconic response.

"I'll see what I can do. What are you building anyway?"

"It's a secret. You are just the operator. Need to know basis. You will find out soon enough anyway. I need to talk to the landscape crew to start with and some other people. We will actually need more debris. Rocks in particular. Spread the word to the Air Force. Any large rocks they want to dispose, bring them over here and dump them in our construction debris pile."

Next day a Case 580 E backhoe front unloader combination mysteriously appeared, parked next to the construction debris pile. It was followed by a convoy of Air Force trucks delivering construction debris which was for the most part rocks. And what rocks they were. The size of Volkswagen beetles. Money under the table to Rolfs pocket must have transpired to solve the Air Force problem and dilemma what to do with their pile of construction debris. After the initial onslaught, however, the traffic from the Air Force trickled to a couple of trucks a day. Phil Rolfs in the meantime, initially with the help of an Air Force operator, had become an expert after a day of practice moving boulders around using both ends of the machine.

Michael took Rolfs as his stick boy and surveyed an circular area of approximately five thousand square feet and drew on the ground with a spray can a circle starting eighty feet away from the South track bend and expanding further South on the way to the dormitory he was staying. He told Rolfs to get back on the 'hop two' and place rocks inside the perimeter of the circle he drew. Rolfs worked all day at his task. At the end of the day Michael had workers throw in the midst of the rocks all the loose rebar they could find in the construction debris pile irregardless of its size or shape. He then asked Rolfs to order for the next day a load of concrete and a concrete pump.

"What are we making?" Was Rolfs single question.

"A natural looking foundation." Michael replied.

"What for?"

"A new park, which will serve as an observatory."

"You are the boss." Rolf replied. "I hope you know what you are doing. If asked, I will pretend that I know."

The next day the circular rock foundation was coated with three to six inches of concrete. Michael asked Rolfs to start depositing construction debris mixed with dirt and other rocks on top, trying to keep the added pile as vertical as possible. After it reached five feet, the landscape crew arrived with the Native American Indian in charge. They started working with Rolfs and directing the next dump and the next, while they were carving paths and laying plastic piping.

"What are you folks building here?" The Warden appeared one morning on his way to the Air Force Golf Course.

"A park." Rolfs replied. "As a means to get rid of all the construction debris we've been accumulating, both here and on Base."

"Good idea. Smart too, Phil. I will pass it on to Regional. They must be facing the same problem we are." The Warden concluded.

Typical government thinking at work, Michael thought. Phil Rolfs stole the idea as his own and passed it on. Michael after all was working for him.  The Warden appropriated the idea as his own to pass it on to his bosses at Regional.  The thinking being that since Rolfs was working for him, the Warden inspired him with the idea.  In the meantime the park was taking shape aiming upwards to the point that was now the highest structure at the Camp.  It was no longer a park.  It was a Mountain.  The word got around.  The Air Force no longer delivered just debris.  They delivered custom ordered rocks, rock benches rock tables flat rocks for picnic area flooring and everything asked of them for 'Michael's Mountain' as everyone referred to it.  There was no construction debris to be found at camp.  Michael designed and incorporates crevices for future debris deposits.  The landscape crew outdid themselves in planting dwarf cypress along the paths and other miniature trees and bushes not native to the desert, but with the watering system they installed, they were thriving.  'Michael's Mountain' became the centerpiece of the Nellis Camp.  The Warden was taking every visitor for a stroll to show off what can be accomplished out of debris.  On the very top of the mountain one hundred fifty feet above ground a single stone chair, almost a throne looking structure with a foot rest, was constructed facing the Las Vegas strip.  It was called Michael's chair and like the one in the Movie Theater it was always   vacant, unless Michael happen to be sitting smoking his cigar and staring at the lights and sounds coming out of the Las Vegas strip.

This was where Krupp found him one day, smoking a cigar.

"What the fuck you think you are doing?"  He barked.

Phil Rolfs was on vacation, he had left the previous day.  In his absence, Krupp took over Construction 4; so technically, Michael was now working for Krupp.

"I am taking a midmorning break and doing some thinking."  He pointed at the engineering pad on his lap, the page filled with notes and numbers.

"Likely story." Krupp replied. "Why don't you admit it. Your regular boss is away and you decided to fuck around. It won't happen while I am around. Phil is gone. Your ass is mine now. Follow me Mr. Engineer and I will get you acquainted with your next assignment. You are to do only that for as long as I deem necessary and nothing else. Am I making myself clear?"

"Yes sir!" Michael said knocking the cigar ashes against his shoe, getting off his throne and following Krupp down the path.

"By the way," Krupp mumbled on the way down the mountain, "who told you to build this God damned monstrosity?" He pointed at the mountain. "Do you have anything in writing from the Warden or one of the staff? I ought to file a charge against you for wasting taxpayers money for a monument to your ego. 'Michael's Mountain', my ass. Every time I hear the name I want to smash something."

Michael stayed silent. He did not wish to offer a readily available and convenient smash target. He wished Lieutenant Teresa Kyle was around. The head of SIS. She was the only one he trusted to set the record straight. 'Monument to my Ego', my foot, he thought. His original idea was to get rid of the construction debris. That's all. The mountain was a project developed as the work progressed and the horizontal real estate limited, the vertical unlimited. The same as every overpopulated city in the world. He had nothing to do with the name. The Air Force came up with it because Rolfs had told them to see a prisoner by the name of Michael as to where to unload the rocks and debris. The mountain appeared out of nowhere and became the landscape symbol of the Air Force dump trucks destination. Michael and the mountain became synonymous. The inmates heard the Air Force drivers talking and asking directions for 'Michael's Mountain'; the name stuck. 'Michael's Mountain'. Now Krupp, who saw Michael as an arrogant SOB was perceiving the name of the mountain as another example of Michael's extreme arrogance; his Hubris, if Krupp even knew the meaning of the word.  However, Krupp was ready, God like, to pass on to Michael the new assignment, as his punishment.

They made their way to the Mess Hall.  They were going to the CMS offices.  Michael relaxed.  His punishment would be some sort of confinement in his office.  Krupp was bound and determined to kill him with boredom.

"Get yourself a mop and a bucket."  Krupp said as soon as they entered the Mess Hall and stopped at the top of the concrete stairway, down to CMS and Michael's office.  "You see this stairway.  You see the mess.  This is unacceptable.  This is the first thing a visitor to our offices sees.  I want this cleaned up."

The stairway was full of muddy foot prints.  As Krupp and Michael were standing there at the top of the stairway, a steady stream of workers were coming from the field adding to the muddy footprints.  An equal number of workers kept coming up the stairway from below.

"Mr. Krupp."  Michael started with a respectful tone of voice.  "The stairway gets cleaned up at the end of the day by a worker on a rotation system.  There is no use to be cleaned up during the day.  If somehow the cleaning person reaches the bottom of the stairway, he has to start all over, because invariably someone has used the stairs.  You cannot stop the foot traffic..."

"Who said anything about stopping the foot traffic!" Krupp barked.

"But...But...in that case the act of cleaning the steps would become a perpetual activity..."

"You may stop at the end of the day."  Krupp added smiling mischievously.  "However, during the day, from now on, until further notice from me and only me, this is your job: To keep the stairway mop clean. Nothing else! Are we clear?" Without waiting for an answer from Michael he walked away.

The stairway, starting from the bottom of the basement, was twelve steps up to a landing. A ninety degree turn from the landing and twelve more steps, brought you up to the first floor which led, to the left, towards the entrance to the dining  room and the kitchen, or to the right, towards the main entrance to the Mess Hall building.

Michael got himself a mop and a bucket which he filled with soapy water. He looked at his watch 9:45 AM. He barely would have had time to get to the location of the new Air Rescue Building, where the dedication ceremony was about to begin at 10:00 AM sharp. The Nellis Air Force Base General had invited him to attend. Michael was planning to do a survey and mark the actual foot print of the new building as the dedication ceremony was taking place.

"Boss! I've been looking for you everywhere. I got the golf cart parked right up front. We better get a move on! If we are going to have the survey done on time." Milton, his current survey stick boy exclaimed. He curiously looked at Michael standing there and getting the mop wet. "What the hell are you doing. Victor will take care of that at the end of the day. It's his turn."

"Milton my boy," Michael spoke from the side of his mouth, the other side holding an unlit cigar, "I am going no where but here. I am doing no other work, but cleaning this stairway. Krupp's orders. From now on, until I am told otherwise by him and only him, I am just a laborer. As such, I am unable to do anything else, including to answer engineering or construction questions."

"What did you do to get this punishment?" Milton asked. "For how long is your punishment?"  He followed with another question, before Michael could respond to the first one.

Michael was explaining to Milton what happened, when another inmate came in looking for Michael, holding a roll of Drawings for the new Motor Pool.  Michael listened and told the inmate to follow the Drawings.

"But…Krupp is asking me questions which I am unable to answer…"

"Just follow the Drawings." Was Michael's repetitive reply. "If you have any questions or concerns, ask Krupp."

Herb Holmes the Chief Draftsman was coming up the stairway steps for consultation wanting to ask Michael a quick question. Now Michael had an audience of three preventing him to continue with his newly assigned task.

"But…Krupp is the problem. He wants to change the Drawings…and he wants your approval…" The first inmate insisted.

Michael pointed out on the Drawing his stamp and his signature. "No changes. Just follow the Drawings." He repeated.

The inmate left dragging the roll of Drawings disgusted. Michael told Herb Holmes who had witnessed the exchange, what had transpired with Mr. Krupp and that he was unavailable for the time being to solve engineering problems. Holmes, instead of going back down to the drafting department, he went out the main Mess Hall door.

"Shit!" Milton exclaimed, following on the footsteps of Herb Holmes. "All construction at Camp and on Base will come to a standstill by tomorrow."

Michael resumed his cleaning job. As soon as he reached the bottom of the stairway, he had to start cleaning going up. Inmate traffic, more than usual Michael noted, was coming in to witness Michael's humiliation, dirtying the steps further in the process. Michael looked up to the top of the stairway. The footprints were there as if he never cleaned the stairway.

"At least the Gods waited until Sisyphus reached the top of the mountain!" He exclaimed in a loud voice stopping the foot traffic in mid-step momentarily. No one realized what he was talking about.

All day long he remained at his task diligently, avoiding to answer questions and after a while the work became so monotonous and repetitive that he quit acknowledging people. For example when the chaplain came over to talk to him, Michael ignored him. All the while Milton, having nothing else to do, remained at the top of the stairway answering questions and providing explanations as to the sequence of events leading to Michael's demise. At the end of the day as Michael was cleaning the stairway for the last time that day, Herb Holmes appeared.

"I went and saw the Warden. I told him that I quit together with the rest of the drafting department over your unfair treatment." It was like he was talking to the wall, Michael, although pleased at the moral support and the turn of events he remained silent.

Michael put the mop and the bucket back in the closet and went to his room to lay down and rest because he was beat, unused to repetitive manual labor. He fell to an immediate dreamless sleep. Next thing he knew when he opened his eyes it was morning. He was a no show for the personal trainer the Camp had hired specifically for him. He missed his morning work out with Milton and the tunnel rat. He owed a dollar, fifty cents to each for his transgression. He missed his morning shower. What would Lieutenant Kyle make of it? He barely had time to go to breakfast. His stomach was growling; warning him that he would be unable to continue his appointed Sisyphean task on an empty stomach.

He sat at a table alone and ate his breakfast, mechanically. He went and retrieved his mop and bucket heading up the stairway which had already some dusty foot prints. He stopped on the landing and looked up. He had visitors.

The Warden was waiting for him at the top of the stairway looking down on him. As he made his way half way up, the main entrance to the Mess Hall opened and an agitated Lieutenant Kyle, the head of the SIS, closely followed by the Chaplain were joining the Warden.

"Do you know that all construction activities have stopped, both at the Camp and on Base!  The drafting department is on strike!  The Red Horse is on a self imposed slow down!  The Air Force General is on the phone to me every hour on the hour since yesterday chewing my ass and wanting your head!"  The Warden was the first to speak and succinctly state the situation.

"Sir.  I don't care what you do to me.  I have reached the point where I don't care if you shoot me.  I am beyond care of what happens to me.  I have hit bottom..."  before Michael could continue, Lieutenant Kyle rushed over and embraced Michael in front of everyone.

"Why didn't you tell me, you silly boy!"  She whispered in his ear squeezing him tight.

"Let's go to your office and discuss this matter like civilized people."  The Warden suggested addressing Michael still entangled in Lieutenant Kyle's hug.

Lieutenant Kyle unlocked Michael's door.  She wanted to broadcast it that she alone and Michael, of course, knew the cypher combination to the door to his office.

"What happened here?" The Warden pled ignorance, in spite of the fact that Michael knew that Herb Holmes had talked and explained to the Warden yesterday the sequence of events and happenings. Like a good bureaucrat the Warden did not react instantly.  Instead he waited a day to see which way the wind was blowing.  When he was met in the morning with a shit storm of unprecedented proportions, he thought prudent to look into the matter.

Michael explained the sequence of events since yesterday morning's encounter with Mr. Krupp.

The Warden was speechless.  Lieutenant Kyle was seething.  Michael thought that if Krupp was in the room, she would have taken her spring loaded sap to him.  The chaplain corroborated Michael's narrative as being a carbon copy of what he had been told by numerous inmates.

The silence in the room was deafening.

"What would it take to put the matter behind us, Michael?" The Warden asked.  Everything to the Warden was a matter of dollars and cents, Michael was thinking.

"I'd tell you what is going to happen." Lieutenant Kyle took charge. "You," she addressed Michael, as she pulled a folded typed page from her breast pocket "read this and sign it, if you are in agreement with the statements."

"Come on Teresa." The Warden interceded.  "Do we want to go that far..."

"It has already gone that far Warden.  It is up to Michael to decide."

"What are we talking about?" Michael asked innocently.  His faith for Justice lay with Lieutenant Kyle.

"It is a formal Complaint I drafted with the help of the chaplain.  The narrative does not go into detail.  The details will be included in my Report to the Department of Justice.  The document you will be signing merely gives me the authority to investigate..."

"Do we really want to get the SIS involved here and the Department of Justice?" The Warden mumbled.  He was concerned and worried about the backdraft of the incident heading his way from the National.  Because that was whom the  Department of Justice would be contacting and dealing with.  He had no other alternative but to embrace whatever got decided and get behind it.  If it was up to him the matter would be resolved in the old boy network way.  The impasse was resolved as soon as Michael put his John Henry on the proffered page which was refolded and neatly placed back in Lieutenant Kyle's breast pocket.  Poor Krupp, the Warden was thinking.  He might as well kiss his career with the BOP goodby.  But it's his own doing, he decided.  The times are a changing.  The old fashioned bull guard is out.  Political correctness is in.  Let's embrace it…

"With the matter out of my hands," the Warden said.  "what's the deal with the new Motor Pool?  Herb Holmes your Chief draftsman came to see me yesterday and he was concerned."

"Mr. Krupp wanted to change the design.  He sent a messenger to get my permission to do so.  I responded by stating to follow the Drawings, repeatedly.  This conversation and my direction was witnessed by Herb Holmes who was standing by to ask me a question and Milton my survey stick boy who wanted me to disregard Mr. Krupp's orders and go do a survey at the Base for the new Air Rescue Building."

"The plot thickens."  Was all the Warden said as he got up.  "Let's take a walk over to the new Motor Pool and see what we shall see."

Michael followed the Warden side by side with Lieutenant Kyle.  The chaplain, his task accomplished and at an end, went the other way.

A convoy of three concrete trucks and a concrete pump greeted them.  A twenty foot high masonry wall by eighty feet long was already built, located in the South of the future Motor Pool building.  Scaffolding was erected to the top of the wall where workers were using the concrete pump hose to pump concrete into every empty CMU cell in the masonry wall.

"STOP!"  Michael screamed at the top of his voice.

Everything and everyone stopped at his command.  The concrete pump hose was dumping concrete at the base of the wall.

"What's the idea!"  Krupp barked appearing out of nowhere.  He was ready to bite Michael's head off for merely being there, instead of mopping the stairwell.  The  presence of the Warden and especially Lieutenant Kyle stopped him dead in his tracks.

"Why did you not follow the Drawings?"  Michael asked.

"I just wanted to make the building stronger." Krupp replied meekly.

"The building now as constructed does not meet the seismic Code requirements and it constitutes a safety hazard." Michael replied Ex Cathedra.

"I don't understand…" Krupp admitted. The bravado that 'I am the Code around here', having long disappeared. Michael almost felt sorry for him, almost.

He dispatched Milton, who was standing in the periphery like a loyal dog, to bring the tripod and the rest of the survey equipment.

"Las Vegas in in a seismic four zone. As such the Code requires concrete and reinforcing steel every thirty two inches vertically and every fourth block row horizontally. This means a reinforced checkerboard pattern of thirty two inches square." He interlaced his fingers and twisted them. "See the flexibility?" He demonstrated with his hands. "By filling every block cell with concrete, particularly unreinforced, you have killed the wall flexibility and just added weight. The wall will topple in an earthquake. Let me show you what the added weight has already done."

Milton had arrived with the survey equipment. Michael invited everybody, and specifically Krupp, to the side of the erected wall. He leveled the transit and took a sighting at the side of the CMU wall. He invited Lieutenant Kyle to take a look at what he was seeing.

"The vertical line of the scope as you see Lieutenant is even with the outer edge of the masonry wall. You are currently looking at the bottom of the masonry wall. If you lower the end of the scope you are looking through, you will progressively reach the top of the wall."

She did as she was told.

"Look at the vertical line of the scope and tell us what it is showing."

"It is past the middle of the concrete block and it's showing, the scope is showing, the inside of the wall." She replied.

"This means that there is over an eight inch deflection already. The wall has already started leaning. The ground is unable to bear and support the weight. This sandy ground, I'd say guesstimating, could support 1,600 psi compressive weight. The wall partially full of concrete, weighs a lot more than the ground is designed to support. If the workers kept pumping concrete into the wall, it would have toppled, trapping them underneath and with all that weight and a twenty foot fall, you would need a spoon to scrape the remains Mr. Krupp. This is the reason I yelled STOP earlier on."

Krupp sprinted towards the stranded inmates on top of the wall and told them to get down, carefully, and the rest of the inmates standing around to get away from the wall. He dispatched the concrete pump and sent the concrete trucks back where they had come from.

"What do we do with the wall?" The Warden asked, when Krupp came back and rejoined the group.

"It most certainly must come down." Michael said. "The sooner the better. If we get rain, the ground will soften and the angle of deflection will increase. The wall is a safety hazard; an accident to happen. If I were you," he said addressing Krupp, "I will do it immediately. Right now, while the concrete is still fresh. Tie ropes along the top on the rebar. Remove the scaffolding and have the crew pull on the ropes, standing of course more than twenty feet away. The wall will come down like 'timber'." He imitated the loggers yell. "Break it up with jackhammers and move the pieces to be used at 'Michael's Mountain'." He spoke with relish.

"Come see me, after you are done with the wall." The Warden ordered addressing Krupp. "What's the damage?" He asked Michael.

"A delay of two weeks in the schedule and our cost in material and labor runs a little under ten bucks per square foot for the wall. Eighty feet long by twenty feet high, is sixteen hundred square feet, times ten bucks per square foot, that's sixteen thousand dollars. The footing runs fifty bucks per linear foot.  That will be eighty linear feet times fifty, four grand.  Total damage twenty thousand dollars." "Don't you love how he got all the numbers at his fingertips and comes up with the answer right away.  No paper involved.  All in his head."  The Warden addressed Lieutenant Kyle.

"He is amazing." She admitted. "That's why I watch over him like a hawk, so no harm comes to him.  I just wish he ignored Krupp and just walked to my office and talked to me.  None of that nonsense and expense we just incurred would have happened."

"With all due respect Lieutenant Kyle, you just are not realistic in your expectations."  Michael alluded.  The Warden winked at him agreeing with his assessment.

"What's all that excavation I've been seeing from my office?"  The Warden asked, changing the topic of the conversation.

They started walking towards the Warden's office.  Two dozen workers were sitting under the spare shade waiting.

"This is the new sewer line for the Air Force Base."  Michael explained.

"Why are all these people standing around and not working?"

"They are waiting for me." Michael admitted. "The sewer line must have a slope towards the Air Force Base equal to three sixteenths of an inch per linear foot on the button.  Less than an eighth of an inch per foot slope, the solids will not move.  More than a quarter of an inch per foot slope, the liquids will outrun the solids with the same results.  They will plug up the first manhole they encounter and will back up towards the new Motor Pool.  They need me or someone with a transit to mark the sewer pipe slope every time they lay a section of pipe."

"What the fuck did we do before you came along?"  The Warden exclaimed.

"You simply did handyman's work type of construction.  No individual project was worth  more than a couple of thousand dollars, with the exception of the Movie Theater and I don't need to remind you of the results on this project before I took over.  You simply did not undertake and rolled over such work volume of complex projects and the price tag is currently into the millions.  You have become an Engineering and Construction concern of the 20 million dollars a year variety."  Michael replied succinctly.

The Warden walked away towards his office leaving Lieutenant Kyle and Michael alone.  Michael felt that if they were standing alone, without two dozen inmates watching, Lieutenant Kyle would have knocked him on the ground and had her way with him.  Michael kept staring at her, waiting.

"What do you expect me to do or say?"  She said looking towards the inmates. "Imagine that I simply kneel at the feet of talent.  I will let you know the results of the investigation of your Complaint."  She informed Michael instead, smiling, following on the footsteps of the Warden.

*   *   *   *

Michael got the results of the investigation of his Complaint while taking his morning shower two weeks later.

1.  Krupp was no longer allowed to talk to Michael directly.
2.  Michael could talk to Krupp if he so chose in association with the work and issue the appropriate directives which were to be followed to the letter without argument or further discussion.
3.  Krupp was to keep a physical distance at one hundred feet from Michael at all times.

"Do you want to know details of what will happen with Krupp?" Lieutenant Kyle asked.

Michael shook his head; he did not care one way or another.

# CHAPTER 24

## The Arch Of Peace

Adjebo, a Nigerian inmate, whom Michael had renamed the 'Nigerian Nightmare'; but that's another story...walked into his office one morning and told him that a vehicle accident took place yesterday on Base.

"What accident?" Michael inquired. "I didn't read anything in the paper."

"That's because they are covering it up." Adjebo replied. "It involved two High School students and the parents at the base are all up in arms. One of the parents knows you." He said cryptically.

"I don't know any parents on the Base." Michael protested.

"Are you sure, she talked to me about you...rater intimately. Her name is Trish Harris. Does the name ring a bell?"

Michael felt his blood rising to his face. "She was my fist job assignment when I first arrived."

"You must have made an impression on her. She wants to see you and ask you to help resolve the problem all parents are facing. Her daughter and the other girl were not seriously injured. I looked over the problem myself and believe I have a solution..."

"If you have a solution, why are you trying to get me involved?" Michael asked.

"Because if it stays with me it will be all talk. You on the other hand, you have a way of making things happen."

"Hop on my golf cart and show me what's what.  No promises though." Michael said.  The Nigerian complied and explained his idea of a pedestrian overpass.

Michael was directed towards the Base housing.  He knew where Trish Harris lived.  He rang her door bell.  Her house was full of females like there was a party in progress.

"I brought him."  Adjebo announced to the room from the front home entrance.  He turned right around and left.

Trish Harris introduced Michael and added that no construction work takes place at the Camp or on Base without his approval.  Adjebo must have blabbed; Michael thought.  However, his suspicion towards the 'Nigerian Nightmare' was dispelled when during the introduction period he found out that a couple of the ladies were married to Air Force personnel from the Red Horse and one was the wife of the man in charge of the construction materials warehouse.

"There is the Base main road which our children have to cross twice every day.  The school is divided into Elementary School, Middle School and High School.  All the schools are separate, but on the same campus accessible from the housing area by crossing the main road.  So you can see the children crossing the highway range from six years old up to eighteen." Trish said.

"Why doesn't the school post crossing guards?"  Michael asked wondering why did they overlook this basic and simple solution.

"They do.  They even have posted a reduced speed limit of twenty five miles per hour.  The cars ignore both the twenty five mile per hour speed limit and the crossing guards." Another concerned parent clarified.

"Well then, this is a matter for the Base Military Police to enforce." Michael concluded.

"They do; sporadically. But for all practical purposes it is a race to cross the street between car gaps. It works most of the time, but accidents happen." A voice in the crowd of women emphasized.

"We want a fool proof solution." Trish interjected. "Something that does not have to depend on the MP's being present or the human factor and consideration of the drivers."

"You are talking about a pedestrian overpass." Michael concluded. "You need permission from the General to start and after you get it, the overpass must be constructed high enough so it does not present an obstruction for trucks and other high load carrying vehicles. A structure with at least forty feet high clearance across the street, straddling the main street of the Base."

The women started chatting enthusiastically about the project.

"Who is going to pay for it?" Michael inquired. "You are talking about a project costing north of half a million dollars here..."

Michael's statement threw a damper to the premature celebration.

"Would you at least design the damn thing?" Trish erupted in frustration.

"Your sequence of activities does not make sense," Michael said, "considering the financial circumstances. I will visit your husband at the warehouse," Michael addressed the woman who was introduced to him as the wife of the man in charge of all the construction material on Base, "and find out firsthand what structural material there may be laying around, designated as surplus. I will design an overpass based on the material on hand, gratis. I will work on it during the weekend as to not be accused of cheating either the Air Force or the Camp. Afterwards, I will submit the Drawings through the Red Horse to the General for his approval. This is phase one of the proposed project."

On that note the meeting broke up and Michael said that he would visit the Air Force warehouse tomorrow so Betty, the wife of the warehouseman, could give her husband a heads up.  Michael returned to the Camp deep in thought as to what he was getting himself into.  He brought the matter up with his roommates to find out what they thought of it.

The discussion reminded him of the bumpersticker he saw in the sixties while riding around the WSU in his motorcycle.  'Cash, Grass or Ass.  No one rides free.'

Giovanni was on the fence.  He was an old accountant who took the fall for the mob, with a controlling interest  of Caesars Palace in Las Vegas, in a money laundering indictment.  As a result, their room beds had Caesars Palace mattresses instead of the the BOP issue, for starters.  Food could be ordered directly from the menus of several restaurants at the Casinos in Las Vegas, delivered hot to their room and the occasional chorus girl delivered in a van in the parking lot behind their dorm after dark and the ten o'clock count.

Joe thought the overpass would cause controversy, since you could not keep the lid on something like the Arch de Triumph, the name would pose a problem since the concerned parents during the meeting at the Base wanted to name it 'The Arch of Peace', over the main highway into the base.  Michael didn't know how   well the proposed name would ring with the General who presided on an Air Force Base with the Moto inscribed at the entrance 'Global Domination'.

Michael was concerned that the Warden and the BOP would be pissed as hell for missing their cut from his involvement with the project.

Joe ran Murder Incorporated out of his Dry Cleaning chain of stores all over Las Vegas.  His murder for hire enterprise was compromised but the feds could not make a case.  So they elected the Conspiracy indictment route with their stable of ready made witnesses for every occasion. Needless to say that the witnesses disappeared shortly after their testimony, but the harm was done.  Joe gave his wife his share of their home, vacation home on Lake Tahoe, cars and all his belongings.

He sold his Dry Cleaning chain to his wife and divorced her at the same time.  The feds could not touch his assets.  The wife was visiting him every other week like nothing happened.  Joe ran the Book at the Camp.  His body guards were in charge of the protection of the room.  A dozen of the meanest motherfuckers, most of them black, with Joe's personal entourage keeping an eye on the watchers.  This was in addition to the BOP at the Camp being on his payroll.

The night of the Mike Tyson fight with an unknown, the action was all on Mike Tyson.  Michael alone had in the false bottom of his closet, half a million dollars in cash to pay the certain winners.  Until that is Mike Tyson bit the ear of the challenger in the second round and was disqualified.  What to do with all that money running into millions in cash in their room, now that they did not have to pay anybody.  That night their room was guarded all afternoon and night by two BOP guards at all times and a contingent of bodyguards behind the closed door.  The door to their room looked wood.  Michael had Construction 4 insert a quarter inch steel plate between the wood panels, invisible on both sides, but resilient to the fiercest portable ram hoe.  The door had spring loaded hinges, like no other door in the dormitory, which automatically shut the room door with a thump, the sound reminiscing of the Mercedes Benz Turbodiesel car doors being shut.  Only the World Series, the Super Bowl and March Madness came close to the cash flow of the Mike Tyson fight night.

Joe's reputation saved the day.  No one dared to try anything.  They daydreamed and planned, but they came short on execution.  The faith of the pilot who had come at Camp after being arrested with a plane load of dope and a year and a day plea bargain sentence was still fresh in their mind.  A year and a day for a plane load of dope meant one thing only 'Ratting' up and down the seller and the   buyer's organization.  Joe got the word and the astronomical price he requested, dispatched a couple of his torpedoes and the pilot willing to talk, was unavailable to testify and all the charges to the co-conspirators were dropped.

Salvatore was a convicted bank robber who slept on the top bunk of Joe's bed and he was the chief enforcer and collector of losing bets. The collection part was rare, because the money was paid up front by the bettor and collected at any one of the Dry Cleaning stores. 'Mad dog Sal' as he was called, wanted to know how did the concerned women parents looked and how far were they willing to put out on their part for the project to go forward.

Dino, the Gambino family lawyer, saw clear sailing for the project to proceed forward.

"What about what Joe said?  Wouldn't the federal government, at the urging of the BOP, bring a case and a charge against me for 'freelancing'?"

"They will consider it.  They may even try to scare the daylights out of you.  But proceeding with it?  No.  It will be a lose - lose proposition for them.  They don't take cases like that.  They know you will take them to trial.  You did it before.  Just make sure you do not receive anything that could be traced back to you; because it will then become the focus in lieu of the deed itself.  Also make sure you do not spent any time on the 'Arch of Peace' project that could be interpreted as taking place during the hours you should be working for the government and getting paid by them.  If you make sure you document these two items, the government can go piss up a rope for all you care.  Haven't you noticed, the government will not go up against Public Opinion.  This is the only deterrent the Department of Justice will consider before they bring a case against you. 'How will it play in Peoria?' Thats all. Not whether you are guilty or innocent. They will use during the trial only select evidence against you and lose the ones which exonerate you. Their only question and concern is: If the media gets ahold of it in open court, how will the government look? In this case they will look bad and they will lose in the process an 'Institutional Need'.  It could also reopen, if the judge is sympathetic, your original case.  If the government is so vindictive to come after you for saving kids lives, how did the treated you during your original case.  No fear buddy.  You are safe.  I guarantee it, and I don't guarantee many things."

"Thanks Dino.  You are my kind of lawyer." Michael exclaimed.  "I only wished I had known you when the government indicted me."

"You would have won your case.  You would have collected triple damages.  You would have possibly collected on the seven million plus of all the Change Orders on all the other Contracts on which the government saved money.  I would have recused the Judge you had and the new Judge would have been sympathetic and knowing the dollar amount, would have come up with some sort of vehicle for punitive damages to make sure you collected.  I am a master at manipulation. The jury would have carried you out of the court room on their shoulders.  There would have been no verdict.  Innocent by Bench decision, before it even went to the jury.  I would only have had one request of you.  Stay out of my way and don't attempt any 'Hubris' while I am around."

Michael's fifth roommate was Ralph, a businessman out of Salt Lake City, Utah. He was a Mormon recently placed in their room by the BOP. Michael was assigned the task by the others to determine whether he was a 'Rat'. Michael befriended him.  Read his PSI and cleared him.  He was a sad case.  He owned with four others an Alternative Energy company.  They had built successfully a couple of geothermal power plants with profits in the stratosphere, when they decided to go public. A geothermal plant operates like any other power plant.  They produce steam and transfer it to condensing turbines to produce electricity. However, they do not use nuclear or fossil fuels to produce steam. Instead they rely on mother earth.  They drill down until they reach a pocket close to the earth core that heats the filtered rain water and converts it into steam. Because the rain water has gone through several layers of the earth to reach and collect in this underground lake, it is artesian; which means very pure.  Hawaii's potable water, for example is artesian water, having gone through layers of lava to collect underground and then pumped with well pumps back on the surface to be distributed by pipes to the public.  Since the water is artesian, the steam produced is very clean.  It is piped directly to the stream turbine with very few impurities and precipitate.  Since there is no fuel involved to produce the steam, the cost to produce power is very reasonable.  Cheaper than the one produced by hydroelectric means.  It is also very clean, since it does not involve combustion, which at its cleanest produces carbon dioxide and water vapor.

Another source of alternative energy is the potential of old dumps.  When the dump has filled with refuge, it is sealed with plastic and layers of clean dirt on top.  It is usually destined to become a park, a golf course or other public source of recreation.  The old refuge underneath decomposes and produces methane, which is a gas.  A power plant is built on top involving a turbine generator being   fueled by this methane and produces power directly without having to go the steam route. The only draw back is that it involves combustion which generates as any organic combustion, carbon dioxide and water.

Naturally, there was a bidding war on who would buy the Alternative Energy Company which from their financial statement looked like a gold mine.  The five partners had to make a hard decision.  Sell or maintain ownership and keep working like Trojan horses.  They voted to sell because they were facing a hostile takeover anyway from the high bidder, Portland Electric, who were bound and determined to acquire the company by any means.  They were going to operate the company themselves.  They had no need of the expertise of the present owners.  The five partners got their money and gave the keys to Portland Electric.

Needless to say Portland Electric through mismanagement made all the projects already in the books losers.  The newly acquired company's bottom line was heading South.  Instead of contacting the five owners for advise, Portland Electric used the newly acquired Alternative Energy Company as the dumping ground for all their losses in all of their other divisions including the parent company.  At the end of the year they went to the government and said that they were defrauded, because the five owners failed to disclose to them that there was a pending law suit which was ongoing and costing them an armload in legal fees.

The Department of Justice asked Ralph, who was the spokesman of the group, why the pending law suit was never disclosed to Portland Electric at the onset. Ralph explained that the pending law suit was nothing more than a Termination for Convenience. A municipality had contracted with them to build a power plant in a park which used to be a dump. The people thought the power plant would be an eye sore and did not want it in the new park. They were threatening to start recall proceedings for the Mayor and the City Council. The Mayor and the City Council ordered the City Manager to cancel the project. Public Works issued a Termination for Convenience Notice to the Alternative Energy Company. The Contract stipulated that in a case of Termination for Convenience, the Owner, in this case the municipality, would be required to reimburse the Alternative Energy Company of all their costs and expense up to the issue date of The Termination for Convenience letter. The reason they did not include it in the sale prospectus was that it was income instead of liability and they had not calculated the revenue as of the date of the sale. How did it turn into a lawsuit was beyond him.

The government gathered the five partners and informed them that they were convening a grand jury and were proceeding with an indictment. They felt they had done nothing wrong, so they had not hired an attorney. Now with the indictment looming, they hired a law firm in a hurry. The law firm they hired was of the type that had a Motto for their white collar criminals: 'Bleed them and Plead them'. They never studied the case. Instead they collected their fee up front from the five partners and went to the government and negotiated from a position of inferior knowledge. They went back to their clients and presented the government offer of two years each and one hundred big ones from each. If the government proceeded with the indictment, based on the amount of money involved, they could go to trial; however, if the government prevailed, which they did on 97% of their cases according to the statistics, they would be asking for millions and twenty years in jail for each.

The fear of the unknown and their attorneys recommendation tipped the scale for all five and they pled guilty. One of the lawyers, feeling guilty over the whole thing, started reading their case after the fact. He called his partners in a meeting and laid out for them the facts of the case. They did not discuss their wrong doing and the disservice they had done for their clients, instead they discussed how they may profit further from the case. They approached Portland Electric and disclosed to them that they had called 'Wolf' to the government where there was a 'golden goose' in its place. How their clients were suffering and how the government reacted towards the ones that called 'Fire' where none existed. To make a long story short Portland Electric sold the Alternative Energy to the Law Firm for a dollar.

The law partners asked for a meeting with their clients, the old Alternate Energy five partners. It was convenient that all were serving their sentences in the same place. 'Camp Snoopy'. They explained to them that the government did not disclose to them all the documents during discovery, so they were steered towards a wrong conclusion regarding the case. They wanted their help to go after the Municipality which issued the Termination for Convenience letter. Because when the Municipality found out that Portland Electric bought the Alternative Energy Company, they remained quiet. When Portland Electric approached them to inquiry the status of the Contract, they lied and said they Terminated the Contract for Default because the Alternative Energy was so far behind schedule. They were not going to pursue the Termination for Default damages they incurred. However, if they had to spent any more time on this issue, they were threatening to sue Portland Electric.

The Law firm told the ex Alternative Energy Company partners, that they were given the company by Portland Electric in lieu of residual legal fees they were owed. The money they were going to collect from the Municipality would serve as their investment capital to reopen the company with all five of the previous partners at the helm. Only now they would be 10% vested, each and the Law firm will hold the remaining stock. That meant that all they had to do was to convince one partner to vote with them. Ralph helped them and they collected over 5 million in Liquidated Damages from the Municipality under threat that they were going to go to the government and complain that the Municipality and its duplicity was the cause of the perils suffered by their clients due to Portland Electric relying on the Municipality's presentations which precipitated them going to the federal government for relief, who in turn reacted with the threat of an indictment. They convinced the Municipality that they were the lynch pin which cascaded the whole mess. Now the five partners were assured of a job when they got out. They were all happy and ready to put the whole thing behind them, because according to their attorneys they had no recourse of going back to the government, once they pled guilty.

This is the short version story of the 'Book Room' and the 'Men of Respect'.

The next day, after work, Michael went to see Steve at the Air Force warehouse and materials yard. The Air Force sergeant's wife must have talked his ears off last night, because he was very friendly and well aware of what Michael was looking for.

"Let's go to the surplus yard and have a look around." Steve suggested.

Michael hopped onto the sergeant's Jeep and headed for the Air Force surplus yard. It resembled a junk yard. There were material there from before the second World War. Michael spotted what he was looking for immediately. The skeleton of an old storage depot. The only problem was that every steel member was circular in shape. He imagined two structural members welded together and measured the base of their arch. One hundred feet. The apex was well over forty. He decided to design the overpass around these four structural members. He tagged them together with some more secondary structural pieces, like beams, grating for the steps and a stack of almost new and shinny checkered solid plate for the overpass floor. There were numerous forty foot length beams to be used as support structure for the overpass floor and the construction of a truss from the overpass floor to the arch steel members above. Steve put his John Henry on the tags; all the material destined to be used for a fictitious project   whose number he scribbled. There was rebar in the surplus yard to build a whole new Base. Michael selected and tagged the number 5, because it was the most available, less rusted and easier to bend in order to make the desired reinforced steel cages for the overpass bridge buttresses.

Michael made a list of the material he had selected and tagged, including their length and size. The lumber for the concrete forms, he didn't bother to tag, it was so much of it in the yard. He located a pile of plywood with distinct wood grain which he thought would give an excellent outside concrete finish to the buttresses.

Michael went back to the Camp. He went to his office on Saturday and started engineering and drafting the pedestrian overpass based on the surplus material in his notes. He also made steel fabrication Drawings. He wanted all the pieces pre-fabricated in order to cut down on the actual onsite time for construction.

Monday morning Michael's first stop was at the Air Rescue Building which was under construction by a combined work force of Camp inmates and the Air Force Red Horse brigade. It was the General's pet project and Michael was sure to find him there. The General had long since had forgiven Michael for missing the ground breaking ceremony. He found out from the Warden that it was out of Michael's hands due to unfairly having been assigned by Krupp, a BOP guard, clean up duties of the stairway from the Mess Hall dining room to the basement and the CMS offices.

Michael asked the General to step into the air conditioned field office of the Air Rescue Building construction site where he explained to him how he was contacted by the parents at the Base after hours and his reconnaissance at the Air Force surplus material yard. He unrolled the Drawings and explained how he had prepared them over the weekend. Michael explained that he could get inmates from Construction 4 to donate a Saturday of labor to build the buttresses, even if he had to pay them out of his own pocket.

The General was no dummy; how else he got to be a General. He immediately saw the PR and good will the project would attach to his name. He immediately embraced the project as his own. He made the Red Horse prefabricate, on their own time, all the steelwork. The buttresses were built the following Saturday under Michael's supervision by the Red Horse airmen. The parents, the Base women that is, prepared a feast and a party after the work was done, which Michael, the guest of honor, declined to participate with the General as his witness.

On Monday after the 'Arch of Peace' was erected, Michael was on the call out to the SIS office. He anticipated the BOP's move and discussed it in detail with his roommate and mentor Dino, the Gambino family lawyer. He had with him affidavits from all the Base ladies that their meetings took place after working hours. He had signed, by whoever guards were on duty at the time, affidavits that he worked in his office during weekends preparing Drawings and writing specifications for the overpass. He had an affidavit signed by the General and countersigned by over one hundred women that he did not participate at the party thrown after the completion of the project. He made copies of all that paperwork folded it safely into his back pocket on his way to see 'wide glide' at her SIS lair.

The door to the SIS was held open by a wedge of wood when he arrived. No psychological games this time. Lieutenant Kyle avoided talking about their impending daily meetings during their shower scene at six thirty in the morning and Michael said nothing about it in turn.

"I drove under the Arch of your Triumph this morning on the way to work." Lieutenant Kyle said with a smile. Her eyes and mouth, however, were not smiling. "Are you going to deny that it's your doing?"

"I believe it was team effort." Michael said smiling also.

"That may be, but the project would not have gotten off the ground without your initiative, engineering and supervision of the construction. The Warden is very angry. He was stuck in traffic on Saturday after his golf game at the Base because a crane was lifting in place the pedestrian overpass. The Airmen stopping the traffic thanked him for building it for their children."

"I hope he accepted the Base personnel thanks gracefully." Michael said ironically, biting his tongue to prevent it straying into the uncharted, dangerous waters associated with 'Hubris'.

"He would have, if he was not taken by total surprise. He summoned me and asked me to bring another charge against you. It would give me great pleasure to do, because it would mean that you would be with us for a long time…"

"What's the charge?" Michael cut off her gloating.

"Well, let's see. I drafted a number of reasons. I'll let you to take your pick."

"I will demand a hearing in front of a Las Vegas federal judge. I will appoint as my lawyer my roommate Dino."

"It's within your constitutional rights to do so." Lieutenant Kyle added bitterly. "However, I was hopping to avoid all that ugliness and instead reach a negotiated settlement between the two of us. How about a year and a day added to your sentence sounds to you?"

"I refuse your offer. I will instead take the BOP to trial."

"Remember what happened the last time you made this decision?"

"This time will be different." Michael insisted with emphasis. "This time I will be in charge of my case and destiny. This time my attorney will be working on my behalf..."

"Let's cut through the chase. What's you got? Consider this a moot court. If you can convince me. I will tell the Warden that I refuse to bring charges against you. If he insists, I will be your advocate and you may call me as a witness."

Michael laid out his case as Dino had advised him. He pulled the wad of affidavits from his back pocket and handed them to her. She took her time reading them. Michael sat quietly waiting for her verdict.

"You are pretty smart." She admitted. "I will keep these as an attachment to my report and advise the Warden that we have no case against you. Think of some way to make it up to him; the embarrassment he felt waiting in the traffic jam and the money he lost for your services to the Air Force."

"Do you know of a way to accomplish this? I am on your side. Do you have kids Teresa? Think of them trying to dodge the traffic to get to school. The poor parents at the Base could not afford what the Warden would be charging them for my time..."

"I believe I do." Lieutenant Kyle cut him off, smiling cryptically. "The Warden has just purchased a Motel 6 in town and he intends to convert it into a halfway house. He is reluctant to ask for your help because it is something personal and   neither does it involve the Camp nor the Base. Maybe you may make the first move and offer your assistance..."

"Thank you Teresa. We make a good team. If only..." Michael left the last part unsaid. "Am I free to go?"

She nodded in the affirmative and Michael got up. The door to the SIS was still open. It had been left open the whole time he was in the room. The 'roll up' squad of goons which was scheduled to materialize to take him away, were still waiting for Lieutenant Kyle's signal telephone call. He did not care if he had been seen by inmates in the SIS room.  They already knew that he was in the 'callout' to be at the SIS.  The Camp was buzzing already with the 'Arch of Peace' saga.

# CHAPTER 25

## The Cadre Program

The 'call - out' stated that Michael was to see the Unit Manager at 9:00 AM.  The Unit Manager, he knew, was in charge of all the councilors which Michael had avoided like the plague.  They were all black and extremely prejudiced towards all white inmates. Asking them for advice was a non issue.  They would invariably try to give the wrong advise, always verbally, so you could not pin them down. They were uneducated, GED or worse and also very lazy.  Michael considered that if not for the BOP they would be on welfare.  They made a point to talk jive to white inmates so someone could only understand half of what they were saying.  The scuttlebutt was that the female counselors were game for a roll of quarters.  They looked and smelled repulsive.

The unit manager was white.  Michael felt welcome and sensed he was well liked before he even knocked on the door.

"Sit down." He said with a smile on his face. " My name is George White. I happened to read your PSI."  This was the report prepared by the probation department in Hawaii upon Michael's conviction. "You are a Chemical Engineer.  My father-in-law was a Chemical Engineer.  The nicest guy I ever met in my life."

Michael relaxed.  The guy appeared on the level.  He smiled encouragingly, for the fellow to keep talking.

"So, I took an interest in you as soon as I found out you were a Chemical Engineer, also. I read your PSI. I could not believe what a bullshit charge you got.  In my twenty years in the system, I've never read so much baloney.  I kept reading and reading and could not believe what I was reading.  As far as I am concerned, you do not belong belong in prison.  You should never have been indicted to begin with; nor convicted and sentenced on top of it.  Thirty three months.  Hard to believe.  I know bank robbers, drug dealers and murderers who got less.  You must have pissed off somebody big.  You must have stepped on somebody's toes.  There is no other explanation I can see.  Then, I don't understand the judge.  He literally threw the book at you.  What have you done to him?"

Michael's ears were ringing, echoing on what he had just heard.

"I feel guilty myself to be part of it."  George White continued.  "I hope you get a chance sometime, down the road to stick it to those bastards.  If it is any consolation, in the meantime, I will try everything within my power to get you out of here."

George White went on to explain the CADRE program.  It was a work release program, handled directly by the BOP for qualified inmates with no violence in their record.  For someone with Michael's qualifications, he should have no problem finding a job in the government sector and spend his sentence working and living at home.

Michael explained to him that all the case mangers were black.  Several of his friends had tried for the CADRE program, but the paperwork was never processed.  They happened to be all white.  He had his doubts if he would not be facing a similar fate.

"I know what you mean."  He said thoughtfully.  "Isn't it funny you had to come to prison to get discriminated against?  Don't worry though.  I will make sure your case manager processes your paperwork and submits it as soon as humanly possible.  I, on the other hand, will promote your talents to various government agencies.  I got contacts with some influence.  Where were you planning to go from here?  Have you thought about it? Are you going back to Hawaii?"

"No. I am not.  My wife has relocated to the Phoenix area.  Specifically, Scottsdale.  I plan to apply to be released there."

He began to shuffle some paperwork on his desk.

"Here it is!" He finally exclaimed. A CADRE request just happened to reach my desk only this morning. The Department of Energy, DOE, is looking for a Chemical Engineer for their Gilbert office. Gilbert is a small town in the Phoenix Metro area. It's in the East valley just South East of Scottsdale where your wife lives. They are paying $400.00 a month and $35.00 a day per diem. This means that you can live at home and they will pay you $35.00 a day, seven days a week, against your room and board. It seems a little low to me. But they say at the bottom that the fee and rates are negotiable."

"I am very much interested." Michael heard himself say, jumping at the opportunity.

"I'll tell you what. Go and write for me a Resume and I will personally make the arrangements." George said in parting.

Michael went to his room and a few minutes later returned with his Resume in hand. The Unit Manager read it and told Michael that it was very impressive. He made some calls with his back turned to Michael. He went to his FAX machine while his telephone was left off the hook on his desk, still connected to whoever he was calling. He returned to his desk and continued his telephone conversation. He hang up and smiled.

"You got the job." He announced to Michael. "In less than a week we will receive their written confirmation. A done deal before you even filled an application. Go see your case manager with a clear heart. No case manager can derail this; it is sawn tighter than the Gordian knot."

Michael left the Unit Manager's office elated. He went straight to his case manager's door and knocked politely. No response. He knocked again harder. Still nothing. Michael tried the door knob. It turned. The door was unlocked. The case manager, a fat black man was laying on his desk chair snoring. Michael quietly closed the door and went to the Unit Manager's office and told him. George got out of his chair and stormed to the case managers office.  He slammed a book on his desk waking him up.  He went on to explain what he needed him to do.  A release request to Phoenix, and an application to the DOE request for a CADRE position.  He then left Michael alone with the case manager.

"You will be replacing someone who retired," were the first words out of his case manager's mouth, "he was a Chemical Engineer making $70,000.00 a year.  What makes you think you are qualified for the job."

"I am a Registered Professional Chemical Engineer while he was not.  As to the money basis, he was making $70,000.00 a year after thirty years on the job; a year ago I was making $250,000.00 a year plus a bonus based on the profit sharing.  For your information that's over $5,000 a week.  At $100.00 a week the DOE is offering me, they are getting quite a bargain.  Don't you agree?"  Michael replied matter of factly.  "If you want to verify my statements, it's all there in my PSI and the DOE job advertisement.   Please note that they could not find a qualified candidate from the outside for over two years.  That was the reasoning for trying the CADRE route."

The case manager was speechless.  He gave Michael the relocation application and the CADRE application for the DOE job.  Michael filled them both out, right there in the case manager's office and handed them back to him.

"It's a done deal."  Michael continued.  "My wife has relocated from Honolulu, Hawaii and is now residing in Scottsdale, Arizona.  Just process the paperwork so they catch up with our verbal agreement. You will be receiving confirmation of what I am telling you in less than a week.   My agreement with the DOE is something like home confinement, but with relative freedom as long as I showed up for work at the DOE office, located in Gilbert, Arizona, five days a week Monday through Friday.  They indicated that their per diem rate was thirty five dollars a day, seven days a week.  The government is saving money and demonstrating good will for advertising, by giving someone a second chance. Win-win situation all the way around."

"What do you need me then?  Why is not George White processing the paperwork?"

"I don't know and I will not venture into the internal politics of the BOP. There are however a couple of outstanding issues. The first is that I have not been approved to reside in Arizona.  The second is we are in negotiations about daily transportation to and from the DOE facility. I have requested a government issue vehicle to use, gas card and maintenance expenses.  Their position was that I was on my own to figure a way to solve the transportation issue.  I had offered the option of one of their employees living in Scottsdale to give me a ride.  They turned it down.  I am waiting to hear from them on my latest request for a government issue vehicle.  Please let me know as soon as you hear from them.  It will probably be a counter offer of some sort, probably in the form of vehicle allowance."

On that note, Michael got up and left the case manager's office.

Michael relayed the news of the CADRE program to his wife during their weekend visit.  When he told her about about the options he had suggested to the DOE, she exploded.

"Choices!"  Michael's wife complained.  "You give the government options and choices to make a decision on, you know what's going to happen..."

"What?"

"Nothing. That's what. They will sit for ever pondering and considering. You might as well kiss the Phoenix area CADRE good by."

Michel shook his head disagreeing. "They want me bad.  They had been unable to fill the position after two years of searching.  Look at the money they'd be saving.  Where are they going to find a Chemical Engineer with experience in air and water pollution?  When they read my Resume that I had invented the scrubber and verified my patent, George White, the Unit Manager, told me that they were drooling, wanting me too start yesterday.  The only way the government can get someone of my caliber to work for them, it's to put him in prison.  Captive talent.  Look how fast they approved me.  They Faxed documents back and forth.  When was the last time the government Faxed anything?"

Michael had a point, his wife acknowledged.  This bought him some grace time with his wife, who was staying on top of it; anxious for further developments.

The other stumbling block was the state of Arizona.  Michael was a Hawaii resident.  In order to be able to work in the Phoenix area, he had to be approved for relocation by the state of Arizona.  His papers were expedited by the BOP together with a glowing report on the work he was doing at Camp and the Air Force Base.  The DOE in turn wrote to the state of Arizona a letter, similar to the one written by the BOP, as a 'friend of the court'.  Reading all that plus Michael's PSI, the state clerk must have been wondering what was Michael doing in prison, because the state of Arizona wrote a letter to the BOP asking exactly that.  The Unit Manager had allowed Michael to read all the pertinent correspondence.  The answer by the BOP was a no answer.  They claimed they had nothing to do with Michael's conviction.  They suggested they write to the Department of Justice and the Hawaii sentencing judge for answers to their question.  Michael read the answer provided by the Department of Justice.  It basically said that Michael had done nothing wrong other than administrative wrong doings which could be up to interpretation.  Michael's interpretation was viewed wrong, at the time.  Since he was sentenced, the Supreme Court had overturned the government's interpretation.  Michael by all rights he should be a free man, but Nellis Air Force Base and the Camp have an 'Institutional Need' of his services.  Michael's stay should be viewed as 'an attitude adjustment', for his extreme arrogance and the monetary damage he has caused the government over the years, rather than punishment for something that he had done wrong.

The parole officer who talked to Michael's wife, told her that the state of Arizona had approved her husband's relocation immediately. He even commented on the speed by which the government processed her husband's application. He had not seen that before. Especially, not when the prisoner had over a year still to serve on his sentence.

Michael's wife informed Michael of all that during the next visit.

"The only thing remaining, as far as I can tell, is transportation to and from the DOE facility." She added,

Michael was waiting all week reading the 'call out' daily to find out when was he supposed to see his case manager. The notice was finally on the Friday's 'call out'. It had to be regarding the DOE response to his request, he thought. The CADRE was hanging in the balance. Michael waited with baited breath till 1:30 PM for his appointment.

"Well...?" Michael asked his case manager. "Yeah or Nah?"

"I don't know." Was the reply.

"Isn't this meeting about my CADRE?"

"Yes it is. I need your signature of approval on something." He said enigmatically.

"More signatures..." Michael protested. "I thought I had signed all the paperwork the DOE had sent."

"Well, here is some more."

He handed Michael a single page document with a place to sign at the bottom. The letterhead was not the now familiar DOE, but one of the VA, the return address was Dallas, Texas.

"What the hell!" Michael blurted with his pen poised in mid air. "That's not the Phoenix CADRE!"

"No. It is not." His case manager said reluctantly. "We have not heard from the DOE, so I thought I'd line up something else, just in case the DOE deal falls through."

"Dallas, Texas?" Was the only thing Michael could think of saying.

"Well, they sent us an inquiry. They plan to expand and renovate the Veterans Hospital in Dallas, Texas. They are looking for a construction engineer to use as a liaison between the General Contractor and themselves..."

"Could I take a look at the VA inquiry?" Michael asked.

The case manager passed Michael the job notice and advertisement. The job description fit him to a tee. But so did the job for the DOE in Phoenix. Actually, he felt overqualified for the one in Dallas which was paying more; like eight hundred per month and fifty bucks per diem for food alone, because they were providing free housing at the premises as an option. But then again Michael would save a shitload of money for the government riding herd on the General Contractor and his subcontractors.

"Has anyone told them about me?" Michael asked, handing back the job advertisement flyer.

"The Warden." The case manager said avoiding to give details. Michael knew that getting information out of him would be like pulling teeth. He stood up and returned the acceptance paper for the job with the VA, unsigned.

"Aren't you going to sign it?" The case manager asked Michael, worried.

"No. I am not going to Dallas, Texas."

"That's your choice of course. But I must warn you. If the Phoenix CADRE falls through, you are saying here for the duration of your sentence."

"So be it." Michael said resignedly. "I cannot ask my wife to relocate a thousand miles away."

"What can I do to change your mind?" The case manager asked staring at him and the acceptance letter, Michael had dropped on his desk, unsigned.

"Level with me...for starters."

The case manager pulled a two page letter from Michael's file and handed it to him wordlessly. Michael sat down and started reading. It was a letter form the Warden to the VA Hospital administrator about Michael. It appeared that the two men knew each other well. The guy in Dallas was in a bind and the Warden was telling him about Michael in the most complimentary terms. "...of course you realize that the individual is the key player to our construction program here at Nellis.", Michael read at the bottom of the first page. "Losing an inmate of that caliber, will certainly set our own construction program back. Accordingly, we must negotiate some sort of equity...", Michael turned the second page to keep on reading. Before he had a chance, his case manager snatched the whole thing out of Michael's hands.

"You can't read the rest." He simply said.

"But why? The Warden says some nice things about me. I was even going to ask you for a copy."

"You got to be kidding. Isn't enough that the letter is in your file?"

Michael smiled. He would have loved to read the rest of it. It looked like some kind of a deal in the works, between the Warden and his old buddy at the VA, with Michael being the commodity traded. Michael made a move towards the door.

"Aren't you going to sign?" His case manager stopped him.

"Let me think about it over the weekend." Michael replied. "My wife is coming for a visit this weekend. I don't want to make a decision on my own, before talking it over with her."

"Monday then!" His case manager waved the typed acceptance, setting it on top of Michael's file.

Michael's wife was furious. "Why did you have to put conditions, that you will need transportation to and from the workplace. Now you got the whole deal soured. Mark my words. You will end up in Dallas."

"How could that be? I haven't signed the acceptance letter for Dallas."

"They will ship you. You got no choice."

"Hold on a second. I don't agree. With the CADRE program you have a choice. You either agree to go or you stay where you are. They cannot force you to go to work where you don't want to. Otherwise, it's slavery. And for your information slavery was abolished sometime ago."

"All right then you are staying right where you are."

"I believe the DOE in Gilbert will come through."

The Unit Manager had a heart attack two weeks from the date of Michael's signing of the DOE acceptance application. In less than a month, he had to leave the BOP for good, because they did not want the liability of him having a second heart attack and blaming work related stress. He was forced to take early retirement. Michael had lost the sole ally to his cause. No more Faxes circumventing the bureaucracy. He simply had to wait to hear from his case manager the DOE response to his request for transportation. No one had been assigned as the new Unit Manager. George White was still listed in name only, but he was unavailable. He never came back after his heart attack.

Michael did not go to his case manager's office on Monday and he avoided him all day. A week later he was in the 'call - out' sheet to see him. This he could not avoid. His case manager was black, so was the

Warden. Blacks ran the prisons, both as staff and as inmates. Not so much at FPC Nellis which was in the category of one of the lowest security risk institutions in the country. At Nellis there was predominately white female staff, for the BOP to meet the federal regulations quota. Michael discovered via insatiable reading that there were more blacks in prison than black college graduates in the country. He would not have believed this statistic a year ago on the outside. He still was reluctant to go and face the music. A hack came to his office and informed Michael that his case officer was looking for him. He had no alternative. He knocked and opened the door to his case manager's office. He was prepared for a confrontation.

"I have some good news and some bad news." The case manager said with no preamble. "Which one do you want first?"

"Let's start with the good news." Michael said hurriedly. He was surprised that his case manager was not sitting there with the VA acceptance document trying to force a pen in his hand to sign.

"Your Phoenix CADRE came through. They Faxed me yesterday evening a reply to your request for transportation. They checked the box that they will provide it and initialed a signature next to it. There is no doubt. They wanted to make sure that you noticed they accepted your terms. You won."

"Hey! That's great!" Michael exclaimed. "I guess I don't have to consider the Dallas CADRE then." Michael said cautiously.

"I guess you don't." He said grinning like a cat who swallowed the canary. He knew something that was not telling Michael and his smugness started to annoy him.

"What are the bad news?" Michael inquired with his fingers crossed.

"I am afraid the whole CADRE may be a moot point." His case manager said. "That's the bad news." He said handing Michael a single piece of paper. It looked like a Memorandum form the National BOP containing a single six line paragraph.  Michael read silently, gloom settling on his face.  The order from the National BOP was effective today.  They were canceling handling of the CADRE programs.  The CADRE program would remain, but it would be henceforth administered directly by the Department of Justice; i.e. the district Federal Judge and the Prosecutor.  Michael immediately made the connection.  The CADRE program would be used as a carrot to induce more plea bargains.

Michael called his wife as soon as he left the case manager's office.  She broke down crying.  He didn't know what to do or tell her, other that hang up and let her be for a while.

# CHAPTER 26

## The A-10 Thunderbolt Affair

He was waiting outside the locked CMS offices. He was a young man not yet out of his teens. But then again Michael had a hard time guesstimating the age of Mexican nationals. They looked like kids to him. He unlocked the main door ignoring the waiting Mexican. He unlocked the drafting room and left the door open to air it out. The Mexican was waiting outside the fortress like door of his office. He was studying the label on the side of the door designating it as the office of the Camp and Base Engineer with Michael's name in the slot underneath.

"Are you looking for me?" Michael inquired.

"I am, if you are the person under the title." He said pointing with his chin at Michael's name.

"Bingo!" Was Michael's response. "What can I do for you?"

"I came over to apply for the position as your assistant." Was the curt reply.

Michael recalled that he had placed a small notice on the bulletin board for an assistant. Joey Scala, his present assistant was due to depart for a halfway house within a week. Michael was too busy to continue doing what he was doing without an assistant. He recalled that his notice in search of one, included that it was mandatory for any applicant to have engineering and/or architectural knowledge. Preferably, a College degree and some on hand experience. The Mexican was the first to apply.

"Why don't you wait at the bottom of the stairway." Michael said. "My current assistant should be here momentarily. I want him to be present during the interview. He would be the best to explain the scope of work and your duties, since he has been doing it for a year now. By the way, what's your name? I have to admit that I have not seen you around."

"My name is Julio and I arrived a couple of days ago."

"Hold on." Michael cautioned him. "Aren't you still in orientation? You have to complete the orientation before being assigned to a job."

"Orientation, so far is a joke. If I wait a couple of weeks, the job would be gone to someone else. Plus I don't want to rely on the BOP to assign me a job. I heard you have such juice at the Camp that if you want me as your assistance, your word is the law with the BOP. No one will say no to you."

Michael started studying the Mexican with some interest. He sure was a go getter. Michael's kind of man. He noticed his two bodyguards had suddenly materialized and have taken up position to intervene, should Michael was of a mind to signal them. Julio noticed the two swarthy inmates looking at Michael and instantly understood that he was skating on thin ice.

"I was a junior at UCLA in Mechanical Engineering before I was kidnapped..." He added to reinforce his qualifications for the job.

Michael heard him, but he could not get passed the trigger word 'kidnapped'. However, he still had to dial the four numbers to the cypher lock of his door and he certainly did not want a witness. 'Wide glide' would have his balls for breakfast with her coffee, he thought, if he did. No one but her and him knew the number. He wanted to keep it this way.

"Why don't you go to the bottom of the stairway like I have asked you before he said."

Instantly, Michael's Italian bodyguards seized Julio by each arm and he was escorted to where he was told to wait. Michael dialed in the number in the cypher lock and entered his office. 'Kidnapped', he mused. He couldn't wait to hear the full explanation.

He heard noise of the draftsmen reporting for work right on time as a group. He could set his watch with their promptness. They had better. They knew Michael would already be in the office, early, as always. Their monthly bonus depended on their promptness, among other things which Michael kept track and submitted to Phill Rolfs, the BOP supervisor, before the end of the month a circled number next to their name, as their monthly bonus which was never altered. Their assignments for the day were waiting for them on their drafting tables, together with the red marked Drawings on which Michael had bled on late yesterday afternoon. Fifteen minutes passed the reporting time, Joey Scala showed up suffering from  the same disease that effects seniors in High School at the end of the semester. He was followed by Julio with the body guards bringing up the rear. Michael signaled to the body guards that it was alright and that they were free to go.

"Sup Boss?"  Joey asked.  "Who is the FNG, fucking new guy?"  He pointed to Julio who was waiting standing, visibly subdued.

"We are about to find out." Michael said. "So far I have found out that his name is Julio. He's been with us a couple of days. He is applying for the job as my assistant. His qualifications are that he was junior in Mechanical Engineering at UCLA, before he was kidnapped. Have I got the jest of it right Julio?"

Julio nodded in the affirmative.

"Let's start with the 'kidnapped' part." Joey started. "Did I hear this right? Who kidnapped you?"

"The U.S. Government." Julio replied.

"The U.S. Government." Joey repeated. "What did you do? I mean what was the indictment for? Did you go to trial? How long is your sentence?" "I was never indicted." Julio replied. "As for the rest...they are a moot point." "Why are you here then?" Was Joey's logical question.

"It was never explained to me.  I was just whisked, strapped with a monitor  and brought in this place."  Julio raised his right pants leg to show his ankle monitor.

Michael was thinking back to the 'Nigerian Nightmare', he had first hand knowledge.  The tale so far was a mirror image of that, sans the beatings and the addition of the ankle monitor.

"Let's start from the beginning."  Michael admonished.  "Staring with your full name and a detail description of what took place, before the kidnapping to being here."

"My full name is Julio Escobar.  I am a Colombian national.  I came over to the U.S. with a Colombian passport to study Mechanical Engineering at UCLA.  I   paid and am paying my own way.  I am not at the top of the class, but I am not flunking out either.  No grade lower than a 'C'.  I am currently a Junior.  Last Saturday I was at a party.  A typical UCLA party as parties go.  A beer keg and drugs in the bathrooms.  I have been invited and attended a number of parties like this, in the past.  Others go for the booze, others for the drugs, others for the girls, others for all three.  I go strictly because of the girls.  Its the only place I have time to socialize, because of the academic load I am carrying.  Last Saturday, around 1:30 AM, the feds wearing baklavas and waving guns, broke the door down with a ram hoe and arrested everyone.  They put them in a van, except me.  They blindfolded me and put me in the back seat of a government sedan with two fellows on either side.  They put me in a single cell somewhere in LA, I couldn't tell you where.  They took all my personal belongings, like my Rolex 18 carat gold President, clothes, shoes and gave me khakis and flip flops instead.  I did not get to make a phone call or nothing.  They said I was not a U.S. citizen, so I had nothing coming. They arraigned me, with no lawyer on my side. Everyone seemed to be in the know, including the judge, except me. Present at my arraignment were all sorts of government agencies talking to the judge in front of the bench so I could not hear. At the end of the arraignment hearing the judge advised me that I was being held as a Material Witness. Evidently, the government convinced the judge that I knew where the booze, because some of the girls at the party were not twenty one, and the drugs had come from. The government kidnapped me and could hold me, according to the judge for a year. They brought me here at Nellis AFB, which was the first place I could call my family and tell them what happened. My uncle is pissed as hell. I wouldn't put it passed him if he does not get his army of faithful to raid this place."

"Do you know who his uncle is?" Joey leaned and whispered in Michael's ear.

"I have no idea.", Michael replied.

"Pablo Escobar."

"So…It still does not ring a bell…"

"The head of the Colombian Medellin Cartel. He is the kingpin and responsible for 90% of the drugs coming into the United Sates." Joey whispered to Michael with fear mixed with reverence. "He is worth thirty billion, give or take. He has thousands of armed soldiers under his command. The U. S. government has a hard on for him. They are trying to extradite him or lure him into U. S. soil and arrest him."

Julio must have caught the gist of their conversation, because he said. "I am not a material witness, I am a hostage of the U.S. Government."

"What happened to the rest of the party goers who were arrested?" Michael asked.

"They kept them overnight and let them go the next day."

"Has anyone from the government talked to you?  Asked you questions about the party?"

"To me personally, no.  However they lied to the judge and said they did. They claimed that it was an on going investigation.  Lies...lies...lies!"

"At any rate," Michael concluded, "it looks like you will be in the system for a year..."

"You wanna bet?  I will be out before the end of the month." Julio said with confidence.

"Dum Spiro Spero." - While I breath I hope, - Michael said. "In the mean time Joey Scala will show you the ropes.  Tell the person in charge at the next orientation that the Engineer wants you at Construction 4."

Julio must have done as he was told because the next day he was on the 'call -out' to report to the Camp Engineer at Construction 4.  Joey Scala took him under his wing and started showing him what he was supposed to be doing.  Julio was smart and an eager worker.  He told Joey that he was fortunate to land at Nellis and be working in the engineering and construction of all the projects at Camp and on Base.  It was like he skipped his senior year and ended at the Graduate School.

A small notice appeared in the Las Vegas Review - Journal on Thursday April 15 stating that an airplane, an A-10 Thunderbolt disappeared from Nellis Air Force Base with four nuclear bombs aboard.  The search for the warplane was joined by a SR-71 'Blackbird', a spy plane that carries a highly sensitive radar.  The SR71 is capable of flying three times the speed of sound and high enough that the pilots can see the curvature of the Earth.  In the meantime, the Air Force had sent ground teams into the snow covered remote terrain over the Rocky Mountains for the missing pilot who may have bailed out.  However, the emergency beacon for both the plane and the pilot have remained silent immediately after the take off, indicating that they have been disabled.

An updated version of the same notice, the next day reported that no crash has been reported.  In an updated version of the neighborhood cop going door-todoor looking for a lost child, Air Force officials were checking all potential landing spots in the Southwest in their search for the missing warplane and its pilot.  In the meantime ground searchers braved winds, knee deep snow and cold temperatures as they continued to scour the mountains southwest of Vail.

A third version of the notice, a couple of days later announced that radar tracking and visual sightings of a gray plane, led authorities to Colorado, where the Air Force, Civil Air Patrol, Air National Guard and other agencies have taken up the search in the area around New York Mountain, a 12,500 foot peak about 15 miles southwest of Vail.  The area however, would have been 800 miles off Captain Craig Button's course.  One story circulating at local bars and restaurants had the pilot stopping in, ordering a bologna sandwich to go, and then hitch-hiking East on Interstate 70.

The facts, as far as Michael could ascertain were as follows.  Captain Creg Button, age 32, stationed at Nellis Air Force Base and his A-10 warplane with four nuclear bombs aboard disappeared on April 2 during a training exercise out of Davis - Mothan Air Force Base in Tucson, Arizona.  According to eye witnesses on the ground, he left the exercise and was last seen heading South.

"Do I see your uncle's handwriting on this saga?" Michael asked Julio.

"I was not told." Julio answered.  "It is something though that he would dream of.

You hold my nephew hostage.  I will hold your warplane hostage."

*   *   *   *

Julio did not show up for work the next day.  Michael was told that he was picked up by a private car late last night and was whisked way. Two weeks later, after an anonymous tip, the A-10 was found intact with all four nuclear bombs aboard, in an abandoned air field outside of Medellin, Colombia, of all places and was flown back by a U.S. Air Force crew, back to Nellis.  None of the above was reported by the Las Vegas Review - Journal.  The A-10 warplane story never appeared in print again.  The whereabouts of Captain Creg Button remain unknown. Three months later, on December 2, Pablo Escobar's stronghold, while celebrating his 44th birthday, was attacked by a Columbian police and military force, joined by the U. S. DEA.  Pablo escaped on the rooftop of the building where the party was being held with a bodyguard.  They were both gunned down and killed.

*    *    *    *

Michael is in search of a new assistant, since Joey Scala has been released.

# CHAPTER 27

## The Sargo Incident Redux

A loud knock sounded on the door to the 'Book Room' and it bust open, before anyone had said 'enter'. James Dean, from Michael's old room stepped in breathless.

"Mike you got to come with me!" He managed to say.

"Sup James." Michael responded, not moving from his reading position laying against the pillow in his bed. It was 9:30 PM. Anytime now and the blue light would come on for the ten o'clock count.

"I found the missing pages of the book you are writing." James continued not missing a beat.

Michael was indeed writing a book, The SARGO Incident. As a matter of fact he had let James read the outline. The tale he wanted to tell was based on a true incident he had witnessed in the CIA area of Pearl Harbor Naval Shipyard while building a power plant and a demineralized water facility across the street from the Incident. It had all the elements for a best seller and a blockbuster movie according to his creative writing instructor here at Camp, who was a published Author. Intrigue, non stop action, twists and turns in the plot, danger, conspiracy, murder and lots of sex. The underlying story, that of a nuclear accident involving the nuclear submarine SARGO was true and a scandal, covered up by the government. It was also instrumental in shaping the future of nuclear powered attack submarines.

"What did you say?" Michael perked up and lowered the book he was reading. "What pages? What are you talking about?"

"There is guy who just came to our room.  For the night only.  He will be gone tomorrow.  He came on a CON - AIR who made an emergency landing in Las Vegas at Nellis Air Force Base.  They parceled the inmate passengers for the night and he happened to land in our room.  We gotten talking and he informed me that he was aboard the SARGO at the time of its accident.  Talk about a coincidence.  You are writing the story of the accident being on the outside looking in.   He was on the inside looking out…I bet he has information for a lot of blanks to fill you in.  I had to come over and clue you in.  I know you write speculative fiction and I read the outline…But still the whole thing was testing the outer bounds of reality.  Was there really a nuclear submarine named SARGO?   Did the Incident you describe really took place?   Now, listening to the sole survivor, I have no doubts in my mind."

"Go back to your room for the count.  I will be there right after the blue light goes off, signaling the end of the ten o'clock count."  Michael said looking at his watch.

A little after ten Michael made tracks for his old room.  Bishop and Babalui, were the only remaining of his old roommates and James Dean of course.  There was a new fellow he had not seen around.  He must be a white collar criminal he thought to be invited to join the room.  He zeroed in on the newcomer via CON - AIR, whom he had also never seen before.  His eyes looked young, but that was as far as it went.  The rest of him, white unkept beard and long tangled white hair, stooped posture and two crutches.  Dead man walking, he was announcing.

"How is the stock market doing?"  Michael addressed the Bishop to make conversation.

"Rally good with the addition of Max here."  He pointed to the white collar newcomer.  "He was a stockbroker, after all.  And a famous one at that."

"What's his claim to fame?  Getting caught?"  Michael said smiling to convey he was only joking.

"He was Hillary Clinton's broker." The Bishop added with pride, because Hillary Clinton's broker was now working for him.

"I always wanted to ask Hillary's broker; how did she turn a $100.00 investment into $100,000.00 in less than a year." Michael asked.

"It's easy." Max announced. "Put the stocks on a dart board and fire away. Buy the ones you land on."

"You are jesting. If it was that easy. Everyone would be doing it."

"I forgot to add," Max said pontificating, "that as soon as you buy, you must fill up a slip with the opposite down side, leaving the name blank."

"Who pays for the slip covering the downside?" Michael asked.

"Our guardian angel. In the case we are talking, Tyson Chicken. At the end of the day, you put Hillary's name on the winning slip and Tyson Chicken on the losing."

"Why would Tyson Chicken be willing to pay $100,000.00?"

"An easy investment for them if they wanted the federal transportation law changed to allow a third trailer added when transporting their chickens."

"That's why the law changed?" Michael asked in amazement.

"I am sure others sweetened the pot through lobbyists." Max added. "Now you know the rest of the story."

"Why are you in for, if I may ask?"

"Insider trading. In other countries and with our Congress it's called 'Market Analysis'. I thought of myself being in that same category, bulletproof. I was mistaken. Anyway, a year and a day, a $50,000 fine and I get to keep my license is part of the cost of doing business. I will be golden when I come out because I kept my mouth shut. I had no choice in the matter. My attorney advised me to plead. Going to trial and explaining in open court would have given me a death sentence, by suicide."

Michael zeroed in on the other fellow who reminding him as a double of what he pictured 'Ben Gun' from the book 'Treasure Island', would look like.

"I heard from James that you were aboard the SARGO during the…Incident." Michael cut through the chase in lieu of introduction. "I was on the other side of the street building the power plant and the demineralized water facility."

"Is that right?  I am Ned by the way."

"Michael."

"What did you see?"

"Two Polaris type attack submarines were approaching to dock across the street from the power plant where I was working.  It was during the first week of December  1979, a little after eight o'clock in the morning, I recall, because it was right after the raising of the flag and the National Anthem.  SWORDFISH was in the lead and SARGO was close behind. They docked and as soon as SARGO tied up, SWORDFISH untied itself and was gone.  Emergency Services showed up and for a while it looked like they were filming ET across the street.  Men in hazmat suits were carrying body bags in stretchers and men wrapped in seethrough plastic.  No visible injuries, though, as far as I could tell, because there was no blood.  The Navy hung magenta signs in the middle of the road and stopped all traffic.  The Resident Officer in Charge of Construction, the ROICC, told us, when I called his office, that it was an emergency simulation…"

When Ned heard that, he started laughing in a hacking way, like he had trouble breathing.

"That's what the Navy told you?"  He said after he got his cough under control.

"That was it. Word for word. When I asked him about the nuclear agent signs, he told me they wanted to simulate a nuclear accident and were trying to be as realistic as possible."

This brought another hacking laugh from Ned.

"I think they carried the whole thing a little too far, if you ask me." Michael concluded. "They painted over the name SARGO and the numbers. They parked the submarine in the middle of Pearl Harbor, close to Ford Island, surrounded it with a floating fence having nuclear magenta signs hanging form it every twenty feet or so. Everyone avoided to navigate in the area. We got used to it and hardly noticed any more; until one day after almost a year, it just was not there any more."

Michael made sure he relayed the events as an observer and nothing more. He left out, for the time being, his personal saga investigating the incident and his findings.

"I got news for you old buddy." Ned started as soon as Michael was done with his narrative. "It was no simulation. It was a nuclear accident. Ask the crew who was walking knee deep in contaminated nuclear waste water, which was used by the pumps as feed water, cooling the reactor."

"Where were you at the time?" Michael interrupted.

"Right in the engine room aboard the Polaris-class nuclear attack submarine 'SARGO.'"

"Go ahead." Michael whispered.

"The Captain, Bill Rudich, was having problems. For the past two days, the secondary circuit circulating water pumps have been cavitating. Which means that a portion of the water was turning into steam pitting the pump impeller. As a result the pump capacity has been progressively diminishing. The feed water pumps were unable to keep up with the submarine's Nuclear Core cooling demand. Consequently, the steam production has being reduced drastically. The turbines with inadequate steam supply could not maintain the submarine's cruising speed.

"The secondary circuit circulating water was deriving its heat from the primary water loop through a heat exchanger in which the heat was passed from one circuit to the other until equilibrium was reached. Since the secondary circuit water was in short supply, the coolant which was circulating through the reactor core, was not removing the nuclear generated heat because it had no place to transfer it outside the Core.

"The Annunciator Alarm of LOW COOLING WATER FLOW had been going off every few minutes annoying everybody. It had since been disconnected, the red flashing light remaining the only Alarm indicator, requiring vigilance by the Control Panel operators on duty. The only water available on board was the drainage water collected in the submarine bilges and pumped out occasionally when the water level reached the overflow point.

"This water was now being used as make-up water to supplement the secondary circuit, with any excess pumped back to the bilges through the sea cocks. Ordinarily, this arrangement could work temporarily. The crew having to be both alert and knowledgable because several automated procedures were now being performed manually.

"The downward spiral of the domino principle could be staved off until the submarine was able to limp to Pearl Harbor Naval Shipyard for repairs. Why then was the SARGO coming in assisted on the last legs of its electric battery, having previously exhausted all the diesel fuel for the back-up engine?"

SARGO and its sister ship Polaris-type nuclear attack submarine SWORDFISH were built in 1967. Their primary propulsion system was a nuclear Pressurized Water Reactor (PWR); developed by the U.S. Navy under the direction of Admiral Hyman Rickover. From the beginning both ships have been experiencing the presence of excess oxygen in the secondary circuit circulating water that had been attacking all the wetted surfaces causing excessive corrosion that was cutting down the life of its equipment. Particularly in the tube sheets of the heat exchanger. They both had a major overhaul in Guam, Micronesia. They were heading for the Pearl Harbor Naval Shipyard for inspection of the repairs and to enter into the Shipyard maintenance schedule.

"SARGO Commander, Captain Bill Rudich together with Lieutenant Jake Patterson, both ambitious and hungry for promotion, the latter for his own command, got together with the Shipyard engineers in Guam and equipped the submarine cooling system with Oxygen scavenging devices which utilized chemicals. One of the chemicals had a Sulfite root which was hungry to reach a state of equilibrium as Sulfate by absorbing Oxygen from the water and becoming an acid in the process. Then by adding Caustic, Calcium Hydroxide a base, to neutralize the acid and gain a neutral pH of 7.

"These chemicals were introduced into the secondary cooling water circulating pump suction. The water in that loop, heated by the primary loop in a heat exchanger, was kept pressurized to prevent it from boiling and turning into steam. A delicate balance was maintained between the water, the water pressure and temperature as it entered the circulating pump suction."

The circulating pumps had a Required, designed by the pump manufacturer, NPSH, Net Positive Suction Head, in FT. The piping configuration and the height between the water level in the condensate receiving tank and the centerline of the pump suction determined the NPSH Available. The NPSH Available, less the friction losses in the interconnecting piping, must always be greater than the NPSH Required. Otherwise the pressurized hot water will flash into steam and the feed water pump will start cavitating, losing portions of its impeller in the process.

In Nuclear Reactors built and operating on land, there is always adequate space in the plant so that the NPSH Available could comfortably surpass the NPSH Required by the pump.  The nuclear submarine, however, was limited in that regard by the overall body design, specifically its height.  The NPSH Available in the  stream lined, low profile body style of the Polaris-type attack submarine was closely tracking the NPSH Required.

"The medium temperature and pressure was, within limits, kept constant.  The water temperature in the secondary circuit circulating pumps was, however, increased without a corresponding increase in the pressure to maintain equilibrium, resulting in the water flashing into steam, cavitating the pump impeller, progressively diminishing the pump's pumping capacity.

"The water in the pumps being hot to begin with, reached the flashing point because of the reaction between the acid and the base is an exothermic reaction, meaning it produces and releases heat, causing at that point the NPSH Required to exceed the NPSH Available, causing the exploding steam bubbles to disintegrate the pump impeller.

"If the problem was analyzed and caught at its inception, the situation presently aboard SARGO could have been averted; by simply introducing the oxygen scavenging chemicals at the circulating water pump discharge in lieu of the suction. This way the exothermic chemical reaction would not interfere with the pump internals.  The Control Panel Annunciator was not equipped with a secondary loop High Temperature Alarm.  The circulating water pumps did not have a pressure gauge at both inlet and outlet, so that the operator may be able to see a pressure differential change.  The sole gauge was at the pump discharge indicating the TDH, Total Developed Head, which dropped ever so slowly that it was not noticed by the operators, until two days ago when the secondary loop water capacity became inadequate to properly cool the water in the primary loop, resulting in the overheating of the Reactor Core. The Central Control Panel Annunciator picked the diminished cooling water flow signal and sounded the Alarm.

"At that instant, the Reactor Room Chief, no other than Lieutenant Jake Patterson, should have initiated emergency Reactor shut down procedures. Although the cooling of the Reactor would have taken several days, the submarine was equipped with a diesel engine as a secondary propulsion system and a back-up electric battery. Granted that under diesel power, SARGO would be forced to periodically raise a snorkel devise to draw in fresh air for the diesel engine combustion and crew to be able to breath and to carry away exhaust gasses. The backup battery could operate an electric motor that could propel the submarine twelve knots maximum for ten hours.

"The Lieutenant realized immediately that the cause for the Reactor overheating was inadequate water quantity in the secondary circuit. Accordingly, instead of shutting down the Reactor, he activated the stand-by water circulating pump.

"The submarine had two water circulating pumps. One on line at all times and the second one as an emergency stand-by. In order to insure readiness of the stand-by pump, it was put on line interchangeably, rendering the active pump and the stand-by to switch. Hence in this case both pumps sustained cavitation, unable to provide the required water volume capacity on demand.

"By the time Lieutenant Chamberlain realized the fact that the stand-by pump was in no better shape than the primary one, the reactor temperature had moved into the red sector indicating imminent meltdown. The Annunciator Horn had long been disconnected, so the grave situation of the engine room was not widely known but for Lieutenant Patterson and three other crew members assigned to the engine room.

"By the time Lieutenant Patterson decided to shut down the Reactor, it was too late. Only the ingenuity of Ensign Bob Pizzano in the engine room, prevented a complete nuclear core melt down. He switched to the diesel powered propulsion system and jury rigged the bilge pumps to pump water into the secondary cooling system, bringing the temperature indicator into the Orange Sector.

"Lieutenant Jake Patterson informed Captain Bill Rudich that he was forced to shut down the Reactor because the secondary cooling water circuit pumps had lost their ability to pump water due to the loss of their impeller as a result of excess oxygen corrosion."

"It was not excess oxygen. It was a rise in the water temperature that turned the water into steam, eroding the pump impeller."

"I do not know the cause of the temperature rise."

"Lieutenant Patterson of course omitted in his Report to the Captain to mention that the Reactor remained for a considerable amount of time with its Core temperature indicator in the Red Sector."

All is well that ends well.

In the case of SARGO though it was not to be.

"The wall between the primary and secondary loop cracked. The secondary water circuit was thus contaminated with radiation. Since it was circulated by the bilge pumps, they were now contaminated together with the bilge walls themselves. Since the cooling for the reactor was now on manual, occasionally there was overflow of secondary cooling water in designated spill areas. These areas now hot and radioactive were cleaned and moped by crew members.

"For the past two days the sick bay was experiencing an unusually large number of cases reporting inability to fulfill their duties. The Captain was informed. Further testing revealed that the ailing crew members were suffering from radiation sickness.

"The Captain was given a progress report just before entering Pearl Harbor Naval Shipyard. He in turn dispatched a May Day distress signal to the Shipyard Nuclear Containment Office. He was ordered to dock in his designated spot and remain there with all the hatches closed, until a portable hospital unit and other emergency vehicles could be dispatched at his location.

"Captain Rudich, while waiting for the Shipyard portable hospital to arrive, in an effort to reduce radiation exposure to the SARGO crew, he orders his men to manually pump the bilges overboard, dumping contaminated water into the Pearl Harbor Naval Shipyard bay.

"As soon as we lost the feed water pumps the reactor overheated and broke the seal contaminating the water. The Captain gave orders to dump it in the bilges. But the water was too much. It soon overflowed the bilges. Then it was up to the Captain to order the bilge pumps to be turned on. But then all the nuclear contaminated water would go out to sea, and we were already approaching the dock at Pearl Harbor Naval Shipyard. The Captain decided to sacrifice himself and the crew so we did not contaminate the Hawaiian environment. He was afraid I think more of what the press will say and its impact upon the tourist industry on Oahu. Good that it did in the end. As soon as we docked at Pearl Harbor and the Rescue Crew arrived, the first thing they did was turn the bilge pumps on and dump all the contaminated water into Pearl Harbor; across from the power plant you were building. They had refused to walk into contaminated nuclear water and rescue the crew. The submarine Captain fought them on this, until he collapsed that is and passed out."

"What happened next?" Michael asked eagerly. He knew some but not all the revelations made by Ned.

"Some died immediately, some survived and were immediately discharged from the Navy. I was one of the survivors. We, the survivors, got together, hired a lawyer and filed a Class Action suit against the government. It's been going on for twenty years now. One by one the surviving crew of SARGO have been dying off. I am the sole survivor. And not long for this world as you can see." "What are you doing on CON - AIR?" Michael asked.

"I am given an attitude adjustment treatment by the government because I am outspoken.  It's the same thing as the 'diesel therapy' on land.  I've been flying to no where for six months now.  No medical treatment for the cancer I developed after the SARGO nuclear accident.  I am not complaining.  I am alive.  The rest of the crew are all dead."

"How did you end up in prison?" Michael asked.

"Your government at work.  As soon as we filed the Class Action law suit, the government put all the survivors in prison to keep an eye on them and control them.  Me, it was bank fraud.  I bought a car and the government claimed I lied on my loan application, because I overstated my net worth.  I had no money to hire a lawyer.  The 'public pretender' they hired for me did not lift a finger to defend me.  The same thing happened to all my crew members.  Planted drugs.  Planted stolen goods. You name it.  On a lot of them the government did not even have to be inventive.  They were criminals, in the life, to begin with.  They just caught them and made them name others to put them away on Conspiracy charges."

"Have you gone to trial yet?"

"Are you kidding.  Continuance upon continuance.  As we come close to trial, the government changes lawyers.  Then they ask the court for a year postponement for the new attorney to get up to speed..."

"Doesn't your attorney object?"

"He does not.  I think the government is paying his fee, under the table. I have not spoken to my attorney in years.  Every time I call, he is either in court or   some other legal malarkey.  I cannot receive phone calls.  I tried changing my voice and name, but the operator announces the call is originating from such and such federal prison facility.  I am sure the secretaries who answer the phone they have all been clued in.  It's hopeless."

"I know what you mean." Michael said sympathetically. "I had a case with the Air Force. My Contract was at Hickam Air Force Base, to change all the water piping with new and install water meters. I left the country to go to my father's funeral. All the projects were at a stand still for a week, until I got back. Hickam Air Force Base looked like a testing ground for tanks when I left. When I returned it looked like no one had ever excavated. Grass sod have been planted over the trenches. I went to the Contracting Office to find out what happened. The Air Force had changed all their personnel. I asked for Dooling, the Contracting Officer officer. I was told there was no Dooling in their employee. I asked about my Contract by its number. I was told there was no Contract under that number. I thought I had walked into an episode of the Twightlight Zone.

"I filed a Complaint against the Air Force with the Armed Services Board of Contract Appeals. The government started pulling the same shit with me. Changing attorneys. I filed for discovery. I found out what happened. The Base General wanted the Base in pristine condition because he had a Pacific Rim Conference scheduled. They just backdated everything and had numerous meeting deciding what to do with me and the open Contract. I was supposed to mark the pages I wanted for the government to make copies for me. Good luck with that I thought. The pertinent pages would just disappear, the government way. So, instead, I took all the original documents folded them and shoved them inside my pants. When I was asked by a secretary at the conclusion of my Discovery if I had marked anything for copying, I told her "Nothing", which as it happens was the truth.

"I then started filing Motions with the ASBCA requesting a copy of such and such meeting by date. The government's response was that no such document existed. I would then send a copy to the ASBCA and to the government attorney on the case at the time. The attorney would rather quit the JAG office at that time in lieu of facing the wrath of loosing in Court. This same thing happened with a couple of other attorneys and I filed a Motion of Government conspiracy with the

Court.  The ASBCA set a date for a hearing on my Motion to take place in Hawaii. It was February after-all. The day before the hearing the new government attorney walked in my office with a signed blank check.  I refused to settle out of Court with the JAG attorney. I told him that I would see him in Court the next day.   I was my own attorney representing the company.  ASBCA allows that for every federal court, to my knowledge.  The JAG attorney told me that I would never make it to court the next day.  "The government has never lost a 'Bad Faith' case since its inception over two hundred years ago." He claimed that he was not about to be the first.  My wife, Christine, hearing the commotion stepped into my office to find out what was happening.

"Who are you?"  The JAG attorney asked her.

"I am the owner of the company." She declared.

"What the fuck am I doing talking to you then." He said addressing me.

He followed my wife to her office and locked the door keeping me out. My wife settled.  She filled in an amount and the JAG attorney left our office all smiles.

"Unfortunately, I cannot do the same, at the moment,"  Ned declared. "Being on air 'diesel therapy', the government would love to have me petition the Court to fire my attorney and take over Pro Se. They would just make sure that I would miss a court deadline to respond and my case would be thrown out of court."

"I know what you mean."  Michael said recalling his experience with the 'Nigerian Nightmare'.

"I understand from Alex that you are the Camp and Base Engineer.  By your own admission you witnessed the SARGO Incident. You must have investigated what happened.  I was a grunt in the trenches at the time.  I would love to hear your overview."

"The cause of the accident was failure of the pumps circulating the coolant.  This caused the nuclear reactor to overheat, cracking the seal between the primary loop, which is radioactive, and the secondary which operates the rest of the power plant.

"The radioactive primary loop water is pressurized to prevent it from boiling. It runs trough a heat exchanger in which the the heat is passed to another, secondary, water circuit. This heat exchanger is essentially a waste heat boiler and the secondary circuit or loop turns the water into steam that actually turns the turbines. So long as a sufficient seal is maintained, the water of the primary loop that is radioactive, cannot contaminate the water in the secondary loop and the  rest of the power plant. Presence of oxygen in the secondary loop had been playing havoc with the seals and corrosion problems have been plaguing the Polaris submarines propulsion system since their launching in 1967.

"The same thing that happened with SARGO, happened, ten years ago with SCORPION, a 5,900 ton, 382 foot Polaris class attack submarine carrying 16 Polaris missiles; lost according to the Navy somewhere in the middle of the Atlantic near the Azores on May 22, 1968. It had been at sea for 30 days with a crew of 100 after having its fuel renewed at the Naval Shipyard in Norfolk, Virginia. It's reactor was shut down and between one third and one fourth of its fuel, containing 0.07 percent fissile U-235 and 99.3 percent non fissile U-238, was replaced. The entire process of shutting down the reactor, in order to allow it to cool, removing the reactor head and transferring the spent fuel took four weeks. The newly installed core could propel the submarine for distances as great as 400,000 miles before needing to be replaced.

"Additionally, during the last refitting at Norfolk, oxygen scavenging chemicals were installed to be injected in the feed water pumps discharge piping in hope of cleaning up the problem. The decision did not come easy as there was another human factor introduced to the operation: Keeping the pH at the desired level. Some of the engineers were of the opinion that the oxygen should be removed by mechanical means, with the addition of a deaerator assembly, sacrificing some stores and living quarters in the way. This solution was not acceptable to other engineers because they were concerned with feed water pump cavitation due to lack of height in a submarine. They were concerned that the Net Positive Suction Head (NPSH) required by the pumps would not be less than the one available, thus the pump impellers would cavitate.

"At 14:34 EST on May 22, 1968 the signal from SCORPION, somewhere in in the Azores at the time, according to the Navy, was lost. The nuclear attack submarine simply disappeared without a trace, with all hands on board.

"I don't believe the Navy's version that was lost near the Azores in the middle of the Atlantic. People lie. The math and the numbers do not. SCORPION was part of the seventh fleet based in Souda Bay on the island of Crete, Greece. At the time of its disappearance was part of a NATO exercise off the coast of Libya to intimidate the Libyan dictator Kadafy who was instigating all sorts of terrorist attacks all over Europe. This means that the nuclear submarine SCORPION was in the Western Mediterranean. This is confirmed by the fact that on May 18, 1968 SCORPION stopped at the US Naval Station Rota in Spain where two crew men were left ashore. One for a family emergency and the other was dispatched to the hospital for health reasons. They stayed there for a couple of days and they left on May 18, 1968 heading East towards their base in Souda Bay on the island of Crete. Shortly before midnight on May 20 and ending after midnight on May 21, 1968 SCORPION attempted to reach a Navy Communication Station in Nea Macri, Greece. The Nea Macri listening post is primarily maned by the CIA and monitors the activities inside the Mediterranean. The SCORPION transmitted message was garbled. At 14:34 EST on May 22, 1968 the signal from the nuclear submarine SCORPION was lost. The nuclear attack submarine SCORPION simply disappeared without a trace, with all ninety nine hands on board.

"The Navy announced a few days later that the SCORPION was lost in the middle of the Atlantic near the Azores. There is no record of the submarine crossing Gibraltar which is maned by the British and the math, based on the cruising speed and range of the submarine, do not add up. I believe the SCORPION was lost in the Mediterranean near the Balearic Islands Archipelago located 260 miles East of Spain.  They are Spain's premiere tourist attraction and it would be unthinkable for the US to admit that the nuclear submarine SCORPION was lost near the Balearic Islands Archipelago.

"In the late 1960's the U.S. intelligence community began to receive disturbing indications that the nuclear submarines of the Soviet Union had a much higher performance capabilities than previously thought.  A debate broke out between Admiral Hyman G. Rickover, the father of the nuclear powered submarine at the Naval Reactors Branch and the Naval Sea Systems Command (NAVSEA) over the direction of the next generation of attack submarines.

"Rickover believed that what was needed was a high speed, over 35 knots, attack submarine, able to support the carrier battle groups deployed by the Navy.  NAVSEA was supporting a design called 'conform', utilizing a natural circulation reactor, which would be safer; sacrificing top speed to only 25 knots at reduced noise levels.  Admiral Rickover won out, and twelve submarines were ordered, its lead boat named USS LOS ANGELES (SSN-688) was planned, with General Dynamics in Groton, Connecticut, as the prime contractor.

"The Los Angeles class boats delivered on their promise of high speed, utilizing the pressurized water system, circulated by pumps; same as the Polaris class submarines.  Some sixty two Los Angeles class submarines would be eventually contracted, before the accident on board USS SARGO which put an end to further production.

"After the 'SARGO Incident', as it became known and the retirement of Admiral Rickover, the Navy developed natural circulation reactors. U.S.

attack submarines of the Ohio class, developed in the late 1980's, were powered by natural circulation reactors. These were safer and inherently quieter than the pressurized water units, because they required no pumps. The reactors were arranged so that the differences in temperature between the portion of the reactor containing the reacting fuel and the rest of the reactor, forced the water to circulate naturally. Typically, in these natural circulation reactors, cooled water from the heat exchanger is fed to the bottom of the reactor, and it rises through the fuel elements as they heat it."

"Now I have an idea of what caused the accident. I was not aware of a similar accident involving SCORPION. How come it did not make front page news at the time? It seems though that it taught the government a lesson from their mistakes. Why don't they admit it, and settle with me?" was Ned's logical reaction to Michael's narrative.

"The reason the SCORPION incident did not make front page news is that the government did not advertise it. They just covered it up. Other more newsworthy items at the time took center stage. With the Viet Nam war raging, the TET Offensive, the student protests, followed by Watergate...As to the government admitting they made a mistake?" Michael responded. "Are you living under a rock? They will never admit it. They will lie and fabricate a story. They firmly believe that if they lie and keep on lying, the lie will eventually become the truth. This is the government Modus Operandi and will not change; not in our lifetime, anyway."

"You know the SARGO Incident inside out." Ned observed. "You would be the best person to write a book about it some day. You would have a best seller."

"Who knows." Michael said wistfully. "One of these days, after I retire and have nothing but time on my hands...I will have to be in hiding though, because I did not tell you all that transpired and especially the government's reaction followed by a systematic cover up."

# CHAPTER 28

## Greeks Bearing Gifts

There was a guard named Nicholas of Greek extraction. He made an effort to seek Michael out and made every overture he could think of to become friends with him. He was a young man, almost thirty and he admitted to Michael that he was a burn out. He was sent to Camp Snoopy to recuperate. He did not have any injuries that someone would notice. He must be suffering from mental fatigue Michael thought. What prison gives its guards mental fatigue he wondered.

"Hi! My name is Nicholas Papas." He introduced himself. "You must be Michael the engineer. I heard a lot about you. Being Greek also, I thought I'd make your acquaintance."

"Where were you before coming here?" Michael inquired.

"You don't want to know." Was the reply. The reply just worked itself to more questions in Michael's mind. However, Nicholas kept his past a closed book. He was very solicitous though, each time they were at the dorm gazebos making a point to light Michael's cigar.

He was easy going with Michael almost like a kid brother he never had. He read Michael's PSI and decided like everyone who had read it, that Michael did not belong in prison and he told him so on several occasions. He became Michael's shadow watching everything he did all day long. Michael became suspicious that unseen forces had placed Nicholas at the Camp to spy on him. He relayed his suspicion to his mentor Dino.

"Leave it up to me. I will find out and let you know." Was Dino's succinct response.

Dino came back to Michael a week later with the results of his investigation.

"You need to keep away from the dude." Dino concluded. "His is bad news. Damaged to the core..."

"I already knew that." Michael declared. "He told me that he was a burn out case from his previous assignment."

"Did he tell you what his previous assignment was?"

"No. That's the funny thing. He never talks what he has been doing for the BOP before coming here."

"He does not exist on paper. My OC, Organized Crime, contacts however, know him from before. His name is Nicholas Papas, like he told you, and he is Greek. That's the only truth he told you. He is known to the mob as 'Nick the Greek'. He got his training in the East Coast working as a freelance contractor for the mob. You know what this means? He is a Contract killer. He disappeared from the scene a couple of years ago. He now surfaced working for the BOP. Avoid him at all costs. That's my advise. He must have been caught at something. The government turned him and is now working for them. I've been watching him. He has no duties. The other guards, both male and female, are avoiding him like the plague. He smells of death."

"You practically run the engineering and construction activities at Camp and on Base." Nicholas told Michael next time he dropped in his office unannounced. "What are they going to do when you are out? For your information, they already filled a replacement request. Good luck with that."

"When are you leaving?" Michael asked Nicholas point blank.

"In a couple of weeks. Why?"

Michael left the question unanswered. Two could play the game he reasoned.

Three days latter at 03:00 AM he was awakened by Nicholas.

"Come with me buddy for a UA."  He talked loudly as if he was announcing it to the whole room.

"You got to be kidding me.  I've been at Camp almost two years now and no one requested a UA of me.  Take a hair follicle and test.  I've never done drugs in my life..." Michael protested.

"Don't tell me.  The computer kicked your name at random.  Go argue with the computer."

By now all the roommates were sitting on their beds watching the exchange.

"If Michael is not back in an hour,"  Dino said, "I am going to the bubble and raise Holly Hell."

Nicholas remained silent.

Michael reassured by Dino's statement got up and threw some clothing over his underwear he was sleeping with.  He did not put his boots though.  He slipped his feet in his flip flops and followed Nicholas out of the room in the hallway.

"I did not wake you up for a UA." Nicholas admitted.  "I am doing a favor for someone.  He begged me because I was Greek, and you were Greek, he thought I would exert some influence on you.  I told him I would try.  You have a reputation around the Camp that you are 'suis generis', your own man.  No one can make you do something that you have decided for whatever reason that you are not going to do.  You told the Supreme Court of the United Sates after all, my way or the highway."

"Who is the guy you are doing the favor for?"

"The guy who has been put on probation on account of the complaint you filed.  He is not allowed to come within 100 feet of you..."

"Krupp!" Michael exclaimed stopping.  "I am going nowhere with you."

"I will owe you." Nicholas said meekly. "He is waiting for us at the gazebo outside. Just talk to him as a favor. That's all I ask. I don't know what he wants from you.  He just came crying to me wanting to arrange a meeting with you. Listen to him. As far as I am concerned you don't have to help him.  You can walk away, back to your room afterwards.  If you do me this favor and meet him, I will answer any question you put to me afterwards, truthfully."

Michael pondered for a while what to do.  His curiosity about Nicholas won out at the end and started walking towards the building exit. Nicholas following in his wake.

"You just don't know what this means to me."  He said in a whisper.

Michael found Krupp sitting at a picnic table under a gazebo smoking a cigarette.  He handed Michael a cigar he kept in a sealed plastic baggie.

"I know it's not up to your standards, but it's the best I could find in Las Vegas."

"Pretty sure of yourself."  Michael said smiling, accepting the offering. He bit the end of the cigar, a Gloria Cubana Maduro sixty gauge, getting a light from Nicholas ever-present butane lighter.

"It's your dime."  Michael said after a few minutes of silent contemplation.

"I would like first to apologize for my inexcusable behavior."  Krupp started. "I know you are thinking he is just saying that because he wants something.  But I am sincere and the apology comes from my heart.  I've never met someone like you in my life before.  All my life I had been kicked to the curb by the CEO's of the world.  You were a CEO on the outside.  I pigeonholed you under the same category.  Only to find out, the hard way that you do not have one mean bone in your body.  Always doing what's best for the project with no ulterior motives.  The 'Bridge of Peace' for example is something unheard of.  To build an overpass for the kids to go to school unharmed out of scrap metal and to look like it was meant to be so.  It would not have looked as good if the Air Force hired an architectural firm to design it and spent an arm and a leg to build it.  And here you built it for them for nothing.  I bet the BOP was pissed as hell not collecting a cut.  I was worried you would be 'rolled up'.  However, here you are, good as gold.  I am so sorry not believing in you and not doing what you told me instead of trying to improve on your ideas.  I am talking about the Motor Pool now.  It cost me my bonus.  I was to receive twenty Gees at the end of last year.  I still did on paper and have to pay taxes on; but I had to endorse the check right back to the fucking BOP in the Warden's office."

Michael kept silent.  He was not dragged out here to listen to Krupp's laments.

He was certain that Krupp wanted something from him and all that talk was  nothing else but clumsy foreplay.  He was not disappointed.  Krupp came to the point in his next sentence.

"I've been with the BOP almost all my life.  In the two years I've been working for you, I have learned more than all my life experience combined.  But I have reached the point of burn out.  I have had it.  I am getting ready to sue the BOP and the government.  My work in construction has affected my life.  Who knows what I have contacted while working under the BOP miserable conditions.  I have three kids and all three are retarded with congenital diseases.  I plan to sue the government.  I need your help.  I heard how you have and are always helping inmates with their legal problems.  I am on my knees in front of you begging for your help."

Michael kept silent.  How the wheel has turned.  Should he kick the man while he was down on his knees, like he took pleasure in kicking the government all the years he was doing defense contract work for them?  The prison experience, certainly has changed him.  He no longer viewed the workers in construction as tiny cogs to be spun at the speed he had decided, in order to roll over the amount of work he had decided, at his whim.  He found himself carrying for the people working for him, sympathetic to their plight. He no longer followed his mother's dictum: 'Familiarity breeds contempt'.  He now always looked after what's best for the client.   Krupp was begging him and if he wanted to assume the client role, what could he do for him?

"Your best bet in my opinion is to concentrate on the hazardous material associated with your work without the proper protection provided by the government."  Michael started.  "You may bring examples to elicit the sympathy of the jury, like your children.  However, never lose track of your target, like a laser beam: You were made by the BOP to work around hazardous materials banned by the EPA, who is part of the government.  I have a report in my office prepared by an independent consulting engineering firm hired by the Air Force in 1988, the year they gave the Camp to the BOP, which lists all the safety hazards and hazardous materials present requiring clean up.  The BOP should have been aware of it.   They did no remediation work. Additionally, I have my own Log Book where I write every day, among other things, the method my which the BOP is handling the hazardous material clean up, particularly in the new dormitory which is being remodeled under Construction 2, which is your division.  Let's go to the CMS offices under the Mess Hall.  I will open my office and hand you the two books. You have the rest of the night to copy or do whatever you wish with them. Kinko's is open 24/7.  I arrive at my office at 7:30 AM. Work starts at 8:00 AM.  I  need both books back in my office sometime between the hours I have stated.  If I don't receive them back or in the same condition as I have given them to you, I am required to report them missing to SIS by 9:00 AM.   Lieutenant Kyle will conduct an investigation and I will cooperate.  Am I making myself clear?"

"Crystal clear."  Krupp said with tears in his eyes.  He picked Michael's right hand and brought it to his lips.

They went all three and retrieved the two books from Michael's office. Michael had them wait at the foot of the stairway so he could enter his code number at the cypher lock. He explained that only Lieutenant Kyle, the head of SIS, and himself knew the number, and he intended to keep it that way. Krupp with the two books in hand left immediately. Michael and Nicholas ended up back at the gazebo.

"That was the most magnanimous and magnificent act, I've just witnessed, in all my life. I have heard about you and Krupp. It's the Camp scuttlebutt among the staff. I have also heard rumors that you are balling the head of SIS. Any truth to that?"

"Nick you are Greek. As such you know the term 'kathicon', obligation. I have an obligation to my wife. She has stood by me through thick and thin. How am I to pay back my obligation? By dumping her and fucking Teresa Kyle? I will not deny it. I am attracted to Teresa and she is attracted to me. But she understands my rational. Nothing happened. She just stays guard every morning while I take a shower. I am a 'Man of Respect' around here. I already have two body guards around the clock. They are watching us now as we speak. They don't know what's going on. But rest assured that if they think that harm is to visit upon me, they will react, and they react violently to the threat. You never see them, until it's too late. But I don't tell that to Lieutenant Kyle. Let her think she is protecting me because I am an 'Institutional Need'; as she explained it to me and others."

They remained silent. The eight hundred pound gorilla was sitting with them in the gazebo.

"You already know what I will be asking you." Michael finally said. "Why don't you start your tale. I am not interested in your life story. I am only interested in your life the moment you joined forces with the BOP."

Michael anticipated. He even expected something bizarre. However, the first words out of Nicholas mouth decked him.

"I am a member of the BOP death squad. Most of the others are ex military, special forces. We are basically, assassins at the beck and call of the BOP through our BOP contact. We get rid of problems that the

BOP does not know how to handle any other way, or it is prohibitive expensive to throw money at the problem. I have been doing this for two years and even with the generous allowance of down time, I feel burned out. Maybe it was the last assignment. Before, I never questioned the assignment or shown any interest to find out the underlying reasons for the hit. I just did as I was told. Most of the fatalities, could be written off as suicides or accidents. Not the last one, however."

"What happened with the last one?" Michael asked having an inkling of what Nicholas had already confessed from his conversation with Dino. However, he was still surprised at its extent. Death squads! Employed by our government? 'Los Desaperasitos' belonged in the 'Banana Republics', not the good old USA. But then again who taught the 'Banana Republics'? Who organized and trained their death squads? What about slave labor disguised under the UNI-COR label? President Clinton was expounding on TV about the Chinese prison labor and that no such thing existed in USA. Nevertheless, Michael had first hand knowledge that prison labor exploitation existed and was thriving in the USA in partnership with Chinese prisoners disassembling radioactive buildings in Area 51, without protective gear and clothing, at the request and invitation of our government. He wondered what Chen was doing. Has he been caught or merely disposed by a BOP hit squad, he was now learning of their existence and activities.

"I believe I have changed during the time I have spent with you." Nicholas admitted. "You are the definition of 'Philotimo'; (translated exactly as 'love of honor', there is no similar word in all the other languages of the world expressing the deeper meaning of the word) the way I learned it on my grandfather's knee. He was born in Greece, and I was listening to his stories from the old country. I was forced by your example to re-examine my own life and concluded that I can no longer do what I have been doing. The last case was nothing more than an attempt to stem the tide in a Class Action law suit."

This last part perked up Michael instantly.  He was getting sleepy and trying hard to stay awake, as he was nodding off.

"The Class Action suit against the BOP was filed under John Doe. However, the federal judge sitting on the federal Court in which the Class Action was filed and was handling the case found out who John Doe was and informed the BOP of his real name.  He was, by the way, a former prisoner. I wasted a good hardworking man who was in the right because the BOP did not want to pay the money the lawsuit was asking and the BOP owed.  This sickened me.  I was burned out after I completed the assignment and here I am.  But you have changed me. I hope for the better.  By the way I see you in the library almost every night, writing.  I am hoping you will write a book some day about your experience at the Camp.  I will be the first to buy it.  You will have the last laugh at government's expense."

Michael decided right there and then not to work with Dino and place himself in harms way by filing a Class Action suit against the BOP and UNI-COR under John Doe.  He felt he would be painting a target on himself, regardless of the reassurances of Dino that his real name would be sealed under Court Order.  There was no such thing, according to Nicholas and he believed him; particularly in his case with the federal judges enhanced pensions on the line.  A federal judge with such lofty ideals has not been appointed to the federal bench, yet. He decided that he would neither discuss his decision nor argue with Dino.  He would just fade away upon his release.

*  *  *  *

Michael made a point to be absent from his office, as soon as he unlocked it the next day in the morning, between 7:30 AM and 8:00 AM. When he returned at eight, he found the Air Force Camp Report and his Log Book on his desk, in the same pristine condition as they were yesterday.

*  *  *  *

A week later Nicholas was gone, as suddenly as he had appeared. Michael asked Lieutenant Kyle the next morning, while he was taking a shower, as to the whereabouts of Nicholas Papas.  She told him she did not know what he was talking about.  There was no one named Nicholas Papas ever at the Camp or in the BOP system, anywhere, as far as she was aware of. **Phoenix, Arizona - August 2024 matrozosmichael24@aol.com**